TZ
SS

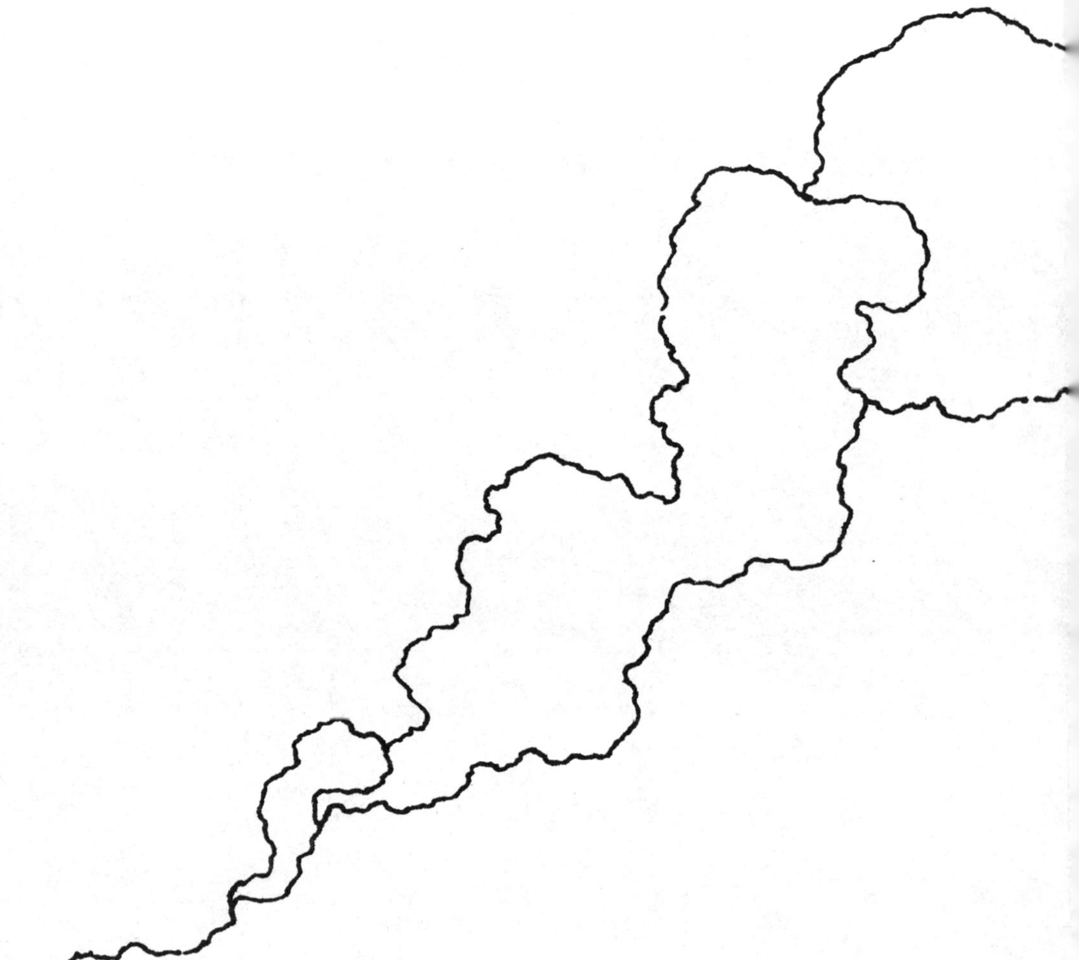

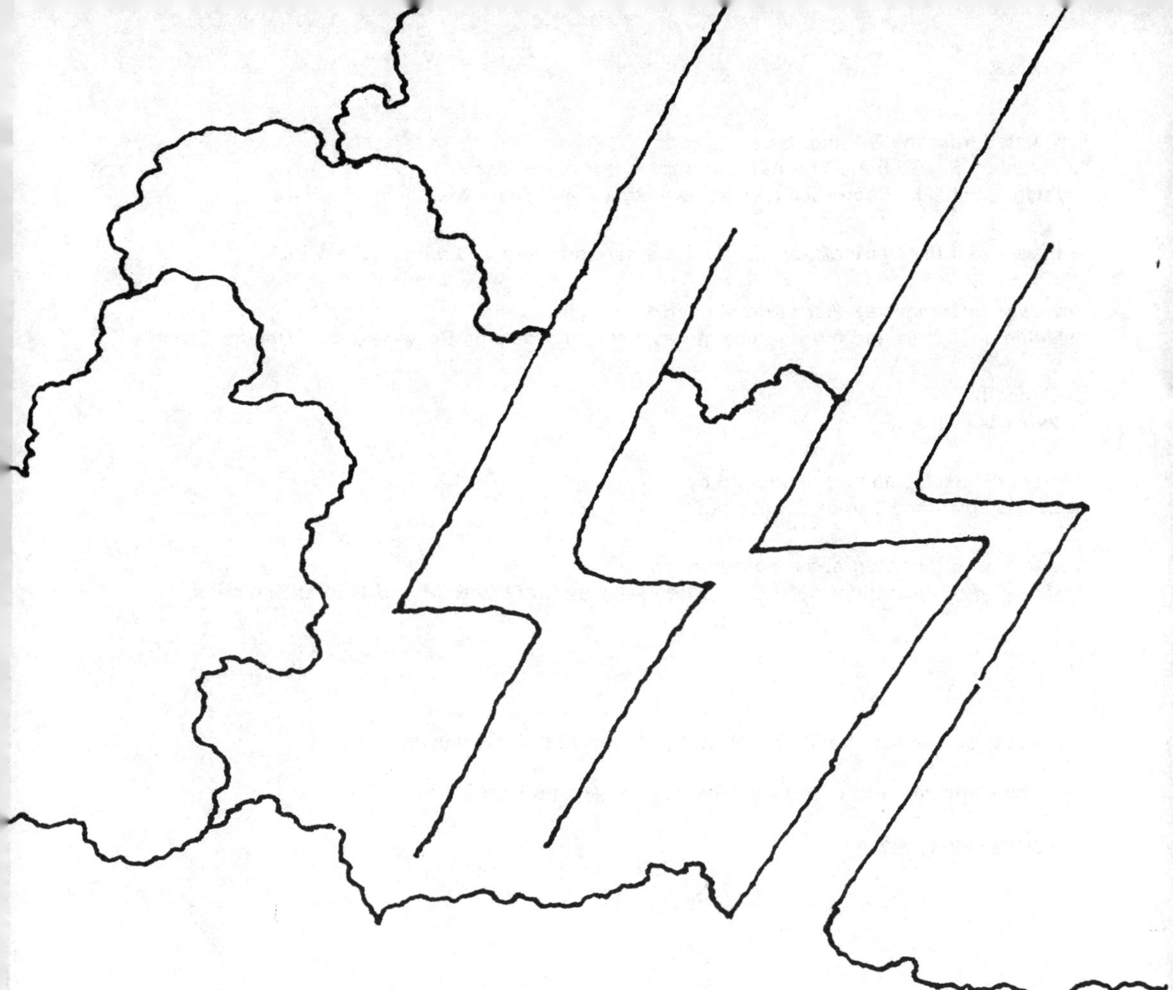

KL AUSCHWITZ SEEN BY THE SS

Rudolf Höss • Pery Broad • Johann Paul Kremer

The Auschwitz-Birkenau State Museum
Oświęcim 1998

Translated from the German by
Constantine FitzGibbon: *The Autobiography of Rudolf Höss*
Krystyna Michalik: *Reminiscences of Pery Broad* and *Diary of Johann Paul Kremer*

Translation of the *Diary of Johann Paul Kremer* corrected by Zbigniew Bezwiński

Reviewed by Władysław Bartoszewski and Mieczysław Kieta
Selected, footnotes and biographical notes edited by Jadwiga Bezwińska and Danuta Czech

Designed by
Jerzy Kępkiewicz

Photographs selected and captioned by
Izabela Smoleń and Teresa Świebocka

Documents and photographs reproduced by
Archives of the Auschwitz-Birkenau State Museum in Oświęcim and Günter Schindler

This book appears also in Polish, French, German and Russian

ISBN 83-85047-32-8

TABLE OF CONTENTS

FOREWORD • Jerzy Rawicz *

We present our readers with three documents in one selection, documents written by SS-men from the concentration camp at Auschwitz. And so we feel we should preface the selection with some information about all three authors: the first commandant of KL Auschwitz, *Rudolf Höss; Pery Broad, a functionary of the Political Section (*Politische Abteilung*), or camp* Gestapo*; and Johann Kremer, a physician.*

It is about Höss that we know the most, thanks to his detailed autobiography, of which the section relating to Auschwitz can be found in the present book. If, despite this, we still give Höss our closest attention, this is due both to his personal importance, and to the enormous significance of his memoirs.

*Rudolf Franz Ferdinand Höss was born in 1900, the son of a retired colonel of the German army. His upbringing at home was strict, Roman-Catholic in spirit. It was the wish of his father to see the future commandant of Auschwitz ordained a priest. The young Höss was sixteen when he volunteered for the army. He took part in the fighting in Turkey and Jerusalem during World War I, and at the age of seventeen became the youngest non-commissioned officer of the German army. He returned to his country after the defeat of the Central Powers and became active in the East Prussian Voluntary Corps (*Freikorps*), a reactionary organization which used all means to fight the opponents of German nationalism and militarism, particularly by attacking revolutionaries in Latvia and Germany, or the Polish insurgents in Silesia and in Great Poland.*

It was as early as 1922 that Höss met Adolf Hitler and joined his party. The number of his party membership card—no. 3240—was a source of pride for the rest of his life. In 1923 Höss was arrested and sentenced to 10 years' imprisonment for his participation in the Fememord *or vengeance-killing of the teacher Kadow whom the members of the Rossbach Corps, Höss's companions, considered to be a traitor. Discharged in 1929, Höss took to farming in Mecklenburg and married. Three of his children were born during his five years' stay there (the fourth was born at Dachau and the fifth at Auschwitz).*

In 1934 Höss was persuaded by Himmler, whom he had met years before, to exchange his farmer's life for active service in the SS. He received training in the concentration camp at Dachau where he was employed at first in a subordinate position. He was transferred to the Sachsenhausen camp in 1938,

---

* Jerzy Rawicz (1914—1980), during World War II, prisoner of *KL Auschwitz* and *KL Mauthausen*. After the war, journalist, contributor to many newspapers and magazines, interested first and foremost in Polish and German questions. Author of a number of books, including *Dno*, a collection of Auschwitz stories, and *Dzień powszedni ludobójcy*, about the commandant of *KL Auschwitz*; also translated from German. In 1961—1965, head of the bureau of the secretariat of the International Auschwitz Committee. Was engaged in the work of the Central Commission for the Investigation of Nazi Crimes in Poland. The following foreword was written in 1970 to the first edition of this book.

was promoted and became aide-de-camp with officer's rank, later serving as deputy commandant with the rank of an SS-Hauptsturmführer.

In May 1940 Höss was assigned the task of organizing the camp at Auschwitz. He remained there till November 1943 and was then transferred as Obersturmbannführer *to the Berlin Central Office where he occupied the position of Head of the DI Office in the Inspectorate of Concentration Camps in the SS Economic and Administrative Head Office (WVHA). It was in this role that he returned once more to Auschwitz to conduct the so-called* Aktion Höss, *that is, mass murders of the Hungarian Jews in the gas chambers of Birkenau.*

After the defeat of the Third Reich Höss went into hiding using the name of sailor Franz Lang, worked as a farmer in the British occupational zone, where he was recognized and arrested on February 11, 1946. He was taken from the Nuremberg prison to be a witness for the defence at the trial of the chief war criminals and was then extradited to Poland. It was in the Polish prison that he wrote his memoirs. Höss was sentenced to death on April 2, 1947, by the Supreme National Tribunal and hanged at Oświęcim on April 16 of the same year.

Johann Paul Kremer, doctor of medicine and philosophy, followed a different walk of life. He was probably the oldest among the SS-men ever on duty at Auschwitz. Born in 1884, he graduated from school only after the end of his voluntary service in the army in 1909. Just before World War I he obtained the degree of doctor of philosophy at the University of Berlin, where he simultaneously studied medicine and biology. During the war he received the diplomas of medical doctor and Doctor of Biology. He became Doctor of Medicine in 1919.

In the years that followed he worked in institutes and laboratories of anatomy, histology and biology, occupying various positions. He became Dozent *of Anatomy in 1929 at the University of Münster, where he had previously been an Assistant, specializing in problems of heredity. In July 1932 he joined the Nazi party, a short time before the Nazi take-over in Germany, the first to do so among the Münster* Dozents, *and in 1935 he became a member of the SS with the rank of* Untersturmführer *(after his service at Auschwitz he was promoted to* Hauptsturmführer*).*

The first three war years passed rather uneventfully for Professor Kremer, but finally the authorities remembered the existence of the 58-year-old reserve officer of the SS, particularly when many younger men had already been killed at the front. He was assigned to service at KL Auschwitz *on August 29, 1942, and stayed there somewhat less than three months. These three months were very likely the most fateful in his life.*

Called away from Auschwitz Kremer returned to Münster, where he engaged in petty controversies, in the belief that the university authorities underestimated his merits as "the oldest party member among the Münster Dozents*" and also his scientific achievements. It was in Münster, too, that he endured the discomforts of the last stages of war, discomforts to which the Germans were also exposed when the Allied air force was bombing the German towns. The end of the war found him in Münster.*

Arrested by the British, who also found his inadequately hidden diary,

Kremer was extradited to Poland and found himself in the dock together with the Auschwitz garrison, at their trial heard by the Supreme National Tribunal in Cracow. Sentenced to death on December 22, 1947, he evaded the hangman's rope reprieved on account of his advanced years. After ten years of imprisonment he was discharged and returned to Germany on January 10, 1958.

He was a model, even humble, prisoner in the Polish prison, just like other Nazi prisoners, but he changed, as if by magic, as soon as he crossed the frontier of the Federal Republic of Germany. He began to enact the role of a martyr of "the German cause", trying to rouse sympathy with his person. This was not a wise move but then wisdom was never Kremer's strong point.

As a result of his autopropaganda he was put in the dock again and was sentenced to ten years in which his term of imprisonment in Poland was included. So he was a free man. His sentence did, however, influence his life. The University of Münster divested him of his doctor's degree, as it could not tolerate an acknowledged war criminal among its staff. Kremer died in the 1960's.

The biography of Pery Broad may be summarized in a few sentences. He was born in 1921 in Rio de Janeiro, the son of a Brazilian merchant and a German woman. He returned to Germany with his mother. Here he joined the Hitlerjugend *(Hitler Youth) while still in school. In 1941 he volunteered for the SS and was detached to do service at* KL Auschwitz *in the following year. He was employed as a guard at first, then he again volunteered to work in the Political Section where he remained till the liquidation of the camp.*

He was arrested by the British after the war and to them he handed the documentary account written by himself, describing the crimes of the SS at Auschwitz. Discharged from captivity he chose a business career in the Federal Republic of Germany. He was thus employed till April 30, 1959, that is, until he was arrested in connection with the Auschwitz investigations then conducted in Frankfurt am Main. For his activity at Auschwitz he was sentenced in 1965 to a term of four years in which his term of investigative detention was included. After discharge he continued working as a trader.

This is the briefest summary of the life stories of the three SS-men whose records we herewith present to our readers. It seemed necessary "to introduce" them to our readers as their life histories show that various people found their way to being employed in the Auschwitz camp of oppression and crime, that they became criminals and executioners on their own initiative or following a false concept of obedience to their superiors.

It is characteristic that Broad was twenty when he took over his duties at KL Auschwitz, *Höss was forty, and Kremer was fifty-eight. Three generations!*

Kremer, from a formal point of view, belonged to the intellectual élite of Germany, being a professor with two doctorates. Höss was something of a military man, something of a farmer and had had a term in prison for assassination behind him. Broad was still very young, but then he had been a product of the upbringing of the Nazi régime.

These are the three "diarists". When taking into consideration the defendants in the trials in Cracow and Frankfurt we notice that the range of age and profession covers nearly the entire profile of German society. We find among them: a revenue officer, an accountant, physicians, a baker, a carpenter, a laboratory assistant, a mechanic, locksmiths, a specialist in the manufacture of musical instruments, farmers, a house-painter, an iron-master, a forwarding agent, waiters, the owner of a restaurant, shopkeepers, a post-office clerk, a nurse, a horse-and-cart driver, farm labourers, white-collar workers, a watch-maker, a motoring instructor, the owner of a transport firm, a bank clerk, a fireman, a stocking-weaver, a specialist in machine construction, a mason, dentists, a pharmacist, a joiner, a customs officer, a textile worker, a legal adviser...

The contingent of potential candidates for genocide included all the generations of Nazi Germany and representatives of nearly all social circles.

*

The literature of evidence, dealing with these "times of contempt," and especially with their condensed symptoms such as the Nazi concentration camps, is enormous today. No bibliography could possibly encompass all the publications in book form, scientific research works, literary writings or memoirs on this subject. Future generations will have a collective document, certifying to events which will seem improbable to the world of the next century, just as our generation found it hard to accept the horror and cruelty of the Middle Ages (of course, this was so only until we went through the experience of World War II). Besides the ethical, educational, political or social values of the relevant documents, their most enduring value is historical.

It has to be stressed that the overwhelming majority of the reports were written by victims of the crimes, that is, by those few who managed to escape with their lives, thanks to some imperfection in that most accurate Nazi machinery of murder. And having survived they considered it their duty to bear witness to the truth. The truth is also to be found in the writings of men, who did not themselves pass through these experiences, nor were they eye-witnesses or victims of the crimes. They were scholars, dedicated to various branches of learning, publicists and creative authors. They acquired knowledge about those times, conducting research and investigations, they digested all they had learnt about the realities of the epoch and attempted to record them in their academic or literary writings, in their works of painting, sculpture or music.

Relatively small—in fact quite minute—is the group of authors in the double meaning of the word, namely authors of crimes and at the same time authors of the documentary records relating to these. Naturally we are referring here to those whose basic activities centred round genocide. Among the leaders, politicians or military men of the Third Reich, who only "accidentally" helped to destroy the enemies of the Third Reich, there were many who after the war published their memoirs, thus trying to augment their own war-time glory and their fortunes in times of peace. Of course, they were careful to omit "embarrassing" details.

For example, Hans B. Gisevius, presenting his friend Arthur Nebe, Head of the Kriminalpolizei *in the Reich Main Security Office, as "a hero of the Resistance Movement," does not even mention that Nebe, while he commanded an* SS Einsatzgruppe *in the occupied territories of the Soviet Union, carried out mass executions of Jews.*[1] *As a rule, however, the professionals of mass murder lapsed into silence, which is hardly surprising.*

The situation would probably have been quite different if Hitler had won. Who can tell how many diaries and memoirs would have appeared in Germany by now, if that had been the case? Some of them would have born such titles, perhaps, as: "I Was in the Politische Abteilung *of* KL Auschwitz*," or "I Destroyed 600,000 Enemies of the Third Reich," or "Buchenwald—Majdanek—Mauthausen: Battle Stages of a Faithful SS-man," or "*Einsatzkommando SS *Carries out the Führer's Orders."*

Hitler lost, however, and consequently diaries or reminiscences of that kind could not appear, even if they were written. Many authors perhaps followed the first impulse of postwar fright and simply destroyed their memoranda, fearing they might fall into the wrong hands, as they were aware that a diary of this sort could be used as evidence at a trial (such, for example, was the case with Kremer's diary). Other memoranda are, perhaps, well hidden, awaiting "better times" to come. It seems probable that some diaries or memoirs exist, for the army of genocides is somehow out of keeping with the lack of documents written by them. Therefore each document of this kind which comes to light is of particular importance.

On the subject of Auschwitz we have only three such documents at our disposal, which we now present to our readers. Each one differs from the others and each is of importance. The earliest document is the diary of Kremer. It differs from the two remaining reports in that it was written not after but during the war, while the events chronicled by the author were actually happening. This document was, moreover, not intended for publication. It was written from day to day, in the form of notes recording events occurring in the author's private life, and it reflects the curious combination of the bizarre, almost degenerate mentality of Kremer and his acquired predilection for method and order.

The next report, in so far as the time of writing is concerned, is the document of Pery Broad, who of his own free will called a British officer and handed him his Auschwitz reminiscences. It is possible that as a prisoner of war he wished to ingratiate himself with the victors in this way.

Finally, the third document, widely known the world over, translated into many languages and published in many countries, is "The Autobiography" written by Rudolf Höss in his Polish prison. This is the document of the greatest significance, both because of the importance of its author and due to the detailed way of relating events (over 200 pages of print). The author's position enabled him to acquire a far wider range of knowledge of all aspects of camp life than the others could possess. And as he was directly connected with the centres where the crimes were planned, he was able to depict the extermination system with greater exactitude.

These three cases of testimony from "the other side" are now presented to younger readers who, in our opinion and in the opinion of former Auschwitz

---

[1] Hans Bernd Gisevius: *Bis zum bitteren Ende*. Darmstadt 1947, Classen u. Würth Verlag. Gisevius had been a high official of the *Gestapo*, later of the *Abwehr*.

prisoners, should learn about the terrible events taking place during their fathers' lifetime.

*

The basic obligation of a research worker is the critical evaluation of the document which he quotes. Critical evaluation means confronting the data in it with data obtained elsewhere, gathered from other kinds of document and testimony. Today we are still able to verify Auschwitz documents not only with others, but also with the memory of people (which sometimes plays tricks, but still supplements a given document). This is the last opportunity to do so, as the Auschwitz generation is slowly disappearing. Former prisoners of German concentration camps only rarely attain extreme old age. As far as the other side, the SS, are concerned, we receive only very meagre materials at the trials when they give evidence as witnesses or defendants. Former SS-men either plead forgetfulness or consciously evade the truth (with few exceptions only). Some shock is often needed to make them change this attitude. This happened during the Auschwitz trial in Frankfurt am Main when two defendants, primitive men with the ranks of non-commissioned officers in the SS, Oswald Kaduk and Stefan Baretzki, were irritated by the fact that defendants of a higher rank not only pleaded not guilty but also maintained they were ignorant of the Auschwitz crimes. They lost their patience when confronted by what they thought to be blatant injustice and denounced the falsehoods of the "bigwigs," who had tried to place all responsibility on the shoulders of the Auschwitz small fry.

And so the need arises to attempt a critical evaluation of the three documents presented here. For the sake of orderliness it should be added that Broad's document is reprinted in its entirety, Kremer's document in entirety in those parts which deal with Auschwitz and in part only where his memoranda are not connected with the camp. The document of Höss is republished in those parts which deal with Auschwitz, jointly with Appendix 1, "The Final Solution of the Jewish Question," but omitting his extensive memoirs covering the times before he entered on active service in the SS.

*

The importance of the document of Höss, which constitutes a reliable testimony of the most unimaginable crimes, has been stressed in scores of writings by historians, lawyers, psychologists and philosophers. This document was the subject of debate in the law courts during the Auschwitz trial and other trials. It also contains a wealth of evidence both against those who devised the crimes and against their various executors. This fact relieves us of the necessity of a detailed analysis of the data about Auschwitz. But we do not feel excused from making an evaluation of the veracity and frankness of its statements. We feel we ought to devote, some space to this aspect of the problem. It should also be explained how it came to pass that Höss, the man who bore the greatest direct responsibility for the mass murders committed on a scale unknown in history, decided not only to accept this responsibility but also to relate all the particulars connected with them.

Höss himself gives the answer:

"I could never have brought myself to make this confession of my most secret thoughts and feelings, had I not been approached with a disarming humanity and understanding that I had never dared to expect. It is because of this humane understanding that I have tried to assist as best I can in throwing some light on matters that seemed obscure."[2]

"I was approached with humanity," said Höss. This happened in the Polish prison where he stayed from May 25, 1946, till April 16, 1947, the day when he was executed.

Taking into consideration this remarkable opening of Höss's mind, the commentators of his memoirs stress the sincerity of his statements. Two Polish scholars in particular mention this fact in their writings, after holding many conversations with Höss in the Polish prison. They were Professor Stanisław Batawia, a psychologist, and Professor Jan Sehn, a lawyer. Professor Batawia stated in his Introduction to the first Polish edition of Höss's Autobiography*:*

"The inhibition, shown at first by Höss, gradually lessened and when he came to trust his interlocutor the investigation proceeded in an atmosphere conducive to frank answers."[3]

Here is another passage from the same source:

"It is of course possible to call in question the truthfulness of the statements of the Auschwitz camp commandant, as they could be verified in part only. But both the investigators and all those who came into contact with Höss thought that his statements were generally true, as opposed to the statements of the majority of the interrogated war criminals. The frankness with which he discussed many matters of essential importance was often regarded, I think wrongly, as cynicism, typical of a man devoid of all moral sense."[4]

Professor Batawia's opinion on the credibility of the statements of Höss was quoted with approval by Professor Sehn who, as a judge and member of the Central Commission for the Investigation of Nazi Crimes, conducted the preparatory investigation before the trial of the former commandant of Auschwitz.

Sehn added:

"Höss ... stated that he did not want to conceal anything or to leave anything unsaid, he made no use of his right to refuse answering any question, although he was duly reminded of this right in the course of the interrogation. He readily gave detailed answers to all the questions of the interrogator."[5]

The argument in favour of Höss's frankness, put forward by the Polish authors, was also shared by foreign commentators. Were they right in all

---

[2] *Commandant of Auschwitz. The Autobiography of Rudolf Höss.* London 1961, Pan Books Ltd., p. 205.

[3] *Biuletyn Głównej Komisji Badania Zbrodni Hitlerowskich w Polsce*, vol. 7, Warszawa 1951, Wydawnictwo Ministerstwa Sprawiedliwości, p. 14.

[4] *Ibid.*, p. 28.

[5] *Wspomnienia Rudolfa Hössa, komendanta obozu oświęcimskiego.* Warszawa 1965, Wydawnictwo Prawnicze, p. 19.

respects? I think they were right whenever they stressed the reliability of source, minuteness of detail, accuracy and perhaps even frankness of the statements of Höss, when he spoke about the "technology" of the system of concentration camps, the methods of genocide and of the destruction of prisoners, when he described the systematic approach to mass extermination, worked out even before the war and perfected (with Höss's active participation) in the years of war. It seems, too, that the estimation made by Höss of particular SS-men, of their characters and role, agreed with what he really thought of them. The merits (I do not hesitate to use this word) of Höss in these matters are in fact considerable. If it were possible for him to do any good before being hanged at Auschwitz, he did so by writing his autobiography, so insolubly connected with the history of mass murder.

Even greater, of course, is the merit of those who managed to induce him to do so, that is of Professors Batawia and Sehn. The role of the latter was especially difficult, as he was the official representative of the Polish administration of justice and so, from a formal point of view, the most dangerous adversary of the defendant who stood to lose everything (Höss was conscious of the fact that the death sentence was the only possibility in his case). This circumstance was a further factor, which brought about the decision by Höss to write down his reminiscences in exactly the way he did.

One gains, nevertheless, the impression that the Polish interlocutors of the former Auschwitz commandant, who were at the same time authors of the initial studies of his autobiography, did not manage to avoid a certain over-estimation of the allegedly absolute credibility of his reminiscences.

Captivated to some degree by the prisoner's veracity, they took all that Höss had written at its face value, all the more so because the statements made by Höss before the trial were also corroborated during the trial by written documents, especially those relating to the structure of the camp, the general course of Auschwitz events and the action of mass murder. This, however, is understandable—Höss was indeed an exceptional figure among the war criminals, as he did not deny responsibility for the millions of Auschwitz victims, nor did he gloss over the activities of the SS, although in the Polish prison he still professed his adherence to National Socialism.

Despite all this there still exists one section of the reminiscences of Höss which is hardly credible, namely, that in which he wrote about himself. It is true that today, in 1970, we have at our disposal a considerably wider knowledge about Auschwitz than the authors of the prefaces quoted above. Auschwitz trials, numerous writings and the growing collection of the State Museum at Oświęcim (particularly the collection of reports by former prisoners) allow us to expose the inner history of certain camp matters, while the untimely death of Professor Sehn prevented his having access to such sources. In the light of the facts which were known to Professor Sehn, the whole truth about the man whose name was Höss hardly coincides with the image which Höss himself attempted to hand down to posterity. When one reads his reminiscences, entering into their spirit, one gets the picture of a man of small stature entangled in the cog-wheels of the vast, all-embracing machinery, of which he had been an indispensable part, acting in accordance with the acquired habit of unquestioning obedience and fanatical belief in the justness and inevitability of his deeds.

In other words, Höss wanted to appear as an unshaken and irreproachable National Socialist, acting disinterestedly and in the firm conviction that his activities were necessary for the good of his country and his nation. He admitted, it is true, that what he had done was terribly wrong, and he felt the burden of his responsibility; but he wanted us to believe that his motives were exclusively ideological. This was not so, however, and it is a pity that the commentators of his memoirs failed to notice this.

I do not intend to elaborate on this view here, although I should hope to return to the problem some other time. At present I wish only to draw attention to some particulars which confirm the justness of my above-mentioned reservations.

The commandant of Auschwitz was not disturbed by the fact that he directed the gassing of millions of people, whose possessions he transferred to the Third Reich; but he was indignant when some SS-man, who had access to the belongings of the victims of mass murder, could not resist the temptation to take some of them.

"... the morals of these women [the so-called Aufseherinnen, *SS wardresses, employed in the women's camp.—J.R.]," said Höss, "were, almost without exception, extremely low. Many of them appeared before the SS tribunal charged with theft in connection with* Aktion Reinhard*..."*[6]

In the report entitled "The Final Solution of the Jewish Question," written by Höss in the Cracow prison somewhat earlier, namely in 1946, the reader will find the following statement:

"The treasures brought in by the Jews gave rise to unavoidable difficulties for the camp. It was demoralizing for the members of the SS, who were not always strong enough to resist the temptation provided by these valuables which lay within such easy reach."[7]

But was the commandant himself sufficiently strong to resist this temptation?

There was no question of his "organizing" things as the common SS-man, who had access to "Canada,"[8] *might do. But then he neither had to, nor was he able to do so. "My family, to be sure, were well provided for in Auschwitz. Every wish that my wife or children expressed was granted them. The children could live a free and untrammelled life. My wife's garden was a paradise of flowers,"*[9] *noted Höss. A paradise in Auschwitz... Mrs. Höss corroborated this statement when, according to the report of the prisoner Stanisław Dubiel, employed in the Höss household, she used to say: "I want to live here till I die."*

What contributed to make the life of the Höss family at Auschwitz "a life in paradise"? It was an open secret among prisoners of longer standing in the camp that the Höss family had its regular caterers who supplied the commandant's household with everything that was asked of them. The chief caterer of the Höss household was a German, Erich Grönke, originally a criminal

---

[6] See p. 63.

[7] See pp. 96—97.

[8] "Canada"—in camp slang—storehouse of Jewish property.

[9] See p. 80.

offender, later a civilian functionary of the camp administration at Auschwitz. It was thanks to Höss that Grönke, formerly a capo known as a cruel killer of his fellow-prisoners, was released from the camp and employed as manager or director of a large factory called Bekleidungswerkstätten—Lederfabrik,[10] *in which more than 800 prisoners were employed. In the premises of a former tannery not only tanners were employed but also, above all, shoemakers and tailors, not to mention artisans of different kinds such as joiners, carpenters, smiths, locksmiths, upholsterers, saddlers, etc. They attended both to the wants of prisoners and to those of the SS. And also to the steadily mounting requirements of the commandant himself. One cannot possibly specify to what extent the Höss family profited from the slave labour of the prisoners employed there. Certainly, from the materials taken from the Jews, victims of the gas chambers, the caterers managed to produce all that the fancy of the commandant, and particularly of the commandant's wife, could dream up.*

The author of this Foreword *himself worked in the* Lederfabrik *squad and witnessed the daily jobs, done by experts, for the commandant on orders from Grönke. It is difficult to enumerate all the things made there. Armchairs covered with leather, chandeliers, brief-cases, handbags, suit-cases, shoes, furniture, all kinds of objects made of leather and metal, toys for children and carpets. Finished articles, found among the possessions of the victims (the premises of the* Lederfabrik *contained part of the so-called "Canada" stores) were also often sent to the commandant's house.*

The prisoners employed in the commandant's house (and there were many indeed) had special "Canadian" underwear assigned to them. This was to make them look decent and above all clean. The Hösses, like all SS-men, were greatly afraid of infection, on account of the many contagious diseases in camp, particularly typhus. Mrs. Höss received the underwear to distribute among the prisoners. But instead of doing so she kept it for herself and gave the prisoners the old, worn underwear, discarded by the family. The Höss family wore the underwear of gassed people, their children wore the clothes of those children who had been murdered by their father.

Mrs. Höss lived in paradise amidst the Auschwitz flowers. But flowers do not suffice for man's needs... The above mentioned Polish prisoner, Stanisław Dubiel, was their gardener. He relates as follows: "Before every reception Mrs. Höss told me what was needed or she would tell me to ask Sophie, the cook. Mrs. Höss never gave any money or coupons which were ordinarily needed to buy food." Through another prisoner Dubiel contacted the manager of the prisoners' food store, SS-Unterscharführer *Schebeck, and letting him believe that promotion awaited him induced him to supply the Höss household with various foodstuffs. Dubiel wrote: "The food store was well supplied at that time, as provisions which had been taken from the Jews ... who in the majority of cases had been directed to the gas chambers were kept there."*

Another caterer for the Höss household was the manager of canteens, SS-Oberscharführer *Engelbrecht, who supplied meat, sausage and cigarettes. The commandant "failed" to notice the abundance of all kinds of foodstuffs,*

---

[10] Clothing Workshop—Tannery.

he was "not interested" to inquire where the meat, southern fruit, wines, etc. on his table had come from, in times when there was strict rationing of bread and skimmed milk in the Third Reich. When Höss went to Hungary to help Eichmann organize transports of Hungarian Jews to the Auschwitz gas chambers, he used to send to his wife, still in Auschwitz, whole crates of wine. When the Hösses had to leave their Auschwitz paradise, several freight cars were needed to transport all kinds of property accumulated by this family, which had started in life as modest farmers until Rudolf Höss joined the SS.

The "disinterestedness," so often stressed by Höss, can therefore be regarded as a myth.

*

The situation concerning a number of other matters is similar. For example, Höss severely denounced any erotic relationship between women prisoners and SS-men: "One of these female supervisors," he wrote with indignation, "sank so low as to become intimate with some of the male prisoners."[11]

Höss accused Rapportführer *Palitzsch, one of the most cruel among the Auschwitz murderers, of sexual relations with a woman prisoner at Birkenau. Several SS-men, however, were acquainted—even while* KL Auschwitz *still existed—with the exceptionally sordid affair between the commandant and a woman prisoner (Eleonore Hodys, thought to be Italian) who was employed at his house. After working for several months in Höss's household she was transferred first to a women's penal company and then to the cellars of Block 11, where Höss used to visit her in secret. When her pregnancy became known, she was put into a* Stehbunker *(standing-cell) and condemned to die of starvation. It was only by accident that the affair became public. There had been some clashes between Höss and the Head of the Political Section, Grabner. The seduced woman had managed to get Grabner, against whom an inquiry in another matter was then under way, interested in her fate. Grabner made use of the acquired information to have his revenge on Höss, towards whom he bore a grudge. He informed the investigating SS judges of the Hodys affair. The Hodys episode was again recalled in 1965, during the Auschwitz trial in Frankfurt, when the former SS judge, Dr. Wiebeck, gave evidence as a witness in this matter.*[12]

Rudolf Höss had not, after all, been a Nazi saint!

*

There is another sphere of matters which raises doubt as to the absolute frankness of the commandant's report. This is the sphere of his attitude to prisoners. In his reminiscences, we continually meet with the statement that he could not have prevented the additional evils rampant in the camp, namely the torturing and murdering of prisoners for alleged offences. According to Höss

---

[11] See p. 63.

[12] Hermann Langbein: *Der Auschwitz-Prozess. Eine Dokumentation.* Wien 1965, Europa-Verlag, vol. 1, p. 145.

things were so because the SS functionaries at his disposal, as well as the German criminal offenders brought from Sachsenhausen ("the founders of the camp") had introduced such a régime, against which he was powerless to act. He wrote: "From the very beginning the camp was dominated by theories which were later to produce the most evil and sinister consequences. Despite all this, it might have been possible to control these men, and indeed even to bring them round to my way of thinking, if the officer in charge of the prison camp and the Rapportführer *had followed my instructions and obeyed my wishes. But this they neither could nor would do, owing to their intellectual limitations, their obstinacy and malice, and above all for reasons of convenience."*[13] *And further: "The commandant ... directs policy ... and bears ultimate responsibility for all that happens. But the real master of the prisoners' whole life, and of the entire internal organization, is the officer in charge of the prison camp or alternatively the* Rapportführer, *if that officer is strong-minded and more intelligent than his immediate superior."*[14]

In this way Höss tried to evade his responsibility for the "sinister consequences" of the inhuman régime introduced in KL Auschwitz *from its very beginning.*

*Is that the truth? Was Höss really helpless? Did he mean well, while others turned his plans to evil? This was not the case. This may be proved by a more thorough analysis of his writings, which are full of inconsistencies. He mentioned, for instance, that towards the end of 1939, before he found his way to Auschwitz, he became commander (*Lagerführer*) of the concentration camp at Sachsenhausen. According to the theory propounded by himself he could have made use of his position to introduce the régime which he considered to be the proper one. And yet—to quote him again—"whereas Dachau was predominantly red, because the majority of the prisoners were politicals, Sachsenhausen was green. The atmosphere in the camp varied accordingly."*[15] *But Höss, who was then* Lagerführer, *did nothing to change this atmosphere: "green" prisoners (criminal offenders) still had the upper hand.*

A similar situation reigned at Auschwitz in the times of Höss. He again backed the "green" prisoners, regarding them as the mainstay of order in the camp. He mistrusted the "red". One of the many examples of this attitude is the case of the murderer of many prisoners, the "green" Grönke mentioned above, a favourite of Höss, released by him from the camp. On the whole the position in Auschwitz was as follows: as long as Höss was the commandant, "green" prisoners ruled, while when he left and Liebehenschel replaced him as commandant, "red" prisoners took over their duties, not only Germans but also prisoners of other nationalities, including Poles and sometimes even Jews. Conditions within the camp became less rigorous as a result. This fact alone suffices to make the point that Höss, in concealing the truth, wanted to clear himself of blame in this respect too.

---

13 See p. 30.

14 See p. 31.

15 *Commandant of Auschwitz, op. cit.*, pp. 109 and 110.

We often met, during the trials of the SS murderers, with the provocative opinion, also held by some of the lawyers, that SS-men were veritable lambs while only the prisoners murdered each other. The peak of hypocrisy was reached by the Nazis, full of sympathy for their fellow murderers. Himmler said about Heydrich that "he had suffered extremely; he had never been really able to enjoy tranquillity and to relax." The SS diarist Paul Blobel, commander of one of the Einsatzkommandos *which slaughtered people in the occupied territories of the Soviet Union, wrote:* "Ich muss sagen, dass unsere Männer, die daran teilgenommen haben, mehr mit ihren Nerven, runter waren als diejenigen, die dort erschossen werden mussten." *(I must say that our men, who took part in the operation, were more of nervous wrecks than those who had to be shot there).*[16]

Höss does not go so far, but nevertheless the thesis that "the victim is guilty, not the murderer" appears so clearly in his autobiography, that it is surprising that it has been missed by earlier commentators.

When he wrote about the cruel extermination of the Soviet prisoners of war, of whom only very few had survived, Höss cynically declared: "But I never got over the feeling that those who had survived had done so only at the expense of their comrades, because they were more ferocious and unscrupulous, and generally 'tougher'."[17]

When speaking of the Jewish prisoners he said: "They were mainly persecuted by members of their own race, their foremen or room seniors."[18] *"They flinched from nothing, no matter how desperate, in their efforts to make such safe jobs fall vacant and then to acquire them for themselves. Victory usually went to the most unscrupulous man or woman."*[19]

He wrote about the special squad: "They were all well aware that once the actions were completed they, too, would meet exactly the same fate as that suffered by those thousands of their own race, to whose destruction they had contributed so greatly. Yet the eagerness with which they carried out their duties never ceased to amaze me."[20] *According to him, "There were three main political groups among the Polish prisoners, and the adherents of each fought violently against the others ... Each group competed with the others for the most influential posts ... Indeed I dare say that many cases of spotted fever or typhus resulting in death, ... could be accounted for by this struggle for power."*[21]

In other words—Soviet prisoners were killing their own countrymen, Jews were murdering Jews, and Poles were murdering other Poles. These lies and slanders of Höss, just like the lie that it needed only courage to escape from Auschwitz, have so far been missed by the commentators ...

---

[16] Robert M. W. Kempner: *SS im Kreuzverhör.* München 1964, Rütten u. Leoning Verlag, p. 91.

[17] See p. 48.

[18] See p. 54.

[19] See p. 58.

[20] See p. 76.

[21] See p. 45.

2*

In reality the Soviet prisoners of war had come to Auschwitz only to die a martyr's death; SS-men and through them the "green" capos had orders to murder such prisoners, and they consistently carried them out. The fact that several score of these survived was an accident, and accidents often decided matters of life and death in the camp.

The Jewish prisoners, being the most defenceless among the camp pariahs, were killed off by the SS-men, and, with their approval and encouragement, by the German criminal offenders in the camp. The greatest number of Jewish prisoners met their deaths at the hands of such murderers.

It is hard to guess on what grounds Höss divided the Polish prisoners into three groups. It is true that the Poles were divided politically into right and left wingers, but it is also true that they were united in general solidarity against the SS-men, their henchmen and the camp administration. Höss's statement that the Polish prisoners, "fighting for power," got rid of their rivals by infecting them with typhoid, is pure exaggeration. There were such incidents, not caused by a "struggle for power," however, but by the fight against agents of the SS, against the spies of the Political Section, who could not be liquidated in any other manner because they were protected by Höss, Grabner and their men.

A deeper analysis of the reminiscences of Höss could offer more examples of his over-superficial treatment of many questions. In giving so much space to these problems, I did not wish to present a one-sided view of the person of the Auschwitz commandant and to paint him in black colours only. But I felt that in the name of the whole truth certain things had to be said. It should also be stated that many of the accusations addressed to Höss during the Warsaw trial by the witnesses, former prisoners of KL Auschwitz, *were the result of misunderstanding. I am thinking of the evidence of my fellow-prisoners, who allegedly saw how Höss used to beat and torture prisoners. This was an error, as far as the person of the torturer is concerned. Höss would never stoop to such things. He had more important and more general duties to perform.*

*

What is the relationship of the other two documents, offered to our readers, to the reminiscences of Höss? Even from a strictly formal point of view, we can hardly regard the reminiscences of Pery Broad or the diary of Johann Kremer as documents of equal value. Both authors occupied far less important positions in the camp hierarchy, Broad being only a non-commissioned officer, while Kremer, though an officer, was not a "professional" concentration camp official. He was a physician, who through accident rather than design found his way into the history of the anus mundi, *the anus of the world, as he had called Auschwitz in his diary. Moreover, Broad was still a young man at the time, and his knowledge of life was limited to what he had learnt in the* Hitlerjugend. *Kremer was much older, but he was still an individual of distinct psychopathic traits, when seen against a background of the perverted characters so frequent among the SS-men. He therefore left his mark, although his stay in Auschwitz was rather short.*

We cannot therefore directly compare the notes of Broad and Kremer with the reminiscences of Höss. They should not, however, be underestimated, above all because of the fact that both authors occupied positions in the most sensitive points of the camp administration, both were components of the Auschwitz death factory, closely bound with its basic function of mass extermination.

Broad, employed in the Political Section, was not only well informed about the crimes perpetrated by this section on its victims, the prisoners, but also played an active part in them. Kremer, the camp physician, was obliged, like all the SS doctors, to be present at the gassing of the newly arrived RSHA transports and of the "selected" prisoners. His "presence" was not limited to passive observation during such events. The physician's finger pointed out those who were to be led straight to the gas chambers, and decided who was to be directed to the camp, thus cooperating in the process of extermination. Kremer's finger was the finger of fate. Those at whom it pointed could live only as long as it took to go through the "formalities" of undressing and being led to the gas chamber, where another SS-man would throw a tin of Cyclon into the sealed room. Both Kremer and Broad had seen and known a great deal. Their notes supplement the reports left by Höss with essential and shocking details.

*

In a certain sense, the reminiscences of Broad resemble those of Höss. Broad tried to write objectively about his experiences and about all he had seen at Auschwitz. But there is one reservation—he did not speak the whole truth about himself and his own part in the events. He did not pretend to be a good man, as Höss did; his tactics were different: he simply omitted to mention his own actions. Generally speaking, however, their common application of distortions or concealments, psychologically quite understandable, is probably the result of the fact that both reports, written after the war and in prison, were destined to be read by the victors.

However, the document handed immediately after the war to an officer of the British Intelligence Service naturally differs from evidence given before the court. The officer in question was not well versed in problems of Auschwitz and was probably enraptured to find one "just man," who moreover knew English. The members of the court, on the other hand, well understood what the role of the Political Section had been in the camp. Besides, there were witnesses of the events present in court, former prisoners. Thus Broad, the defendant, could count on having his reminiscences corrected during the Frankfurt trial.

When the ex-SS-Unterscharführer *vividly described in his memoirs the mass executions of Polish prisoners under the wall of death of Block 11, he forgot to mention his own activity there. But he could not avoid being more outspoken during the trial. Faced by the statements of witnesses who had seen him taking part (together with all the other functionaries of the Political Section) in acts of terror he was forced to admit that this had been the case.*

Broad described the tortures inflicted by the camp Gestapo *with indignation. Not a word about himself! Witnesses — former prisoners — charged him with complicity in them. It was proved beyond all doubt that he, too, had beaten and tortured prisoners. But liability for this crime had become prescribed in the Federal Republic of Germany by the time that the Frankfurt court was in session; only murder could still be prosecuted. In its verdict the court stated that "there existed a strong suspicion that Broad had killed people during the interrogations, but final evidence was lacking."[22] Broad was not convicted on that charge. Nevertheless, we possess sufficient information to be able to assess his real attitude.*

Broad gives us a horrifying picture of the transports sent directly from the unloading ramp to the gas chambers. Where was he on these occasions? Did he not actively participate in mass murder? Again no mention of that. The Frankfurt court came to the conclusion that "it has been proved that Broad served at the ramp ... As it was not possible to ascertain how often he was on duty at the ramp, the court decided in his favour that he had been there at least twice. As this happened during the arrival of Hungarian transports which were on the whole more numerous, it is assumed that each time at least one thousand people were destined to die."[23]

A comparison of Broad's notes with the findings of the court makes it possible to supplement the gaps which exist in his report regarding his own activities.

Once again it should be stressed that Broad's report of the events which he had witnessed or about which he had heard was truthful, although he omitted to mention his own role in the life of Auschwitz. This conclusion becomes apparent if we compare his notes with the reminiscences of former camp prisoners and with the documents which the SS did not manage to destroy. His report, when contrasted with the document of Höss, is naturally fragmentary, but even so it broadens our knowledge of Auschwitz, offering new elements omitted by Höss and not known to the ex-prisoners, such as, for example, the history of the revolt of the Ukrainian SS-men or details of the massacre of women prisoners at Budy.

Kremer's notes are altogether different in character. They do not expand our knowledge of the history of KL *Auschwitz as much as the other two documents. But the fact that an SS physician wrote about the role of the Nazi "sanitary authorities," confirming their collaboration in crimes, is particularly valuable. Unlike the other documents, Kremer's diary tells us much about its author. He wrote it for his own use, with no intention of publishing it, and so it was entirely honest.*

It is not a diary written ex post, *like the others, but noted day by day, under the fresh impression of new events. It was brought to light by chance. Kremer—as opposed to Höss and Broad—did not evaluate the Auschwitz events, but only recorded them in so far as they involved his own person. He gives vent to his own feelings only rarely, as for instance in the entry of September 2, 1942:*

"Was present for the first time at a special action at 3 a.m. By comparison Dante's Inferno seems almost a comedy. Auschwitz is justly called an extermination camp!"[24] And the entry of September 5, 1942: "This noon was present at

---

22 Hermann Langbein, *op. cit.*, p. 886.

23 *Ibid.*

24 See p. 162.

a special action in the women's camp (Moslems)—the most horrible of all horrors. Hschf. Thilo, military surgeon, is right when he said to me today that we are located here in the anus mundi.*"*[25]

Such examples of personal involvement are very infrequent. More often a bald note of a "special action" appears alongside a detailed account of the contents of the menu of the SS canteen. The doctor of philosophy and medicine from Münster was not deprived of appetite either by his active presence at the events of the anus mundi *or "the most horrible of all horrors."*

It so happened that I had the opportunity to evaluate both Kremer's diary and the reminiscences of Broad, as I translated and wrote commentaries on both documents.[26] *I shall not be able to add here anything fresh or sensational to our present knowledge of these documents and their authors. I shall, however, repeat some of my earlier remarks on the subject of Kremer:*

"... A very incomplete enumeration of RSHA transports, in the selection of which Kremer had participated (no data given about 4 transports), shows that during his short stay at Auschwitz he had managed to send to the gas chamber 10,717 men, women and children out of 12,291 deportees. Let us add that this number does not include the 'Moslems,' prisoners selected by Kremer to be gassed or for the lethal injection ...

"A separate and exceptionally abominable episode in Kremer's Auschwitz crimes was his exploitation of the criminal conditions prevailing there for 'scientific' purposes. We know that not only Kremer made use of this opportunity, but that tens, even hundreds of Nazi 'scientists,' not to mention the big pharmaceutical enterprises, also used the defenceless prisoners as the 'guinea-pigs' for their experiments."[27]

This German professor went so far in his scientific research that he would point out the "objects" of interest to him—i.e. starving prisoners; then after first interviewing them, he would order their immediate murder, to obtain FRESH SAMPLES of spleen, pancreas and liver, taken from the corpses. He examined these for changes in the human organism under the influence of starvation. Kremer's lebendfrisches Material *constitutes a really striking proof of the degeneration of science in the Third Reich.*

It is true, as we said before, that Kremer was an individual with psychopathic traits. But he was also a Dozent *of a university, and had held various posts. It was the criminal Nazi ideology and practice that incited such individuals. When* Reichsführer-SS *Heinrich Himmler, speaking of the Slavs, called them* Menschentiere *(human animals),*[28] *not to mention the "sub-human Jews," then*

---

[25] See p. 162—163.

[26] Jerzy Rawicz translated both manuscripts from German into Polish. The Reminiscences of Pery Broad were first published in *Zeszyty Oświęcimskie*, no. 9, while excerpts from Kremer's diary appeared in *Zeszyty Oświęcimskie*, no. 13. The Reminiscences of Pery Broad were first published in English in 1965, under the title *KZ Auschwitz: Reminiscences of Pery Broad, SS-man in the Auschwitz Concentration Camp*.

[27] Jerzy Rawicz: Dokument hańby (foreword to Kremer's Diary). *Zeszyty Oświęcimskie*, Oświęcim 1970, no. 13, p. 12.

[28] Himmler's speech to SS generals in Poznań, October 4, 1943 (IMT DOC 1919-PS). Quoted after Edward Crankshaw: *Die Gestapo.* Berlin 1959, Colloquium Verlag, p. 24.

normal persons, like Höss, who were overcome by a ruthless concept of obedience, and psychopathic individuals like Kremer had the opportunity to act savagely. Sub-human beings and human animals could, or even should, be gassed, shot, killed with phenol injections or with the handle of a spade. They could and should be treated as experimental material, for: "Unsere Sorge, unsere Pflicht ist unser Volk und unser Blut; dafür haben wir zu sorgen und zu denken, zu arbeiten und zu kämpfen und für nichts anderes."[29]

Hence the duality of Kremer's evaluations. Kremer, as already pointed out, felt no repugnance when prisoners were killed for lebendfrisches Material, *but when* Herr Dozent *returned after his Auschwitz adventure to his august Münster, bombed by American aircraft towards the end of the war, he most severely censured the "air gangsters" (entries of January 22, and March 26, 1945), condemning them for their lack of humanity. It is not, then, important what is done; it only matters who does it and who is the victim.*

If Germans, and among them Kremer himself, committed the most outrageous crimes, everything was in order; if the Allies, however, wishing to put an end to those crimes, fought against Germans, then they lacked humanity.

Let us add that the quasi-critical remarks on the subject of conditions in the Third Reich, strewn over the pages of Kremer's diary, have nothing in common with the alleged opposition of the author to the régime, as he tried to prove during his trials. They are only the result of the zealous ambition of that pseudo-scientist. His strange notion—the discovery of the hereditary nature of acquired injuries (those cats with stumpy tails)—could not, quite apart from its absurdity, have found recognition in the Nazi war state, where hundreds and thousands of men, mutilated at the fronts, haunted the towns and villages, their arms and legs amputated. In reality Kremer was an obedient National-Socialist, with a grudge for not having been suitably rewarded for his fidelity. Envious and pusillanimous, he saw how others were promoted and so felt wronged, perhaps even a victim of a plot hatched by the opponents of Nazism.

*

Had Adolf Hitler not seized power in Germany in 1933, no person in the world would have known of the existence of men like Rudolf Höss, Pery Broad and Johann Kremer.

To tell the truth, Höss was already known in 1923, when he was sentenced to a long term in prison for his participation in an assassination. But there were many assassins of that type in those days. If it had not been for the triumph of the Nazi in 1933, Höss, after having served his term in prison, would have fallen into oblivion.

Even less can be said about Pery Broad, born in the other hemisphere, who returned to Germany with his mother and was preparing to enter a merchant's career. He would have lived out his insignificant life, and nobody would have noticed him.

---

29 "Our concern, our duty, is our people and our blood, so we have to care and think, to work and fight for this and for nothing else." *Ibid.*

Johann Kremer? He would not have been successful in his career under normal circumstances. Chasing his stumpy-tailed cats he would have become the laughing-stock of his learned colleagues, perhaps like one of those "professors," so pointedly ridiculed in former times by Heinrich Heine, the poet of genius anathematized by Hitler.

Who would have been acquainted with all those names—symbols of evil—the Himmlers, Heydrichs, Eichmanns and Müllers, or to stick to Auschwitz, the Kaduks, Bogers, Grabners, Palitzsches? They were created by a criminal system, thanks to which those who were of no account in society suddenly became lords over the life and death of thousands, hundreds of thousands, millions. They did their task not only with thoughtless obedience, but also willingly and sometimes—as was the case with Höss—with unexpected inventiveness. They became indispensable cogs in the machinery of destruction, they reached the peaks of their lives endowed with unlimited power. They used it freely, growing in their own opinion and wallowing in inhuman cruelty.

The fascist system had created Höss, Broad, Kremer and others like them. And then they all became the tools of that system. Just as well that their infamous activities have left their traces not only in the memory of their few surviving victims, but also in the reports written by the criminals themselves. The world will, perhaps, be able to draw its conclusions from this most terrible lesson of history, realizing to what extremes a system of injustice, evil, and contempt for other human beings can lead. Perhaps this will prove to be an effective warning for the future?

Let us hope so!

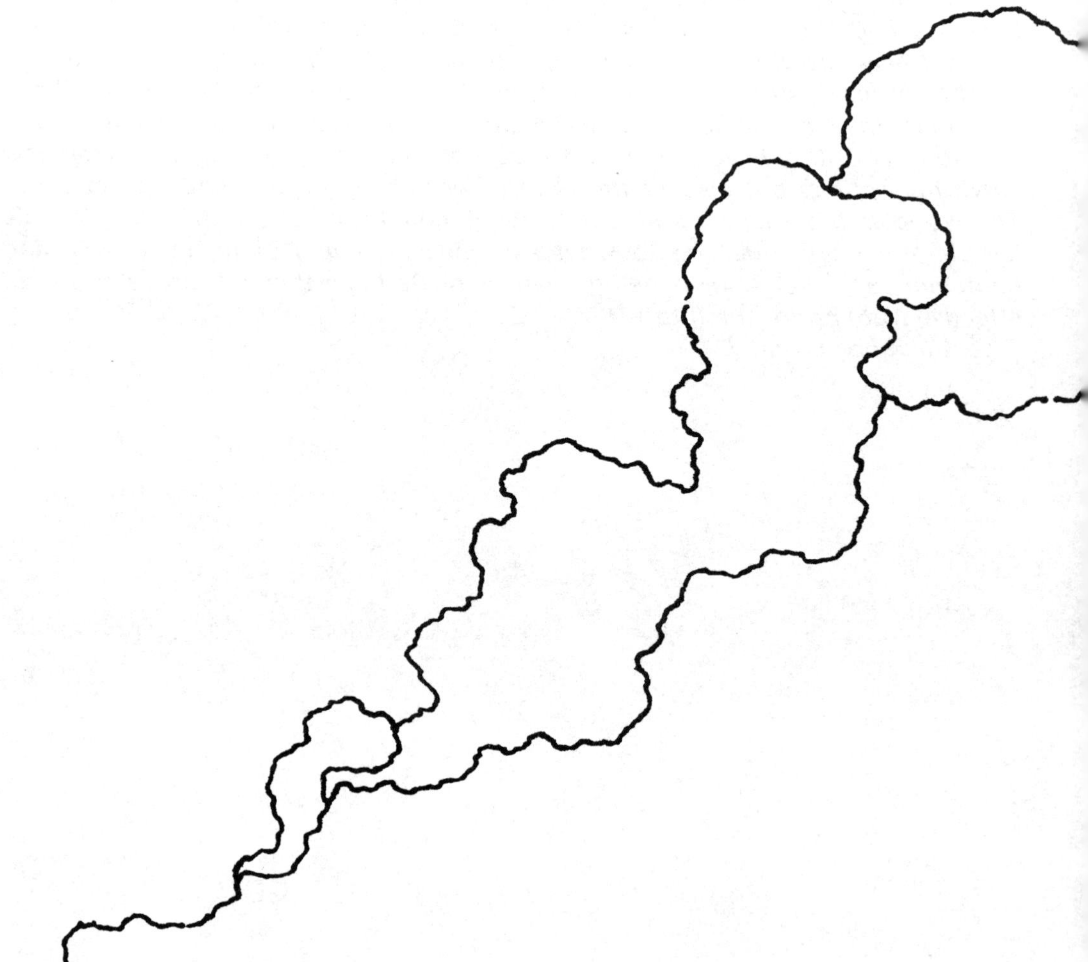

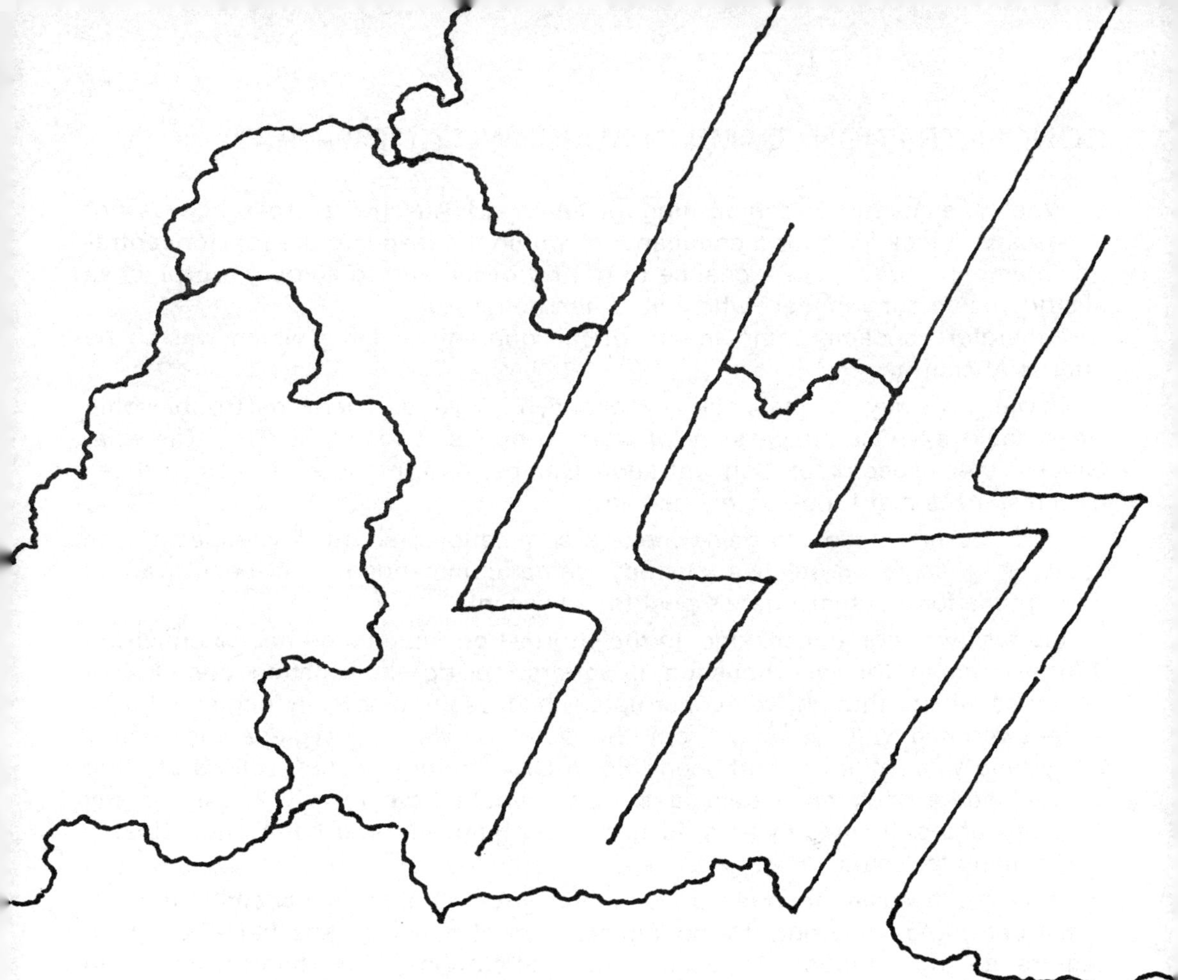

AUTOBIOGRAPHY
of Rudolf Höss

CONCENTRATION[1] CAMP IN AUSCHWITZ (1940—1943)

When the matter of establishing [a camp at] Auschwitz arose, it was not necessary to look long for a commandant within the Inspectorate [of Concentration Camps]. Loritz[2] had a chance to get rid of me and to acquire a protective custody camp commander[3] who suited him better . . .

I therefore became commandant of the quarantine camp which was to be built at Auschwitz.

It was far away, in the back of beyond, in Poland. There the troublesome Höss could exercise his passion for work to his heart's content. That was what Glücks, the Inspector of Concentration Camps, had intended. It was in these circumstances that I took up my new task.

I had never anticipated being made a commandant so quickly, especially as some very senior protective custody camp commanders had been waiting a long time for a commandant's post to fall vacant.

My task was not an easy one. In the shortest possible time I had to construct a transit camp for ten thousand prisoners,[4] using the existing complex of buildings which, though well-constructed, had been completely neglected, and were swarming with vermin. From the point of view of hygiene, practically everything was lacking. I had been told in Oranienburg,[5] before setting off, that I could not expect much help, and that I would have to rely largely on my own resources. In Poland I would find everything that had been unobtainable in Germany for years!

It is much easier to build a completely new concentration camp than to construct one quickly out of a conglomeration of buildings and barracks which require a large amount of constructional alteration. I had hardly arrived in Auschwitz before the Inspector of the Security Police and of the Security Service in Breslau[6] was inquiring when the first transports could be sent to me!

It was clear to me from the very beginning that Auschwitz could be made into a useful camp only through the hard and untiring efforts of everyone, from the commandant down to the lowest prisoner.

---

[1] *Konzentrationslager—KL*. In Nazi terminology concentration camps were also sometimes designated by the letters KZ.

[2] Commandant of *KL Sachsenhausen*, *SS-Oberführer* Hans Loritz.

Further information about persons mentioned in the reminiscences of Höss, also in those of Broad and Kremer, is appended at the end of this book in the form of biographical notes.

[3] *Schutzhaftlagerführer*. SS officers were entrusted with this function.

[4] The camp was located on the site of former Polish military barracks, taken over by the German army (Wehrmacht). The barracks consisted of a block of over ten buildings, both wooden and brick-built, situated in the Zasole district of the town of Auschwitz (Oświęcim). According to the original plans of the Inspector of Concentration Camps, Auschwitz was to be a quarantine camp, that is, a transit camp for prisoners of Polish nationality.

[5] That is, in the Inspectorate of Concentration Camps.

[6] *SS-Oberführer* Arpad Wigand held this position at that time.

But in order to harness all the available manpower to this task, I had to ignore all concentration camp tradition and customs. If I was to get the maximum effort out of my officers and men, I had to set them a good example. When reveille sounded for the SS rankers, I too got out of bed. Before they had started their day's work, I had already begun mine. It was late at night before I finished. There were very few nights in Auschwitz when I could sleep undisturbed by urgent telephone calls.

If I wanted to get good and useful work out of the prisoners, then, contrary to the usual and universal practice in concentration camps, they had to be given better treatment. I assumed that I would succeed in both housing and feeding them better than in the other camps.

Everything that, from my point of view, seemed wrong in the other camps, I wished to handle differently here.

I believed that in such conditions I could obtain the willing cooperation of the prisoners in the construction work that had to be done. I also felt that I could then demand the maximum effort from them.

I had complete confidence in these assumptions. Nevertheless, within a few months, I might even say during the first weeks, I became bitterly aware that all my good faith and best intentions were doomed to be dashed to pieces against the human inadequacy and sheer stupidity of most of the officers and men under me.[7]

I used every means at my disposal to make my fellow-colleagues understand my wishes and intentions, and I attempted to make it clear to them that this was the only practicable way of getting everyone to cooperate fruitfully in completing the task assigned us.

My good intentions were in vain. Over the years the teaching of Eicke,[8] Koch[9] and Loritz had penetrated so deeply into the minds of the "old hands," and had become so much a part of their flesh and blood, that even the best-willed of them simply could not behave otherwise than in the way to which they had become accustomed during long service in the concentration camps. The "beginners" were quick to learn from the "old hands," but the lessons they learnt were unfortunately not the best.

All my endeavours to obtain at least a few good and competent officers and non-commissioned officers for Auschwitz from the Inspector of Concentration Camps were to no avail. Glücks simply would not cooperate. It was the same with the prisoners who acted as supervisors of the others. The *Rapportführer*[10]

---

[7] Officers, non-commissioned officers and other rank, detailed to concentration camps, were members of the SS. See p. 31, note 14.

[8] The first Inspector of Concentration Camps.

[9] Then the commandant of *KL Buchenwald*.

[10] Reporting officer. This used to be a non-commissioned officer of the SS. His duties consisted above all in checking the prisoners' number in camp at morning and evening roll-call. The *Rapportführer* was directly subordinate to the *Lagerführer*, while all the block leaders (*Blockführer*) were responsible to the *Rapportführer*.

Palitzsch was to find thirty useful professional criminals of all trades, since the RSHA[11] would not let me have politicals for this purpose at Auschwitz.

He brought back thirty[12] of these, whom he considered the best among those offered to him at Sachsenhausen.[13]

Less than ten of them were suited to my wishes and intentions. Palitzsch had selected these men according to his own opinions and his own ideas as to how prisoners should be treated, which he had already acquired and to which he had grown used. He was by disposition incapable of behaving in any other way.

So the whole backbone about which the camp was to be built was defective from the start. From the very beginning the camp was dominated by theories which were later to produce the most evil and sinister consequences.

Despite all this, it might have been possible to control these men, and indeed even to bring them round to my way of thinking, if the officer in charge of the prison camp and the *Rapportführer* had followed my instructions and obeyed my wishes.

But this they neither could nor would do, owing to their intellectual limitations, their obstinacy and malice, and above all for reasons of convenience.

---

[11] *Reichssicherheitshauptamt* (RSHA)—Reich Main Security Office was called into being in 1939. Its first director was the Head of the Security Police and Security Service (*Chef der Sicherheitspolizei und des Sicherheitsdienstes—CdSuSD*), *SS-Obergruppenführer* Reinhard Heydrich. After Heydrich had been killed in Prague on June 5, 1942, by the Czech Resistance Movement, this function was assigned (in January 1943) to *SS-Obergruppenführer* Ernst Kaltenbrunner, who was sentenced to death in 1946 by the International Military Tribunal in Nuremberg.

The RSHA—like the WVHA (see p. 61, note 96)—had been organized as one of the twelve main offices in the central office of the SS administration (*Reichsführung SS*) and at the same time as a department in the Internal Affairs Ministry of the Third Reich. The head office in question consisted of seven offices, among which the Office of the State Secret Police (*Geheime Staatspolizeiamt*) was designated by number IV, the Office of the Criminal Police of the Reich (*Reichskriminalpolizeiamt*) by number V and the Security Service (*Sicherheitsdienst*) by III, VI and VII.

[12] The thirty prisoners mentioned here were brought to *KL Auschwitz* on May 20, 1940, and had camp numbers from 1 to 30. All of them were criminal offenders of German nationality and they held various functions in the camp, such as camp senior (*Lagerältester*), block senior (*Blockältester*), capo, etc. Almost all of them revealed remarkable sadism and brutality in their treatment of other camp prisoners.

[13] *KL Sachsenhausen*, established in 1936, was one of the concentration camps which were organized within the territory of the Third Reich after Hitler seized power. In July 1936 prisoners were brought here from one of the oldest camps at Esterwegen. Then further political prisoners, mainly communists, began to arrive. As a model camp (*Musterlager*) it was raised to the rank of a unit supervising the organization of concentration camps, and this had a decisive influence on the choice of Oranienburg by the highest SS authorities as the seat of the Inspectorate of Concentration Camps (*Inspektorat der Konzentrationslager*—IKL). In 1939 *KL Sachsenhausen* became an international camp.

A total of over 200,000 registered prisoners passed through this camp. In fact the numbers were much greater, for up to the end of 1939 the camp numbers of ex-prisoners (now dead, released or transferred) were given to new arrivals. Moreover, a great number of persons who perished in the camp (either gassed or shot) were not noted in the records. Over 110,000 people died here during the 9 years of its existence.

Its successive commandants were : *SS-Standartenführer* Karl Otto Koch, *SS-Oberführer* Hermann Baranowsky, *SS-Oberführer* Hans Loritz, and *SS-Standartenführer* Keindl.

For these men the key-prisoners we had been sent were exactly right, right, that is, for the purposes which they envisaged, and for their attitude.

The real ruler of every concentration camp is the officer in charge of the prison camp. The commandant may leave his stamp upon the outer form of communal camp life, and this will be more or less obvious according to the energy and enthusiasm he devotes to his job. It is he who directs policy, has final authority, and bears ultimate responsibility for all that happens. But the real master of the prisoners' whole life, and of the entire internal organization, is the officer in charge of the prison camp or alternatively the *Rapportführer*, if that officer is strong-minded and more intelligent than his immediate superior. The commandant may decide the lines on which the camp is to be run and issue the necessary general orders and regulations concerning the life of the prisoners, as he thinks best. But the way in which his orders are carried out depends entirely on the officers in charge of the prison camp. The commandant is thus entirely dependent on their goodwill and intelligence.

It follows that if he does not trust them, or considers them incapable, he must take over their duties himself. Only thus can he be certain that his instructions and orders will be carried out correctly in the manner he intends, particularly when they relate to matters other than mere routine. How much harder it is for the commandant of a concentration camp to know that all his orders concerning the prisoners, orders which are often of the greatest consequence, will be correctly interpreted and carried out regardless! The capos always prove particularly difficult to control. For reasons of prestige as well as for disciplinary reasons, the commandant can never interrogate the prisoners concerning their SS[14] guards; only in extreme cases, with a view to a criminal investigation, can this be done. Even then the prisoners, almost without exception, will say they know nothing or will give evasive replies, for they inevitably fear reprisals.[15]

I had learnt enough about all this at first hand in Dachau[16] and Sachsen-

---

[14] The Guard Detachments of the National-Socialist German Workers' Party (*Die Schutzstaffeln der Nationalsozialistischen Deutschen Arbeiterpartei*), generally known as the SS, were organized in 1925 by Adolf Hitler as the Party's fighting squads. Their aim was to ensure the protection and security of party meetings. After Hitler took over in 1933, the SS became a large organization consisting of three formations: 1. The General SS (*Allgemeine SS*). 2. Military Formations of the SS (*SS-Verfügungstruppe, Waffen-SS*). Until the first stages of World War II, members of these formations did four years voluntary military service, which was equivalent to compulsory military service. These formations constituted the main part of the SS armed forces (*Waffen-SS*), which fought at the fronts. 3. The Death's-Head formations (*SS-Totenkopfverbände*) which constituted the garrisons of concentration camps. In 1934 they were excluded from the ranks of the General SS and considerably enlarged due to the endeavours of Theodor Eicke.

Tattooing was introduced in the SS when World War II began. It denoted the blood-group of the individual, and was placed beneath the left armpit.

[15] The aim of all concentration camps, including the Auschwitz camp, was to destroy the mind and the body of the prisoner. The camp authorities achieved this end by using terror, both generally and individually. As a rule every SS-man was the master over a prisoner's destiny; he could "dispose of" the prisoner at any time, should the latter dare to complain to the camp authorities about bad treatment.

[16] *KL Dachau*, established on March 22, 1933, on the premises of a former gun-powder factory, was one of the first concentration camps organized within the territory of the Third Reich. It was a model camp in which the SS staff was trained to serve in other camps. From March 1933 to

hausen, as block leader,[17] *Rapportführer* and commander of the protective custody camp. I know very well how easy it is in a camp for unwelcome orders to be deliberately misinterpreted, and even to be given an entirely opposite construction, without the issuing authority ever being aware of this. In Auschwitz I was very soon quite sure that this was being done.

Such a state of affairs could only be radically altered by an immediate change in the entire staff of the protective custody camp. And the Inspector of Concentration Camps would never in any circumstances have permitted this.

It was impossible for me personally to see that my orders were carried out down to the smallest detail, since this would have meant diverting my attention from my main task, the building of a serviceable camp as rapidly as possible, and acting as officer in charge of the protective custody camp myself.

It was during the early period, when the prison camp was being got under way, that I should have spent my whole time in the camp, precisely because of the mentality of the camp staff.

But it was precisely then that I was compelled to be almost always away from the camp owing to the inefficiency of most of the officials with whom I had to deal.

In order to get the camp started I had already had to negotiate with various economic offices, and with the local and district authorities. My executive officer[18] was a complete halfwit and I was thus forced to take matters out of his hand and to organize the entire victualling of troops and prisoners myself.

Whether it was a question of bread or meat or potatoes, it was I who had to go and find them. Yes, I even had to visit the farms in order to collect straw. Since I could expect no help of any kind from the Inspectorate, I had to make do as best I could on my own. I had to "organize" the trucks and lorries I needed, and the fuel for them. I had to drive as far as Zakopane and Rabka to acquire cooking-pots for the prisoners' kitchen, and to the Sudetenland for bed-frames and mattresses.

Since my architect could not acquire the materials he needed most urgently, I had to drive out with him to look for them. In Berlin they were still quarrelling

---

February 1940 it was a place of isolation for Germans who were hostile towards Nazism, and for German Jews. Austrians and Czechs were its next victims. Around 2,000 Poles, citizens of the Third Reich, were held there at the outbreak of war. On September 27, 1939, the camp was taken over by Theodor Eicke, in order to form here a front-line division of the *Waffen-SS*. About 100 prisoners were left in the camp to do the most important work (e.g. tending to the hot-houses), while more than 4,000 were sent to other camps. In February 1940 the SS troops were dispatched to the front-line and the empty barracks were filled again with prisoners brought from *KL Buchenwald, Flossenbürg, Mauthausen* and *Sachsenhausen*. More than 200,000 prisoners had passed through Dachau by April 1944; of these about 150,000 had perished. The first commandant of *KL Dachau* was *SS-Standartenführer* Hilmar Wäckerle. He was succeeded by *SS-Oberführer* Heinrich Deubel, *SS-Oberführer* Hans Loritz, *SS-Sturmbannführer* Alex Piotrowsky, *SS-Obersturmbannführer* Martin Weiss, and *SS-Obersturmbannführer* Eduard Weiter.

[17] An SS non-commissioned officer, the direct superior of prisoners living in a given block.

[18] *Verwaltungsführer*. In the initial stage this was *SS-Untersturmführer* Max Meyer, detailed to *KL Auschwitz* from the Inspectorate of Concentration Camps.

about the responsibility for the construction of Auschwitz, for it had been agreed that the whole project was an army affair and had only been handed over to the SS for the duration of the war.

The RSHA, the Commander of the Security Police in Cracow, and the Inspector of the Security Police and the Security Service in Breslau were repeatedly inquiring when ever-larger groups of prisoners could be accepted at the camp.

Yet I still could not lay my hands on a hundred yards of barbed wire. There were mountains of it in the Engineer Depot at Gleiwitz. But I could not touch it without first getting authority to have it decontrolled from the Senior Engineer Staff in Berlin. The Inspectorate of Concentration Camps refused to help in this matter. So the urgently needed barbed wire just had to be pilfered. Wherever I found old field fortifications I ordered them to be dismantled and the pill-boxes broken up, and thus I acquired the steel they contained. Whenever I came across installations containing material I urgently needed, I simply had it taken away at once without worrying about the formalities. I had to help myself.

Furthermore, the evacuation of the first zone of the area assigned to the camp was going on. The second zone had also begun to be cleared. I had to work out how all this additional agricultural land was to be used.[19]

At the end of November 1940 the first progress report was submitted to the *Reichsführer SS*[20], and an expansion of the whole camp area was begun as ordered.

I thought that the construction and completion of the camp itself were more than enough to keep me occupied, but this first progress report served only to set in motion an endless and unbroken chain of fresh tasks and further projects.

From the very beginning I was so absorbed, I might say obsessed with my task, that every fresh difficulty only increased my zeal. I was determined that nothing should get me down. My pride would not allow it. I lived only for my work.

It will be understood that my many and diverse duties left me but little time for the camp and the prisoners themselves.

---

[19] In connection with the establishing of *KL Auschwitz* the area round the camp was cleared of the Polish inhabitants. The displacement of the population took place in several stages. The first stage occurred in June 1940. About 2,000 persons, inhabiting the cottages situated near the former military barracks and the buildings of the Polish Tobacco Monopoly, were then deported. The next displacement took place in July 1940 and concerned the inhabitants of the following streets: Legionów, Krótka and Polna. In November of the same year a third displacement was effected, during which the inhabitants of the Zasole district had to leave. This operation continued through March and April 1941, when the inhabitants of the villages of Babice, Budy, Rajsko, Brzezinka, Broszkowice, Pławy and Harmęże were deported.

The entire area amounted to 40 square kilometres and was called the camp interest or activity zone (*Interessengebiet*). In the years 1941—1943 agricultural and live-stock farms and fisheries were established in which prisoners, men and women, were employed. The camp authorities established sub-camps for prisoners employed on the farms in the years 1942—1943.

[20] Heinrich Himmler.

I had to leave them entirely in the hands of individuals such as Fritzsch,[21] Meier,[22] Seidler[23] and Palitzsch, distasteful persons in every respect, and I had to do this even though I was well aware that they would not run the camp as I wished and intended.

But I could only dedicate myself completely and wholly to one task. Either I had to devote myself solely to the prisoners, or I had to use all my energies in the construction and completion of the camp. Either task required my entire and undivided attention. It was not possible to attempt both. But my job was, and always remained, to complete the construction and enlargement of the camp.

Over the years many other tasks occupied my attention, but the primary one remained the same throughout. All my thoughts and aspirations were directed towards this one end, and everything else had to take second place. I had to direct the whole undertaking from this standpoint alone. I therefore observed everything from this one point of view.

Glücks often told me that my greatest mistake was in doing everything myself instead of delegating the work to my responsible subordinates. The mistakes that they would make through their incompetence, I should simply accept. I should become reconciled to that. Matters cannot be expected to run just as one wants, always.

He refused to accept the validity of my arguments when I objected that in Auschwitz I had certainly been given the worst type of human material to act as capos and as junior officers : and that it was not only their incompetence, but far more their deliberate carelessness and malice, that compelled me to handle all the more important and urgent tasks myself.

According to him, the commandant should direct and control the whole camp by telephone from his office desk. It should be quite enough if he took an occasional walk through the camp. What innocence! Glücks was only able to hold this view because he had never worked in a concentration camp. That was why he could never understand or appreciate my real needs.

This inability on the part of my superior to understand me brought me to the verge of despair. I put all my ability and my will into my work, I lived for it entirely; yet he regarded it as though this were a game or even a hobby of mine, in which I had become too absorbed and which prevented me from taking the broader view.

When as a result of the visit of the *Reichsführer SS* in March 1941, new and greater tasks were assigned[24] to me without any extra help in the most

---

[21] The first *Schutzhaftlagerführer* (see p. 28, note 3). He held this position in the years 1940—1941.

[22] The correct spelling is Maier. He held the position of the second *Schutzhaftlagerführer*.

[23] He succeeded Maier as the third *Schutzhaftlagerführer*.

[24] Höss had here in mind Himmler's first inspection of *KL Auschwitz* which took place on March 1, 1941. As a result of the inspection of the camp and its interest or activity zone Himmler gave orders to develop the camp at Auschwitz so as to accommodate 30,000 prisoners. He gave orders to build a camp for 100,000 prisoners of war on the site of the village of Brzezinka (Birkenau), and to supply IG-Farbenindustrie, which was then building industrial plants at Dwory near the town of

vital matters being given, my last hope of obtaining better and more reliable assistants vanished.

I had to resign myself to the "bigwigs" and to my continuing quarrels with them. I had a few good and reliable colleagues to support me, but unfortunately these were not in the most important and responsible positions. I was now forced to load and indeed to overload them with work, and I was slow often in appreciating that I was making the mistake of demanding too much of them.

Because of the general untrustworthiness that surrounded me, I became a different person in Auschwitz.

Up to then I had always been ready to see the best in my fellow creatures, and especially in my comrades, until I was convinced of the contrary. I was often badly let down by my credulity. But in Auschwitz, where I found my so-called colleagues constantly going behind my back, and where each day I suffered fresh disappointments, I began to change. I became distrustful and highly suspicious, and saw only the worst in everyone. I thus snubbed and hurt many honest and decent men. I had lost all my confidence and trust.

The sense of comradeship, which up to then I had regarded as something holy, now seemed to me to be a farce. The reason was that so many of old comrades had deceived and doublecrossed me.

Any form of friendly contact became repugnant to me. I repeatedly refused to attend social gatherings, and was glad when I could find a plausible excuse for staying away. My comrades strongly and repeatedly reproached me for this. Even Glücks drew my attention more than once to the lack of that friendly comradeship which should have linked the commandant and his officers at Auschwitz. But I simply could not do it any more. I had been too deeply disillusioned.

I withdrew further and further into myself. I hedged myself in, became unapproachable, and visibly harder.

My family, and especially my wife, suffered on account of this, since my behaviour was often intolerable. I had eyes only for my work, my task.

All human emotions were forced into the background.

My wife was perpetually trying to draw me out of my seclusion. She invited old friends from outside the camp to visit us, as well as my comrades in the camp, hoping that I would be able to relax in their company.[25] She arranged parties away from the camp with the same end in view. She did this in spite of the fact that she had never cared for this sort social life any more than I did.

These efforts did succeed for a time in making me abandon my self-imposed

---

Auschwitz, with 10,000 prisoners. He also recommended that the entire area round the camp should be developed agriculturally and in any other way and that various camp workshops should be enlarged. He also stressed that large armaments factories should be erected round the camp, so that the SS could take the lead also in the field of providing armaments for the German army.

[25] It is evident from the report of Aniela Bednarska, who was employed in the Höss household as a domestic help, that Höss gave parties for groups of SS-men and their families twice monthly. At such parties there used to be present, among others, *SS-Hauptsturmführer* Schwarz and wife, *SS-Obersturmführer* Schwarzhuber, *SS-Hauptsturmführer* Seidler, and *SS-Hauptsturmführer* Kramer and wife. The guests also included the directors of local industrial plants, e.g. the director of the Brzeszcze mine, Otto Heine.

seclusion occasionally, but new disillusionments quickly sent me back behind my glass wall.

Even people who hardly knew me felt sorry for me. But I no longer desired to change, for my disillusionment had, to a certain extent, made me into an unsociable person.

It often happened that when I was with friends whom I had invited, and who were close friends of ours, I would suddenly become tongue-tied and even rude. My only desire then was to run away, and be alone, and never see anyone again. With an effort I would pull myself together and try, with the help of alcohol, to put my ill-humour aside: I would then become talkative and merry and even boisterous. Alcohol, more than anything else, was able to put me in a happy and contented frame of mind. Drink has never made me quarrel with anyone. It has, however, made me admit to things that I would never have divulged when sober. I have never been a solitary drinker, nor have I ever had a craving for drink. I have never been drunk or given way to alcoholic excesses. When I had had enough, I would quietly disappear. There was no question of neglecting my duties through over-indulgence in alcohol. However late I returned home, I was always completely fresh for work and ready for duty next morning. I always expected my officers to behave in the same way. This was on disciplinary grounds. Nothing has a more demoralizing effect on subordinates than the absence of their superior officers at the beginning of the day's work due to over-indulgence in alcoholic consumption on the previous night.

Nevertheless, I found little sympathy for my views.

They only obeyed me because they knew that I was watching them, and they cursed "the old man's bad temper." If I wanted to carry out my task properly, I had to be the engine, tirelessly and ceaselessly pushing on the work of construction and constantly dragging everyone else along with me. Whether SS-man or prisoner, it made no difference.

Not only had I to struggle with all the tedious wartime difficulties in connection with the construction work, but also, daily and even hourly, with the indifference, sloppiness and lack of cooperation of my subordinates.

Active opposition is something that can be met head-on and dealt with but against passive resistance a man is powerless, it eludes his grasp, even though its presence can be felt everywhere. I had to urge on the reluctant shirkers; when there was no alternative, I used force.

Before the war, the concentration camps had served the purpose of self-protection, but during the war, according to the will of the *Reichsführer SS* they became a means to an end. They were now primarily to serve the war effort, the munitions production. As many prisoners as possible were to become armaments workers.[26] Every commandant had to run his camp ruthlessly with this end in view.

---

[26] The exploiting of prisoner labour was not uniformly conducted in the years 1933—45. Three basic stages are easily recognizable in that period. The concentration camps established in the years 1933—39 were originally aimed not only at isolating Hitler's opponents, but also at collecting together anti-social and criminal elements in order to "re-educate" them through work. As the number or prisoners increased it was decided to make use of the prisoners kept in

The intention of the *Reichsführer SS* was that Auschwitz should become one immense prison-cum-munitions centre. What he said during his visit in March of 1941 made this perfectly plain. The camp for 100,000 prisoners of war, the enlargement of the old camp to hold 30,000 prisoners, the ear-marking of 10,000 prisoners for the synthetic rubber factory,[27] all this emphasized his point. But the numbers envisaged were at this time something entirely new in the history of concentration camps.

A camp containing 10,000 prisoners was then considered exceptionally large.

The insistence of the *Reichsführer SS* that the construction work must be pushed on regardless of all present or future difficulties, many of which were and would be well-nigh insuperable, gave me much food for thought even then.

The way in which he dismissed the very considerable objections raised by the *Gauleiters*[28] and by the local authorities[29] was itself enough to indicate that something unusual was afoot.

I was accustomed to the ways of the SS and of the *Reichsführer SS*. But his stern and implacable insistence that these orders be carried out as speedily as possible was new even in him. Glücks himself noticed this. And it was I and I alone who was to be responsible for it all. Out of nothing, and with nothing

---

concentration camps to carry out the tasks set by the NSDAP. The SS established concentration camps at Mauthausen, Flossenbürg and Gross-Rosen, where there were quarries, because Himmler, in the name of the SS, promised Hitler that he would supply the stone needed for party buildings all over the Third Reich. In the years 1940—1942 the camps played a major role in the process of exterminating through work of prisoners from countries subjugated and occupied by Hitler; but even then prisoners were already being employed in industrial plants. In the period from December 1942 until the capitulation—because of the total mobilization within the Third Reich—the concentration camps became the main source of cheap labour, sold by the SS to military and civilian enterprises. This period began with Himmler's order of December 14, 1942, on the strength of which the RSHA requested that 35,000 prisoners capable of work should be sent to concentration camps by the end of January 1943. Rounding up hundreds of thousands of prisoners at the time of the victories of the Soviet army at Stalingrad, and sending them to concentration camps, was the direct result of the demand for manpower in the armaments industry.

[27] The so-called Buna or the Buna-Werke at Dwory near Auschwitz, property of IG-Farbenindustrie, where in a newly built factory the production of synthetic rubber, called "buna," and synthetic petrol had been undertaken. The construction of Buna-Werke had started as early as April 1941, employing prisoners from the Auschwitz camp which was situated at a distance of about 7 kilometres from Dwory. Prisoners were at first brought on foot to the building site, later they were brought by rail in goods-vans. The firm demanded that a sub-camp should be built in the vicinity of the factory. This was done, and the prisoners of *KL Auschwitz* employed in the *Buna* factory were accommodated there in October 1942.

This camp was at first a sub-camp of *KL Auschwitz*, but in November 1943, as a result of the division of *KL Auschwitz* into three camps, it was renamed *KL Auschwitz III—Aussenlager*, and became the headquarters for other Auschwitz sub-camps which were being formed at industrial plants, foundries and mines. According to the evidence of Dr. Otto Ambros, a member of the board of *IG-Farbenindustrie*, the joint payment received by the SS for the labour of Auschwitz prisoners amounted to 20 million marks in the course of two years and six months. According to statements by former prisoners the total number of prisoners killed at *Buna* amounted to circa 30,000.

[28] Höss meant here the *Gauleiter* of Upper Silesia, Fritz Bracht.

[29] *Regierungspräsident*. At that time Dr. Springorum held this post in the Kattowitz region.

something vaster than ever before had to be built in the shortest possible time, with these people to work with and, to judge by previous experience, without any help worth mentioning from higher authorities.

And what was the situation as regards my labour force? What had been happening to the protective custody camp in the meantime?

The officers of the camp had taken great care to observe the Eicke tradition in their treatment of the prisoners.[30] Fritzsch from Dachau, Palitzsch from Sachsenhausen and Meier from Buchenwald had competed among themselves in the employment of ever-better "methods" of dealing with the prisoners along the lines laid down by Eicke.

My repeated instructions that Eicke's views should be abandoned as hopelessly out-of-date in view of the new functions of the concentration camps, fell on deaf ears.

It was impossible for their limited minds to forget the principles that Eicke had taught them, for these were admirably suited to their mentality. All my orders and instructions were "turned about" if they ran contrary to these principles.

For it was not I, but they, who ran the camp. It was they who taught the capos, from the chief block senior, down to the last block clerk, how to behave.

They trained the block leaders and told them how to treat the prisoners.

But I have said and written enough on this subject.[31] Against this passive resistance I was powerless.

This will only seem comprehensible and credible to men who have themselves served for years in a protective custody camp.

I have already described the influence which the capos generally exercised over the lives of their fellow-inmates. This influence was especially noticeable in this concentration camp. It was a factor of decisive importance in Auschwitz-Birkenau where the masses of prisoners could not be easily supervised. One would have thought a common fate and the miseries shared by all would have led to a steadfast and unshakable feeling of comradeship and cooperation, but this was far from being the case.

Nowhere is crass egotism so nakedly self-evident as in prison. And for reasons of self-preservation, the harder the life the crasser that egotism would become.

Even people, who in ordinary life outside the camp were at all times considerate and good-natured, became capable, in the hard conditions of

---

[30] Writing in prison Höss gives the following account of how Eicke regarded the prisoners: "... *Die Häftlinge sind für ihn allezeit Staatsfeinde, die sicher zu verwahren, hart zu behandeln und bei Widersetzlichkeit zu vernichten sind. So belehrt und erzieht er seine SS-Führer und SS-Männer.*" (In his view, the prisoners were sworn enemies of the State, who were to be treated with great severity and destroyed if they showed resistance. He instilled the same attitude of mind into his officers and men). *Commandant of Auschwitz*. Appendix 8, p. 263.

Höss's attitude towards the prisoners was exactly the same, despite his statements to the contrary. The living conditions and fate of prisoners in *KL Auschwitz* bear witness to this fact.

[31] Höss is thinking here of excerpts from his reminiscences dealing with his service in the camps of Dachau and Sachsenhausen.

imprisonment, of bullying their fellow-prisoners mercilessly, if by so doing they could make their own lives a little easier.

More merciless yet was the behaviour of those who were naturally egotistical, cold and even criminally inclined, and who rode roughshod and without pity over the misery of their fellow-prisoners if they could thereby gain even the pettiest advantage for themselves. Quite apart from the physical effects of such mean and vile treatment, its psychological results were unspeakably worse for those of their fellow-prisoners whose sensibilities had not yet been blunted by the harshness of camp life. The treatment they received from the guards, however brutal, arbitrary and cruel, never affected them psychologically to the same extent as did this attitude on the part of their fellow-inmates.

The very fact of having to watch helplessly and without any power to intervene, while capos of this sort tormented their fellows, had a thoroughly crushing effect on the prisoners' spirit. Woe betide the prisoner who tried to interfere, to stand up for the oppressed! The system of terror that prevailed within the prison camp was far too great for any man to take such a risk.

Why do privileged prisoners and capos treat their fellow-prisoners and fellow-sufferers in this fashion? Because they want to make a favourable impression on the guards and supervisors whose attitude is known to them, and to show how well-suited they are for the privileged positions that they hold. And also because of the advantages to be obtained in this way, and which will make their prison existence more pleasant. But such advantages are always obtainable only at the cost of their fellow-prisoners.

However, it is the guards and the supervisors who create the opportunity for such behaviour. They do so either out of indifference, since they are too lazy to stop such activities, or else, being themselves base and cruel by nature, they permit it because they enjoy the spectacle provided, and indeed even encourage the bullying, since they derive a satanic pleasure from watching the prisoners torment one another.

There were many capos who needed no encouragement. Their mean, brutal and cowardly natures and their criminal tendencies led them to torment their fellow-prisoners both physically and mentally, and even to harass them to death out of pure sadism.

During my present imprisonment I have had, and have now, ample opportunity of confirming, from a necessarily personal viewpoint, the truth of what I have just written.

In no place is the real " Adam " [32] so apparent as in prison. All the characteristics that a prisoner has acquired or affected are stripped from him, everything that is not an essential part of his real being. Prison in the long run compels him to discard all simulation and pretence. He stands naked, as he really is, for better or for worse.

How did the communal camp life of Auschwitz affect the various categories of prisoner?

For Germans from the Reich it was no problem, no matter what their

---

[32] The word " Adam " is used by Höss to denote primitive man.

category.[33] Almost without exception they held "high" positions, and were thus provided with all the physical necessities of life. Anything they could not obtain officially they would "organize"[34]. This skill in "organization" was indeed shown by all the "high" capos in Auschwitz, regardless of category or nationality. Their relative success varied only in accordance with their intelligence, daring and unscrupulousness. Opportunity was never lacking.

Once the Jewish Action[35] was under way, there was practically no limit to what a man might obtain for himself. And the senior capos also had the necessary freedom of movement for this.[36]

Until early 1942 the largest single group of prisoners were Poles.[37]

They all knew that they would remain in the concentration camp at least for the duration of the war. Most of them believed that Germany would lose the war and, after Stalingrad, virtually all of them were conviced of this. They were kept fully informed about Germany's "true position" by the enemy news broadcasts. It was not difficult to listen to these enemy broadcasts, since there were plenty of wireless sets in Auschwitz.[38] They were listened to even in my

---

[33] Prisoners put into concentration camps were marked by triangles of different colour depending on their category, i.e. on the reason why they were sent to the camp. Thus political prisoners wore red triangles, criminal offenders wore green, anti-social prisoners wore black, Jehovah's witnesses wore violet and homosexuals wore pink.

[34] "Organizing"— an expression used in camp slang for obtaining food, clothes, medicines or articles of daily use from the camp stores, never by stealing from other prisoners.

[35] Höss writes here of the so-called "Final Solution of the Jewish Question," a cryptonym used by the Nazis to denote the action of bringing to *KL Auschwitz* transports of Jews, destined to be exterminated in the gas chambers of Birkenau (*cf.* that part of the reminiscences of Höss entitled "The Final Solution of the Jewish Question in the Auschwitz Concentration Camp," printed on p. 81). The property of the victims was collected by the camp authorities in 35 ware-houses known as "Canada." These were located at Birkenau, sectors BIIg, as well as BIIb, BIIc and BIIe.

[36] Contrary to these statements by Höss, the possibilities of "organizing" supplies were limited because prisoners were not allowed to move freely about the Auschwitz camp, nor among the various sectors of the Birkenau camp. Even prisoners entrusted with special duties went from one camp to the other under the supervision of SS-men. This fact made "organizing" difficult and also compelled prisoners to bribe some members of the SS.

[37] Prisoners of Polish nationality were in the majority in the Auschwitz camp until March 1942. Besides them there were also Germans, Czechs, Yugoslavs and Soviet prisoners of war. From April 1942 mass transports of Jews from many countries of occupied Europe began arriving in connection with the so-called "Final Solution of the Jewish Question." Among the newcomers were many Jews who were Polish nationals.

Polish prisoners tried hard, using all the means available to them, to avoid being sent to other camps situated within the Third Reich. It should be mentioned here that political prisoners prevailed among the Poles. Thanks to their experiences before their arrest, these were able to organize even in the difficult conditions of camp life, a resistance movement which soon got in touch with representatives of other nationalities, and thus became an international section coordinating illegal conspiratorial work on the camp. The Poles formed the nucleus within the Camp Resistance Movement and directed all conspiratorial work.

All these factors contributed in no small measure to the situation whereby Poles represented the most numerous national group, right up to the end of the camp's existence.

[38] Radio sets were in the possession of the SS camp garrison. The prisoners had no chance of listening in. Only very few could do so thanks to their special circumstances, e.g. of working in the offices or private homes of SS-men, where they would sometimes be left without supervision for a while. If such prisoners dared to listen in to a non-German broadcasting station, they could transmit the acquired news to their closest friends in the utmost secrecy.

own house. Furthermore there was ample opportunity, with the help of the civilian workers and even of the SS-men, for the extensive smuggling of letters.[39] There were thus many sources of news. New arrivals also always brought in the latest information with them. Since, according to enemy propaganda, the collapse of the Axis powers was only a matter of time, the Polish prisoners felt in consequence that they had no cause for despair.[40] The only question was : which prisoners would have the luck to survive their imprisonment? It was this uncertainty and fear which, psychologically speaking, made imprisonment so hard for the Pole. He lived in a perpetual state of anxiety as to what might befall him each day. He might at any time be swept away by an epidemic against which his weakened physical condition could offer no resistance. He might suddenly be shot or hanged as a hostage. He might also be unexpectedly brought before a court-martial in connection with the resistance movement, and condemned to death. He might be shot as a reprisal. He could meet with a fatal accident at work, brought about by someone who bore him a grudge. He could die as the result of ill-treatment. And there were many other similar fates perpetually hanging over his head.

The crucial question was whether he could physically survive in view of the steadily deteriorating diet, the increasingly crowded living quarters, the worsening of the already highly defective sanitary arrangements, and the hard work, which often had to be done in all weathers.

---

[39] Prisoners were officially allowed to send letters written on special forms once a fortnight, always to the same address. The letters had to be written in German and could not contain any information as to conditions in camp. A letter usually consisted of the conventional statement that "the prisoner was in good health and felt well." All other information which prisoners tried to slip through in their letters was deleted from the text by the camp censor. We must not forget that a number of prisoners, including all Jews, were forbidden to send letters at all. Illegal letters could be sent only by those few prisoners who came in touch during their working hours with Polish civilian workers or the Polish inhabitants of nearby villages. If the SS-men caught them sending letters in this way, they would be put into the "bunkers" (i.e. cells) of Block 11 (Block of Death) and interrogated. Interrogation would usually end for the prisoner with a sentence of flogging, of a transfer to work in a penal company(*Strafkompanie*—SK) or of some other equally severe punishment. Those who undertook to forward illegal letters were also liable to suffer reprisals, including imprisonment in a camp. It happened occasionally that an SS-man would agree to transmit illegal correspondence, not out of pity, but for remuneration in cash, food or other things.

[40] According to the anticipations of the authorities, a prisoner was expected to live in camp for no more than three months. The first camp leader, *SS-Hauptsturmführer* Fritzsch, used to welcome newcomers with the following words: "You have come to a German concentration camp, not to a sanatorium, and there is only one way out—through the chimney. Anyone who does not like it can try hanging himself on the wires. If there are Jews in this draft, they have no right to live longer than a fortnight; if there are priests, their period is one month—the rest, three months." Prisoners mostly perished soon after their arrival in camp owing to starvation, beating, ill-treatment and harassment by the camp authorities. Those who survived the initial stage of life in camp (Quarantine) were later decimated by diseases (diarrhoea—*Durchfall*—typhus and typhoid fever, scabies, phlegmon). Disastrous sanitary conditions, hard work, starvation and insufficient clothing increased the death rate. Many additional dangers threatened the lives of prisoners, both at work and in the blocks, and so only a few managed to survive. Out of the total number of 405,222 prisoners registered in the camp records (this official figure was in fact far less than the actual number of victims), only c. 60,000 survived. Of that number many died directly after liberation or a few months later, due to illness and complete exhaustion.

To this must be added perpetual worry about his family and dependants. Were they still living where he had left them? Had they also been arrested and sent to forced labour somewhere or other? Were they indeed still alive?

Many were tempted into flight in order to escape from such worries. Flight was not very difficult from Auschwitz, where opportunities for escape were innumerable.[41] The necessary preparations were easily made, and it was a simple matter to avoid or outwit the guards.

A little courage and a bit of luck were all that was needed. When a man stakes everything on one throw, he must also of course reckon that if it goes wrong the result may be death.

But these plans of escape always involved the prospect of reprisals, the arrest of family and relations, and the liquidation of ten or more fellow-sufferers.

Many of those who tried to escape cared little about reprisals,[42] and were prepared to try their luck. Once beyond the ring of sentry posts, the local civilian population would help them on their way. The rest was no problem. If they had bad luck, then it was all up with them. One way or another, it was the solution of their problems.

The other prisoners had to parade past the corpses of those who had been shot while trying to escape, so that they would all see how such an attempt might end. Many were frightened by this spectacle, and abandoned their plans as a result.

---

[41] This information of Höss is not true. In the Auschwitz camp, just as in the other concentration camps, a number of drastic measures were taken to prevent escapes. The most important were the deporting of Polish inhabitants from the area around the camp (*cf.* p. 33, note 19) and encircling the camp area with barbed wire, electrified fences and rows of watch-towers, which formed the so-called small sentry chain (*kleine Postenkette*). This chain of sentries was removed during the day, when the camp and the adjoining area, the prisoners' place of work, was surrounded with the so-called large sentry chain (*grosse Postenkette*). This was formed by armed SS sentries and raised platforms, spaced every two hundred metres. Strong searchlights were lit at night at the camp fences, and should any prisoner venture near the wires the sentry on duty would discharge a volley from his machine-gun. If a prisoner managed to reach the fences unobserved, he would perish after touching the live wires.

As the camp was shut off from the outside world, it is difficult to believe that there were "innumerable opportunities" for escape. This seems even more unlikely, if we consider that prisoners had difficulties both in escaping and in hiding in the area outside the camp on account of their camp clothes (with stripes), shorn hair and in the later stages because of their camp number, tattooed on the forearm.

The escape would inevitably be noticed, however lucky the prisoner might be, not later than after 12 hours, as roll-calls were held in the camp every morning and evening, when the numbers of each block were checked. When the absence of a prisoner was discovered, the alarm was given by sounding the camp siren. SS patrols would then leave the camp, entering the adjacent area, and the large sentry chain would not be removed until the runaway was found. If the escapee was not recaptured, the large sentry chain would be removed only after three days.

[42] The escapes were not indicative of the unscrupulousness of the fugitives—"indifferent" to the fate of their fellows left behind in the camp—but mostly resulted from danger in the camp, e.g. an expected execution. The fear of being arrested and put in the bunkers of Block 11 for interrogation and of suffering the most horrible tortures, very often proved to be the decisive factor in an attempt to escape. Should a prisoner, suspected of planning an escape or caught after escaping, manage to survive the interrogation, he would be executed by shooting or hanging. The fugitive's colleagues, working in the same squad or living in the same block, would perish in the same way.

But there were others who did not hesitate to make the attempt despite everything, hoping that they would be among the lucky ninety per cent who succeeded.[43]

What can have passed through the minds of the prisoners as they marched past the corpse of a dead comrade? If I read their expression rightly, I saw horror at his fate, sympathy for the unlucky man, and a determination to exact revenge when the time came.

I saw the same expression on the faces of the prisoners when they were paraded to watch the hangings. Only terror, and fear lest a similar fate overtake themselves, were here more in evidence.

I must refer here to the court-martial tribunal, and to the liquidation of hostages, since these affected solely the Polish prisoners.

Most of the hostages had been in the camp for a considerable time, and the fact that they were hostages was unknown both to them and to the camp authorities. Then one day a teleprinter message would arrive from the Security Police or from the Reich Main Security Office, stating that the prisoners named therein were to be shot or hanged as hostages.[44]

A report that the executions had been carried out had to be forwarded within a few hours. The prisoners concerned would be taken away from their work or called out during the roll-call and placed in custody. Those who had been in the camp for some time usually knew what this meant, or had at least a very shrewd idea.

The order for their execution was made known to them after they had been arrested. At first, in 1940 and 1941, they were shot by firing squad. Later they were either hanged or shot in the back of the neck with a small-calibre revolver.[45] The bedridden were liquidated in the hospital building[46] by means of an injection.[47]

---

[43] The percentage of successful escapes given by Höss finds no corroboration in investigations conducted in this field. The total number of those who escaped in the years 1940—1945 from the Auschwitz camp (jointly with Birkenau, Monowitz and the sub-camps) amounted to 667 men and women. It is certain that the Nazis recaptured 270 persons out of that number, which is more than 40 per cent. Lack of data about the recapturing of the others does not prove that these escapes were successful.

[44] Among other examples, a group of 198 painters, men of letters, lawyers and military men can be mentioned here. They were brought to the camp on April 24 and 25, 1942, after having been arrested in an artists' café in Cracow, in connection with an attempt on the life of an SS officer of higher rank at the airport of Rakowice near Cracow. Of this group, 169 prisoners were shot on May 27, 1942, at the Death Wall in the courtyard of Block 11.

[45] An execution was conducted in this manner for the first time on November 11, 1941. The executioner was the *Rapportführer*, *SS-Hauptscharführer* Gerhard Palitzsch.

[46] The so-called *Revier*—this name was borrowed by the prisoners from the SS-men. Officially the prisoners' hospital was called *Häftlingskrankenbau* (HKB).

[47] Not only. Executions of sick prisoners, performed within Block 11, also occurred in the history of *KL Auschwitz*. An example is the case widely known in the camp, of the shooting of Professor Marian Gieszczykiewicz on July 31, 1942. His fellow-prisoners tried to save him from the execution by putting him in HKB, but the SS ordered the professor who was actually in good health to be brought on a stretcher to the yard of Block 11, where Palitzsch shot him with a small-calibre gun.

The Kattowitz military court visited Auschwitz every four to six weeks and sat in the punishment cell building.[48]

The accused prisoners, most of whom were already camp inmates (although some had only recently been sent there for trial), were brought before the tribunal and interrogated through an interpreter concerning their statements and the admissions they had made. All the prisoners whom I saw tried admitted to their actions quite freely, openly and firmly.

In particular, some of the women answered bravely for what they had done. In most cases the death sentence was pronounced and carried out forthwith. Like the hostages, they all met their death with calm and resignation, convinced that they were sacrificing themselves for their country. I often saw in their eyes a fanaticism that reminded me of Jehovah's Witnesses when they went to their death.

But criminals condemned by the tribunal, men who had taken part in robberies with violence, gang crimes and so on, died in a very different way. They were either callous and sullen to the last, or else they whined and cried out for mercy.

The picture here was the same as it had been during the executions in Sachsenhausen: those who died for their ideals were brave, upstanding and calm,[49] while the anti-socials were stupefied or struggling against their fate.

Although the general conditions in Auschwitz were far from good, none of the Polish prisoners was willingly transferred to another camp. As soon as they heard that they were to be moved, they did everything in their power to be left out of the transport and kept in the camp. When, in 1943, a general order was issued that all Poles were to be taken to camps in Germany, I was overwhelmed by every works department with requests for the retention of prisoners described as indispensable. No one could spare his Poles. Finally the transfer had to be carried out compulsorily, and a fixed percentage was moved.

I never heard of a Polish prisoner voluntarily requesting transfer to another camp. I have never understood the reason for this desire to hang on in Auschwitz.[50]

---

48 This was the *Polizeistandgericht*—Police Summary Court—from Kattowitz which sentenced Polish civilians from the so-called Kattowitz regency. They were brought from the investigative detention centre at Myslowitz to *KL Auschwitz* and a "trial," which was a travesty of justice, was staged there. A vivid description of this court, of its sentences and of the performing of executions, was given by one of the SS-men, a functionary of the Political Section (*Politische Abteilung*) in *KL Auschwitz*, *SS-Unterscharführer* Pery Broad (see pp. 112 and 117, "The Police Summary Court" and "Shambles in the Old Crematorium").

49 *Cf.* Broad's reminiscences, pp. 110—111.

50 This can easily be explained. First of all *KL Auschwitz* was situated in Polish territory, although these regions were incorporated into the Third Reich. The prisoners were conscious of the fact that, in spite of their isolation from the outside world, they were in their own country and this helped them to survive. At the same time they could hope for greater possibilities of finding help, in case they should decide to escape, than they could receive from the hostile German population inside the Third Reich. Another factor not without significance was the consideration that prisoners became in a certain sense accustomed to their Auschwitz fellow-prisoners, and therefore each change of camp meant a worsening of their situation and a lowering of their chances for survival.

There were three main political groups among the Polish prisoners, and the adherents of each fought violently against the others. The strongest was the chauvinistic-nationalist group. Each group competed with the others for the most influential posts. When one man managed to obtain an important position in the camp, he would quickly bring in other members of his own group and would remove his opponents from his domain. This was often accomplished by base intrigue. Indeed, I dare say that many cases of spotted fever or typhus resulting in death, and other such incidents, could be accounted for by this struggle for power. I often heard from the doctors that this battle for supremacy was always waged most fiercely in the hospital building itself. It was the same story in regard to the control of work. That and the hospital building offered the most important positions of power in the entire life of the camp. Whoever controlled these, ruled the rest. And they did rule too, in no half-hearted fashion. A man who held one of these important positions could see to it that his friends were put wherever he wished them to be. He could also get rid of those he disliked, or even finish them off entirely. In Auschwitz everything was possible.[51] These political struggles for power took place not only in Auschwitz and among the Poles, but in every camp and among all nationalities. Even among the Spanish communists in Mauthausen there were two violently opposed groups. In prison I myself have experienced how the right and left wings fight each other.

In the concentration camps these enmities were keenly encouraged and kept going by the authorities, in order to hinder any strong combination on the part of all the prisoners. Not only the political differences, but also the antagonisms between the various categories of prisoners, played a large part in this.[52]

However strong the camp authorities might be, it would not have been possible to control or direct these thousands of prisoners without making use

---

[51] Höss represents this problem in a rather one-sided manner, noticing only fighting and friction among the representatives of the various groups of prisoners. When discussing this problem one should not forget that the Camp Resistance Movement helped many prisoners by placing them in so-called " better " squads, where work was easier or was conducted under the shelter of a roof. Among the attempts to make the fate of political prisoners easier to bear, one should mention the struggle to remove criminal offenders (who maltreated their fellow-prisoners in order to gain the favour of the SS-men) from their posts as capos, foremen, block seniors, etc., and giving such functions to political prisoners who were conscious of the role they should play in the camp.

The campaign to help prisoners embraced many spheres of camp life, thanks to the efforts of the political prisoners. This was especially true of the hospital, where they tried to save from extermination many eminent public figures (scientists, artists, politicians, civic leaders) who would otherwise never have survived the murderous tempo of manual work.

Political prisoners were instrumental in eliminating camp informers, whose activities could have had disastrous results for their fellow-prisoners. Dr. Alfred Fiderkiewicz, one of the prisoner doctors in camp, wrote of such cases in his reminiscences about his work in the camp hospital. *Cf.* Alfred Fiderkiewicz : *Reminiscences concerning a prisoner-doctor's work in tuberculous Blocks of the Prisoners' Camp Hospital at Birkenau (1943—1944). From the History of KL Auschwitz*, vol. II, p. 274.

[52] Höss has in mind here the hostility between political prisoners (marked with red triangles) and criminal prisoners (with green triangles). See note 51.

of their mutual antagonisms. The greater the number of antagonisms, and the more ferocious the struggle for power, the easier it was to control the camp. *Divide et impera!*[53] This maxim has the same importance, which must never be underestimated, in the conduct of a concentration camp as in high politics.

The next largest contingent consisted of the Russian prisoners of war, who were employed in building the prisoner-of-war camp at Birkenau.

They arrived from the military prisoner-of-war camps at Lambsdorf[54] in Upper Silesia, and were in very poor condition. They reached the camp after many weeks' marching. They had been given hardly any food on the march; during halts on the way they were simply turned out into the nearest fields and there told to "graze" like cattle on anything edible they could find. In the Lambsdorf camp there must have been about 200,000 Russian prisoners of war. This camp was simply a square area of ground in which most of them huddled as best they could in earth hovels they had built themselves. Feeding arrangements were completely inadequate and the distribution of food was irregular. They cooked for themselves in holes in the ground. Most of them—it could not be called eating—devoured their portions raw. The army was not prepared for the immense numbers of prisoners captured in 1941. The organization of the army department responsible for prisoners of war was too rigid and inflexible, and could not improvise speedily. Incidentally, it was the same story with the German prisoners of war after the collapse, in May 1945. The Allies, too, were unable to cope with such massive numbers. The prisoners were simply herded on a convenient patch of ground, enclosed with a few rolls of barbed wire, and left to their own devices. They were treated exactly as the Russians had been.[55]

It was with these prisoners, many of whom could hardly stand, that I was now supposed to build the Birkenau prisoner-of-war camp. The *Reichsführer SS*

---

[53] In translation "divide and rule": cause dissension, create political parties and rule over them. The old Roman maxim was widely used by the SS-men in their internal camp policy, directed against prisoners. Thus for example the camp authorities would entrust the function of block senior to a prisoner of a different nationality from that of the block inmates. Similar conditions also prevailed in the work squads.

[54] Łambinowice in Polish. Here the Nazis established one of the biggest camps for prisoners of war. It included *Stalag VIIIB*, *Stalag VIIIF* and *Stalag 344*. The first to arrive were 40,000 Polish prisoners of war in 1939, and then successively French, Dutch, Yugoslav and British soldiers. After the Third Reich had attacked the Soviet Union, Soviet prisoners of war began pouring into Łambinowice in great numbers. They were put in a new part of the camp (*Stalag VIIIF*), in the open air, in an area surrounded by barbed wire. The last transport of prisoners of war to arrive at Łambinowice, in the autumn of 1944, consisted of 4,000 former participants of the Warsaw Uprising. During World War II circa 300,000 prisoners of war of 18 nationalities, including some 200,000 Soviet troops, passed through the camp at Łambinowice. Of that total, about 100,000 perished there due to back-breaking labour and hunger. *Cf.* Stanisław Łukowski: *Zbrodnie hitlerowskie w Łambinowicach i Sławięcicach na Opolszczyźnie w latach 1939—1945.* Katowice 1965, Wydawnictwo "Śląsk," and *Łambinowice*. Warszawa 1967, Wydawnictwo "Sport i Turystyka."

[55] Höss seems to have forgotten or deliberately omitted the fact that according to the plans of the leaders of the Third Reich the Soviet prisoners of war were doomed to be exterminated, while the German prisoners of war were put into camps for a definite period of time. If it became evident that they were not war criminals, they were set free. German prisoners of war were not subjected to starvation or murder. The situation mentioned by Höss occurred in the initial stages after the capitulation.

ordered that only the strongest of the Russian prisoners, those who were particularly capable of hard work, were to be sent to me. The officers who accompanied them said these were the best available at Lambsdorf. They were willing to work, but were incapable of doing so because of their weakened condition. I remember very clearly how we were continually giving them food when first they arrived at the base camp, but in vain.[56] Their weakened bodies could no longer function. Their whole constitution was finished and done for. They died like flies from general physical exhaustion, or from the most trifling maladies which their debilitated constitutions could no longer resist. I saw countless Russians die while in the act of swallowing root vegetables or potatoes. For some time I employed 5,000 Russians almost daily unloading trainloads of swedes. The railway tracks were blocked, mountains of swedes lay on the lines, and there was nothing to be done about it. The Russians were physically all in. They wandered aimlessly about, crept into a safe corner to swallow something edible that they found—which was a great effort for them—or sought a quiet spot where they might die in peace. The worst time was during the mud-period at the beginning and end of the winter of 1941—1942. The Russians could endure the cold more or less, but not the damp and being constantly wet through. In the unfinished, simple stone barracks, hastily constructed in the early days of Birkenau, the death rate constantly rose. Even those who had hitherto shown some powers of resistance now declined rapidly in numbers day by day. Extra rations were of no avail ; they swallowed everything they could lay their hands on, but their hunger was never satisfied.

On the road between Auschwitz and Birkenau I once saw an entire column of Russians, several hundred strong, suddenly make a rush for some nearby stacks of potatoes on the far side of the railway line. Their guards were taken by surprise, overrun, and could do nothing. I luckily happened to come along at this moment and was able to restore the situation. The Russians had thrown themselves onto the stacks, from which they could hardly be torn away. Some of them died in the confusion, while chewing, their hands full of potatoes. Overcome by the crudest instinct of self-preservation, they came to care nothing for one another, and in their selfishness now thought only of themselves. Cases of cannibalism were not rare in Birkenau. I myself came across a Russian lying

---

[56] This information cannot be corroborated by our present knowledge about the camp. In order to achieve the mass extermination of Soviet prisoners of war the High Command of the Armed Forces (*Oberkommando der Wehrmacht*—OKW) together with the Ministry of Food of the Third Reich determined the food rations for Soviet prisoners of war, which were worse both in quantity and quality than those of prisoners of war from other countries. On August 6, 1941, OKW issued an order concerning food quotas for Soviet prisoners of war. They were to receive for the period of 28 days (per person) : 6 kilogrammes of bread, 400 grammes of meat, 440 grammes of fat and 600 grammes of sugar. The bread was to contain only 50% rye flour, the rest being valueless additions. The meat could only be horse meat and the fat synthetic. Assuming that food rations were not pilfered by other parties, a Soviet prisoner of war would get 515 calories daily.

The food rations of the Soviet prisoners of war at Auschwitz were even worse than those of ordinary prisoners. They received daily 1/2 litre of soup, cooked with rotten turnips, 300—350 grammes of bread with a small quantity of margarine or 50 grammes of sausage. The physical condition of prisoners of war, who were already exhausted when they arrived in camp, soon led to death. These men could hardly walk and were completely indifferent to what went on around them after a few weeks' stay in the camp.

between piles of bricks, whose body had been ripped open and the liver removed. They would beat each other to death for food. Once, riding past the camp, I saw a Russian hit another on the head with a tile, so as to snatch a piece of bread which the man had been secretly chewing behind a heap of stones. I happened to be outside the wire and by the time I found a gate and reached the spot the man was dead, his skull bashed in. I could not identify his assassin among the crowds of Russians swarming around. When the foundations for the first group of buildings were being dug, the men often found the bodies of Russians who had been killed by their fellows, partly eaten and then stuffed into a hole in the mud.

The mysterious disappearance of many Russians was explained in this way. I once saw, from a window in my house, a Russian dragging a food-bucket behind the block next to the command building and scratching about inside it. Suddenly another Russian came round the corner, hesitated for a moment, then hurled himself upon the one scrabbling in the bucket, and pushed him into the electrified wire before vanishing with the bucket. The guard in the watch-tower had also seen this, but was not in a position to fire at the man who had run away. I at once telephoned the duty block leader and had the electric current cut off. I then went myself into the camp, to find the man who had done this. The one who had been thrown against the wire was dead, and the other was nowhere to be found.

They were no longer human beings. They had become animals, who sought only food.

Of more than 10,000 Russian prisoners of war who were to provide the main labour force for building the prisoner-of-war camp at Birkenau, only a few hundred were still alive by the summer of 1942.[57]

Those who did remain were the best. They were splendid workers and were used as mobile squads wherever something had to be finished quickly. But I never got over the feeling that those who had survived had done so only at the expense of their comrades, because they were more ferocious and unscrupulous, and generally "tougher."

It was, I believe, in the summer of 1942 that a mass break-out by the remaining Russians took place.[58] A great part of them were shot, but many managed to get clear away. Those who were recaptured gave as the reason for

---

[57] The camp documents contain evidence that 11,957 prisoners of war, registered in camp, were brought to *KL Auschwitz*. Out of that number 49 were transferred from *KL Auschwitz* to *KL Flossenbürg*, 29 escaped and on January 17, 1945, at the last roll-call before the evacuation of the camp, there were 92 prisoners of war left at Auschwitz. The number of escapees was probably greater, but only 29 appear in the camp documents as such. Besides the above number of 11,957 prisoners of war at *KL Auschwitz*, over 1,818 were not entered in the camp registers but were immediately shot, gassed or killed in other ways. 900 commissars of the Soviet army were among that group. Thus 13,775 prisoners of war altogether were brought to *KL Auschwitz*.

[58] On the basis of information given by the only living participant of that escape, Andrei Aleksandrovich Pogozhev, this occurred on November 6, 1942. About one hundred Soviet prisoners of war took part in the mass escape, and managed to flee from the camp area. The fate of the escapees is not known. The only certain fact is that Pogozhev and another prisoner, Victor Kuznetsov, managed to reach Rybnik after two weeks, but there they were captured by the German police and sent to the prisoner-of-war camp at Łambinowice.

their escape the fear that they were to be gassed, for they had been told that they were to be transferred to a newly built sector of the camp. They took it that this transfer was merely a deceptive measure. It was, however, never intended that these Russians should be gassed. But it is certain that they knew of the liquidation of the Russian *politruks* [political officers] and commissars.[59] They feared that they were to suffer the same fate.

It is in this way that a mass psychosis develops and spreads.

The next largest contingent were the Gypsies.

Long before the war Gypsies were being rounded up and put into concentration camps as part of the campaign against asocials. One department of the Reich Criminal Police Office was solely concerned with the supervision of Gypsies. Repeated searches were made in the Gypsy encampments for persons who were not true Gypsies, and these were sent to concentration camps as shirkers or asocials. Moreover, the Gypsy encampments were constantly being combed through for biological reasons. The *Reichsführer SS* wanted to ensure that the two main Gypsy stocks be preserved: I cannot recall their names.[60] In his view they were the direct descendants of the original Indo-Germanic race, and had preserved their ways and customs more or less pure and intact. He now wished to have them all collected together for research purposes. They were to be precisely registered and preserved as an historic monument.

Later they were to be collected from all over Europe, and allotted limited areas in which to dwell.

In 1937 and 1938 all itinerant Gypsies were collected into so-called habitation camps [*Wohnlager*] near the larger towns, to facilitate supervision.

In 1942, however, an order was given that all Gypsy-type persons on German territory, including Gypsy half-castes, were to be arrested and transported to Auschwitz, irrespective of sex or age.[61] The only exceptions were those who

---

[59] *Cf.* pp. 69—71, where Höss mentions the treatment of political officers and commissars of the Soviet army and their fate.

[60] Martin Broszat, researcher from the Institute of Recent History (*Institut für Zeitgeschichte*) in Munich and editor of the German edition of the Autobiography of Höss, is of the opinion that the Gypsies in question belonged to the tribe of Sinti and Lallerie. *Kommandant in Auschwitz. Autobiographische Aufzeichnungen von Rudolf Höss*. Stuttgart 1958, Deutsche Verlagsanstalt, p. 104, note 4.

[61] The order of *Reichsführer SS* (RFSS) Himmler of December 14, 1942, is meant here. It was issued in keeping with the agreement of September 18, 1942, between Thierack, Minister of Justice of the Third Reich, and Himmler. This agreement contained, among other things, the following provisions: Item 2: "The exclusion of asocial elements from general jurisdiction and their transfer to that of RFSS, to be annihilated through work [*Zur Vernichtung durch Arbeit*]. All interned Jews, Gypsies, Russians and Ukrainians, then Poles sentenced to more than three years of imprisonment, also Czechs or Germans sentenced to more than eight years, depending on the decision of the minister of justice, shall be handed over." Item 14: "It was therefore agreed that in view of the objectives outlined by the government regarding the solution of the Eastern problems, Jews, Gypsies, Russians, Poles and Ukrainians shall not be tried by ordinary courts in cases relating to criminal offences, but shall be placed under the authority of RFSS [*Sondern durch den RFSS erledigt werden*]." Nuremberg Trial, Case No. IV. Doc. PS-654.

On January 29, 1943, the Reich Main Security Office issued instructions to arrest all Gypsies inhabiting the Third Reich and the occupied territories, and to liquidate them in concentration camps. The first transports of Gypsies arrived at *KL Auschwitz* towards the end of February and the beginning of March 1943.

had been officially recognized as pure-blooded members of the two main tribes. These were to be settled in the Ödenburg district on the Neusiedlersee. Those transported to Auschwitz were to be kept there for the rest of the war in a family camp.

But the regulations governing their arrest were not drawn up with sufficient precision. Various offices of the Criminal Police interpreted them in different ways, and as a result persons were arrested who could not possibly be regarded as belonging to the category that it was intended to intern.

Many men were arrested while on leave from the front, despite high decorations and several wounds, simply because their father or mother or grandfather had been a Gypsy half-caste. Even a very senior Party member, whose Gypsy grandfather had settled in Leipzig, was among them. He himself had a large business in Leipzig, and had been decorated more than once during World War I. Another was a girl student who had been a leader in the Berlin League of German Girls. There were many more such cases.[62] I made a report to the Reich Criminal Police Office.[63] As a result the Gypsy camp was constantly under examination and many releases took place. But these were scarcely noticeable, so great was the number of those who remained.

I cannot say how many Gypsies, including half-castes, were in Auschwitz.[64] I only know that they completely filled one section of the camp designed to hold 10,000.[65] Conditions in Birkenau were utterly unsuitable for a family camp. Every prerequisite was lacking, even if it was intended that the Gypsies be kept there only for the duration of the war. It was quite impossible to provide proper food for the children, although by referring to the *Reichsführer SS* I managed for a time to bamboozle the food offices into giving me food for the very young ones. This was soon stopped, however, for the Food Ministry laid down that no special children's food might be issued to the concentration camps.

In July 1942 the *Reichsführer SS* visited the camp. I took him all over the Gypsy camp.[66] He made a most thorough inspection of everything, noting the

---

[62] Broad also wrote about them. *Cf.* the chapter of his reminiscences entitled " Liquidation of the Gypsies " on pp. 139—141.

[63] *Reichskriminalpolizeiamt* belonged, as Office V, to the Reich Main Security Office (RSHA).

[64] Research has shown that a total of 22,667 Gypsies were brought to the camp at Birkenau, 10,873 women and 10,094 men. They all had separate numbers of the Z series (*Zigeuner*), different for men and women. Apart from these, 1,700 Gypsies were brought to camp (men, women and children) and immediately killed in gas chambers, as they were suspected of carrying spotted fever.

[65] The Gypsy camp, or *Zigeunerlager*, was located at Birkenau, sector BIIe. The Gypsy families, when brought to Auschwitz, were not separated (men, women and children lived together). They lived here in disastrous sanitary conditions, which caused epidemics of contagious diseases. Persons suspected of being ill were sent to the gas chambers. A more detailed account of the fate of Gypsies at Birkenau is given by Jerzy Ficowski : *Cyganie na polskich drogach*, Kraków 1965. Wydawnictwo Literackie, pp. 117—129.

[66] Himmler's second visit to *KL Auschwitz* took place on July 17—18, 1942. Höss made a significant mistake in his Autobiography, as in July 1942 he could not have shown Himmler the Gypsy camp. There were no Gypsies in Auschwitz at that time (see p. 49, note 61). The facts described by Höss could have occurred in the spring of 1944, when Höss had again taken over the function of commandant of the

overcrowded barrack-huts, the unhygienic conditions, the cramped hospital building. He saw those who were sick with infectious diseases, and the children suffering from noma[67]—which always made me shudder, since it reminded me of leprosy and of the lepers I had seen in Palestine[68]—their little bodies wasted away, with gaping holes in their cheeks big enough for a man to see through, a slow putrefaction of the living body.

He noted the mortality rate, which was relatively low in comparison with that of the camp as a whole. The child mortality rate, however, was extraordinarily high. I do not believe that many new-born babies survived more than a few weeks.

He saw it all, in detail, and as it really was—and he ordered me to destroy them. Those capable of work were first to be separated from the others, as with the Jews.

I pointed out to him that the personnel of the Gypsy camp was not precisely what he had envisaged being sent to Auschwitz. He thereupon ordered that the Reich Criminal Police Office should carry out a sorting as quickly as possible. This in fact took two years.[69] The Gypsies capable of work were transferred to another camp. About 4,000 Gypsies were left by August 1944, and these had to go to the gas chambers. Up to that moment they were unaware of what was in store for them. They first realized what was happening when they made their way, barrack-hut by barrack-hut, towards Crematorium I.[70] It was not easy to drive them into the gas chambers. I myself did not see it, but Schwarzhuber[71] told me that it was more difficult than any previous mass destruction of the Jews, and it was particularly hard on him, because he knew almost every one

---

SS garrison, replacing *SS-Obersturmbannführer* Arthur Liebehenschel, who became commandant of *KL Lublin* (Majdanek), as well as of the labour camps in Warsaw, Radom, Budzyń and Bliżyn.

[67] Noma or watery cancer (*Cancer aquaticus*) is the most serious form of an ulcerous disease of the oral cavity. It occurs, particularly affecting children, as a result of starvation and exhaustion. It is generally fatal.

[68] Höss was in Palestine as a soldier during World War I. He wrote about that period of his life in his Autobiography. *Commandant of Auschwitz*, *op. cit.*, pp. 36—39.

[69] The operation of liquidating the Gypsy camp was commenced in the afternoon of August 2, 1944, so the whole affair lasted only three months, not two years. The course of the liquidation was as follows: in the afternoon of August 2, an empty goods train was brought to the railway ramp at Birkenau and 1,408 Gypsies (813 men, 105 boys of 9—14 years and 490 women) were taken from the base camp (*Stammlager*) in Auschwitz. They were to be transferred to concentration camps in the interior of the Third Reich. The Gypsies who remained at Birkenau took leave of those departing across the barbed-wire fencing of the camp. The train left at 4 p.m. The Gypsies who left that day were in fact brought to *KL Buchenwald*.

In the evening, at 7 p.m., the camp authorities gave orders of *Lagersperre* (prohibition of entering or leaving the camp) in the Gypsy camp at Birkenau, sector BIIe. Vans and a group of SS-men, who were to take part in the "liquidation," arrived at the Gypsy camp. 2,897 men, women and children were taken to the crematoria and killed in the gas chambers. The Gypsy camp at Birkenau ceased to exist.

[70] This operation took place in Crematoria IV and V. Höss was then absent from the camp, because on July 29, 1944, he returned to Oranienburg as Head of Office DI, a post he had held since November 1943. He gave the wrong number of the crematorium in which the Gypsies perished.

[71] *Lagerführer* in the men's camp at Birkenau.

of them individually and had been on good terms with them. They were by their nature as trusting as children.

Despite the unfavourable conditions the majority of the Gypsies did not, so far as I could observe, suffer much psychologically as a result of imprisonment, apart from the fact that it restricted their roving habits.

The overcrowding, poor sanitary arrangements and even to a certain extent the food shortage were conditions to which they had become accustomed in their normal, primitive way of life. Nor did they regard the sickness and the high mortality rate as particularly tragic. Their whole attitude was really that of children, volatile, in thought and deed. They loved to play, even at work, which they never took quite seriously. Even in bad times they always tried to look on the bright side. They were optimists.

I never saw a scowling, hateful expression on a Gypsy's face. If one went into their camp, they would often run out of their barracks to play their musical instruments, or to let their children dance, or perform their usual tricks. There was a large playground where the children could run about to their heart's content and play with toys of every description.[72] When spoken to they would reply openly and trustingly and would make all sorts of requests. It always seemed to me that they did not really understand about their imprisonment.

They fought fiercely among themselves. Their hot blood and pugnacious natures made this inevitable in view of the many different tribes and clans thrown together here. The members of each clan kept very much together and supported each other. When it came to sorting out the able-bodied, the resulting separations and dislocations within the clan gave rise to many touching scenes and to much pain and tears.

They were consoled and comforted to a certain extent when they were told that later they would all be together again.

For a while we kept the Gypsies who were capable of work in the base camp at Auschwitz. They did their utmost to get a glimpse of their clan-mates from time to time, even if only from a distance. We often had to carry out a search after roll-call for homesick Gypsies who had cunningly slipped back to join their clan.[73]

Indeed, often, when I was in Oranienburg with the Inspectorate of Concentration Camps, I was approached by Gypsies who had known me in Auschwitz, and asked for news of other members of their clan. Even when these had been gassed long ago. Just because of their complete trust, it was always hard for me to give them an evasive answer.

Although they were a source of great trouble to me at Auschwitz, they were nevertheless my best-loved prisoners—if I may put it that way. They never managed to keep at any job for long. They "gypsied around" too much for

[72] "The children's playground" was established in the Gypsy camp in June 1944, only one month before the camp's final liquidation. It was a travesty in the conditions of camp life, as the sick and starving children had no strength left to play or exercise. Ficowski : *op. cit.*, p. 125.

[73] Not very probable, as the distance between Auschwitz and Birkenau was three kilometres ; prisoners were, besides, not allowed to leave the camp.

that, whatever they did. Their greatest wish was to be in a transport company, where they could travel all over the place, and satisfy their endless curiosity, and have a chance of stealing. Stealing and vagrancy are in their blood and cannot be eradicated. Their moral attitude is also completely different from that of other people. They do not regard stealing as in any way wicked. They cannot understand why a man should be punished for it. I am here referring to the majority of those interned, the real wandering Gypsies, as well as to those of mixed blood who had become akin to them. I do not refer to those who had settled in the towns. These had already learnt too much of civilization, and what they learnt was unfortunately not of the best.

I would have taken great interest in observing their customs and habits if I had not been aware of the impending horror, namely the Extermination Order, which until mid-1944 was known only to myself and the doctors in Auschwitz.

By command of the *Reichsführer SS* the doctors were to dispose of the sick, and especially the children, as inconspicuously as possible.

And it was precisely they who had such trust in the doctors.

Nothing surely is harder than to grit one's teeth and go through with such a thing, coldly, pitilessly and without sympathy.

What effect did imprisonment have upon the Jews, who from 1942 on composed the greater part of the inmates of Auschwitz?[74] How did they behave?

From the very beginning there were Jews in the concentration camps. I knew them well since Dachau days. But then the Jews still had the possibility of emigrating to any country in the world, provided only that they obtained the necessary entry permit. The duration of their stay in the camp was therefore only a question of time, or of money and foreign connections. Many obtained the necessary visa within a few weeks, and were set free. Only those who had been guilty of a racial offence,[75] who had been particularly active politically during the pre-Hitler period or who had been involved in one of the public scandals, were forced to remain in the camp.

Those with some prospect of emigrating did their best to ensure that their life in custody went as "smoothly" as possible. They worked as diligently as they were capable of doing—the majority were unaccustomed to any sort of physical labour—and behaved as unobtrusively as they could, carrying out their duties quietly and steadily.

---

[74] This was the result of the beginning of the so-called *Endlösung der Judenfrage*, a cryptonym used by the Nazis to designate the total extermination in camps of the Jewish population inhabiting the Third Reich and the occupied countries. After selection, able-bodied men and women from transports arriving in Auschwitz were directed to work in the camp. The number of those kept in the camp depended on the demand for manpower.

[75] Höss meant here offence against Paragraphs 1 and 2 of the Nuremberg Statutes of September 15, 1933, providing for the protection of German blood and German honour. The Nuremberg Statutes not only forbade marriage between persons of German and Jewish nationality, but also prohibited sexual intercourse between representatives of those nationalities. Offences against the Nuremberg Statutes were termed "defiling the race" (*Rassenschande*).

The Jews in Dachau did not have an easy time. They had to work in the gravel pit which, for them, was very strenuous physical labour. The guards, influenced by Eicke and by *Der Stürmer*, which was on show everywhere in their barracks and the canteens, were particularly rough with them. They were sufficiently persecuted and tormented already as "corrupters of the German people," even by their fellow-prisoners. When a display case containing *Der Stürmer*[76] was put up in the protective custody camp, its effect on those prisoners who had hitherto been not at all anti-Semitic was immediately apparent. The Jews, of course, protected themselves in typically Jewish fashion by bribing their fellow-prisoners. They all had plenty of money, and could buy whatever they wanted in the canteen. It was therefore not hard for them to find penniless prisoners, who were only too glad to render services in return for tobacco, sweets, sausage and suchlike. In this way they were able to arrange for the capos to give them easier work, or for the prisoner nursing staff to get them admitted to the camp hospital. On one occasion a Jew had the nails drawn from his big toes by one of the prisoner nurses in exchange for a packet of cigarettes, so that he might get into the hospital.

They were mainly persecuted by members of their own race, their foremen or room seniors. Eschen, their block senior, distinguished himself in this respect. He was to hang himself later, because he feared punishment on account of some homosexual affair in which he had become involved. This block senior used every possible means, no matter how low, to terrorize the other prisoners, not only physically but above all mentally. He kept the screws on the whole time. He would entice them into disobeying the camp regulations, and then report them. He goaded them into acts of violence against one another, or against the capos, so as to have an excuse to report them for punishment. He would not send his report in at once, however, but would keep it hanging over their heads as a means of blackmail. He was the "devil" incarnate. He showed a repulsive zeal towards the members of the SS, but was ready to inflict any kind of iniquity on his fellow-prisoners and members of his own race.

I wanted to sack him more than once, but it was impossible. Eicke himself insisted on his retention.

Eicke invented a special form of collective punishment for the Jews. Each time an atrocity propaganda campaign about the concentration camps was inaugurated abroad, the Jews would be forced to lie in bed for anything from one to three months, and would be permitted to get up and leave their block only at meal times and for roll-call.

They were forbidden to ventilate their quarters and the windows were screwed down. This was a cruel punishment, with particularly severe psychological effects. As a result of this compulsory staying in bed for long periods, they became so nervous and overwrought that they could no longer bear the

[76] *Der Stürmer*, a weekly paper published in the Third Reich since 1923 and dedicated to anti-Semitic propaganda.

sight of each other, and could not stand one another's company. Many violent brawls broke out in consequence.

It was Eicke's opinion that responsibility for the propaganda campaign must lie with those Jews who had emigrated after being in Dachau, and that it was therefore only right that the remaining Jews should suffer this distressing collective punishment.

In this connection I must make the following statement. I was opposed to *Der Stürmer*, Streicher's anti-Semitic weekly, because of the disgusting sensationalism with which it played on people's basest instincts. Then, too, there was its perpetual and often savagely pornographic emphasis on sex. This paper caused a lot of mischief and, far from serving serious anti-Semitism, it did it a great deal of harm. It is small wonder that after the collapse it was learnt that a Jew edited the paper and that he also wrote the worst of the inflammatory articles it contained.[77]

As a fanatical National-Socialist I was firmly convinced that our ideals would gradually be accepted and would prevail throughout the world, after having been suitably modified in conformity with the national characteristics of the other peoples concerned. Jewish supremacy would thus be abolished. There was nothing new in anti-Semitism. It had always existed all over the world, but only came into the limelight when the Jews pushed themselves forward too much in their quest for power, and when their evil machinations became too obvious for the general public to stomach.

In my opinion the cause of anti-Semitism is ill-served by such frenzied persecution, as was provided by *Der Stürmer*.

If one wished to combat Jewry spiritually, then better weapons must be used. I believed that our ideas would prevail because they were both better and stronger.

I had no hope that Eicke's collective punishments would have the slightest effect on the foreign newspaper campaigns. These would go on, though hundreds or even thousands were shot on that account. Nevertheless, I thought it right that the Jews we had in our power should be punished for the dissemination of these atrocity stories by men of the same race.

Then came the "Crystal Night," staged by Goebbels[78] in November 1938, when, as a reprisal for the shooting of von Rath[79] in Paris by a Jew, Jewish shops throughout the country were destroyed or at least had their windows smashed, and when fires broke out in all the synagogues and the fire-fighting services were deliberately prevented from putting them out. "For their own protection, and to save them from the wrath of the people," all Jews who played

---

[77] According to Martin Broszat, the information given here by Höss has still not been corroborated. *Kommandant in Auschwitz*, *op. cit*., p. 109, note 1.

[78] Minister for Propaganda in the government of the Third Reich.

[79] Ernst von Rath was secretary at the embassy of the Third Reich in Paris. On November 7, 1938, he was shot by a Jew, Herschel Grynszpan, and died two days later. This incident became the excuse for the leaders of the Third Reich to engage in open anti-Jewish excesses.

any part in trade, industry or the business life of the country were arrested and brought into the concentration camps as "protective custody Jews."

Thus did I first get to know them in the mass.

Up to then Sachsenhausen had been almost free of Jews, but now came the Jewish invasion. Hitherto bribery had been almost unknown in Sachsenhausen. Now it was widespread, and took every form.

The "green" prisoners welcomed the Jews with delight as objects to be plundered. Their money had to be taken away from them, since otherwise it would have been impossible to prevent the camp from falling into a state of chaos.

They did their best to do each other in the eye whenever they could. Each tried to wangle a little position for himself and, with the tacit consent of the capos, they had won over, even invented new posts for themselves so as to avoid having to work. They did not hesitate to get rid of their fellow-prisoners by making false accusation against them, if this would enable them to obtain a nice, easy job. Once they had "got somewhere," they proceeded to harry and persecute their own people quite mercilessly. They far surpassed the "green" prisoners in every way.

Many Jews were driven to despair by this behaviour and in order to escape further persecution they "ran into the wires"[80], or attempted flight, hoping to be shot, or hanged themselves.

The numerous incidents of this nature were duly reported to Eicke by the commandant. Eicke merely remarked: "Let them carry on. The Jews can quietly devour each other."

I must emphasize here that I have never personally hated the Jews. It is true that I looked upon them as the enemies of our people. But just because of this I saw no difference between them and the other prisoners, and I treated them all in the same way. I never drew any distinctions. In any case the emotion of hatred is foreign to my nature. But I know what hate is, and what it looks like. I have seen it and I have suffered it myself.

When the *Reichsführer SS* modified his original Extermination Order of 1941, by which all Jews without exception were to be destroyed, and ordered instead that those capable of work were to be separated from the rest and employed in the armaments industry, Auschwitz became a Jewish camp. It was a collecting place for Jews, exceeding in scale anything previously known.[81]

Whereas the Jews who had been imprisoned in former years were able to count on being released one day[82] and were thus far less affected psycho-

---

[80] "To run into the wires" in camp slang meant committing suicide by touching the high-voltage fencing. It frequently happened that the prisoner was killed by a series of shots, fired by SS-men on duty at the watch-towers, before he could reach the wires.

[81] Himmler changed his decision because there was a growing demand for manpower in armaments factories and such industries which supplied the army. It became necessary to employ a large number of new workers to replace the Germans called up for military service.

[82] Such possibilities existed solely in the period preceding the so-called Crystal Night, also known as the Night of Broken Glass (*Kristallnacht*).

logically by the hardships of captivity, the Jews in Auschwitz no longer had any such hope. They knew, without exception, that they were condemned to death, that they would live only so long as they could work.

Nor did the majority have any hope of a change in their sad lot. They were fatalists. Patiently and apathetically, they submitted to all the misery, distress and terror. The hopelessness with which they accepted their impending fate made them psychologically quite indifferent to their surroundings. This mental collapse accelerated its physical equivalent. They no longer had the will to live, everything had become a matter of indifference to them, and they would succumb to the slightest physical shock. Sooner or later, death was inevitable. I firmly maintain from what I have seen that the high mortality among the Jews was due not only to the hard work, to which most of them were unaccustomed, and to the insufficient food, the overcrowded quarters and all the severities and abuses of camp life, but principally and decisively to their psychological state.[83]

For the mortality rate among the Jews was not much lower in other work places and other camps, where general conditions were far more favourable. It was always considerably higher with them than with other types of prisoners. I observed this again and again during my journeys of inspection as DI.[84]

This was even more noticeable in the case of the Jewish women. They deteriorated far more rapidly than the men, although from my observations they generally had far greater toughness and powers of endurance than the men, both physically and mentally. What I have just written applies to the bulk, the mass of the Jewish prisoners.

The more intelligent ones, psychologically stronger and with a keener desire

---

[83] The high death rate among the Jewish population was also caused by the extremely harsh conditions in the ghettos, where Jews were not only strictly separated from the rest of the population, but also had to do the hardest work while receiving starvation rations. Even before being brought to the camp the Jews were starving and terrified by all that had been inflicted on them and their families during their stay in the ghettos, where they were decimated in the course of successive deportation operations which finally took them to labour or extermination camps. When transported to *KL Auschwitz* many of them perished due to the horrible conditions in which they travelled from their former homes or camps. They passed through selection in the camp, which meant separation from their families (who were sent to the gas chambers). All this weakened their mental resistance. Jews in camp were moreover deprived of the chance to obtain additional food, because they were not allowed to receive parcels. A detailed description of life in ghettos and conditions of transportation to Auschwitz, as well as of the selection carried out on the railway ramp, is to be found in the manuscripts of members of the *Sonderkommando*, published in *Amidst a Nightmare of Crime. Notes of Prisoners of Sonderkommando Found at Auschwitz*. Oświęcim 1973.

[84] In November 1943, upon Pohl's suggestion, the Auschwitz camp was divided into three parts and a change of the camp commandant was effected. On November 11, *SS-Obersturmbannführer* Arthur Liebehenschel, hitherto the Head of Office DI in the Inspectorate of Concentration Camps at Oranienburg, took over from Höss as Auschwitz camp commandant, while Höss was entrusted with the post previously held by Liebehenschel. The Auschwitz camp was divided into three parts on November 22: 1. *Konzentrationslager (KL) Auschwitz—Stammlager* (commandant *SS-Obersturmbannführer* Arthur Liebehenschel); 2. *Konzentrationslager Auschwitz II—Birkenau* (commandant *SS-Sturmbannführer* Fritz Hartjenstein). At the same time Birkenau was divided into a camp for men (*SS-Untersturmführer* Johann Schwarzhuber) and a camp for women (*SS-Untersturmführer* Franz Hössler); 3. *Konzentrationslager Auschwitz III—Monowitz* (commandant *SS-Untersturmführer* Heinrich Schwarz).

for life, that is to say in most cases those from the western countries, reacted differently.

These people, especially if they were doctors, had no illusions concerning their fate. But they continued to hope, reckoning on a change of fortune that somehow or other would save their lives. They also reckoned on the collapse of Germany, for it was not difficult for them to listen to enemy propaganda.

For them the most important thing was to obtain a position which would lift them out of the crowd and give them special privileges, a job that would protect them to a certain extent from accidents and mortal hazards, and improve the physical conditions in which they lived.

They employed all their ability and all their will to obtain what can truly be described as a "living." The safer the position, the more eagerly and fiercely it was fought for. No quarter was shown, for this was a struggle in which everything was at stake. They flinched from nothing, no matter how desperate, in their efforts to make such safe jobs fall vacant and then to acquire them for themselves. Victory usually went to the most unscrupulous man or woman. Time and again I heard of these struggles to oust a rival and win his job.

In the various camps I had become well acquainted with the struggles for supremacy waged between the different categories of prisoners and political groups, and with the intrigues that went on to secure the higher posts. But I found that the Jews in Auschwitz could still teach me a lot. "Necessity is the mother of invention," and here it was an actual question of sheer survival.

Nevertheless, it frequently happened that persons who had acquired these safe positions would suddenly lose their grip, or would gradually fade away, when they learnt of the death of their closest relations. This would happen without any physical cause such as illness or bad living conditions. The Jews have always had very strong family feelings. The death of a near relative makes them feel that their own lives are no longer worth living, and are therefore not worth fighting for.

I have also seen quite the contrary, during the mass exterminations, but I shall refer to this later.

What I have written above applies particularly to the female inmates of all types.

But then everything was much more difficult, harsher and more depressing for the women, since general living conditions in the women's camp were incomparably worse. They were far more tightly packed, and the sanitary and hygienic conditions were notably inferior.[85] Furthermore, the disastrous over-

---

85 On August 16, 1942, the women prisoners were transferred from the base camp in Auschwitz, where they had occupied Blocks 1 to 10 separated by a wall from the camp for men, to Birkenau, sector Bla. The women were accommodated in one-storey brick barracks, equipped with bunks instead of beds. These were three-tier bunks in which an average of eight women slept on a handful of rotten straw. One such barrack was originally meant to accommodate 550 persons, later 744, but in reality about one thousand women were held in each.

Because of the humid climate and the impermeable, clayey subsoil of Birkenau, the camp was for the greater part of the year immersed in mud which literally flowed into the barracks and swamped the lowest bunks. In its beginnings the Birkenau camp had no sewage system and the prisoners suffered a severe water shortage. Women lived in atrociously inadequate sanitary conditions, which caused frequent epidemics of typhus and skin diseases. Sick and exhausted women prisoners

crowding and its consequences, which existed from the very beginning, prevented any proper order being established in the women's camp.

The general congestion was far greater than in the men's camp. When the women had reached the bottom, they would let themselves go completely. They would then stumble about like ghosts, without any will of their own, and had to be pushed everywhere by the others, until the day came when they quietly passed away. These stumbling corpses were a terrible sight.

The "green" female prisoners were of a special sort. I believe that Ravensbrück[86] was combed through to find the "best" for Auschwitz.[87] They far surpassed their male equivalents in toughness, squalor, vindictiveness and depravity. Most were prostitutes with many convictions, and some were truly repulsive creatures. Needless to say, these dreadful women gave full vent to their evil desires on the prisoners under them, which was unavoidable. The *Reichsführer SS* regarded them as particularly well-suited to act as capos over the Jewish women, when he visited Auschwitz in 1942.[88] Not many of these women died, except from disease.

They were soulless and had no feelings whatsoever.

The Budy blood-bath is still before my eyes. I find it incredible that human beings could ever turn into such beasts. The way the "greens" knocked the French Jewesses about, tearing them to pieces, killing them with axes, and throttling them—it was simply gruesome.[89] I do not believe that men could turn into such beasts.

Luckily not all the "greens" and "blacks"[90] were such utter brutes. There

---

were sent to the gas chambers after the frequent selections carried out both in the living quarters and in the hospital wards.

[86] *KL Ravensbrück*, established in 1939 as the only camp for women in the Third Reich, was situated in Mecklenburg near the small town of Fürstenberg, at the distance of about 85 kilometres north-west of Berlin and some 45 kilometres from *KL Sachsenhausen*. The building of the camp had started in the autumn of 1938, with prisoners from neighbouring *KL Sachsenhausen* supplying the manpower. In 1942 a men's camp was established in the immediate vicinity of the camp for women. In the first stages of its existence until the outbreak of World War II, the camp at Ravensbrück became a place of isolation for German women who were hostile towards National Socialism, and for German Jewesses. From the outbreak of war to August 1944 women of various nationalities were brought to the camp from countries occupied by the Nazis. From August 1944 women transferred from other camps, or brought from Warsaw after the Uprising, began to arrive in large numbers. The evacuation and liquidation of the camp began in April 1945. In the women's camp at Ravensbrück the Nazis had kept a total of about 132,000 women prisoners. At first *SS-Obersturmbannführer* Otto Koegel was the camp commandant, then *SS-Hauptsturmführer* Fritz Suhren, who was intermittently replaced by *SS-Sturmbannführer* Sauer.

[87] Höss means the first transport of 999 women brought to *KL Auschwitz* on March 26, 1942. Among them were the women prisoners who would occupy special posts in the women's camp.

[88] This was the second visit of Himmler to *KL Auschwitz*. It took place on July 17 and 18, 1942, when he inspected the camp for women which was then located in the base camp of Auschwitz. He asked to be shown the punishment of flogging women prisoners, and then reserved for himself for the future the right to confirm sentences of such punishment in the case of women.

[89] Another version of the events at Budy was given by Broad in the chapter of his reminiscences entitled "Revolt at Budy" (see pp. 120—123).

[90] Höss speaks here of asocial women prisoners, marked in the camp by black triangles and the letters *ASO* (*asoziale*). Prostitutes were the main category in this group.

were capable ones among them, who preserved a measure of sympathy for their fellow-prisoners. But such women were, of course, continually and cruelly persecuted by other members of their colour. Nor could the majority of female supervisors really understand them.

A welcome contrast were the female Jehovah's Witnesses,[91] who were nicknamed " bible-bees " or " bible-worms."

Unfortunately there were too few of them. Despite their more or less fanatical attitude they were much in demand. They were employed as servants in the homes of SS-men with large families, in the *Waffen-SS* club-house, and even in the SS officers' mess. But they worked above all on the land.

They worked on the poultry farm at Harmense,[92] and on various other farms.[93] They needed no supervision or guards. They were diligent and willing workers, for such was the will of Jehovah. Most of them were middle-aged German women but there were also a number of younger Dutch girls. I had two of the older women working for more than three years in my own household. My wife often said that she herself could not have seen to everything better than did these two women. The care that they bestowed on the children, both big and small, was particularly touching. The children loved them as though they were members of the family. At first we were afraid that they might try to save the children for Jehovah. But we were wrong. They never talked to the children about religion. This was really remarkable, considering their fanatical attitude. There were other wonderful beings among them. One of them worked for an SS officer, doing everything that had to be done without needing to be told, but she absolutely refused to clean his uniform, cap or boots or indeed even to touch anything that had any connection with the military life. On the whole they were contented with their lot. They hoped that, by suffering in captivity for Jehovah's sake, they would be given good positions in His kingdom, which they expected to enter very soon.

Strangely enough they were all convinced it was right that the Jews should now suffer and die, since their forefathers had betrayed Jehovah.

I have always regarded Jehovah's Witnesses as poor, misguided creatures, who are nevertheless happy in their own way.

The rest of the female prisoners, Poles, Czechs, Ukrainians and Russians, were employed so far as possible on agricultural work. They thus escaped the congestion and the evil effects of camp life. They were far better off in their billets on the farms and in Rajsko. I had always found that the prisoners engaged in agricultural work and living away from the camp made a very different impression from the others. They were certainly not subjected to the

---

91 They wore violet triangles and were marked with the letters IBV (for the *Internationaler Bibelforscherverein*, or the International Bible Students association).

92 The poultry farm Harmęże (*Geflügelfarm Harmense*), where on December 8, 1941, a sub-camp was established. The history of this camp was published in *Hefte von Auschwitz*, no. 11.

93 These were sub-camps established on the estate of Babice (*Wirtschaftshof Babitz*), on the agricultural farm at Budy (*Wirtschaftshof Budy*), the agricultural farm at Pławy (*Wirtschaftshof Plawy*) and the plant growing station at Rajsko (*Pflanzenzuchtstation Rajsko*). The history of all these sub-camps (except Pławy) was published in *Hefte von Auschwitz*, nos. 9—11.

same psychological strains as their fellows in the massive camps. They would not otherwise have been so willing to do the work demanded of them.

The women's camp, tightly crammed from the very beginning, meant psychological destruction for the mass of the female prisoners, and this led sooner or later to their physical collapse.

From every point of view, and at all times, the worst conditions prevailed in the women's camp. This was so even at the very beginning, when it still formed part of the base camp. Once the Jewish transports from Slovakia began to arrive, it was filled to the roof within a matter of days.[94] Wash-houses and latrines were sufficient, at the most, for a third of the number of inmates that the camp contained.

To have put these swarming ant-hills into proper order would have required more than the few female supervisors[95] allotted me from Ravensbrück. And I must emphasize once again that the women I was sent were not the best.

These supervisors had been thoroughly spoiled at Ravensbrück. Everything had been done for them, to persuade them to remain in the women's concentration camp, and by offering them extremely good living conditions it was hoped to attract new recruits. They were given the best accommodation, and were paid a salary they could have never earned elsewhere. Their work was not particularly onerous. In short, the *Reichsführer SS*, and Pohl[96] in particular, wished to see the female supervisors treated with the utmost consideration.

Up to that time conditions in Ravensbrück had been normal, and there was no question of overcrowding.

These supervisors were now posted to Auschwitz—none came voluntarily—and had the job of getting the women's camp started under the most difficult conditions.

From the very beginning most of them wanted to run away and return to the quiet comforts and the easy life at Ravensbrück.

The chief female supervisor[97] of the period, Frau Langenfeld,[98] was in no way capable of coping with the situation, yet she refused to accept any instructions given her by the commander of the protective custody camp.

---

[94] In the period from March 26 to April 29, 1942, 6,250 Jewesses from Slovakia were brought in nine RSHA transports. The Jewesses were directed to the camp through the Jewish Section (known as B4) in Office IV (*Geheime Staatspolizei*) of the Reich Main Security Office, which was responsible for the liquidation of the Jewish population.

[95] *Aufseherinnen* in German.

[96] Head of the SS Economic and Administrative Head Office (*SS-Wirtschaftsverwaltungshauptamt*—WVHA). WVHA was one of the offices in the SS headquarters (*Reichsführung SS*) and at the same time a department of the Internal Affairs Ministry. Organized in 1942, it was divided into five groups of which office group D (*Amtsgruppe D*) was concerned with matters of concentration camps in their entirety, while office group W (*Amtsgruppe W*) directed and supervised all enterprises belonging to the SS.

[97] An overseer (*Oberaufseherin*). This position corresponded to that of the *Schutzhaftlagerführer* in the camp for men.

[98] Correst spelling Langefeld. The first supervisor (*Lagerführerin*) of the camp for women in Auschwitz and later at Birkenau.

Acting on my own initiative, I simply put the women's camp under his jurisdiction, since this seemed the only method of ending the disorderly way in which it was being run. Hardly a day passed without discrepancies appearing in the numbers of inmates shown on the strength-return. The supervisors ran hither and thither in all this confusion like a lot of flustered hens, and had no idea what to do. The three or four good ones among them were driven crazy by the rest. The chief supervisor regarded herself as an independent camp commander, and consequently objected to being placed under a man of the same rank as herself. In the end I actually had to cancel her subordination to him. When the *Reichsführer SS* visited the camp in July 1942 I reported all this to him, in the presence of the chief female supervisor, and I told him that Frau Langenfeld was and always would be completely incapable of commanding and organizing the women's camp at Auschwitz, as this should be done. I requested that she be once again subordinated to the first commander of the camp.

The *Reichsführer SS* absolutely refused to allow this, despite the striking proofs he was given of the inadequacy of the chief supervisor and of the female supervisors in general. He wished the women's camp to be commanded by a woman, and I was to detail an SS officer to act as her assistant.

But which of my officers would be willing to take his orders from a woman? Every officer whom I had to appoint to this post begged to be released as soon as possible. When the really large numbers of prisoners began to arrive, I myself devoted as much time as I could to helping in the running of this camp.

Thus from the very beginning the women's camp was managed by the prisoners themselves. The larger the camp became, the more difficult it was for the supervisors to exercise control, and self-rule by the prisoners became more and more apparent. Since it was the "green" who had the supremacy, and who therefore ran the camp by reason of their greater slyness and unscrupulousness, it was they who were the real masters in the women's camp, despite the fact that the camp senior and other key officials were "red." The women controllers, as the female capos were called, were mostly "green" or "black." It was thus inevitable that the most wretched conditions prevailed in the women's camp.[99]

The original female supervisors were, even so, far and away superior to those we got later. In spite of keen recruiting by the National Socialist women's organizations, very few candidates volunteered for concentration camp service, and compulsion had to be used to obtain the ever increasing numbers required.

Each armaments firm to which female prisoners were allotted for work had in exchange to surrender a certain percentage of their other female employees to act as supervisors. It will be understood that, in view of the general wartime shortage of efficient female labour, these firms did not give us their best workers.

These supervisors were now given a few weeks' "training" in Ravensbrück and then let loose on the prisoners. Since the selection and allocation took place at Ravensbrück, Auschwitz was once again at the end of the queue.

---

[99] By means of such interpretation of camp reality, Höss tried to exonerate the authorities of responsibility for the appalling conditions.

Obviously Ravensbrück kept what seemed to it the best ones for employment in the new women's labour camp, which was being set up there.

Such was the position regarding the supervisory staff in the women's camp at Auschwitz.

As was only to be expected, the morals of these women were, almost without exception, extremely low. Many of them appeared before the SS tribunal charged with theft in connection with *Aktion Reinhard*.[100] But these were only the few who happened to be caught. In spite of the most fearful punishments, stealing went on, and the supervisors continued to use the prisoners as go-betweens for this purpose.

I will give one very bad case as an illustration.

One of these female supervisors sank so low as to become intimate with some of the male prisoners, mostly "green" capos. In return for sexual intercourse, in which she was only too anxious to take part, she received jewellery, gold and other valuable objects. As a cover for her shameless behaviour, she started an affair with a senior non-commissioned officer of the SS guard unit and used his house as a safe place in which to lock up her hard-earned winnings. This poor fool was completely unaware of what his sweetheart was up to, and was very surprised when all these pretty things were discovered in his house.

The supervisor was sentenced by the *Reichsführer SS* to life imprisonment in a concentration camp, and to twice twenty-five strokes of the lash.

Like homosexuality among the men, an epidemic of lesbianism was rampant in the women's camp. The most severe measures, including transfer to a penal company,[101] were inadequate to put a stop to this.

Time and again I received reports of intercourse of this sort between supervisors and female prisoners. This in itself indicates the low level of these supervisors.

Obviously they did not take their work or duties very seriously and most of them were inefficient as well. There were only a few punishments that could be inflicted for dereliction of duty. Confinement to their quarters was not

---

[100] "Action Reinhard" (*Aktion Reinhard*)—cryptonym referring to the extermination of Jews and the appropriation by the SS of wealth belonging to persons murdered in the camps (see p. 95). The name was taken from the first name of *SS-Gruppenführer* Heydrich, assassinated in Prague by the Czech Resistance Movement.

[101] The penal company (*Strafkompanie—SK*) for women was at first located at Budy (*Kommando Budy*) at a distance of about seven kilometres from Auschwitz. It was established in June 1942 in retaliation for the escape of a woman prisoner, Joanna Nowak of Łódź. 200 women, Polish political prisoners, were then sent to the penal company. They were brought in transports from Cracow on April 27 and May 28, 1942. Later Germans, as well as Jewesses from Slovakia and France, were also interned here. Altogether the SK numbered about 400 women prisoners, who were employed in cleaning, dredging ponds and moving earth. In the evening of August 16, 1942, i.e. on the same day when the camp for women was transferred from Auschwitz to Birkenau (to sector BIa) the Polish women prisoners from the penal company from Budy were also taken there. From 200 Polish women who were sent to the penal company in June, only 137 persons survived. At Birkenau, they were housed in ordinary barracks which meant that they were released from the penal company. The penal company for women stayed at Budy till the end of March or even early April, 1943, when it was transferred to Birkenau to sector BIa. About 90 women prisoners were killed during the massacre which took place at Budy in October 1942. *Cf.* Broad's reminiscences, p. 140; and Teresa Cegłowska: Karne kompanie w KL Auschwitz. *Zeszyty Oświęcimskie*, 1975, no. 17, pp. 193—195.

looked on as a punishment at all, since it meant that they did not have to go out when the weather was bad. All punishments had first to be countersigned by the Inspector of Concentration Camps or Pohl. Punishment was to be kept to a minimum. "Irregularities" were to be put right by careful training and good leadership. The female supervisors knew all about this, of course, and the majority of them reacted as might be expected.

I have always had a great respect for women in general. In Auschwitz, however, I learnt that I would have to modify my views, and that even a woman must be carefully examined before she is entitled to enjoy a full measure of respect.

What I have said certainly applied to the majority of the female supervisor staff. It is true that there were good, decent, reliable women among them, but they were very few.[102] There is no need to emphasize that these suffered greatly from their surroundings and from the general conditions at Auschwitz. But they could not escape, being bound by their war service obligations. Many of them complained to me about their troubles, and even more to my wife. We could only tell them to hope that the war would soon be over. This was indeed a poor means of consolation.

Attached to the women's camp, for the purpose of guarding the working parties employed outside the camp, were the dog-handlers.

Already at Ravensbrück the female supervisors in charge of outside working parties had dogs allotted them, so as to reduce the number of guards. These supervisors were, of course, armed with pistols, but the *Reichsführer SS* believed that a greater terror-effect would be produced by the use of dogs. For most women have a powerful respect for dogs, whereas men do not bother about them so much.

Because of the mass of prisoners at Auschwitz, how to guard the outside working parties effectively was a constant problem. There were never enough troops. Chains of sentry posts were useful, in that they could be used to enclose the larger working areas. But the constant moving of work parties from one site to another, and the mobility necessitated by the nature of the work itself made proper supervision impossible in the case of agricultural work, digging ditches and so on. Owing to the small number of female supervisors available it was necessary to employ as many dog-handlers as possible. Even our one hundred and fifty-odd dogs were not enough.[103] The *Reichsführer SS* calculated

---

[102] The existing state of information concerning the camp, including evidence and reports by former women prisoners, does not allow us to mention a single female supervisor who could be regarded as a decent person. The alleged favourable reputation of some of them was not corroborated during the trial of the SS garrison of Auschwitz-Birkenau, heard by the Supreme National Tribunal in Cracow. During that trial Marie Mandel and Therese Brandl were sentenced to death, Luise Danz received a life sentence, while Alice Orlowski and Hildegard Marthe Luise Lächert were sentenced to 15 years' imprisonment. The majority of supervisors escaped trial at the time, but some were later charged at the trials of *KL Bergen-Belsen* and *KL Ravensbrück*.

[103] In accordance with a Berlin headquarters order dated October 16, 1942, luxuriously fitted kennels were built at Birkenau at the cost of 81,000 marks. They were to house 250 guard dogs. The files concerning the building show that when the kennels were planned, advice was sought from the camp veterinary surgeon and everything was done to ensure proper sanitary conditions. Adequate green areas were provided as well as a suitably fitted dogs' hospital and a special

that one dog should be able to replace two sentries. This was probably so, as far as the female working parties were concerned, owing to the universal fear caused by the presence of the dogs.

The Auschwitz Dog Squad contained the most astonishing military material. Astonishing in the negative sense. When volunteers were sought for training as dog-handlers, half the SS regiment applied. They imagined that such work would be easier and less monotonous. Since it was impossible to take on all the volunteers, the companies hit upon a cunning solution, and gave up all their black sheep, so as to be rid of them. Someone else could have the headaches now. Most of these men had been punished for some offence or other. If the commander of the guard unit had looked at these men's conduct sheets a little more closely, he would never on any account have allowed them to be sent away for training.

At the Training and Experimental Establishment for Dog-handlers at Oranienburg some of the trainees were returned to their units before they have even finished their course, because of total unsuitability.

When those who had completed their training returned to Auschwitz, they were formed into a unit, the *Hundestaffel*, and it was not hard to see what a splendid new formation had been created. And now it was time for them to be put to work. Either they played games with their dogs, or they found an easy hide-out and went to sleep, their dogs waking them up on the approach of an " enemy ", or else passed the time in pleasant conversation with the female supervisors of the prisoners. A great many of them formed a regular liaison with the " green " controllers. Since the dog-handlers were always employed in the women's camp, it was not difficult for them to continue this liaison.

When they were bored, or wanted to have some fun, they would set the dogs on the prisoners. If they were caught doing this, they would maintain that the dog had done it of its own accord, owing to the peculiar behaviour of the prisoner, or that its lead had been lost, and so on. They always had an excuse.[104] Every day, according to the regulations, they had to give their dogs further training.

Because of the time and trouble it took to train fresh dog-handlers, they could only be relieved of their posts if they had been guilty of some grave offence, such as one that entailed punishment by SS court martial, or alternatively if they had badly ill-treated or neglected their dogs. The kennelman, a former police sergeant, who had looked after dogs for more than twenty-five years, was often driven to despair by the behaviour of the dog-handlers. But they

---

cook-house. Because of delay in repairs to the roof of the kennels the section commander threatened resignation, because, as he said, he could not be responsible for sickness to which the dogs were exposed by leaking roofs. *Cf.* Jan Sehn: *Obóz koncentracyjny Oświęcim-Brzezinka (Auschwitz-Birkenau).* Warszawa 1964, Wydawnictwo Prawnicze, pp. 49—50.

What strikes us most in the relevant text is the far from casual concern of the camp authorities for the well-being of animals, while they were completely indifferent to the sanitary and hygienic conditions in which, at the same time, thousands of Auschwitz camp prisoners lived (see p. 58, note 85).

[104] Höss seems to have forgotten that dogs were specially trained to attack prisoners. Setting dogs on defenceless women was not an occasional, but a regular occurrence in the camp.

knew that nothing much could happen to them, and that they were unlikely to actually lose their jobs. A better commanding officer might have been able to knock this gang into shape. But the gentleman concerned had far more important things to think about. I had much trouble with the *Hundestaffel* and many clashes with the commander of the guard regiment, over this.[105] I had no understanding of what was actually required of troops, at least according to Glücks' way of thinking. Hence I was never able to get him to post away officers as soon as they became intolerable at Auschwitz.

A very great deal of trouble could have been avoided if Glücks' attitude towards me had been different.

As the war went on, the *Reichsführer SS* was constantly insisting on ever greater economies in the manpower employed on guard duties. The men were to be replaced by devices such as wire fencing, by encircling permanent places of work with electrified wire, by minefields, and by ever larger numbers of dogs. Should a commandant manage to devise a really efficient method of economizing in the use of guards, he was given immediate promotion. But all this achieved nothing at all.

The *Reichsführer SS* even imagined that dogs could be trained to circle around the prisoners, as though they were sheep, and thus prevent them from escaping. One sentry, aided by several dogs, was supposed to be able to guard up to 100 prisoners with safety. The attempt came to nothing. Men are not sheep. However well trained the dogs were in recognizing the prisoners by their uniforms and their smell and so on, and however accurately they were taught to know how close prisoners might be allowed to approach, they were all only dogs, and could not think like human beings. If the prisoners purposely attracted them to one spot, the dogs would then leave a wide section unguarded through which they could escape.

Nor were the dogs any use in preventing a mass break-out. They would of course savagely maul some of the escapees, but they would be immediately slaughtered along with their "shepherds."

It was also proposed that dogs should replace the guards in the watch-towers. They were to be allowed to run loose between the double wire fencing that encircled the camp of the permanent places of work, each dog guarding a certain sector, and would give warning of the approach of a prisoner, thus preventing a break through the wire. This, too, came to nothing. The dogs either found a spot in which to go to sleep, or they let themselves be tricked. If the wind was in the wrong quarter, the dog would notice nothing, or its barking would not be heard by sentry.

The laying of mines was two-edged weapon. They had to be accurately laid and their precise situation plotted on the plan of the minefield, since after three months at the most they became defective and had to be replaced. It was also necessary to walk through the minefield from time to time, and this gave the prisoners a chance to observe the lanes where no mines had beeh laid.

Globocnik[106] had used mines in this way at his extermination centres. But

---

[105] At that time it was *SS-Obersturmbannführer* Fritz Hartjenstein.

[106] Then SS and Police Leader in the Lublin district. A district was an administrative unit

despite the carefully laid minefields at Sobibór, the Jews knew where the lanes through the minefield ran, and were able by force to achieve a major break-out, during which almost all the guard personnel were wiped out.[107]

Neither mechanical devices nor animals can replace human intelligence.

Even the double electrified fence can be neutralized in dry weather with a few simple tools, provided a man is sufficiently cold-blooded and gives the problem a little thought. This has frequently succeeded. Often, too, the sentries outside the wire have come too close to it, and have had to pay for their lack of caution with their lives.

I have referred several times to what I regarded as my main task: namely to push on, with all the means at my disposal, with the construction of all the installations belonging to the SS in the Auschwitz camp area.

Sometimes, during a period of quiet, I used to think that I could see an end in sight to the constructional work resulting from the numerous schemes and plans that the *Reichsführer SS* had laid down for Auschwitz, but at that point new plans would arrive, involving further urgent action.

The perpetual rush in which I lived, brought about by the demands of the *Reichsführer SS*, by wartime difficulties, by almost daily problems in the camps and above all by the unending stream of prisoners flowing into the whole camp area, left me no time to think of anything except my work. I concentrated exclusively on this.

Harassed thus by circumstances, I passed on my harassment in double measure to all who came under my jurisdiction, whether SS, civilians, officials, business firms or prisoners. I had only one end in view: to drive everything and everyone forward in my determination to improve the general conditions, so that I could carry out the measures laid down. The *Reichsführer SS* required every man to do his duty and if necessary to sacrifice himself entirely in so doing. Every German had to commit himself heart and soul, so that we might win the war.

In accordance with the will of the *Reichsführer SS* the concentration camps were to become armaments plants. Everything else was to be subordinated to this. All other considerations must be set aside.

---

into which the occupied Polish lands were divided; such districts formed the so-called *General-gouvernement*.

[107] In March 1942, the Nazis began building a mass extermination centre at Sobibór, Lublin district, which started functioning in May 1942. Initially its area covered more than 12 hectares, but later it grew to 58 hectares. Sobibór was used until the middle of October 1943. At least 250,000 victims were killed there with exhaust gases. A revolt broke out in the camp on October 14, 1943, organized by a secret society of prisoners. It was led by a Soviet prisoner of war, Sasha Pechersky (a captain in the Soviet Army) and by a Jewish prisoner, Leon Feldhandler, a native of Żółkiewka. About 150 Dutch, Polish and Russian Jews belonged to the organization. The outbreak of the revolt was precipitated by the fact that Jewish transports destined for extermination had stopped. This led to the supposition that the camp with its remaining inmates would soon be liquidated. The prisoners killed more than ten SS-men and several Ukrainian nationalists from the camp guard. Less than twenty prisoners managed to survive the revolt, namely those who were able to cross the minefield around the camp area and hide in the woods. The rest of the prisoners were murdered by SS-men. The extermination centre did not continue its activity after the revolt. Gerald Reitlinger: *The Final Solution*. London 1953, Sphere Books Ltd., p. 153 and note.

His words made it quite clear that the unwarrantable general conditions in the camps were of secondary importance. Armaments came first, and every obstacle to this must be overcome. I dared not allow myself to think otherwise. I had to become harder, colder and even more merciless in my attitude towards the needs of the prisoners. I saw it all very clearly, often far too clearly, but I knew that I must not let it get me down. I dared not let my feelings get the better of me. Everything had to be sacrificed to one end, the winning of the war. This was how I looked on my work at that time. I could not be at the front, so I must do everything at home to support those who were fighting. I see now that all my driving and pushing could not have won the war for us. But at the time, I had implicit faith in our final victory, and I knew I must stop at nothing in my work to help us achieve this.

By the will of the *Reichsführer SS*, Auschwitz became the greatest human extermination centre of all time.

When, in the summer of 1941, he himself gave me the order to prepare installations at Auschwitz where mass exterminations could take place, and personally to carry out these exterminations, I did not have the slightest idea of their scale or consequences.[108] It was certainly an extraordinary and monstrous order. Nevertheless, the reasons behind the extermination programme seemed to me right. I did not reflect on it at the time; I had been given an order, and I had to carry it out. Whether this mass extermination of the Jews was necessary or not was something on which I could not allow myself to form an opinion, for I lacked the necessary breadth of view.

If the *Führer* had himself given the order for the "final solution of the Jewish question," then, for a veteran National-Socialist and even more so for an SS officer, there could be no question of considering its merits. "The *Führer* commands, we follow" was never a mere phrase or slogan. It was meant in bitter earnest.

Since my arrest it has been said to me repeatedly that I could have disobeyed this order, and that I might even have assassinated Himmler. I do not believe that of all the thousands of SS officers there could have been found a single one capable of such a thought. It was completely impossible. Certainly many SS officers grumbled and complained about some of the harsh orders that came from the *Reichsführer SS*, but they nevertheless always carried them out.

Many orders of the *Reichsführer SS* deeply offended a great number of his SS officers, but I am perfectly certain that not a single one of them would have dared to raise a hand against him, or would have even contemplated doing so in his most secret thoughts. As *Reichsführer SS* his person was inviolable. His basic orders, issued in the name of the *Führer*, were sacred. They brooked no consideration, no argument, no interpretation. They were carried out ruthlessly and regardless of consequences, even though these might well mean the death of the officer concerned, as happened to not a few SS officers during the war.

---

[108] These matters were described in detail by Höss in *The Final Solution of the Jewish Question* (see pp. 81—101).

It was not for nothing that during training the self-sacrifice of the Japanese for their country and their emperor, who was also their god, was held up as a shining example to the SS.

SS training was not comparable to university course which can have as little lasting effect on the students as water on a duck's back. It was, on the contrary, something that was deeply engrained, and the *Reichsführer SS* knew very well what he could demand of his men.

But outsiders simply cannot understand that there was not a single SS officer who would disobey an order from the *Reichsführer SS*, far less consider getting rid of him because of the gruesomely hard nature of one such order.

What the *Führer*, or in our case his second-in-command, the *Reichsführer SS*, ordered was always right.

Democratic England also has a basic national concept: *My country, right or wrong!*[109] and this is adhered to by every nationally-conscious Englishman.

Before the mass extermination of the Jews began, the Russian *politruks* and political commissars were liquidated in almost all the concentration camps during 1941 and 1942.

In accordance with a secret order issued by Hitler, these Russian *politruks* and political commissars were combed out of all the prisoner-of-war camps by special detachments from the Gestapo.[110] When identified, they were transferred to the nearest concentration camp for liquidation. It was made known that these measures were taken because the Russians had been killing all German soldiers, who were party members or belonged to special sections of the NSDAP,[111] especially members of the SS, and also because the political officials of the Red Army had been ordered, if taken prisoner, to create every kind of disturbance in the prisoner-of-war camps and their places of employment and to carry out sabotage wherever possible.

The political officials of the Red Army thus identified were brought to Auschwitz for liquidation. The first, smaller transports of them were executed by firing squads.

---

[109] These words were written by Höss in English.

[110] The manner of treating this group of Soviet prisoners of war was determined by "The Principles of Treating Political Commissars," dated June 6, 1941, worked out by the High Command of the Armed Forces (OKW) on the basis of Hitler's instructions of March 30, 1941. On these grounds *SS-Gruppenführer* Reinhard Heydrich, Head of the Reich Main Security Office, issued on July 17, 1941 (i.e. after the Third Reich had already attacked the Soviet Union) an order to kill those Soviet prisoners of war who were likely to endanger National Socialism. This order pertained to all important party and state functionaries, particularly "professional revolutionaries," all people's commissars of the Soviet army, Jews, the Soviet intelligentsia and persons of whom it was discovered that they were agitators or "fanatic communists." On January 15, 1942, in his capacity as inspector of concentrations camps, Glücks gave the order to select Soviet prisoners of war sent to concentration camps for extermination. But even earlier, in November 1941, a Special Gestapo Commission (*Sonderkommission der Gestapoleitstelle Kattowitz*) came to Auschwitz from Kattowitz, whose aim it was probably, in accordance with Heydrich's instruction of July 17, 1941, to interrogate prisoners of war and to classify them into suitable categories.

[111] *Nationalsozialistische Deutsche Arbeiterpartei* (*NSDAP*)—National Socialist German Workers' Party (Nazi Party). Founded in January 1919 as the German Workers' Party (*Deutsche Arbeiterpartei*).

While I was away on duty my deputy Fritzsch, the commander of the protective custody camp, first tried gas for these killings.[112] It was a preparation of prussic acid, called Cyclon B,[113] which was used in the camp as an insecticide and of which there was always a stock on hand. On my return Fritzsch reported this to me, and the gas was used again for the next transport.

The gassing was carried out in the detention cells of Block 11.[114] Protected by a gas-mask, I watched the killing myself. In the crowded cells death came instantaneously the moment the Cyclon B was thrown in. A short, almost smothered cry, and it was all over. During this first experience of gassing people, I did not fully realize what was happening, perphaps because I was too

---

[112] In the light of present research it appears that the first attempt to kill with gas took place in the cellars of Block 11; no other attempt at gassing prisoners in the cellars of that block was recorded. Although Höss denies having been present at the first attempt, he nevertheless states a few sentences further on that he was present when gas was used for the first time. He wrote: "During this first experience of gassing people, I did not fully realize what was happening, perhaps because I was too impressed by the whole procedure. I have a clearer recollection of the gassing of nine hundred Russians which took place shortly afterwards in the old crematorium, since the use of Block 11 for this purpose caused too much trouble."

[113] HCN—hydrocyanic acid, prussic acid, one of the most swiftly acting poisons. In *KL Auschwitz* Cyclon B was used in the form of diatomite, saturated with hydrocyanic acid. Cyclon B was produced by the German Company for Controlling Pests (*Deutsche Gesellschaft für Schädlingsbekämpfung*—Degesch), part of IG-Farbenindustrie. The company *Tesch und Stabenow* (Testa) were the agents supplying the concentration camps with Cyclon B. From existing documents it transpires that SS vans used to bring Cyclon from the storehouses of Testa in Dessau. From the records of sales by Degesch and Testa it has been ascertained that in the respective years they supplied *KL Auschwitz* with the following quantities of Cyclon B: 7,478.6 kilos in 1942, 12,174.09 kilos in 1943. The net profit of both these firms derived from the sale of Cyclon amounted to 45,735.78 marks in 1942 and 127,985.79 marks in 1943.

[114] The first attempt to kill people with Cyclon B was made in the cellars of Block 11 on September 3, 1941. The procedure was as follows: On September 2, the *Lagerführer, SS-Hauptsturmführer* Karl Fritzsch, selected nine persons out of the 19 prisoners put into the bunker of Block 11 the day before. The remaining ten prisoners were sent back to the bunker. In the afternoon of the same day Fritzsch gave the order for those nine prisoners and some others from the penal company to carry the beds from Block 11 to the garret. In the evening of that day the penal company, hitherto housed in Block 11, was transferred, directly after work, to Block 5a, which was still under construction. On September 3, the sanitary orderlies were requested by the SS to fetch 250 sick prisoners from hospital blocks and to put them into the bunkers of Block 11. Then around 600 Soviet prisoners of war (officers and political commissars, selected on the strength of *Einsatzbefehl* no. 8, dated July 17, 1941, see p. 69, note 110) were driven into the bunkers whereupon the windows of the cellars were covered up with earth. After the SS-men had discharged Cyclon B inside, the door was closed. On September 4, *Rapportführer* Palitzsch, wearing a gas-mask, opened the door and saw that some of the prisoners were still alive. So a further dose of the gas was added and the doors were again sealed. Next evening, i.e. September 5, 20 prisoners of the penal company were taken from Block 5a, together with sanitary orderlies from hospital blocks, and they were led to the yard of Block 11. They were informed that they would do some special work about which they were not to talk to anybody, under pain of death. They were promised additional food rations after doing that work. The following officers were in the yard of Block 11: Fritzsch, Maier, *SS-Hauptscharführer* Palitzsch and the camp doctor. The prisoners received gas-masks and were told to go down into the cellars of Block 11 and bring the bodies out into the yard. There they took the military uniforms from the bodies, which they placed on wagons. The corpses were left in their underwear. The transportation of the corpses to the crematorium lasted till late into the night.

impressed by the whole procedure. I have a clearer recollection of the gassing of nine hundred Russians which took place shortly afterwards in the old crematorium, since the use of Block 11 for this purpose caused too much trouble.[115] While the transport was detraining, holes were pierced in the earth and concrete ceiling of the mortuary. The Russians were ordered to undress in an anteroom: they then quietly entered the mortuary, for they had been told they were to be deloused. The whole transport exactly filled the mortuary to capacity. The doors were then sealed and the gas shaken down through the holes in the roof. I do not know how long this killing took. For a little while a humming sound could be heard. When the powder was thrown in there were cries of "Gas!", then a great bellowing, and the trapped prisoners hurled themselves against both the doors. But the doors held. They were opened several hours later, so that the place might be aired. It was then that I saw, for the first time, gassed bodies in the mass.

It made me feel uncomfortable and I shuddered, although I had imagined that death by gassing would be worse than it was. I had always thought that the victims would experience a terrible choking sensation. But the bodies, without exception, showed no signs of convulsion. The doctors explained to me that the prussic acid had a paralyzing effect on the lungs, but its action was so quick and strong that death came before the convulsions could set in, and in this effects differed from those produced by carbon monoxide or by a general oxygen deficiency.

The killing of these Russian prisoners of war did not cause me much concern at the time. The order had been given, and I had to carry it out. I must even admit that this gassing set my mind at rest, for the mass extermination of the Jews was to start soon and at that time neither Eichmann[116] nor I was certain how these mass killings were to be carried out . It would be gas, but we did not know which gas or how it was to be used. Now we had the gas, and we had established a procedure. I always shuddered at the prospect of carrying out exterminations by shooting, when I thought of the vast numbers concerned, and of the women and children. The shooting of hostages, and the group executions ordered by the *Reichsführer SS* or by the Reich Main Security Office,[117] had been enough for me. I was therefore relieved to think that we were to be spared all these blood-baths, and the victims too would be spared suffering, until their last moment came. It was precisely this which had caused me the greatest concern, when I had heard Eichmann's description

---

[115] This event took place in September 1941, when an attempt to gas about 900 Soviet prisoners of war was made in the mortuary of crematorium I in the base camp. Like the 600 prisoners of war killed with gas on September 3—5, they were not entered into the camp records. Records of Soviet prisoners of war, brought to *KL Auschwitz*, were not started until October 1941.

[116] Head of the so-called Jewish Section in the RSHA.

[117] This statement proves that numerous executions of hostages, mass shootings of civilians (particularly members of the Resistance Movement), also of Soviet prisoners and prisoners of war, were taking place in *KL Auschwitz*. Broad also mentions this fact in his reminiscences. See excerpt entitled "Shambles in the Old Crematorium" (pp. 117—120).

of Jews being mown down by the Special Squads[118] armed with machine-guns and machine-pistols. Many gruesome scenes are said to have taken place: people running away after being shot, the finishing off of the wounded and particularly of the women and children. Many members of the *Einsatzkommandos*, unable to endure wading through blood any longer, had committed suicide. Some had even gone mad. Most of the members of these *Kommandos* had to rely on alcohol when carrying out their horrible work. According to Höfle's[119] description, the men employed at Globocnik's extermination centres[120] consumed amazing quantities of alcohol.

In the spring of 1942 the first transport of Jews, all ear-marked for extermination, arrived from Upper Silesia.

They were taken from the detraining platform to the "Cottage"—to Bunker 1[121]—across the meadows where later Building Sector III[122] was located.

---

118 Operational detachments (*Einsatzkommandos*) formed part, like *Sonderkommandos*, *Teilkommandos*, and *Vorkommandos*, of the so-called Action Groups (*Einsatzgruppen*). The establishing of Action Groups was connected with the planned aggression against Poland. In 1939 an agreement was reached between the High Command of the Armed Forces and the Head of the Security Police and Security Service, Reinhard Heydrich. On the strength of that agreement it was determined that a special unit, consisting of the police and the SS, should be attached to each army. Its task would be "liquidation of hostile and destructive elements," present in the Eastern territories occupied by the Wehrmacht. The full name of the Action Group was *Einsatzgruppe der Sicherheitspolizei und des SD*. The Action Groups consisted of members of the Secret State Police (Gestapo), the Security Service (SD) and the Criminal Police (Kripo), who were assigned to this service. Together with the German armies, five of which had invaded Poland, there were five Action Groups and one for special purposes (*Einsatzgruppe z.b.V.*), the task of which was to secure the industrial centres of Upper Silesia. They were organized as early as August 1939. In the course of reorganizing the military administration in the occupied Polish lands, further *Einsatzgruppen* were created. The activities of *Einsatzgruppen* in the occupied areas of the Soviet Union were particularly bloody and continued for the entire duration of the occupation.

Each *Einsatzgruppe* was divided into two to four *Einsatzkommandos* and these in turn were subdivided into smaller detachments (sometimes with less than ten or less than twenty members), called *Nebenstelle* or *Aussenstelle*.

They were found guilty of murdering 2 million men, women and children in the trial of their commandants (Case IX), in accordance with the verdict of the American Military Tribunal in Nuremberg, April 10, 1948.

119 Staff officer with *SS-Gruppenführer* Globocnik.

120 Here Höss meant the extermination camps at Sobibór, Bełżec, Treblinka and partly also that at Majdanek, which were centres designated for the mass extermination of the Jewish population. They were situated within the Lublin district where Globocnik held the post of Higher SS and Police Leader.

121 Bunker 1 was located in a cottage, especially adapted for gassing, just as was Bunker 2, situated at some distance away from it. These were the first installations for killing with Cyclon B in Birkenau. Broad also wrote about gassings in these premises in the excerpt of his reminiscences entitled "The Two Little Farmhouses" (see pp. 131—135) as did the camp surgeon *SS-Obersturmführer* Johann Paul Kremer in his diary (see p. 162).

122 The camp at Birkenau was to consist of four building sectors. Sector I (in which a camp for men and women was located) was put into use in 1942; the camps located in sector II were ready in the years 1943—1944 (the Gypsy camp, men's quarantine camp, men's camp, men's hospital camp, the family camp for Jews from Theresienstadt, the store-house of Jewish property, the so-called *Effektenlager* or "Canada," and the *Depotlager* for Hungarian Jews). Work on sector III was started in 1944. In the unfinished barracks Jewesses were temporarily kept in June and July 1944.

The transport was conducted by Aumeier[123] and Palitzsch and some of the block leaders. They talked with the Jews about general topics, inquiring about their qualifications and trades, with a view to misleading them. On arrival at the "Cottage," they were told to undress. At first they went calmly into the rooms where they were supposed to be disinfected. But some of them showed signs of alarm, and spoke of death by suffocation and of annihilation. A sort of panic set in at once. Immediately all the Jews still outside were pushed into the chambers, and the doors were screwed shut. With subsequent transports the difficult individuals were picked out early on and most carefully supervised. At the first sign of unrest, those responsible were unobtrusively led behind the building and killed with a small-calibre gun, that was inaudible to the others. The presence and calm behaviour of the Special Detachment[124] served to reassure those who were worried or who suspected what was about to happen. A further calming effect was obtained by members of the Special Detachment accompanying them into the rooms and remaining with them until the last moment, while an SS-man also stood in the doorway until the end.

It was most important that the whole business of arriving and undressing should take place in an atmosphere of the greatest possible calm. People reluctant to take off their clothes had to be helped by those of their companions who had already undressed, or by men of the Special Detachment.

The refractory ones were calmed down and encouraged to undress. The prisoners of the Special Detachment also saw to it that the process of undressing

---

They were not entered in the camp records. This camp was also called *Depotlager*, later "Mexico." Work on sector IV was never begun. See the plan of the camp following p. 128.

[123] He succeeded Fritzsch as *Lagerführer* at *KL Auschwitz*.

[124] *Sonderkommando* (special squad) employed in work connected with the cremating of corpses in crematoria or on pyres. The members of the *Sonderkommando* were recruited from among prisoners arriving in Jewish transports sent by the Reich Main Security Office to be exterminated. Such prisoners were detailed to work in *Sonderkommandos* almost directly after their arrival in camp, and so they had no understanding of the kind of work they were to do. From time to time, in order to get rid of eyewitnesses of crimes, the camp authorities would liquidate part of the *Sonderkommando* and then would select fresh prisoners from newly arrived transports. During the successive killings of *Sonderkommando* members part of the skilled workmen, such as capos and stokers of the crematorium ovens, would be retained by the Nazis. The prisoners in the *Sonderkommandos* enjoyed much better living conditions than other prisoners. On account of the kind of work they were engaged in, they were completely separated from their fellow-prisoners and were deprived of all contacts with the camp on pain of death. In spite of all these precautions on the part of the camp authorities, information about the work done by the *Sonderkommandos* filtered through into the camp and the outside world. More than ten prisoners, who had worked in that squad, survived the camp and after the war they made statements (e.g. Stanisław Jankowski, vel Alter Feinsilber, Szlama Dragon, Henryk Tauber, Henryk Mandelsbaum) or even published reminiscences dealing with the Auschwitz camp (e.g. Dr. Miklós Nyiszli in the book entitled *Auschwitz. A Doctor's Eyewitness Account*, New York 1960, Frederick Tell, Inc., Publishers). Six manuscripts were also found after the war in the camp at Birkenau, written by prisoners of the *Sonderkommando* who were eyewitnesses of the mass extermination conducted by the Nazis. The manuscripts were buried on the site of crematoria II and III at Birkenau. They are a moving accusation from beyond the grave, as all authors of the manuscripts were killed before the liberation of the camp. The manuscripts found so far have been published, in excerpts dealing with the Auschwitz camp, in: *Amidst a Nightmare of Crime*, *op. cit.* They enable us to learn in greater detail about the work and life of members of the *Sonderkommando*.

was carried out quickly, so that the victims would have little time to wonder what was happening.

The eager help given by the Special Detachment in encouraging them to undress and in conducting them into the gas chambers was most remarkable. I have never known, nor heard, of any of its members giving these people who were about to be gassed the slightest hint of what lay ahead of them. On the contrary, they did everything in their power to deceive them and particularly to pacify the suspicious ones. Though they might refuse to believe the SS-men, they had complete faith in these members of their own race, and to reassure them and keep them calm the Special Detachments therefore always consisted of Jews who themselves came from the same districts as did the people on whom a particular action was to be carried out.

They would talk about life in the camp, and most of them asked for news of friends or relations who had arrived in earlier transports. It was interesting to hear the lies that the Special Detachment told with such conviction, and to see the emphatic gestures with which they underlined them.[125]

Many of the women hid their babies among the piles of clothing. The men of the Special Detachment were particularly on the look-out for this, and would speak words of encouragement to the woman until they had persuaded her to take the child with her. The women believed that the disinfectant might be bad for their smaller children, hence their efforts to conceal them.

The smaller children usually cried because of the strangeness of being undressed in this fashion, but when their mothers or members of the Special Detachment comforted them, they became calm and entered the gas chambers, playing or joking with one another and carrying their toys.

I noticed that women who either guessed or knew what awaited them nevertheless found the courage to joke with the children to encourage them, despite the mortal terror visible in their own eyes.

One woman approached me as she walked past and, pointing to her four children who were manfully helping the smallest one over the rough ground, whispered :

" How can you bring yourself to kill such beautiful, darling children ? Have you no heart at all ? "

---

[125] The activities and behaviour attributed by Höss to members of the *Sonderkommando* refer to the SS-men, who were on duty at the railway ramp and who escorted people to extermination in the gas chambers. The camp surgeon, *SS-Obersturmführer* Johann Paul Kremer, wrote how SS-men vied for this work because it entailed rations of vodka, cigarettes, sausage and bread (see pp. 162—163, entry dated September 5, 1942).

Members of the *Sonderkommando* did not participate in the procedure of killing, but were employed to remove bodies from the gas chambers, to clean the latter, burn the bodies, extract ashes left after the burning of bodies and convey the ashes outside the crematoria. They were, moreover, engaged in the so-called exploiting of corpses, that is, extracting gold teeth, cutting off hair, searching the bodies of those killed for hidden valuables. They also melted gold into ingots.

In the last phase of the camp's existence, in December 1944 and January 1945, the camp authorities made use of prisoners of the *Sonderkommando* to obliterate traces of crimes, which meant pulling down crematoria and levelling the places which used to contain pits and pyres for burning the corpses.

One old man, as he passed by me, hissed :

" Germany will pay a heavy penance for this mass murder of the Jews."

His eyes glowed with hatred as he said this.[126] Nevertheless he walked calmly into the gas chamber, without worrying about the others.

One young woman caught my attention particularly as she ran busily hither and thither, helping the smallest children and the old women to undress. During the selection she had had two small children with her, and her agitated behaviour and appearance had brought her to my notice at once. She did not look in the least like a Jewess. Now her children were no longer with her. She waited until the end, helping the women who were not undressed and who had several children with them, encouraging them and calming the children. She went with the very last ones into the gas chamber. Standing in the doorway, she said :

" I knew all the time that we were being brought to Auschwitz to be gassed. When the selection took place I avoided being put with the able-bodied ones, as I wished to look after the children. I wanted to go through it all, fully conscious of what was happening. I hope that it will be quick. Goodbye ! "

From time to time women would suddenly give the most terrible shrieks while undressing, or tear their hair, or scream like maniacs. These were immediately led away behind the building and shot in the back of the neck with a small-calibre weapon.

It sometimes happened that, as the men of the Special Detachment left the gas chamber, the women would suddenly realize what was happening, and would call down every imaginable curse upon our heads.

I remember, too, a woman who tried to throw her children out of the gas chamber, just as the door was closing. Weeping she called out, " At least let my precious children live."

There were many such shattering scenes, which affected all who witnessed them.

During the spring of 1942 hundreds of vigorous men and women walked all unsuspecting to their death in the gas chambers, under the blossom-laden fruit trees of the " Cottage " orchard. This picture of death in the midst of life remains with me to this day.

---

126 Similar scenes are described by an unknown member of the *Sonderkommando* in his manuscript : " It was Passover 1944. A transport from Vittel in France had arrived. There were many Jewish dignitaries in it, including the late Moshe Friedman, the Rabbi of Bayonne, one of the greatest authorities in the history of Polish Jewry, a rare example of a patriarch. He undressed together with the others. Then a certain *Obersturmführer* arrived. The Rabbi approached him and, taking hold of the lapels of his uniform, said in German : ' You common, cruel murderers of mankind, do not think you will succeed in extinguishing our nation, the Jewish nation will live forever and will not disappear from the world's arena. And you, villainous murderers, will pay very dearly, for every innocent Jew you will pay with ten Germans, you will disappear not only as a power but even as a separate nation. The day of reckoning is approaching, the blood shed will cry for retribution. Our blood will not have peace until the flaming wrath of destruction overflows upon your nation and annihilates your beastly blood.' He spoke these words in a strong lion's voice and with great energy." Manuscript of an unknown author. *Amidst a Nightmare of Crime*, *op. cit.*, pp. 115—116.

The process of selection, which took place on the unloading platforms, was in itself rich in incident.

The breaking up of families, and the separation of the men from the women and children, caused much agitation and spread anxiety throughout the whole transport. This was increased by the further separation from the others of those capable of work. Families wished at all costs to remain together. Those who had been selected ran back to rejoin their relations. Mothers with children tried to join their husbands, or old people attempted to find those of their children who had been selected for work, and who had been led away.

Often the confusion was so great that the selections had to be begun all over again. The limited area of standing room did not permit better sorting arrangements. All attempts to pacify these agitated mobs were useless. It was often necessary to use force to restore order.[127]

As I have already frequently said, the Jews have strongly developed family feelings. They stick together like limpets. Nevertheless, according to my observations, they lack solidarity. One would have thought that in a situation such as this they would inevitably help and protect one another. But no, quite the contrary. I have often known and heard of Jews, particularly those from Western Europe, who revealed the addresses of those members of their race still in hiding.

One woman, already in the gas chamber, shouted out to a non-commissioned officer the address of a Jewish family. A man who, to judge by his clothes and deportment, appeared to be of very good standing, gave me, while actually undressing, a piece of paper on which was a list of the addresses of Dutch families who were hiding Jews.

I do not know what induced the Jews to give such information. Was it for reasons of personal revenge, or were they jealous that those others should survive?

The attitude of the men of the Special Detachment was also strange. They were all well aware that once the actions were completed they, too, would meet exactly the same fate as that suffered by these thousands of their own race, to whose destruction they had contributed so greatly. Yet the eagerness with which they carried out their duties never ceased to amaze me. Not only did they never divulge to the victims their impending fate, and were considerately helpful to them while they undressed, but they were also quite prepared to use violence on those who resisted. Then again, when it was a question of removing the trouble-makers and holding them while they were shot, they would lead them out in such a way that the victims never saw the non-commissioned officer standing there with his gun ready, and he was able to place its muzzle against the back of their necks without their noticing it. It was the same story when they dealt with the sick and the invalids, who could not be

---

127 A full description of selections and tragedies on the ramp, to which thousands of separated families were subjected, is given in the manuscript of another member of the *Sonderkommando*, Salmen Gradowski: Manuscript of Salmen Gradowski. *Ibid.*, pp. 94—95. Broad also mentions the tragedies on the ramp. *Cf.* the excerpt from his reminiscences entitled "The Two Little Farmhouses," pp. 131—135.

taken into gas chambers. And it was all done in such a matter-of-course manner that they might themselves have been the exterminators.

Then the bodies had to be taken from the gas chambers, and after the gold teeth had been extracted, and the hair cut off, they had to be dragged to the pits or the crematoria. Then the fires in the pits had to be stoked, the surplus fat drained off, and the mountain of burning corpses constantly turned over so that the draught might fan the flames.

They carried out all these tasks with a callous indifference as though it were all part of an ordinary day's work. While they dragged the corpses about, they ate or they smoked. They did not stop eating even when engaged on the grisly job of burning corpses which had been lying for some time in mass graves.[128]

It happened repeatedly that Jews of the Special Detachment would come upon the bodies of close relatives among the corpses, and even among the living as they entered the gas chambers. They were obviously affected by this, but it never led to any incident.

I myself saw a case of this sort. Once when bodies were being carried from a gas chamber to the fire pit, a man of the Special Detachment suddenly stopped and stood for a moment as though rooted to the spot. Then he continued to drag out a body with his comrades. I asked the capo what was up. He explained that the corpse was that of the Jew's wife. I watched him for a while, but noticed nothing peculiar in his behaviour. He continued to drag corpses along, just as he had done before. When I visited the Detachment a little later, he was sitting with the others and eating, as though nothing had happened. Was he really able to hide his emotions so completely, or had he become too brutalized to care even about this?

Where did the Jews of the Special Detachment derive the strength to carry on night and day with their grisly work? Did they hope that some whim of fortune might at the last moment snatch them from the jaws of death? Or had they become so dulled by the accumulation of horror that they were no longer capable even of ending their own lives and thus escaping from this "existence"?[129]

I have certainly watched them closely enough, but I have never really been able to get to the bottom of their behaviour.

The Jew's way of living and of dying was a true riddle that I never managed to solve.

All these experiences and incidents which I have described could be multi-

---

[128] At the beginning of 1942, when the mass killing of transports by means of gas (in Bunkers 1 and 2) had started in Birkenau, the bodies of murdered persons were not cremated, but were buried in pits specially dug for the purpose. Therefore Höss means here the new *Sonderkommando*, which in the autumn of 1942 was employed in digging up and burning bodies of persons buried by the former *Sonderkommando. Amidst a Nightmare of Crime*, *op. cit.*, p. 149, note 27.

[129] One of the members of the *Sonderkommando*, Salmen Lewental, attempted in his manuscript to analyze the psychology of a prisoner, a member of the squad. He sought to answer those very questions to which Höss had found no answers. Lewental's reflections are a pathetic testimony to the inhuman attitude of the camp authorities to persons imprisoned there. Manuscript of Salmen Lewental (22)—(36). *Ibid.*, pp. 155—156.

plied many times over. They are excerpts only, taken from the whole vast business of the extermination, sidelights as it were.

This mass extermination, with all its attendant circumstances, did not, as I know, fail to affect those who took a part in it. With very few exceptions, nearly all of those detailed to do this monstrous "work," this "service," and who, like myself, have given sufficient thought to the matter, have been deeply marked by these events.

Many of the men involved approached me as I went my rounds through the extermination buildings, and poured out their anxieties and impressions to me, in the hope that I could allay them.

Again and again during these confidential conversations I was asked: is it necessary that we do all this? Is it necessary that hundreds of thousands of women and children be destroyed? And I, who in my innermost being had on countless occasions asked myself exactly this question, could only fob them off and attempt to console them by repeating that it was done on Hitler's order. I had to tell them that this extermination of Jewry had to be, so that Germany and our posterity might be freed forever from their relentless adversaries.

There was no doubt in the mind of any of us that Hitler's order had to be obeyed regardless, and that it was the duty of the SS to carry it out. Nevertheless we were all tormented by secret doubts.

I myself dared not admit to such doubts. In order to make my subordinates carry on with their task, it was psychologically essential that I myself appear convinced of the necessity for this gruesomely harsh order.

Everyone watched me. They observed the impression produced upon me by the kind of scenes that I have described above, and my reactions. Every word I said on the subject was discussed. I had to exercise intense self-control in order to prevent my innermost doubts and feelings of oppression from becoming apparent.

I had to appear cold and indifferent to events that must have wrung the heart of anyone possessed of human feelings. I might not even look away when afraid lest my natural emotions got the upper hand. I had to watch coldly, while the mothers with laughing or crying children went into the gas chambers.

On one occasion two small children were so absorbed in some game that they quite refused to let their mother tear them away from it. Even the Jews of the Special Detachment were reluctant to pick the children up. The imploring look in the eyes of the mother, who certainly knew what was happening, is something I shall never forget. The people were already in the gas chamber and becoming restive, and I had to act. Everyone was looking at me. I nodded to the junior non-commissioned officer on duty and he picked up the screaming, struggling children in his arms and carried them into the gas chamber, accompanied by their mother who was weeping in the most heart-rending fashion. My pity was so great that I longed to vanish from the scene: yet I might not show the slightest trace of emotion.

I had to see everything. I had to watch hour after hour, by day and by night, the removal and burning of the bodies, the extraction of the teeth, the cutting of the hair, the whole grisly, interminable business. I had to stand for hours on end in the ghastly stench, while the mass graves were being opened and the bodies dragged out and burned.

I had to look through the peep-hole of the gas chambers and watch the process of death itself, because the doctors wanted me to see it.

I had to do all this because I was the one to whom everyone looked, because I had to show them all that I did not merely issue the orders and make the regulations, but was also prepared myself to be present at whatever task I had assigned to my subordinates.

The *Reichsführer SS* sent various high-ranking Party leaders and SS officers to Auschwitz, so that they might see for themselves the process of extermination of the Jews.[130] They were all deeply impressed by what they saw. Some who had previously spoken most loudly about the necessity for this extermination fell silent once they had actually seen the "final solution of the Jewish problem." I was repeatedly asked how I and my men could go on watching these operations, and how we were able to stand it.

My invariable answer was that the iron determination with which we must carry out Hitler's orders could only be obtained by a stifling of all human emotions. Each of these gentlemen declared that he was glad the job had not been given him.

Even Mildner[131] and Eichmann, who were certainly tough enough, had no wish to change places with me. This was one job which nobody envied me.

I had many detailed discussions with Eichmann concerning all matters connected with the "final solution of the Jewish problem," but without ever disclosing my inner anxieties. I tried in every way to discover Eichmann's innermost and real convictions about this "solution."

Yes, every way. Yet even when we were quite alone together and the drink had been flowing freely, so that he was in his most expansive mood, he showed that he was completely obsessed with the idea of destroying every single Jew that he could lay his hands on. Without pity and in cold blood we must complete this extermination as rapidly as possible. Any compromise, even the slightest, would have to be paid for bitterly at a later date.

In the face of such grim determination I was forced to bury all my human considerations as deeply as possible.

Indeed, I must freely confess that after these conversations with Eichmann I almost came to regard such emotions as a betrayal of the *Führer*.

There was no escape for me from this dilemma.

I had to go on with the process of extermination. I had to continue this

---

[130] The following important persons were among those who witnessed the extermination procedure in *KL Auschwitz*: June 16, 1942, *SS-Gruppenführer* Glücks, Inspector of Concentration Camps; July 17, 1942, *Reichsführer SS* Himmler; September 11, 1942, *SS-Standartenführer* Enno Lolling, Head of Office DIII (WVHA Sanitary Office); September 23, 1942, *SS-Gruppenführer* Pohl, Head of WVHA; September 25, 1942, *SS-Gruppenführer*, Doctor of Medicine, Professor Ernst Robert von Grawitz, SS Senior Surgeon (*Reichsarzt-SS*), Head of the SS Sanitary Head Office (*SS-Sanitätshauptamt*) and Chairman of the German Red Cross (see entries in Kremer's diary under respective dates); also *SS-Obersturmbannführer* Adolf Eichmann, Head of Section IVB4 in RSHA; *SS-Gruppenführer* Odilo Globocnik, Higher SS and Police Leader in the Lublin district; and others.

[131] Head of the State Police (*Staatspolizeileitstelle*) in Kattowitz.

mass murder and coldly to watch it, without regard for the doubts that were seething deep inside me.

I had to observe every happening with a cold indifference. Even those petty incidents that others might not notice I found hard to forget. In Auschwitz I truly had no reason to complain that I was bored.

If I was deeply affected by some incident, I found it impossible to go back to my home and my family. I would mount my horse and ride, until I had chased the terrible picture away. Often, at night I would walk through the stables and seek relief among my beloved animals.

It would often happen, when at home, that my thoughts suddenly turned to incidents that had occurred during the extermination. I then had to go out. I could no longer bear to be in my homely family circle. When I saw my children happily playing, or observed my wife's delight over our youngest, the thought would often come to me: how long will our happiness last? My wife could never understand these gloomy moods of mine, and ascribed them to some annoyance connected with my work.

When at night I stood out there beside the transports, or by the gas chambers or the fires, I was often compelled to think of my wife and children, without, however, allowing myself to connect them closely with all that was happening.

It was the same with the married men who worked in the crematoria or at the cremation pits.

When they saw the women and children going into the gas chambers, their thoughts instinctively turned to their own families.

I was no longer happy in Auschwitz once the mass exterminations had begun.

I had become dissatisfied with myself. To this must be added that I was worried because of anxiety about my principal task, the never-ending work, and the untrustworthiness of my colleagues.

Then the refusal to understand, or even to listen to me, on the part of my superiors. It was in truth not a happy or desirable state of affairs. Yet everyone in Auschwitz believed that the commandant lived a wonderful life.

My family, to be sure, were well provided for in Auschwitz. Every wish that my wife or children expressed was granted them. The children could live a free and untrammelled life. My wife's garden was a paradise of flowers. The prisoners never missed an opportunity for doing some little act of kindness to my wife or children, and thus attracting their attention.

No former prisoner can ever say that he was in any way or at any time badly treated in our house. My wife's greatest pleasure would have been to give a present to every prisoner, who was in any way connected with our household.

The children were perpetually begging me for cigarettes for the prisoners. They were particularly fond of the ones who worked in the garden.

My whole family displayed a keen love of agriculture, and was particularly fond of animals of all sorts. Every Sunday I had to walk them all across the fields, and visit the stables; and we might never miss out the kennels where the dogs were kept. Our two horses and the foal were especially beloved.

The children always kept animals in the garden, creatures the prisoners were forever bringing them. Tortoises, martens, cats, lizards: there was always something new and interesting to be seen there. In summer they splashed in the paddling pool in the garden, or in the Sola. But their greatest joy was when Daddy bathed with them. He had, however, so little time for all these childish pleasures. Today I deeply regret that I did not devote more time to my family. I always felt that I had to be on duty the whole time. This exaggerated sense of duty has always made life more difficult for me than it actually need have been. Again and again my wife reproached me and said, " You must think not only of the service always, but of your family too."

Yet what did my wife know about all that lay so heavily on my mind? She has never been told.

" THE FINAL SOLUTION OF THE JEWISH QUESTION " IN THE AUSCHWITZ CONCENTRATION CAMP

In the summer of 1941, I cannot remember the exact date, I was suddenly summoned to the *Reichsführer SS*, directly by his adjutant's office. Contrary to his usual custom, Himmler received me without his adjutant being present, and said in effect:

" The *Führer*[1] has ordered that the Jewish question be solved once and for all and that we, the SS, are to implement that order.

" The existing extermination centres in the East[2] are not in a position to carry out the large actions which are anticipated. I have therefore ear-marked Auschwitz for this purpose, both because of its good position as regards communications and because the area can be easily isolated and camouflaged. At first I thought of calling in a senior SS officer for this job, but I changed my mind in order to avoid difficulties concerning the terms of reference. I have now decided to entrust this task to you. It is difficult and onerous and calls for complete devotion notwithstanding the difficulties that may arise. You will learn further details from *Sturmbannführer* Eichmann of the Reich Main Security Office who will call on you in the immediate future.

" The departments concerned will be notified by me in due course. You will treat this order as absolutely secret, even from your superiors. After your talk with Eichmann you will immediately forward to me the plans of the projected installations.

" The Jews are the sworn enemies of the German people and must be eradicated. Every Jew that we can lay our hands on is to be destroyed now during the war, without exception. If we cannot now obliterate the biological basis of Jewry, the Jews will one day destroy the German people."

On receiving these grave instructions, I returned forthwith to Auschwitz, without reporting to my superior at Oranienburg.

---

1 Adolf Hitler.

2 Himmler was most likely thinking here of the Soviet Union, where *Einsatzgruppen* were " liquidating " civilian inhabitants regarded as " undesirable elements." The " liquidating " first took the form of mass shooting, then victims were killed with exhaust gases in lorries specially adapted for the purpose.

Shortly afterwards Eichmann came to Auschwitz and disclosed to me the plans for the operations as they affected the various countries concerned. I cannot remember the exact order in which they were to take place. First was to come the eastern part of Upper Silesia and the neighbouring parts of Polish territory under German rule, then, depending on the situation, simultaneously Jews from Germany and Czechoslovakia, and finally the Jews from the West: France, Belgium and Holland. He also told me the approximate numbers of transports that might be expected, but I can no longer remember these.

We discussed the ways and means of effecting the extermination. This could only be done by gassing, since it would have been absolutely impossible to dispose by shooting of the large numbers of people that were expected, and it would have placed too heavy a burden on the SS-men who had to carry it out, especially because of the women and children among the victims.

Eichmann told me about the method of killing people with exhaust fumes in lorries,[3] which had previously been used in the East. But there was no question of being able to use this for these mass transports that were due to arrive in Auschwitz. Killing with showers of carbon monoxide while bathing, as was done with mental patients in some places in the Reich,[4] would necessitate too many buildings and it was also very doubtful whether the supply of gas for such a vast number of people would be available. We left the matter unresolved. Eichmann decided to try to find a gas which was in ready supply and which would not entail special installations for its use, and to inform me when he had done so.[5] We inspected the area in order to choose a likely spot. We decided that a peasant farmstead situated in the north-west corner of what

---

[3] Their official name was *Sonderwagen* (special vehicle). The cars, used as gas chambers, were made use of in the *Warthegau* as early as March 1940. Then they were used to destroy mental patients of the hospital "Kochanówka" near Łódź, while in September 1941 they were utilized for the mass extermination of Jews in a wood near Kazimierz Biskupi, about 40 kilometres from Chełmno. These lorries were brought from Berlin. In the course of investigations conducted after the war it was ascertained that there had been two types of such lorries: a smaller one into which about 80—100 persons could be squeezed and a bigger one accommodating around 150 persons. The bodies of such vehicles were constructed with narrow boards joined together with tongues. They were lined with sheet iron on the inside. The door, situated at the back of the body, was air-tight. The exhaust pipe from the engine ran underneath the lorry and had an inlet through the floor leading to the interior. To prevent blocking by the prisoners inside, this spot was secured by a piece of perforated sheet iron. A wooden grill covered the floor of the lorry. Drivers of such lorries underwent special training.

[4] Not only with mental patients. On Himmler's orders a special commission came to *KL Auschwitz* on July 28, 1941, with the participation of Dr. Horst Schumann. The commission took invalids, cripples and chronic cases selected from among the prisoners, under the pretext of transferring them to another camp and using them for easier work. The transport of 575 prisoners was escorted, on Dr. Schumann's request, by the *Rapportführer* Hössler to the Mental Institution in Sonnenstein. According to Hössler's report, submitted to Höss, the prisoners were gassed in a bath-house with carbon monoxide (*Kohlenoxyd*), led into the room through shower holes.

[5] From the contents of the Höss Autobiography it transpires that this visit by Eichmann to Auschwitz must have taken place before September 3, 1941, that is, before the first attempt to use gas in the cellars of Block 11.

later became the third building sector at Birkenau would be the most suitable.[6] It was isolated and screened by woods and hedges, and it was also not far from the railway. The bodies could be placed in long, deep pits dug in the nearby meadows. We had not at that time thought of burning the corpses. We calculated that after gas-proofing the premises then available, it would be possible to kill about 800 people simultaneously with a suitable gas. These figures were borne out later in practice.

Eichmann could not then give me the starting date for the operation, because everything was still in the preliminary stages, and the *Reichsführer SS* had not yet issued the necessary orders.

Eichmann returned to Berlin to report our conversation to the *Reichsführer SS*.

A few days later I sent to the *Reichsführer SS* by courier a detailed location plan and description of the installation. I have never received an acknowledgement or a decision on my report. Eichmann told me later that the *Reichsführer SS* was in agreement with my proposals.

At the end of November a conference was held in Eichmann's Berlin office, attended by the entire Jewish Section, to which I, too, was summoned. Eichmann's representatives in the various countries reported on the current stage of the operation and the difficulties encountered in executing it, such as the housing of the prisoners, the provision of trains for the transports and the planning of timetables, etc. I could not find out when a start was to be made, and Eichmann had not yet discovered a suitable kind of gas.[7]

In the autumn of 1941 a secret order was issued instructing the *Gestapo* to weed out the Russian *politruks*, commissars and certain political officials from the prisoner-of-war camps, and to transfer them to the nearest concentration camp for liquidation.[8] Small drafts of these prisoners were continually arriving in Auschwitz and they were shot in the gravel pit[9] near the Monopoly buildings or in the courtyard of Block 11. When I was absent on duty my representative, *Hauptsturmführer* Fritzsch, on his own initiative, used gas for killing these Russian prisoners of war.[10] He crammed the underground detention cells with Russians and, protected by a gas-mask, discharged Cyclon B gas into the cells, killing the victims instantly.

Cyclon B gas was supplied by the firm of Tesch & Stabenow and was constantly

---

[6] So-called Bunker 1 is meant here, the first gas chamber in which Cyclon B was tried out. A farmhouse, whose owners Józef Wichaj and Rydzoń had been deported, was adapted for the purpose.

[7] It seems probable that Höss was mistaken over the dates of facts described in this part of his Autobiography. If the conference did take place in November, then perhaps Höss neglected to inform Eichmann about the first attempt to use Cyclon B on September 3. But it is also possible that the conference took place at the beginning of September, because a little further on in his Autobiography Höss wrote: "During Eichmann's next visit I told him about this use of Cyclon B and we decided to employ it for the mass extermination operation." See p. 84.

[8] Compare the section of the Autobiography of Höss on p. 69, and note 110.

[9] So-called *Kiesgrube*.

[10] This tactics of presenting the first attempt at using gas as having occurred during Höss's absence has already received comment. See p. 70, note 112.

used in Auschwitz for the destruction of vermin, and there was consequently always a supply of these tins of gas on hand. In the beginning, this poisonous gas, which was a preparation of prussic acid, was only handled by employees of Tesch&Stabenow under rigid safety precautions, but later some members of the Medical Service[11] were trained by the firm in its use and thereafter the destruction of vermin and disinfection were carried out by them.

During Eichmann's next visit I told him about this use of Cyclon B and we decided to employ it for the mass extermination operation.

The killing by Cyclon B gas of the Russian prisoners of war transported to Auschwitz was continued, but no longer in Block 11, since after the gassing the whole building had to be ventilated for at least two days.

The mortuary of the crematorium next to the hospital block[12] was therefore used as a gassing room, after the door had been made gas-proof and some holes had been pierced in the ceiling through which the gas could be discharged.

I can, however, only recall one transport consisting of nine hundred Russian prisoners being gassed there, and I remember that it took several days to cremate their corpses. Russians were not gassed in the peasant farmstead, which had now been converted for the extermination of the Jews.

I cannot say on what date the extermination of the Jews began. Probably it was in December 1941, but it may not have been until January 1942. The Jews from Upper Silesia were the first to be dealt with. These Jews were arrested by the Kattowitz Police Unit[13] and taken in drafts by train to a siding on the west side of the Auschwitz-Dziedzice railway line,[14] where they were unloaded. So far as I can remember, these drafts never consisted of more than 1,000 prisoners.

On the platform the Jews were taken over from the police by a detachment from the camp, and were brought by the commander of the camp in two sections to the bunker, as the extermination building was called.

Their luggage was left on the platform, whence it was taken to the sorting office called " Canada " situated between the DAW[15] and the timber-yard.[16]

The Jews were made to undress near the bunker, after they had been told that they had to go into the rooms (as they were also called) in order to be deloused.

All the rooms, there were five of them, were filled at the same time, the

---

[11] These were SS-men trained to be sanitary orderlies, in camp terminology, *Sanitätsdienstgrade* (SDG).

[12] This was the so-called old crematorium, designated as crematorium I. It was located at *KL Auschwitz*, opposite the SS hospital.

[13] State Police (*Staatspolizei*—Stapo). This term refers to the political police (as distinct from the Criminal, Kripo—*Kriminalpolizei*, and the Order, or Uniformed Police, *Ordnungspolizei*). In the Third Reich the Secret State Police (*Geheimestaatspolizei*—Gestapo) later became (from 1936), the Security Police (*Sicherheitspolizei*—Sipo), originating from a fusion of the Secret State Police (Gestapo) with the Criminal Police (Kripo).

[14] This was the goods station in Auschwitz (town).

[15] Buildings belonging to the *Deutsche Ausrüstungswerke* (DAW). This firm, owned by the SS, employed prisoners from Auschwitz.

[16] *Bauhof.*

gas-proof doors were then screwed up and the contents of the gas containers discharged into the rooms through special vents.

After half an hour the doors were re-opened (there were two doors in each room), the dead bodies were taken out, and brought to the pits in small trolleys which ran on rails.

The victims' clothing was taken in lorries to the sorting office. The whole operation, including assistance given during undressing, the filling of the bunker, the emptying of the bunker, the removal of the corpses, as well as the preparation and filling up of the mass graves, was carried out by a special detachment of Jews, who were separately accommodated and who, in accordance with Eichmann's orders, were themselves liquidated after every big action.

While the first transports were being disposed of, Eichmann arrived with an order from the *Reichsführer SS* stating that the gold teeth[17] were to be removed from the corpses and the hair[18] cut from the women. This job was also undertaken by the special detachment.

The extermination process was at that time carried out under the supervision of the commander of the protective custody camp[19] or the *Rapportführer*.[20] Those who were too ill to be brought into the gas chambers were shot in the back of the neck by a small-calibre weapon.

An SS doctor also had to be present. The trained disinfectors (SDG's) were responsible for discharging the gas into the gas chamber.

During the spring of 1942 the actions were comparatively small, but the transports increased in the summer, and we were compelled to construct a further extermination building. The peasant farmstead[21] west of the future site of crematoria III [IV] and IV [V][22] was selected and made ready. Two huts

---

[17] After gassing and before throwing the corpses into the crematorium ovens, members of the *Sonderkommando* extracted the teeth of the victims. Gold teeth were melted into ingots, at first by SS-men, then by dentists. After the introduction of crematorium III a special laboratory for melting gold was built. The gold ingots were sent to the SS Sanitary Head Office.

[18] Women killed in the gas chambers had their hair cut off. The hair was dried in the lofts of the crematoria, packed into bags and sent to the Third Reich to be processed; among other uses, it was the raw material for the production of felt and haircloth. On the basis of investigations we know that the following factories processed human hair:

Held in Friedland (now Mieroszów near Wrocław),

Alex Zink at Roth near Nuremberg,

the dye-works of the Forst Company Ltd. at Lausitz,

the felt factory at Katscher (now Śląskie Zakłady Pluszu i Dywanów in Kietrz).

KL Auschwitz probably sent the hair to factories in Silesia. Firms bought it at the price of 0.50 mark per kilogramme. Bags containing 7,000 kilogrammes of human hair were found within the Auschwitz camp after the liberation. The authorities were unable to dispose of them in time.

[19] *SS-Hauptsturmführer* Hans Aumeier held this post at the time.

[20] Post then held by *SS-Hauptscharführer* Gerhard Arno Max Palitzsch.

[21] This was so-called Bunker 2, formerly a farmhouse owned by a deported farmer, Harmata, which was adapted as another gas chamber.

[22] To maintain uniformity in the numbering of crematoria as used in the original camp documents, and in keeping with the terminology used in the publications of the State Museum at Oświęcim, the proper numbering of the crematoria at Birkenau, used in the original plans, is given in square brackets alongside those given by Höss.

near Bunker I and three near Bunker II were erected, in which the victims undressed. Bunker II was the larger and could hold about 1,200 people.

During the summer of 1942 the bodies were still being placed in the mass graves. Towards the end of the summer, however, we started to burn them, at first on wood pyres bearing some 2,000 corpses, and later in pits together with bodies previously buried. In the early days oil refuse was poured on the bodies, but later methanol was used. Bodies were burnt in pits, day and night, continuously.

By the end of November all the mass graves had been emptied. The number of corpses in the mass graves amounted to 107,000. This figure not only included the transports of Jews gassed up to the time when cremation was first employed, but also the bodies of those prisoners in Auschwitz who died during the winter of 1941—1942, when the crematorium near the hospital building was out of action for a considerable time. It also included all the prisoners who died in the Birkenau camp.

During his visit to the camp in the summer of 1942, the *Reichsführer SS* watched every detail of the whole process of destruction from the time when the prisoners were unloaded to the emptying of Bunker II. At that time the bodies were not being burnt. He had no criticism to make, nor did he discuss the matter. *Gauleiter* Bracht and *Obergruppenführer* Schmauser[23] were present with him.

Shortly after the visit of the *Reichsführer SS*, *Standartenführer* Blobel[24] arrived from Eichmann's office with an order from the *Reichsführer SS* stating that all the mass graves were to be opened and the corpses burnt. In addition the ashes were to be disposed of in such a way that it would be impossible at some future time to calculate the number of corpses burnt.

Blobel had already experimented with different methods of cremation in Kulmhof[25] and Eichmann had authorized him to show me the apparatus he used.

Hössler and I went to Kulmhof on a tour of inspection.[26] Blobel had various makeshift ovens constructed, which were fired with wood and petrol refuse. He had also attempted to dispose of the bodies with explosives, but their destruction had been very incomplete. The ashes were distributed over the neighbouring countryside after first being ground to a powder in a bone mill.

---

[23] Higher SS and Police Leader in the south-eastern district in Wrocław.

[24] One of the commanders of the *Sonderkommandos* belonging to the *Einsatzgruppen* operating in the East.

[25] Chełmno-on-Ner near Łódź. The organizing of this mass extermination camp was begun in November 1941. It was active from December 8, 1941, to January 1945. The victims were killed with combustion gases in lorries specially adapted for this purpose. The bodies were cremated in the Rzuchów forests, near the road connecting Koło with Dąbie. Altogether about 360,000 people were killed at Chełmno, chiefly Jews from the provinces of Łódź and Poznań, but also children from the Zamość district and the Czech village of Lidice, as well as Poles seized in street round-ups and inhabitants of the Home for the Aged at Włocławek. *Cf. Guide to Sites of Struggle and Martyrdom. War Years in Poland 1939—1945*, Warsaw 1966, p. 298.

[26] Höss left on September 16, 1942. He was accompanied by *SS-Untersturmführer* Hössler and *SS-Untersturmführer* Walter Dejaco from the SS garrison of *KL Auschwitz*.

Standartenführer Blobel had been authorized to seek out and obliterate all the mass graves in the whole of the eastern districts. His department was given the code number "1005"[27]. The work itself was carried out by a special detachment of Jews who were shot after each section of the work had been completed. The Auschwitz concentration camp was continuously called upon to provide Jews for department "1005."

On my visit to Kulmhof I was also shown the extermination apparatus constructed out of lorries, which was designed to kill by using the exhaust gases from the engines. The officer in charge there, however, described this method as being extremely unreliable, for the density of the gas varied considerably and was often insufficient to be lethal.

How many bodies lay in the mass graves at Kulmhof or how many had already been cremated, I was unable to ascertain.

Standartenführer Blobel had a fairly exact knowledge of the number of mass graves in the eastern districts, but he was sworn to the greatest secrecy in the matter.

Originally all the Jews transported to Auschwitz on the authority of Eichmann's office were, in accordance with orders of the *Reichsführer SS*, to be destroyed without exception. This also applied to the Jews from Upper Silesia[28]; but on the arrival of the first transports of German Jews, the order was given that all those who were able-bodied, whether men or women, were to be segregated and employed on war work. This happened before the construction of the women's camp,[29] since the need for a women's camp in Auschwitz only arose as a result of this order.

Owing to the extensive armaments industry which had developed in the concentration camps and which was being progressively increased, and owing to the recent employment of prisoners in armaments factories outside the camps, a serious lack of prisoners suddenly made itself felt, whereas previously the commandants in the old camps in the Reich had often had to seek out possibilities for employment in order to keep all their prisoners occupied.

The Jews, however, were only to be employed in the Auschwitz camp.

---

[27] This was *Sonderkommando 1005* (the so-called death brigade) whose tasks included the uncovering of mass graves in the Lwów region, the burning of the corpses buried in them and the obliteration of all traces of the murders which had taken place in the region. The work of this brigade was described in the memoirs of Leon vel Arje Lejb Weliczker, who was detailed to *Sonderkommando 1005* together with other Jews. He stayed with it from June 15 to November 20, 1943, that is to the day of his escape from Las Krzywicki, the place where the brigade was then working. Leon Weliczker: *Brygada śmierci—Sonderkommando 1005. Pamiętnik*. Łódź 1946, Wydawnictwo Żydowskiej Komisji Historycznej przy Centralnym Komitecie Żydów Polskich.

[28] The first transports of Jews from Upper Silesia came in January 1942 and were gassed in Bunker 1 at Birkenau.

[29] Höss is mistaken here. The women's camp at Birkenau (Bla) existed as early as August 1942. The first Jewish transports from the Third Reich arrived much later, in October of that year. They brought Jews from various concentration camps in Germany, in connection with the action of "cleansing" (*Judenrein*) the camps in the Third Reich by removing Jews from them. However, transportation of the Jewish civilian population from the territory of the Third Reich to *KL Auschwitz* did not commence until February 1943.

Auschwitz-Birkenau was to become an entirely Jewlsh camp and prisoners of all other nationalities were to be transferred to other camps. This order was never completely carried out, and later Jews were even employed in armaments industries outside the camp, because of the lack of any other labour.

The selection of able-bodied Jews was supposed to be made by SS doctors. But it repeatedly happened that officers of the protective custody camp and of the labour department themselves selected the prisoners without my knowledge or even my approval. This was the cause of constant friction between the SS doctors and the officers of the labour department. The divergence of opinion among the officers in Auschwitz was developed and fostered by the contradictory interpretation of the *Reichsführer SS*'s order by authoritative quarters in Berlin. The Reich Main Security Office (Müller[30] and Eichmann) had, for security reasons, the greatest interest in the destruction of as many Jews as possible. The *Reichsarzt SS*,[31] who laid down the policy of selection, held the view that only those Jews who were completely fit and able to work should be selected for employment. The weak and the old and those who were only relatively robust would very soon become incapable of work, which would cause a further deterioration in the general standard of health, and an unnecessary increase in the hospital accommodation, requiring further medical personnel and medicines, and all for no purpose since they would in the end have to be killed.

The Economic and Administrative Head Office (Pohl and Maurer[32]) was only interested in mustering the largest possible labour force for employment in the armaments industry, regardless of the fact that these people would later on become incapable of working. This conflict of interest was further sharpened by the immensely increased demands for prisoner labour made by the Ministry for Armaments Production[33] and the Todt Organization.[34] The *Reichsführer SS* was always promising both these departments numbers which could never be supplied. *Standartenführer* Maurer (the head of department DII) was in the difficult position of being able only partially to fulfil the insistent demands of the departments referred to, and consequently he was perpetually harassing the labour office to provide him with the greatest possible number of workers.

It was impossible to get the *Reichsführer SS* to make a definite decision in this matter.

I myself held the view that only really strong and healthy Jews ought to be selected for employment.

The sorting process proceeded as follows. The railway carriages were unloaded one after the other. After depositing their baggage, the Jews had to pass individually in front of an SS doctor, who decided on their physical

---

[30] Head of Office IV (Secret State Police) in the Reich Main Security Office.

[31] This post was held by *SS-Obergruppenführer* Professor Ernst Robert von Grawitz, M.D.

[32] Head of Office DII (employment of prisoners) in the Inspectorate of Concentration Camps.

[33] The head of this Ministry was Fritz Todt. After his death (he was killed in an air crash) in February 1942, the architect Albert Speer was nominated for the post.

[34] The Todt Organization (*Organisation Todt*) was founded by the Minister for Armaments Production in the government of the Third Reich, Fritz Todt. It was a para-military organization, above all comprising foreign manpower.

fitness as they marched past him. Those considered capable of employment were immediately taken off into the camp in small groups.

Taking an average of all the transports, between twenty-five and thirty per cent were found fit for work, but this figure fluctuated considerably. The figure for Greek Jews, for example, was only fifteen per cent, whereas there were transports from Slovakia with a fitness of a hundred per cent.[35] Jewish doctors and administrative personnel [other hospital staff] were without exception taken into the camp.

It became apparent during the first cremations in the open air that in the long run it would not be possible to continue in that manner. During bad weather or when a strong wind was blowing, the stench of burning flesh was carried for many miles and caused the whole neighbourhood to talk about the burning of Jews, despite official counter-propaganda. It is true that all members of the SS detailed for the extermination were bound to keep strict secrecy about the whole matter,[36] but later court trials showed that these regulations were not adhered to and even the most severe punishment was not able to stop their love of gossip.

Moreover the air defence services protested against the fires, which could be seen from great distances at night. Nevertheless, burnings had to go on, even at night, unless further transports were to be refused. The schedule of individual operations, fixed at a conference by the Ministry of Communications, had to be rigidly adhered to in order to avoid, for military reasons, obstruction and confusion of the railways concerned. These reasons led to the energetic planning and eventual construction of the two large crematoria, and in 1943 to the building of two further smaller installations.[37] Yet another one was

---

[35] In spite of the sound physical condition of which Höss speaks, these prisoners perished very quickly. The records of the proceedings of Höss's trial show that the death rate among the Jewish prisoners from Slovakia, sent to the camp without selection, in the period from April 17 to June 20, 1942, was as follows:

of 973 persons brought on April 17, 885 (91%) perished within 17 weeks;
of 464 persons brought on April 19, 454 (98%) perished within 16 weeks;
of 543 persons brought on April 23, 502 (92.5%) perished within 16 weeks;
of 442 persons brought on April 24, 419 (94.8%) perished within 16 weeks;
of 423 persons brought on April 29, 403 (95.3%) perished within 15 weeks;
of 404 persons brought on June 20, 359 (88.9%) perished within 8 weeks.

In other words, of the 3,249 Slovakian Jews sent to camp without selection at the railway ramp, only 227 persons were still alive on August 15, 1942.

[36] The archives of the State Museum at Oświęcim contain a photocopy of a declaration signed by a member of the SS garrison, *SS-Unterscharführer* Gerhard Appel, which reads as follows:

"(1) I am acquainted with the fact, and I was thus instructed today, that I shall suffer the death penalty if I lay hands on Jewish property.

"(2) I am obliged to observe absolute silence concerning all actions carried out in connection with the evacuation of the Jews, even talking with my comrades.

"(3) I undertake not to spare myself, and to cooperate with all my strength in the efficient and honest execution of such actions." Trial of Höss, vol. 12, card 178.

[37] Höss gives wrong dates of the completion of the Birkenau crematoria, as all of them were ready for use in 1943. Höss called crematoria II and III "large" crematoria, and crematoria IV and V "small." They were completed on the following dates: crematorium II on March 31, 1943, crematorium III on June 25, 1943, crematorium IV on March 22, 1943, and crematorium V on April 4, 1943; therefore, to use the terminology of Höss, the first to be ready was "small" crematorium (IV), next a "large" one (II), then another "small" one (V), while the other "large" crematorium (III) came last.

planned, which would far exceed the others in size, but it was never completed,[38] for in the autumn of 1944, the *Reichsführer SS* called an immediate halt to the extermination of the Jews.[39]

The two large crematoria I [II] and II [III][40] were built in the winter of 1942—1943 and brought into use in the spring of 1943.[41] They had five three-retort ovens and could cremate about 2,000 bodies in less than twenty-four hours. Technical difficulties made it impossible to increase their capacity. Attempts to do this caused severe damage to the installations, and on several occasions put them out of action altogether. Crematoria I [II] and II [III] both had underground undressing rooms and gas chambers in which the air could be completely changed. The bodies were taken to the ovens on the floor above by means of a lift. The gas chambers could hold about 3,000 people, but this number was never reached, since the individual transports were never as large as that.

The two smaller crematoria III [IV] and IV [V] were capable, according to calculations made by the construction firm of *Topf* of Erfurt, of burning about 1,500 bodies within twenty-four hours. Owing to the war-time shortage of materials, the builders were compelled to economize during the construction of crematoria III [IV] and IV [V] and they were therefore built above ground and the ovens were of a less solid construction. It soon became apparent, however, that the flimsy build of these two four-retort ovens did not come up to the requirements. Number III [IV] failed completely after a short time and later ceased to be used altogether. Number IV [V] had to be repeatedly shut down, since after its fires had been burning for four to six weeks, the ovens or the chimneys burnt out. The gassed bodies were mostly burnt in pits behind crematorium IV [V].

The provisional structure number I[42] was demolished when work was started on building sector III in Birkenau.

Crematorium II,[43] later designated bunker V, was used up to the last and was also kept as a stand-by when break-downs occurred in crematoria I [II] to IV [V].[44] When larger numbers of transports were being received, gassing was carried out by day in number V and numbers I [II] to IV [V] were used for those transports which arrived during the night. The capacity of number V[45] was practically unlimited, so long as cremations could be carried out both by day and night. Because of enemy air attacks, no further cremations were permitted during

---

[38] Höss is referring here to the construction of crematorium VI, which was planned as early as 1943. The plan was never realized.

[39] According to the evidence of *SS-Standartenführer* Kurt Becher, Himmler arrived at this decision on November 26, 1944.

[40] *Cf.* note 37.

[41] *Cf.* note 37.

[42] i.e. Bunker 1, *cf.* note 121 on p. 72.

[43] i.e. Bunker 2, *cf.* note 21 on p. 85.

[44] These were put into action again in 1944, when the extermination of Hungarian Jews was in progress.

[45] In fact, cremation in the open is meant here, i.e. near Bunker 5, not in it.

the night after 1944. The highest total of people gassed and cremated within twenty-four hours was rather more than 9,000. This figure was attained in the summer of 1944, during the action in Hungary,[46] using all the installations except number III [IV]. On that day, owing to delays on the line, five trains arrived, instead of three, as expected, and in addition the carriages were more crowded than usual.

The crematoria were erected at the end of the two main thoroughfares in the Birkenau camp, firstly in order not to increase the area of the camp (and consequently the safety precautions required), and secondly so that they would not be too far from the camp, since it was planned to use the gas chambers and undressing rooms as bath-houses when the extermination actions came to an end.

The buildings were to be screened from view by a wall or hedges. Lack of material prevented this from being done. As a temporary measure, all extermination buildings were hidden under camouflage nets.

The three railway tracks between building sectors I and II in the Birkenau camp were to be reconstructed as a station and roofed over. The lines were to be extended to crematoria III [IV] and IV [V], so that the unloading would also be hidden from the eyes of unauthorized people. Once again shortage of materials prevented this plan from being carried out.

Because of the increasing insistence of the *Reichsführer SS* on the employment of prisoners in the armaments industry, *Obergruppenführer* Pohl found himself compelled to resort to Jews who had become unfit for work. The

---

[46] Also called *Aktion Höss* on account of the fact that Himmler nominated ex-commandant Höss as plenipotentiary for the extermination action of Hungarian Jews; for this reason he was detailed to *KL Auschwitz* from the Inspectorate of Concentration Camps at Oranienburg for the duration of the operation. Höss came to Auschwitz on May 8, 1944, took over the duties of commander of the garrison (*Standortältester*) and began preparing the extermination installations at Birkenau to receive transports from Hungary. He personally supervised the reactivation of the ovens of crematorium V after their breakdown, the digging of five pits near the crematorium for burning corpses and the preparation of Bunker 2, which had not been used recently for killing with gas. A hut for undressing was also built nearby, cremation pits were dug, and the construction of the railway ramp for unloading and of a three-track siding within the camp was speeded up.

Moreover, Höss recalled *SS-Hauptscharführer* Otto Moll, formerly in charge of the crematoria, from the *Gleiwitz I* sub-camp and made him *Kommandoführer* responsible for the cremation in the open of the bodies of gassed people. He requested an increase in numbers of the prisoners' squad employed in the crematoria (*Sonderkommando*) and also of the squad which sorted the looted property of the victims (*Kommando "Kanada"*).

During the Hungarian action Höss used to travel frequently to Budapest to ensure the smooth arrival of the transports. Eichmann himself came to *KL Auschwitz* when the first trains with Hungarian Jews began to arrive, to personally check and speed up the extermination action. The transports began on May 16, 1944. Two to five trains would arrive daily. Each consisted of forty to fifty goods-vans. There were about 100 persons in each. Part of the transports was marched straight to the gas chambers, i.e. without selection. On some days a greater number of transports would arrive and then the closed vans with people inside had to stop for several hours at the railway siding. In some transports the newcomers were already segregated according to sex and age. The Hungarian Jews were brought to Auschwitz under the pretext of "settling" in the East, so they were told to bring timber with them. In reality the timber was used for cremating the bodies of persons killed with gas. The Hungarian Action continued without interruption until the middle of September.

order was given that if the latter could be made fit and employable within six weeks, they were to be given special care and feeding.[47] Up to then all Jews who had become incapable of working were gassed with the next transports, or killed by injection if they happened to be lying ill in the sick block. As far as Auschwitz-Birkenau was concerned, this order was sheer mockery. Everything was lacking. There were practically no medical supplies. The accommodation was such that there was scarcely even room for those who were most seriously ill. The food was completely insufficient, and every month the Food Ministry cut down the supplies still further. But all protests were unavailing and an attempt to carry out the order had to be made. The resultant overcrowding of the healthy prisoners could no longer be avoided. The general standard of health was thereby lowered, and diseases spread like wildfire. As a result of this order the death rate was sent up with a jerk and a tremendous deterioration in the general conditions developed. I do not believe that a single sick Jew was ever made fit again for work in the armaments industry.

*

[48] *Transport-Juden*[49] [Jews from transports], thus had all Jews been designated who were taken to the camp from Eichmann's Office — RSHA IV B4. The reports announcing the arrival bore the notice: "The transport corresponds to the given instructions and is to be subjected to special treatment [*Sonderbehandlung — SB*]!" All other Jews of earlier times, that is before the extermination orders were given, were called *Schutzhaft*[50]*-Juden* [Jews in protective custody] or Jews belonging to other categories of prisoners.[51]

---

[47] Such orders were issued as late as December 9 and 14, 1944, that is, at a time when the extermination action had already been largely interrupted, due to the general situation at the fronts and the growing need for manpower in the armaments industry.

[48] This part of the manuscript, from the top line to the end of paragraph, was omitted in the English edition of the Autobiography of Höss.

[49] The authorities of the Third Reich used this cryptonym to designate persons doomed to be exterminated. Among similar cryptonyms were the following: "special action" (*Sonderaktion*), "special treatment" (*Sonderbehandlung—SB*), and "separate accommodation" (*Gesonderte Unterbringung—GU*). All such cryptonyms meant death.

[50] Protective custody—*Schutzhaft*. This was the origin of the German term for a concentration camp prisoner—*Schutzhäftling*.

[51] The categories in which prisoners were classified depended on the cause of their arrest. In principle a prisoner was committed to a concentration camp on a written warrant issued by Office IV (of the Secret State Police) or Office V (of the Reich Criminal Police) in the Reich Main Security Office. The warrant stated the grounds for the arrest, which then determined the respective category to which the arrested person was to belong in the concentration camp.

Office IV had the authority to issue decisions concerning the keeping in preventive custody of political prisoners, homosexuals (regarded as belonging to the category of the so-called asocial prisoners), Jehovah's Witnesses, persons arrested for "re-education" (so-called *Erziehungshäftlinge*) and prisoners who might possibly have to be extradited because of their foreign citizenship.

During previous interrogations I have put the number of Jews, who arrived in Auschwitz for extermination, at two and a half millions.[52] This figure was supplied by Eichmann who gave it to my superior officer, *Gruppenführer* Glücks, when he was ordered to make a report to the *Reichsführer SS* shortly before Berlin was surrounded. Eichmann, and his permanent deputy Günther,[53] were the only ones who possessed the necessary information on which to calculate the total number destroyed. In accordance with orders given by the *Reichsführer SS*, after every major action all evidence in Auschwitz on which a calculation of the number of victims might be based had to be burnt.

As head of Department DI, I personally destroyed every bit of evidence which could be found in my office. The heads of other offices did the same.

According to Eichmann, the *Reichsführer SS* and the Reich Main Security Office also had all their data destroyed.

Only his personal notes could give the required information. It is possible that, owing to the negligence of some department or other, a few isolated documents, teleprinter messages, or wireless messages have been left undestroyed, but they could not give sufficient information on which to make a calculation.

I myself never knew the total number and I have nothing to help me make an estimate of it.

I can only remember the figures involved in the larger actions, which were repeated to me by Eichmann or his deputies.

Office V ordered the preventive custody (Vorbeugungshaft) of common criminals, Gypsies, asocial prisoners (excepting homosexuals) and certain prisoners imprisoned for "re-education" or prevention (*Sicherungsverwahrte*), who were sent to concentration camps after they had completed their prison sentence pronounced by a court. A separate group of so-called police prisoners (*Polizeihäftlinge*) held during the period of investigation, also existed in the camps. See Broad's reminiscences, chapter entitled "The Police Summary Court," p. 112—117, and J. Sehn: *op. cit.*, pp. 40—41.

52 The State Museum at Oświęcim does not possess a full set of records, which would enable an exact computation of the number of victims at *KL Auschwitz* and its sub-camps. Estimates of the Soviet Extraordinary State Commission for the Investigation of Crimes Committed by the German Nazi Aggressors, by the International Military Tribunal in Nuremberg during the trial of the chief war criminals, and by the Supreme National Tribunal in Poland, were based on the partly preserved documents of the SS high authorities, on the documents of the commandant's office at *KL Auschwitz*, the documents of the Camp Resistance Movement, evidence and reports of witnesses, court experts' reports and opinions, also on the explanations offered by SS-men during their trials. Until recently authors writing on *KL Auschwitz* quoted the figure of three to four million. Historians from various countries, having examined the surviving Nazi documentation, have established the number of camp victims at at least 1.5 million.

53 *SS-Hauptsturmführer* Hans Günther. In the third Polish edition of the Autobiography of Rudolf Höss, Rolf Günther figures by mistake as an *SS-Hauptsturmführer* (who also participated in the "liquidation" of Jews).

From Upper Silesia[54] and *Generalgouvernement*[55]	250,000
Germany[56] and Theresienstadt[57]	100,000
Holland[58]	95,000
Belgium[59]	20,000
France[60]	110,000
Greece[61]	65,000
Hungary[62]	400,000
Slovakia[63]	90,000

---

54 The Jewish RSHA transports from Upper Silesia, destined for extermination, began arriving in *KL Auschwitz* at the end of 1941 and the beginning of 1942. The first transports were killed in the gas chamber of crematorium I in the base camp.

55 Polish territory under German rule. RSHA transports with the Jewish population from the *Generalgouvernement* arrived at *KL Auschwitz* in the years 1943—1944.

56 The first RSHA transports to arrive with Jewish inhabitants of the Third Reich came in February 1943.

57 Terezin, a town situated in Czechoslovakia, of which the German name was Theresienstadt. During World War II the Nazis organized there, in November 1941, a sort of ghetto which was a transit camp for the Jewish population of the so-called Protectorate of Bohemia and Moravia. From February 6, 1942, the Nazis sent Jews of mixed marriages from the Third Reich, Austria and Holland to Theresienstadt. Altogether around 140,000 Jews were settled there (70,000 from the Protectorate itself). Of this total 34,000 persons perished due to inhuman living conditions. Only 17,000 survived. The rest, that is circa 90,000 persons, were taken by the Nazis to concentration camps and extermination centres, including *KL Auschwitz*. The first RSHA transport from Theresienstadt came to Auschwitz on October 28, 1942. A special camp for Jews from Theresienstadt was opened, on September 9, 1943, at Birkenau in sector BIIb, called later *Familienlager-Theresienstadt*.

Jews put in this camp enjoyed better treatment than other prisoners. They were permitted to keep their belongings, they lived together with their families, their hair was not shorn, they could write to their families every fortnight and could receive parcels. A playing ground was organized for their children who initially received better food. In spite of all this the death rate among prisoners of this sector was high. In 1944 the prisoners still surviving were liquidated in the course of two operations, which took place on March 9, and July 11/12. After the liquidation of *Familienlager-Theresienstadt* a new RSHA transport from the ghetto in Theresienstadt was brought on September 30. Transports from Theresienstadt kept coming until the end of October 1944.

58 The first RSHA transport from Holland came to the camp on July 17, 1942. Transports of the Jewish population of Holland continued to arrive till September 1944.

59 The first RSHA transport from Belgium arrived on August 5, 1942. Transports with Jewish inhabitants of Belgium kept coming till August 1944.

60 The first RSHA transport from France came on March 30, 1942. Transports with the Jewish population of France continued until September 1944.

61 The first transport of Jewish inhabitants from Greece arrived at *KL Auschwitz* on March 20, 1943. Since then at least 22 transports with a total of 54,533 persons had come by August 16, 1944. Of that figure 41,776 were killed in the gas chambers and 12,757 were sent to work in the camp. The numbers of Jews from Greece given above do not embrace all Greek Jews brought to the camp, but refer only to those transports which underwent selections. It is likely that a greater number of transports was in fact brought, some of which were destined to be exterminated in their entirety. Danuta Czech: Deportation und Vernichtung der griechischen Juden in KL Auschwitz. *Hefte von Auschwitz*, Oświęcim 1970, no. 11, p. 24 and the following.

62 See p. 91, note 46.

63 The first RSHA transport from Slovakia arrived on March 26, 1942. Transports with Jews from Slovakia kept coming until October 1944.

I can no longer remember the figures for the smaller actions, but they were insignificant by comparison with the numbers given above.[64]

I regard a total of two and a half millions as far too high. Even Auschwitz had limits to its destructive possibilities.

Figures given by former prisoners are figments of the imagination and lack any foundation.

*

Aktion Reinhard was the code-name given to the collecting, sorting and utilization of all articles which were acquired as the result of the transports of Jews and their extermination.

Any member of the SS who laid hands on this Jewish property was, by order of the *Reichsführer SS*, punished with death.

Valuables worth many millions of pounds were seized.

An immense amount of property was stolen by members of the SS and by the police, and also by prisoners, civilian employees and railway personnel. A great deal of this still lies hidden and buried in the Auschwitz-Birkenau camp area.

When the Jewish transports unloaded on arrival, their luggage was left on the platform until all the Jews had been taken to the extermination buildings or into the camp. During the early days all the luggage would then be brought by a transport detachment to the sorting office, "Canada" I,[65] where it would be sorted and disinfected. The clothing of those who had been gassed in bunkers I and II or in crematoria I [II] to IV [V] was also brought to the sorting office.

By 1942, "Canada" I could no longer keep up with the sorting. Although new huts and sheds were constantly being added and prisoners were sorting day and night, and although the number of persons employed was constantly stepped up and several trucks (often as many as twenty) were loaded daily with the items sorted out, the piles of unsorted luggage went on mounting up. So in 1942, the construction of "Canada" II warehouse was begun at the west end of building sector II at Birkenau.[66] A start was also made on the erection of extermination buildings and a bath-house for the new arrivals.[67] Thirty newly-built huts were crammed to capacity immediately after completion, while mountains of unsorted effects piled up between them.[68] In spite of the augmented

---

[64] In the list of figures given here by Höss he fails to mention such countries as Austria, Bulgaria, Yugoslavia, Lithuania, Latvia, Norway, Russia, Trieste, Ukraine and Italy.

[65] "Canada" I was located near the base camp at Auschwitz.

[66] "Canada" II (*Effektenlager*) was located in sector BIIg.

[67] It was called *Sauna* in the camp.

[68] "Canada" in Birkenau comprised 35 barracks. On January 23, 1945, five days before the liberation of the camp by the Soviet Army, SS-men set fire to 30 store-houses filled with property seized from murdered people. The barracks burnt for several days. In six, partly burnt barracks the following objects were found after liberation: 1,185,345 men's suits and women's clothes, 43,255 pairs of men's and women's shoes, 13,694 carpets and great quantities of brushes, shaving-brushes and other articles of daily use.

labour gangs, it was out of the question to complete the job during the course of the individual actions, which always took from four to six weeks. Only during the longer intervals was it possible to achieve some semblance of order.

Clothing and footwear were examined for hidden valuables (although only cursorily in view of the quantities involved) and then stored or handed over to the camp to complete the inmates' clothing. Later on, it was also sent to other camps. A considerable part of the clothing was passed to welfare organizations for resettlers and later for victims of air raids. Large and important munition plants received considerable quantities for their foreign workers.

Blankets and mattresses, etc., were also sent to the welfare organizations. In so far as the camp required articles of this nature they were retained to complete their inventory, but other camps also received large consignments.

Valuables were taken over by a special section of the camp command and sorted out by experts, and a similar procedure was followed with the money that was found.

The jewellery was usually of great value, particularly if its Jewish owners came from the west: precious stones worth thousands of pounds, priceless gold and platinum watches set with diamonds, rings, earrings and necklaces of great rarity. Currency from all countries amounted to many thousands of pounds. Often tens of thousands of pounds in value, mostly in thousand-dollar notes, were found on single individuals. Every possible hiding place in their clothes and luggage and on their bodies was made use of.

When the sorting process that followed each major operation had been completed, the valuables and money were packed into trunks and taken by lorry to the Economic and Administrative Head Office in Berlin and thence to the Reichsbank, where a special department dealt exclusively with items taken during action against the Jews. Eichmann told me on one occasion that the jewellery and currency were sold in Switzerland, and that the entire Swiss jewellery market was dominated by these sales.

Ordinary watches were likewise sent in their thousands to Sachsenhausen. A large watchmaker's shop had been set up there, which employed hundreds of prisoners and was directly administered by Department DII (Maurer). The watches were sorted out and repaired in the workshop, the majority being later dispatched for service use by front-line SS and army troops.

Gold from the teeth was melted into bars by the dentists in the SS hospital and forwarded monthly to the Sanitary Head Office.

Precious stones of great value were also to be found hidden in teeth that had been stopped.

Hair cut from the women was sent to a firm in Bavaria to be used in the war effort.

Unserviceable clothing was sent for salvage, and useless footwear was taken to pieces and remade as far as possible, and what was left over was converted into leather dust.

The treasures brought in by the Jews gave rise to unavoidable difficulties for the camp itself. It was demoralizing for the members of the SS, who were not always strong enough to resist the temptation provided by these valuables which lay within such easy reach. Not even the death penalty or a heavy prison sentence was enough to deter them.[69]

The arrival of these Jews with their riches offered undreamed of opportunities to the other prisoners.[70] Most of the escapes that were made were probably connected with these circumstances. With the assistance of this easily acquired money, watches or rings, etc., anything could be arranged with the SS-men or the civilian workers. Alcohol, tobacco, food, false papers, guns and ammunition were all in the day's work. In Birkenau the male prisoners obtained access to the women's camp at night by bribing some of the female supervisors. This kind of thing naturally affected the whole camp discipline. Those who possessed valuables could obtain better jobs for themselves, and were able to buy goodwill of the capos and block seniors, and even arrange for a lengthy stay in the hospital where they would be given the best food. Not even the strictest supervision could alter this state of affairs. Jewish gold was a catastrophe for the camp.

In addition to Auschwitz there existed, as far as I am aware, the following extermination centres for Jews:

Kulmhof near Litzmannstadt[71]	Engine exhaust gases
Treblinka on the Bug[72]	Engine exhaust gases
Sobibór near Lublin[73]	Engine exhaust gases
Bełżec near Lemberg[74]	Engine exhaust gases
Lublin (Majdanek)[75]	Cyclon B

---

[69] Pery Broad wrote about the activity of a special commission, which was supposed to liquidate corrupt practices, in his reminiscences, see the chapter entitled " An SS Man's Honour " (pp. 145—147). So far investigations have failed to reveal a single case of an SS-man being put to death for theft of Jewish property from the " Canada " stores.

[70] There is no foundation for accepting this statement, as very few prisoners had access to the valuables taken from the Jews (mainly only those who worked in the " Canada " squad).

[71] See p. 86, note 25.

[72] In the summer of 1941, in the old gravel pit near the railway station at Treblinka, the Nazis established a penal labour camp, first for Poles and later for Jews too. On average there were 1,000 to 1,200 prisoners kept there at any one time. Men were employed in the gravel pits and camp workshops while women worked on an SS farm. Some 10,000 prisoners perished in this camp. In the late spring of 1942, another, special camp, *Treblinka II*, a camp for direct extermination, was set up in the vicinity of the penal camp. The first transport of Jews from the Warsaw ghetto arrived at *Treblinka II* on July 23, 1942. The victims were killed in gas chambers and their bodies were cremated on special pyres and in a large pit. During the period of its operation, from July 1942 to August 1943, the Nazis murdered at *Treblinka II* more than 800,000 Jews from many countries of Europe. On August 2, 1943, a revolt organized jointly by the prisoners of *Treblinka I* and *Treblinka II* broke out. The suppression of the revolt was followed by a systematic liquidation of the camp concluded in November 1943. *Treblinka*, Warszawa 1967, Wydawnictwo " Sport i Turystyka."

[73] See p. 67, note 107.

[74] In the autumn of 1941 the Nazis started to build an extermination camp for the Jewish population at Bełżec, Lublin district. Around the middle of March 1942 the first transports of Jewish inhabitants from the neighbourhood were brought to the camp. They were killed in gas chambers with combustion gases. The bodies of the victims were buried in trenches and beginning in the autumn of 1942 cremated on pyres. The extermination persisted till the spring of 1943, that is up to the time when the camp was liquidated. Altogether about 600,000 Jews from various parts of Poland and from other European countries perished here. Around 1,500 Poles were also killed here as

In addition, many centres of extermination were situated in the eastern territories, for example in the vicinity of Riga. There Jews were shot and their bodies were burned on wooden pyres.

I myself have only seen Kulmhof and Treblinka. Kulmhof had ceased to be used, but in Treblinka I saw the whole operation.

The latter had several chambers, capable of holding some hundreds of people, built directly by the railway track. The Jews went straight into the gas chambers without undressing, by way of a platform which was level with the trucks. A motor room had been built next to the gas chambers, equipped with various engines taken from large lorries and tanks. These were started up and the exhaust gases were led by pipes into the gas chambers, thereby killing the people inside. The process was continued for half an hour until all was silent inside the rooms. In an hour's time the gas chambers were opened up and the bodies taken out, undressed and burnt on a framework made of railway lines.

The fires were stoked with wood, the bodies being sprayed every now and then with petrol refuse. During my visit all those who had been gassed were dead. But I was told that the performance of the engines was not always uniform, so that the exhaust gases were often insufficiently strong to kill everyone in the chambers. Many of them were only rendered unconscious and had to be finished off by shooting. I heard the same story in Kulmhof and I was also told by Eichmann that these defects had occurred in other places.

In Kulmhof, too, the Jews sometimes broke the sides of the trucks in an attempt to escape.

Experience had shown that the preparation of prussic acid called Cyclon B caused death with far greater speed and certainty, especially if the rooms were kept dry and gas-tight and closely packed with people, and provided they were fitted with as large a number of intake vents as possible. So far as Auschwitz is concerned, I have never known or heard of a single person being found alive when the gas chambers were opened half an hour after the gas had been inducted.[76]

---

punishment for help given to Jews. Biuletyn Głównej Komisji Badania Zbrodni Niemieckich w Polsce, vol. 3, pp. 41—45, and *Scenes of Fighting*, *op. cit.*, p. 274.

[75] *KL* Lublin (Majdanek), established early in the autumn of 1941, was originally a camp for prisoners of war (*Kriegsgefangenenlager*). Its first inmates were some 2,000 Soviet prisoners of war. In November and December 1941, a group of over a hundred prisoners arrived from other camps, which included 50 German criminal offenders who were entrusted with various functions in the camp. These were followed by Poles and representatives of 51 other nationalities (men, women and children), including a large number of Jews. In mid-1943 Majdanek became a concentration camp and beginning in the autumn of 1942 it also served as a mass extermination camp. In this period its gas chambers were put into action, where victims were killed with carbon monoxide and Cyclon B. The bodies were burnt in crematoria and on pyres within the camp or in the nearby forest. Over half a million persons passed through the camp, of whom 360,000 perished: 200,000 as a result of appalling condition in the camp and the remainder as victims of the direct extermination operation. Zofia Murawska and Edward Gryń: *Obóz koncentracyjny Majdanek*, Lublin 1972, Państwowe Muzeum na Majdanku.

[76] Such a case was reported by an eyewitness—a member of the *Sonderkommando*—Dr. Miklós Nyiszli, in his book, *Auschwitz. A Doctor's Eyewitness Account*, *op. cit.*

*

The extermination process in Auschwitz took place as follows:

Jews selected for gassing were taken as quietly as possible to the crematoria, the men being separated from the women. In the undressing room prisoners of the special detachment, detailed for this purpose, would tell them in their own language that they were going to be bathed and deloused, that they must leave their clothes neatly together and above all remember where they had put them, so that they would be able to find them again quickly after delousing. The prisoners of the special detachment had the greatest interest in seeing that the operation proceeded smoothly and quickly.[77] After undressing, the Jews went into the gas chambers, which were furnished with showers and water pipes and gave a realistic impression of a bath-house.

The women went in first with their children, followed by the men who were always fewer in number. This part of the operation nearly always went smoothly, for the prisoners of the special detachment would calm those who betrayed any anxiety or who perhaps had some inkling of their fate. As an additional precaution these prisoners of the special detachment and an SS-man always remained in the chamber until the last moment.

The door would now be quickly screwed up and the gas immediately discharged by the waiting disinfectors through vents in the ceilings of the gas chambers, down a shaft that led to the floor. This ensured the rapid distribution of the gas. It could be observed through the peep-hole in the door that those who were standing nearest to the induction vents were killed at once. It can be said that about one third died straight away. The remainder staggered about and began to scream and struggle for air. The screaming, however, soon changed to the death rattle and in a few minutes all lay still. After twenty minutes at the latest no movement could be discerned. The time required for the gas to have effect varied according to the weather, and depended on whether it was damp or dry, cold or warm. It also depended on the quality of the gas, which was never exactly the same, and on the composition of the transports which might contain a high proportion of healthy Jews, or old and sick, or children. The victims became unconscious after a few minutes, according to their distance from the intake shaft. Those who screamed and those who were old or sick or weak, or the small children, died quicker than those who were healthy or young.

The door was opened half an hour after the induction of the gas, and the ventilation switched on. Work was immediately begun on removing the corpses. There was no noticeable change in the bodies and no sign of convulsions or discoloration. Only after the bodies had been left lying for some time, that is

---

[77] The camp authorities were interested in conducting the extermination operations in such a way, because of the need to rapidly unload the railway vans with the successive transports, thus ensuring the rhythmic activity of the gas chambers and crematorium ovens, which often worked twenty-four hours non-stop, e.g. at the time when the transports from Hungary were arriving. Members of the *Sonderkommando* could perhaps have wished to spare those sent to the gas chambers the torture of awaiting death, and so they preferred to have the victims enter unaware of their fate.

to say after several hours, did the usual death stains appear in the places where they had lain. Soiling through opening of the bowels was also rare. There were no signs of wounding of any kind. The faces showed no distortion.

The special detachment now set about removing the gold teeth and cutting the hair from the women. After this, the bodies were taken up by lift and laid in front of the ovens, which had meanwhile been stoked up. Depending on the size of the bodies, up to three corpses could be put into one oven retort at the same time. The time required for cremation also depended on this, but on an average it took twenty minutes. As previously stated, crematoria I [II] and II [III] could cremate about 2,000 bodies in twenty-four hours, but a higher number was not possible without causing damage to the installations. Numbers III [IV] and IV [V] should have been able to cremate 1,500 bodies in twenty-four hours, but, as far as I know, these figures were never attained.[78]

During the period when the fires were kept burning continuously, without a break, the ashes fell through the grates and were constantly removed and crushed to powder. The ashes were taken in lorries to the Vistula, where they immediately drifted away and dissolved. The ashes taken from the burning pits near bunker II and crematorium IV [V] were dealt with in the same way.

The process of destruction in bunkers I and II was exactly the same as in the crematoria, except that the effects of the weather on the operation were more noticeable.

The whole of the work connected with the extermination process was performed by special detachments of Jews.

They carried out their grisly task with dumb indifference. Their one object was to finish the work as quickly as possible, so that they could have a longer interval in which to search the clothing of the gassed victims for something to smoke or eat. Although they were well fed and given many additional allowances, they could often be seen shifting corpses with one hand while they gnawed at something they held in the other. Even when they were engaged in the most gruesome work of digging out and burning the corpses buried in the mass graves, they never stopped eating.

Even the cremation of their near relations failed to shake them.[79]

*

When I went to Budapest in the summer of 1943 and called on Eichmann he told me about the further actions which had been planned in connection with the Jews.

---

[78] According to the expert evidence of Dr. Roman Dawidowski, professor at the Academy of Mining and Metallurgy in Cracow, the average amount of corpses cremated within twenty-four hours in the thirty ovens of crematoria II and III totalled 5,000, while the number cremated in the sixteen ovens of crematoria IV and V was 3,000. In his calculations Professor Dawidowski allowed for a break of three hours for every twenty-four hours, caused by the necessity of deslagging the generators and by smaller stoppages, inevitable considering the constant exploitation of the installations. The same figures are given, in their evidence, by eyewitnesses, members of the *Sonderkommando* working in crematoria II to V, namely by Henryk Tauber and Alter Feinsilber vel Stanisław Jankowski.

[79] The state of mind of prisoners of the *Sonderkommando* and their experiences during work connected with extermination are best described in the memoirs of its members (*Amidst a Nightmare of Crime*, *op. cit*.).

At that period there were rather more than 200,000 Jews from the Carpathian Ukraine, who were detained there and housed in some brickworks, while awaiting transport to Auschwitz.

Eichmann expected to receive from Hungary, according to the estimate of the Hungarian police, who had carried out the arrests, about 3,000,000 Jews.

The arrests and transportation should have been completed by 1943, but because of the Hungarian government's political difficulties, the date was always being postponed.

In particular the Hungarian army, or rather the senior officers, were opposed to the extradition of these people, and gave most of the male Jews a refuge in the labour companies of the front-line divisions, thus keeping them out of the clutches of the police. When, in the autumn of 1944, an action was started in Budapest itself, the only male Jews left were the old and the sick.

Altogether there were probably not more than half a million Jews transported out of Hungary.

The next country on the list was Romania. According to the reports from his representative in Bucharest, Eichmann expected to get about 4,000,000 Jews from there.

Negotiations with the Romanian authorities, however, were likely to be difficult. The anti-Semitic elements wanted the extermination of the Jews to be carried out in their own country. There had already been serious anti-Jewish rioting, and abducted Jews had been thrown into the deep and isolated ravines of the Carpathians and killed. A section of the government, however, was in favour of transporting unwanted Jews to Germany.

In the meantime Bulgaria was to follow with an estimated two and a half million Jews. The authorities there were agreeable to the transport, but wanted to wait on the result of the negotiations with Romania.

In addition, Mussolini was supposed to have promised the extradition of the Italian Jews and those from the Italian occupied part of Greece, although not even an estimate had been made of their numbers. But the Vatican and the royal family, and consequently all those opposed to Mussolini, wanted at all costs to prevent these Jews from being surrendered.

Eichmann did not count on getting these Jews.

Finally there was Spain. Influential circles were approached by German representatives over the question of getting rid of the Jews. But Franco and his followers were against it. Eichmann had little faith in being able to arrange for an extradition.

The course taken by the war destroyed these plans and saved the lives of millions of Jews.[80]

---

[80] The figures given by Höss differ from those in the official minutes of the conference at Wannsee, dated January 20, 1942, and dealing with "The Final Solution of the Jewish Question." The minutes contain the following quotas of Jews, destined to be exterminated, from the respective countries: 48,000 from Bulgaria, 6,000 from Spain, 342,000 from Romania, 742,800 from Hungary, and 58,000 from Italy (together with Sardinia).

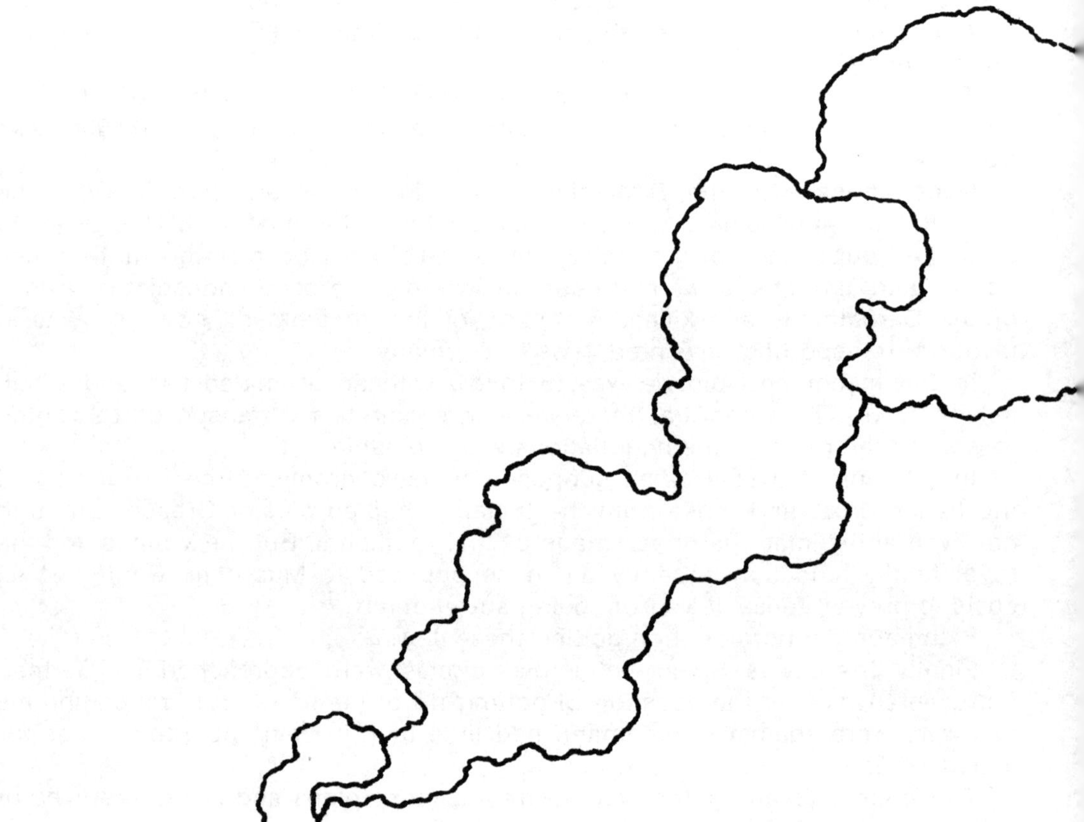

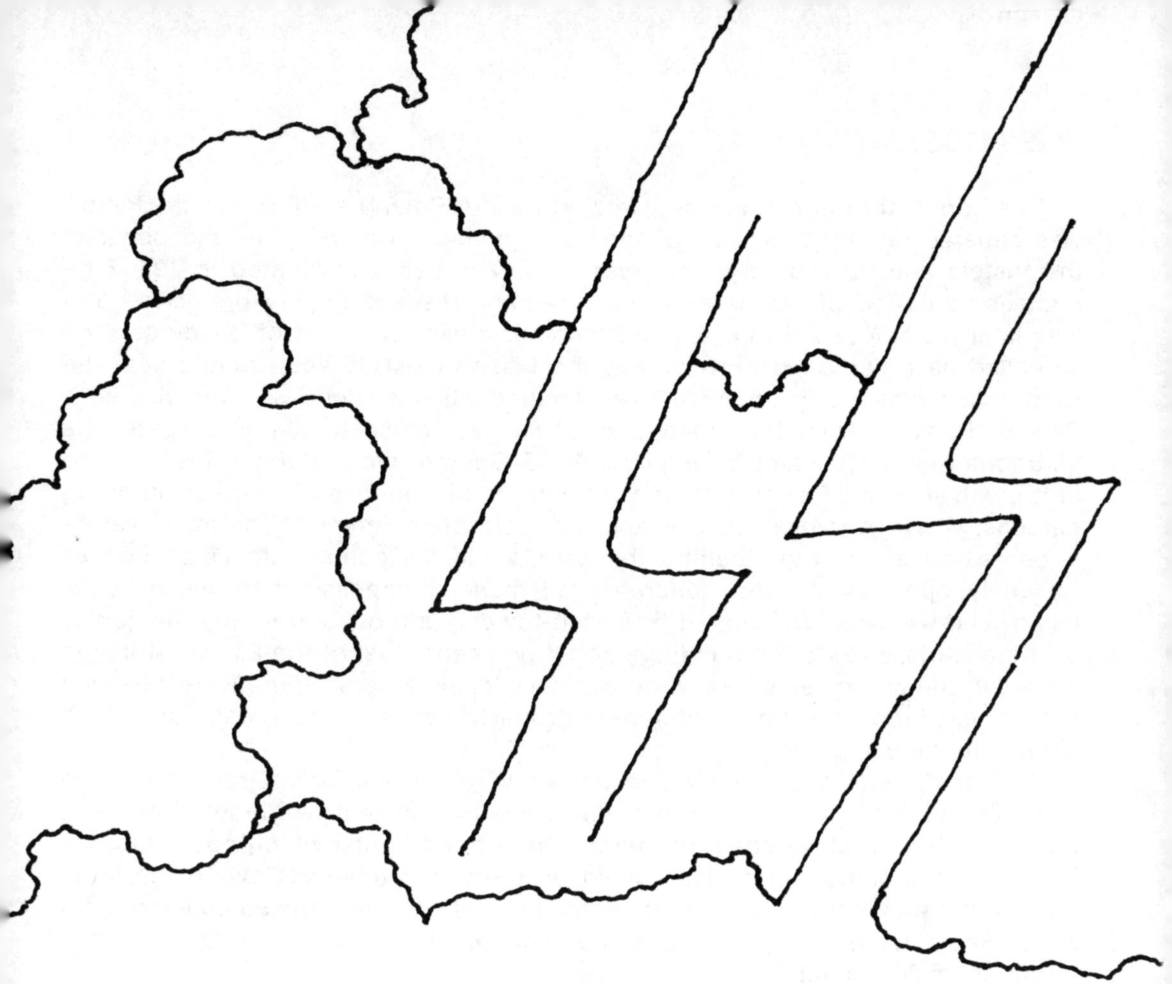

REMINISCENCES
of Pery Broad

[KZ AUSCHWITZ][1]

The concentration camp Auschwitz, known in Poland as the "Death Camp," was situated nearby the town of the same name, on marshy ground between the Vistula and its tributary, the river Sola. The camp originated in 1940.[2] Its nucleus consisted of old garrison barracks and disused factory premises,[3] and was later on developed into a vast complex of various kinds of buildings. The so-called base camp Auschwitz[4] was the first to exist. It was situated near the road which runs along the Sola river, connecting Auschwitz with the village of Rajsko. Looking from this road one could see, close to the main gate, the luxurious villa of the camp commandant, *SS-Obersturmbannführer* Höss. A road block with several SS guards closed the entry to the camp, and all in- or outgoing persons, whether soldiers or civilians, were closely examined. The main watch-house stood to the right behind the gate, while the commandant's office was obliquely opposite. A long concrete wall made it impossible to see into the camp. The wall was overlooked by watch-towers, and beyond it only the gables of the cheerless red brick buildings could be seen. Most of the 28 two-storeyed blocks in the camp served as living quarters for prisoners. Some were reserved for the sick, for offices, for the prisoners' property store etc. There was a prisoners' kitchen in the camp, too.

The camp was secured by two barbed-wire fences, which reached above a man's height[5] and were charged with electric current. At night they were brilliantly lit by a close chain of lamps. Great flood-lights, which could brightly illuminate the camp, were also placed on the watch-towers. Beyond the inner fence there was a strip of gravel, three metres wide, forming the so-called neutral zone. Shots were fired at anyone stepping on it. The base camp contained 20,000 to 25,000 inmates.

At a distance of five or six kilometres from the base camp, the notorious camp of Birkenau[6] was formed in 1941/1942. It later contained 30,000 women prisoners and 50,000 to 60,000 men prisoners. If one went by train from Bielitz to Auschwitz in the evening, then one could see to the left an endless string of glaring lamps, like a string of beads, and a row of whitewashed concrete posts, which formed the fence of the Birkenau camp. The prisoners' living quarters consisted of hundreds of windowless horse stables used as barracks, and of

---

[1] The document published here, written in German, has no title and is not divided into chapters. To make the document clearer the Editors have divided it into sections with titles. It should be added that the translator was often obliged to forego clarity and correctness of style for the sake of fidelity to the original.

[2] The first prisoners were put into the camp on June 14, 1940. They were of Polish nationality and were brought from the prison in Tarnów. Their arrival was preceded by an earlier transport of 30 prisoners of German nationality, criminal offenders directed to *KL Auschwitz* from *KL Sachsenhausen*, and from these the SS formed its subsidiary machinery, i.e. prisoners with special duties. *Cf.* p. 30 and note 12 on p. 30.

[3] These were the former buildings of the Polish Tobacco Monopoly.

[4] *Stammlager Auschwitz*.

[5] The fencing reached a height of 4 metres.

[6] Birkenau, also called *Auschwitz II*, was a branch of the base camp.

primitive stone houses.[7] The camp was divided into three construction sectors. The first sector accommodated women prisoners. Sector 2 was divided into six compounds which were used for different purposes. For example, one compound of this sector was used as a hospital, another served as the Gypsy camp, while yet another contained the quarantine blocks for new arrivals.[8] Sector 3 was still under construction when Auschwitz and Birkenau were hurriedly evacuated on January 17, 1945. The wooden barracks, by now already finished, served as a weaving workshop, and were also occasionally used for housing prisoners.[9]

Conditions in Birkenau were considerably worse than in Auschwitz, where they were bad enough. Feet sank into a sticky bog at every step. There was hardly any water for washing. The prisoners slept, six to a bed, on wooden planks placed in three tiers. Most of the beds were without straw pallets. The roll-call, held twice daily, meant standing for hours in wet and cold weather with mire underfoot. If it rained in the daytime, the prisoners would be obliged to lie on the beds in their wet clothes. No wonder that several hundred of them died every day.

The watch-towers which surrounded both the base camp and Birkenau formed the so-called "small sentry chain." In the daytime the guards of the small sentry chain were called in, while the "large sentry chain" was manned. This chain surrounded a vast area within which the majority of the prisoners, supervised by capos and foremen,[10] had to work in factories and on fields. Along the "large sentry chain" boards were put up with a threatening death's head and the notice: "*Interessengebiet des KL Auschwitz. Weitergehen verboten—Es wird ohne Anruf scharf geschossen!*"[11].

But even if there had been no such notices, civilians would hardly have come close to this haunted region of the country. It was only too easy to be suspected of wanting to get in touch with the prisoners in some way, or of being a spy, and then the suspects would be spirited away into the camp. The work squads,[12] which were employed outside the large sentry chain, were always conducted to and from work by guards whose number depended on the number of prisoners. When in the evening all squads had returned in their full numbers from outside the large sentry chain, the sentries left the watch-towers and the guards of the small chain then took up their posts.

The block leader counted the returning prisoners in front of the block-leaders' office at the entrance. If one of the prisoners was missing, the large sentry chain

---

[7] Two kinds of barracks were built at Birkenau, of brick and of wood.

[8] Newcomers, so-called *Zugang*, were put into quarantine for several weeks and only then transferred to the camp proper and sent to work. The few discharged prisoners were also obliged to undergo quarantine, which was called quarantine before release.

[9] Hungarian Jewesses lived in this sector in the unfinished barracks during the period from July to October 3, 1944 (this was the so-called *Depotlager*). The weaving shop was established later, probably in November of that year.

[10] *Vorarbeiter*.

[11] "Interest zone of the concentration camp Auschwitz. No admittance. Shots will be fired without warning."

[12] *Aussenkommando*.

would remain at its post and a search party with dogs would comb the grounds. But prisoners sometimes managed to leave their squads unnoticed, to find a hiding-place in the partly wooded grounds from where they would sneak at night through the sentries placed at a distance of 30 to 40 metres from one another, thus escaping from the camp. The other prisoners then had to stand all night long in the open as a punishment. Work began immediately in the morning, despite the night's hardships.[13]

Barbarous hygienic conditions, insufficient food rations and hard work, together with other torments, meant that the majority of people sent to Auschwitz met a sad end after a few weeks or a few months at the most. Even women, dressed in discarded Russian army coats or in rags, were obliged to work hard, carrying stones or digging pits. Prisoners who were lucky enough to get some special post in camp, or who worked in the few better squads, were able to keep alive a little longer. Auschwitz was an extermination camp! The biggest in the history of the world. Two or three million Jews[14] were murdered there in the course of its existence! Not to mention thousands of Poles, Russians, Czechs, Yugoslavs, etc.

The sight of the barbed-wire fences with the notice: "*Achtung! Lebensgefahr!*"[15], the guards with their machine-guns and automatic pistols, the lifeless, naked-looking brick barracks, could not but impress all newcomers with a feeling of hopelessness, a feeling that they would never leave this camp behind to return to freedom. People who were not strong enough to resist the paralyzing effect of their surroundings, soon tried to put an end to their sufferings by voluntary death. When working in the outside squads they ran through the chain of sentries in order to be shot by them, or they "ran into the wires"[16], as it was called in camp slang. The high voltage current or the shots of machine-guns saved them from further misery. If shots were heard at night, everybody knew that despair had again driven a man into the live-wire fences and that he would now be lying, a lifeless bundle, in the neutral zone. Innumerable human beings took the decision to end their subhuman existence, driven to suicide by their longing for freedom and for their homes, by starvation, by some painful illness for which they received hardly any treatment, or by cruel blows. Some were found in the morning strung up with their belts on the planks of their bunks. The cases of suicide were then laconically reported to the camp leader by the block senior at roll-call. The officers of the *Erkennungsdients*[17] hurried to the place and photographed the body from all angles; witnesses were interrogated at length to make sure that the victim had not been killed by other prisoners.

---

[13] To have to stand for a considerable time was only one form of punishment in retaliation for an escape. In 1941, if the escape of a prisoner was discovered, the camp authorities (commandant, camp leader) would select from the block in which the escapee had lived, or from his work squad, ten or even twenty prisoners. They were put into the cellars of Block 11 where they would die of starvation.

[14] See p. 93, note 52.

[15] "Attention! Danger!"

[16] "Running into the wires" occurred in the camps surrounded by live wires.

[17] Investigation service. One of the departments of the Political Section, housed in Block 26.

This was truly a farce full of unsurpassed cynicism![18] As if the SS authorities in the camp, where every day thousands were systematically tortured to death, cared what happened to one unhappy man!

[BLOCK 11]

Anyone acquainted with the former concentration camp Auschwitz knows what Block 11 meant. Externally it hardly differed from the other blocks. A few stone steps led to its entrance at the front side of the building. To the right of the door there hung an insignificant, small black sign with the number 11. Through the glass panes of the door one could see the corridor which divided the whole building into two parts. The door of Block 11 was always locked, while in other blocks of the camp this was not the case. If you rang the bell, you saw an SS guard approaching and his steps echoed in the seemingly deserted building. The guard looked at every newcomer with distrust and more often than not sent him about his business. The talking was done through a small peep-hole. If he let a person in, only in rare cases of the strictest necessity, the person would see in the dim light a strong iron lattice with a door, which separated the back of the building from the front. The fact that the windows were almost entirely bricked up, with the exception of a narrow strip not wider than a palm to let daylight in, must have made an uncanny impression from the outside. Even the cellar windows were heavily barred.[19] Here and there strange looking tin cases were affixed at the level of the cellar windows, and it was hard to guess what purpose they served.[20]

The yard between Block 11 and the parallel Block 10[21] next door was

---

[18] Broad was fully aware of the fact that SS-men got three or more days' leave for killing a prisoner who had approached the wire fences. It was officially termed a reward for "preventing a prisoner's escape."

[19] The bars were embedded in the walls on the inside of the windows. Moreover, the windows were hidden on the outside behind brick screens so that prisoners in the cells had no chance of seeing what was going on around the block. The windows of the ground floor were also barred, and later the first-storey windows were bricked up to two thirds of their height.

[20] These cases, shaped like baskets, covered the openings through which air penetrated into the dark cells and also the standing cells.

[21] In the years 1940—1942 Block 10 contained living quarters. The newly organized re-education work squad, *Erziehungskompanie*, was located there for a short time in 1941. From March to August 1942 it housed women prisoners of the women's camp which occupied Blocks 1—10. Medical apparatus was installed there towards the end of 1942; there were also an X-ray room, an operating theatre, tables and other appliances required in a gynaecological hospital ward. In April 1943 Block 10 was handed over to Professor Dr. Carl Clauberg to be used for his sterilization experiments conducted on women prisoners, chiefly Jewesses, selected by him. *SS-Sturmbannführer* Dr. Eduard Wirths, garrison surgeon in *KL Auschwitz*, also conducted research work here into cancer, and he operated on women prisoners suspected of being afflicted with it. Horst Schumann, M.D., operated on women prisoners who had previously been sterilized with X-rays in the experimental station of the women's camp at Birkenau. In April 1943 part of the premises of Block 10 was allocated to the SS Institute of Hygiene (*Hygiene-Bakteriologische Untersuchungsstelle der Waffen-SS Süd-Ost*), which was to do research connected with bacteriology, chemistry, pathological anatomy, etc. A month later, that is in May, the Institute was transferred to Rajsko near Auschwitz.

surrounded by high stone walls, which connected the front parts of both buildings and protected them from curious eyes. A massive wooden gate, with a peep-hole closed from the inside, barred the entrance to the yard. When you noticed that the windows of the next block were secured by crossing boards, then you were convinced that the yard must serve some special purpose.[22]

Even after coming to the office (to the right of the entrance) on business, all the visitor would know about this block was that he had been in the notorious KA,[23] that is the camp prison, where prisoners were detained somewhere in cells. But on leaving the stuffy atmosphere of the Block and on finding himself in the open again, he would involuntarily take a deep breath.

In the office of the leader of Section II[24] of the camp command, all the desk officers and clerks[25] had gathered. The boss, *SS-Untersturmführer* Max Grabner, was holding a briefing session. He sat behind his desk, a man of medium height, and kept swaggering and throwing his weight about. The disconnected sentences of his oration and his vulgar German betrayed his complete lack of education, nevertheless he had silver stripes on his uniform. The initiated knew that in his civilian past he had been a cowherd in the mountains. Now he proudly wore the uniform of the SD[26] and was a criminal investigator in the Gestapo. He found the work of his section unsatisfactory. He had not received a sufficient number of criminal reports against prisoners, or requests for executions. He accused his subordinates of softness; they kept their eyes riveted on a point in front of them and did not dare to answer back or justify themselves. His command to show more hardness in future was silently accepted and heels were clicked.

Grabner had become the most outstanding man in Auschwitz thanks to his unscrupulous brutality, his morbid ambition, his need for self-assertion and his proverbial double-dealing. Even the commandant, *SS-Sturmbannführer* Höss, who was his equal in sadistic cruelty and unscrupulousness, avoided, wherever he could, being at cross-purposes with this experienced Gestapo-man.

The briefing session was taking place, as usual, on a Saturday morning. Grabner's custom was to use every weekend for, as he cynically said, "dusting out the bunker"[27]. After the session the whole staff went to Block 11. In fact only three or four officers were needed, but Grabner usually took everybody as he felt happy amongst a numerous staff of subordinates.

The camp leader, *SS-Hauptsturmführer* Aumeier, was expected in the office of Block 11. To stress his importance he made us wait a while, and then the short Bavarian energetically marched into the room. His sharp, croaking voice

---

[22] The windows of Block 10, which overlooked the yard of Block 11, were boarded up to prevent prisoners in that block from observing what was going on in the yard of Block 11, and particularly from seeing executions which took place there. In spite of this precaution prisoners risked their lives, watching the shooting of their fellow-prisoners through chinks between the boards.

[23] *Kommandanturarrest*.

[24] That is, of the Political Section (*Politische Abteilung*).

[25] *Sacharbeiter* und *Schreiber*.

[26] *Sicherheitsdienst*—SS Security Service. See p. 31, note 14.

[27] Prisoners in the camp described this operation as "cleaning out" or "emptying" the bunker (i.e. cells).

proclaimed the fact that he was a drunkard. It was obvious that he was a cruel man—his eyes and the features of his face told the tale. He boasted of being an intimate friend of Himmler's and he was the proud recipient of the golden party badge. He was officiously followed by the reporting officer, *SS-Unterscharführer* Stiwitz. An SS physician made his appearance too. The rest of the party consisted of the prison warders and some block leaders, and all proceeded to the cellars which were to be "dusted." The broad corridor in the middle, which as on the ground floor was divided up by strong iron lattices with doors, branched out here into short, parallel corridors. Three to five cells were situated in each of them. They had stout oak doors with steel fittings and peep-holes. The air in these underground corridors was so stifling that breathing was almost impossible. The uncanny atmosphere was enhanced by the suppressed whisperings behind the cell doors, the glaring light of the bulbs, the sharp contrast between the black floor and the white walls, and finally by the death's heads glittering on the caps of the SS-men.

A prison warder opened the first cell door with a key selected from a large key-ring. Then two iron bolts were drawn. Escape from this prison was impossible, particularly as it was situated in the middle of the camp with its live-wire fences. A choking stench issued from the crowded, narrow cell. One prisoner shouted "*Achtung!*"[28] and the rest, their faces apathetic, stood up in a line—emaciated men, clad in dirty white and blue rags. One could see that some of them were barely able to stand erect. They accepted with apathy the procedure, which might decide whether they would live or die, and which they had, with better luck perhaps, already gone through before. It was the apathy of men whose will to survive had been destroyed. Aumeier held against the door the list of men who would be tried that day.

The first prisoner gave his name and stated how long he had been in prison. The camp leader briefly questioned the reporting officer as to the cause of his arrest. If any prisoner was arrested by Section II, which was usually the case with recaptured fugitives, then the matter was in Grabner's hands. Both camp dignitaries then took their decision—either penal report 1 or penal report 2. Prisoners of either group left the cell and formed ranks in two groups in the corridor. The rest remained "in prison pending the investigation."

The "criminal activities" of prisoners from group 1 amounted to stealing a few potatoes, obtaining one undergarment too many or smoking a cigarette during work, not to mention other trifles of this sort. They were lucky if they escaped with flogging or a term in a penal company,[29] which meant excessively hard work.[30]

---

[28] Attention!

[29] *Strafkompanie* (SK). This was formed around August 1940. Originally it was situated in one of the rooms of the present Block 3a, then on the ground floor of Block 11. On May 8, 1942, it was transferred to Birkenau, sector BIb. When women prisoners occupied that sector, the SK was moved to Block 11 in the men's camp, sector BIId.

[30] Among its other tasks the penal company was employed in digging a drainage ditch at Birkenau, which was called *Königsgraben*. The penal company worked all day long, even when other prisoners were resting. The SK was supervised by the most bestial SS-men, such as *SS-Hauptscharführer* Otto Moll, and also by the capos and block seniors.

But the unlucky ones, whose further fate was decided by the code-word "penal report 2," would fare much worse. Aumeier drew with his blue pencil a thick cross at every name, putting small lines round the corners of the cross, and everybody could see it. It was no secret what "penal report 2" meant. The group of the less important cases, whose lives were saved once more, were led into the camp where they would receive their punishment.

Large communal cells overlooking the yard on the ground and first floor, where more than a hundred people were sometimes crowded together, were then emptied and the prisoners or civilian detainees, both sexes separately, were conducted into the cells on the other side of the corridor.

Those who had been sentenced to death were taken to the lavatory on the ground floor. Prisoners whose function it was to act as clerks and to clean the premises, covered up the windows and made their fellow-sufferers undress. The victims seemed already to have said goodbye to the world and it was perhaps a relief to them to know that in a few minutes they would be freed from their tortures and from their sufferings. The helpers wrote the prisoners' numbers with indelible pencils on the naked bodies of the victims, to make the identification of the bodies in the mortuary or in the crematorium possible.[31]

Aumeier, Grabner and some of the SS-men had meanwhile gone into the yard. The majority of the SS-men had already left. Nobody cared to be in Grabner's company; it was dangerous to be constantly reproached with slackness by that Gestapo-man. And among Grabner's subordinates most were fanatics, who could hardly be accused of being soft!

One side of the stone wall of Block 11 was black. This wall-face, constructed of black isolation plates, had become the journey's end for thousands of guiltless people. Among them were patriots, who would not betray the country they loved for material gain, men who had managed to escape from the hell of Auschwitz and who had been unfortunate enough to be recaptured, men and women conscious of their nationality, from all the countries then occupied by the Germans.

The shooting of the condemned was carried out by the reporting officer or by a prison warder.[32] In order not to arouse the attention of passers-by, who might then be walking along the road not far behind the stone wall, the weapon used was a small-calibre gun with 10 or 15 cartridges. Aumeier, Grabner and the actual executioner, holding his gun ready to fire behind his back, took their positions, fully enjoying their feeling of omnipotence. In the background several frightened carriers were ready with their stretchers to fulfil their gruesome task.[33] They were unable to hide the horror, clearly visible on their faces. A prisoner would stand near the black wall with a spade in his hand. Another prisoner, belonging to the cleaning squad and specially chosen for his strength, approached at a run, quickly pushing the first two victims forward. He kept

---

[31] This concerns the period before the tattooing of prisoners was introduced, that is, before March 1942.

[32] This is not the whole truth. The functionaries of the Political Section, where Broad was himself employed, also performed executions.

[33] Broad means the prisoners employed to take away the corpses.

a fast hold on their arms and then pressed their faces to the wall. "*Proste*" (straight) was the command, should one of them turn his head to the side. Some of those walking skeletons had spent months in the stinking cells, where not even animals would be kept, and they could barely manage to stand straight. And yet, at that last moment, many of them shouted "Long live Poland," or "Long live freedom." The executioner was then in a particular hurry to shoot them in the back of their necks, or he tried to silence them with brutal blows. Fully conscious of their power, the SS-men nervously laughed in such cases, but they did not like to hear such cries which were evidence that national pride and love of freedom could not be broken, not even by the utmost terror.

Thus did the Poles die and the Jews too, of whom Nazi propaganda maintained that they were base slaves, whining for mercy, and that they had no right at all to live; only Germans had that right! The SS-men almost always had the same spectacle before them—men and women, young and old, people who managed to gather their last resources in order to die honourably. There was no abject pleading for mercy, but often instead a last look of abysmal contempt, which made those primitive thugs fly into a sadistic rage. Shot after shot was fired with hardly any noise. The victims fell down with a groan. The executioner made sure that the shots he had fired from a distance of a few centimetres were effective. He stepped on the forehead of the man lying on the ground, pulled his eyelids back and thus ascertained whether the victim was dead. Aumeier and Grabner looked on expertly. If a ruckle was still heard, one of the SS leaders would give the order—"That one must get one more!" A shot in the temple or in the eye finally put an end to a wretched life.

The carriers ran to and fro as quickly as possible. They loaded the corpses on the stretchers and carried them to a heap at the other end of the yard. More and more blood-stained bodies were brought. Blood kept running in a thin stream from the wound at the back of the head and down the back for several minutes after the shooting. Silently and outwardly unmoved, the prisoner with the spade stepped nearer, when the two bodies were taken away, and covered up the puddles of foaming blood with sand. The executioner mechanically reloaded his gun again and again, and one execution followed another. If a pause in his work became necessary, he would put down the gun and whistle a tune, or talk with the men around him about quite indifferent matters. By his cynical attitude he wanted to show that it did not affect him at all to be "finishing off that rabble"; he wanted to boast how "tough" he was. He was quite proud of the fact that his conscience did not trouble him when he was murdering the innocent victims. If one of them did not hold his head still, he would press the muzzle of his gun into the prisoner's neck and push his face up against the wall. This happened above all when he heard those patriotic shouts. SS-men were aware that prisoners behind the wall, listening to the last demonstrations of the fanatic faith of the martyred men, were morally uplifted and strengthened in their own patriotic feelings.

The last seconds of the victims standing before the black wall were often drawn out in a cruel way. They felt the cold, bloody muzzle of the gun against their necks, they heard the pulling of the trigger... the gun was blocked! The bored executioner then put the gun away and slowly tried to fix it, telling his companions it was high time to get a new gun. Nobody cared that the victim suffered unbearably during the protracted execution. The iron grip on his arms never relaxed. The gun was finally set right and it functioned properly this time, although sometimes further blocks would occur again. The whole indescribably gruesome show was over after an hour or so.

Grabner had " dusted out " the bunker and could enjoy a substantial breakfast. The yard of Block 11 was again deserted. The sand in front of the black wall, which stood there with such indifference, was freshly raked. A swarm of flies was buzzing above some big, black-red spots at the other end of the yard. A wide, dark track led through the camp beginning at the massive wooden gate with the peep-hole, the gate which barred entry to the yard. The track led in the direction of the exit from the camp, to the crematorium.

At the camp gate a prisoners' band played a jolly German marching tune, to the accompaniment of which work squads marched to their afternoon work. It was not easy for them to keep in step in their clumsy wooden shoes, and with blistered feet. If one of the prisoners failed to do this, he was mercilessly kicked or beaten in the face.

In the lavatory of Block 11 the cleaners were by now sorting out the bedraggled clothes of the murdered victims. The executioner removed some blood stains from his clothes, and in the best of moods made ready to attend an educational lecture for the soldiers. The subject of the lecture was: " The European tasks of the SS . . ."

[THE POLICE SUMMARY COURT]

Once or twice a month the " Police Summary Court "[34] of the State Police in Kattowitz held its sessions in the Auschwitz concentration camp. The omnipotent ruler of Upper Silesia, *SS-Obersturmbannführer* and State Councillor[35] Dr. Mildner, would put in an appearance. The man was one of the most blood-thirsty butchers that existed in the Third Reich. He looked like the embodiment of despotism. His mighty skull was most impressive and so were his ice-cold, cruel eyes with their searching look. He was the head of the Kattowitz Police and chairman of the Summary Court. The session always took place in Auschwitz as the sentences could be carried out there immediately. The Reich Main Security Office had issued an order to the Gestapo to carry out sentences inside the concentration camps, with the exception of executions which were to be performed in public in order to intimidate the population. The Summary Court passed sentences on Poles and *Volksdeutsche* [people who had signed German nationality lists], found guilty of " political and criminal offences." A political " offence " was, for example, to listen to the enemy's radio programmes and to talk about them, or to be suspected of being a member of the Polish resistance movement, of serving as a courier for the resistance movement or of helping it with money. Criminal transgressors included, among

[34] *Polizeistandgericht.*

[35] *Oberregierungsrat.*

others, those who where accused of black marketeering. But even the most drastic punishments did not succeed in suppressing the black market. Poles got at the most only half of a German's food rations and could not survive on them alone.

The task of Criminal Court secretary[36] Kauz, who also belonged to the Kattowitz Gestapo, was to organize and prepare the sessions of the Summary Court. Kauz wore an SD uniform. It was impossible to guess from the appearance of that rather insignificant clerk, with his harmless-looking thick glasses, that such a special task had been assigned to him. The victims of the Summary Court were taken in lorries from prisons, particularly from the court prison at Myslowitz, to Auschwitz.[37] Their emaciated, deathly-pale faces testified to their prolonged stay in prison and to the tortures they had endured during the interrogation. They wore civilian clothes and in spite of their pitiful physical condition were, all of them, heavily handcuffed. During some transports the SS-men who brought them to the communal cells of Block 11 were warned to avoid contagion. Prisoners ill with typhus were quite common among those detained by the Summary Court and as a rule typhus and other epidemics were rampant both in prisons and in concentration camps.

On the whole, the men and women detainees, who were to stand trial before the Summary Court, had already been interrogated and had given "their evidence." From time to time, however, Auschwitz was visited by commissions which had the task of conducting inquiries on behalf of the Gestapo.

The persons they wanted to interrogate had been brought directly to Auschwitz after their arrest and were imprisoned in the camp as police prisoners. Before every session of the Summary Court Kauz used to bring a list of people who were already detained in the camp and who even hoped to have escaped death. They then had to be transferred from their work squads to the prison of Block 11. Here every prisoner had to be prepared to become either the victim of Grabner or that of the Summary Court. One mention of the prisoner's name at another interrogation, a vague suspicion or some other accident could easily seal his fate.

In the middle of 1943 a strange procession could be observed every morning in the Auschwitz concentration camp. The procession moved from the gate, above which large letters proclaimed that "*Arbeit macht frei*"[38], towards the former post-office barrack then used as the place where defendants were interrogated. At the head of the procession you could see eight prisoners carrying two mysterious wooden structures, somewhat resembling hurdles. Sixty or eighty police prisoners followed them. They were barely able to walk to the barrack ; some were supported by their fellow-sufferers. A considerable number of Gestapo officers in uniform, walking behind them, closed the fated column.

---

[36] *Kriminalsekretär.*

[37] The ground floor of Block 11 was mostly used to house prisoners who had been brought from the police prison in Myslowitz. Probably because of overcrowding, the Myslowitz prison reserved the ground floor of Block 11 in the concentration camp as a sort of "extension" of its own premises. This part of Block 11 which was occupied by prisoners of the Police Summary Court, was termed in official correspondence *Polizei-Ersatz-Gefängnis Myslowitz in Auschwitz.*

[38] "Work gives freedom."

Some of the Gestapo officers had riding crops at their belts, and some had the specially prepared bull-hide whips, so widely known in concentration camps. Their equipment was completed by typewriters and thick dossiers. Guards with automatic pistols escorted the prisoners, though the latter were certainly too weak to offer any resistance. The Gestapo officers entered the building into which the wooden structures were also brought. The prisoners who were first to be interrogated followed. The rest had to wait outside, guarded by the sentries.

Soon after the bellowing voices of the Gestapo interrogators were heard, together with the crash of overturned chairs and the sound of blows. The horrible cries of the cruelly tortured men could be heard from afar. All of them met with the most terrible treatment if they were not immediately ready to confess their "guilt," or if they were suspected of knowing the hiding places of weapons or the names of "members of the gangs." Not many realized what purpose the wooden structures served. The initiated knew that they were "swings," as those implements of the Inquisition were cynically called.

A certain Gestapo officer was responsible for the idea of constructing the "swings" at Auschwitz.[39] He had come from some State Police Office to interrogate a prisoner in Auschwitz. A strange, subdued groaning was suddenly heard from the room which had been put at his disposal. When the concentration camp officers entered the room, they saw a spectacle which surprised even them, tough as they were. Two tables had been placed side by side with a gap of one metre between them. The victim had to sit down on the floor and cross his hands in front of his drawn up knees. His wrists were then bound. A thick bar was put between his elbows and knees. The ends of the bar lay on both tables. He was helplessly swinging between the tables, his head downwards. Then his posterior and naked feet soles were flogged with a bull-hide whip. The blows were so violent that the tortured man rotated wheelwise. Every time his posterior came into a convenient position—a powerful blow was dealt, with all the strength the torturer could muster. When the cries grew too piercing, the fiendish Gestapo-man smothered them by putting a gas-mask on the victim's head. The mask was taken off from time to time and the tortured man would be asked whether he was ready to confess. He was accused of possessing a weapon; probably he had fallen victim to an unscrupulous informer.

After some 15 minutes the convulsive movements of the tortured man were no longer visible. He was unable to speak and only shook his head weakly when the gas-mask was removed, and he was told to make his confession. His trousers were a dark red colour and blood was dripping to the floor. His head finally hung down motionless; he had fainted.

But the Gestapo officer was not moved by this sight. With a knowing leer he took from his pocket a small bottle of a strong-smelling liquid and held it to the prisoner's nose, who indeed regained consciousness after a few minutes. His buttocks were in such a state that further flogging would hardly have

---

[39] During the Auschwitz trial in Frankfurt, witnesses testified that the swing was an invention of Boger from the Political Section. It was definitely Boger who introduced the swing into Auschwitz.

increased the pain and so the inquisitor had a better idea. He dripped hot water into the victim's nose. The burning pain must have been indescribable. The inquisitor got what he wanted.

After another question, sneeringly asked with full certainty of victory over the fiendishly tormented man, the latter nodded that he would confess. The bar was then taken from the tables and upended on the floor, so that the man slid down. It was only with some difficulty that they succeeded in taking the handcuffs from the purplish, thickly swollen wrists of the victim who lay lifeless on the floor. Since he did not react when they shouted at him to come to the table and sign his "confession," he was flogged with the bull-hide whip. The blows fell indiscriminately on his head and back; he was kicked, too. He finally managed to straighten himself up and to sign his "confession." The shaky handwriting and the perspiration stain, where his hand had rested on the page, made it clear to the expert that the interrogation had been of the "intensified" kind. In official documents they often called it "an interrogation conducted with the assistance of all available means," or "penetrating questioning."[40] This method of questioning became popular in Auschwitz. However, the device with the two tables, between which the iron bar kept sliding and finally fell to the floor together with the victim, was found to be too primitive. The prisoners working in the building workshops[41] were therefore instructed to make two wooden frames with a movable steel bar. Thus the torments could be increased because the tortured person was made to turn a complete circle.

Such were the methods used during the interrogations in the post-office hut. The Gestapo commission carried on their nefarious business for two or three weeks. It was a special action. Six hundred persons of both sexes, Poles and those who had signed the German nationality lists [*Volksdeutsche*],[42] were suddenly arrested and accused of "activities endangering the Reich," or of "political conspiracy against the Reich." As the court prison in Myslowitz had been closed due to typhus epidemics and overcrowding, the detainees were brought straight to Auschwitz.[43] The first floor of Block 2, which consisted of one large hall without any partition walls, was furnished with thin straw pallets and used to accommodate that crowd. It was thought undesirable that the Summary Court prisoners should come into contact with the camp inmates. For weeks all 600 people had to lie on their bellies in that large hall. They were obliged to eat without changing their position. Guards with machine-guns were instructed to shoot as soon as one of them dared to talk or straighten himself up. The sufferings they had already gone through and those that still awaited them, as well as the certain death which threatened so many of them instilled complete apathy in the majority of the victims. There were pregnant women among them. The guards fulfilled their duties most unwillingly. They were bored for one thing and besides, the first floor was full of creeping and jumping insects.

---

[40] *Eindringliche Befragung.*

[41] *Bauleitung.*

[42] Many Poles in Silesia were forced to sign the lists of *Volksdeutsche*, i.e. persons of German nationality.

[43] The event described by Broad occurred on February 12, 1943.

The day finally came when 210 of these prisoners were to appear before the Summary Court. As a result of preparatory investigations the rest were to remain in camp in protective custody. The candidates for the Summary Court trial were led to a room in Block 11. A large room opposite was made ready for the court. A long table with water glasses on it and a row of chairs behind it, with the chairman's seat for Mildner in the middle, was the main feature of the room. Himmler and Hitler graciously looked down from the walls. Through both barred windows, which were not boarded up (as was the case with the rest of the windows in the block), one had a direct view of the tall barbed-wire fences. A concrete wall kept the rest of the camp from view.

The light-blue Opel Admiral car finally drove up to Block 11 and Mildner got out. With his upraised arm he pompously greeted the respectfully standing SS-men, ascended the stone steps and entered the block. He also greeted Grabner and Aumeier, who were allowed to participate in the session. Kauz carried in the heavy dossiers. "*Geheime Staatspolizei Kattowitz*"[44] was the formidable title on their covers. Mildner took his seat. *Sturmbannführer* Dr. Eisenschmidt sat next to him. The rest of those present merrily exchanged greetings, talked of old times and also took their seats at the table. There was some shop talk, some boasting about the latest successes, some critical remarks as to the activities of absent colleagues; then everybody froze into an attitude of the utmost hardness and importance—Mildner had opened the proceedings. With a self-satisfied smile he congratulated the Summary Court on its two hundredth session. Then he signalled to the SS guard at the door to bring in the defendants.

Kauz called the first name. The SS guard repeated the name to the clerk who was standing in the other room with the defendants. From among the softly murmuring crowd of people who, after long unspeakable torments, were waiting for their death sentence, a weak voice called: "*Hier*"[45], and one of the sunken-eyed creatures came reeling forward. The clerk helped him to the door of the court room. The clerk was a prisoner himself and a similar fate might soon be in store for him. The hapless person had to stand near the door. Mildner read out the judge's summing up of the sentence: "As a result of investigations carried out by the State Police, the Pole . . . has been found guilty of acting against the laws of the German Reich by . . . ".

This was the usual beginning, and it ended with the sentence pronounced in a monotonous and unfeeling voice: "The Police Summary Court of the State Police in Kattowitz pronounces the death sentence."

With an expression on his face which brooked no criticism, the despot so brave in killing looked right and left, accepting the consenting nods of his associates as a matter of course. The sentenced man was not allowed to say a word. Each case took up to one minute at the most. Kauz often had a hard task to find the dossier among the heap quickly enough. He perspired when Mildner showed his impatience by a discontented glance or by drumming with his fingers on the table.

If the defendant, called to the court room, did not report immediately, the

---

[44] Secret State Police Kattowitz.

[45] *Hier*, i.e. "present."

other prisoners would impatiently repeat the name. They were no longer eager to delay their end by unnecessary minutes.

A youth of sixteen was led into the room. Unbearable hunger had driven him to steal some food from a shop, he therefore fell into the category of the "criminal" cases. After reading the death sentence, Mildner slowly put the paper on the table and directed his penetrating gaze at the pale poorly-clad boy standing there at the door. Slowly stressing every word he asked: "Have you a mother?" The boy lowered his eyes and replied in a quiet voice, almost smothered by tears, "Yes." "Are you afraid to die?" asked the relentless, bull-necked butcher, who seemed to derive a sadistic pleasure from the suffering of his victim. The youth was silent, but his body trembled slightly. "You shall be shot today," said Mildner, trying to give his voice a full, fateful significance. "You would be hanged anyway, some day. You will be dead in a hour!"

Mildner sometimes liked "to converse" in that way with the people he had sentenced to death. He could not hide the satisfaction he felt in having supreme power over the life or death of everyone. His sadistic tendencies were particularly blatant when he had to deal with women. He would tell them in the most drastic manner about their imminent deaths by shooting.

[SHAMBLES IN THE OLD CREMATORIUM]

The session was over in less than two hours: 206 persons out of the 210 had been sentenced to death, four were to be detained in the camp. Mildner was in a hurry to get to the place of execution. He would never miss an execution, not for anything in the world.

The condemned stood in the yard of Block 11, five persons in a line. That day the execution was to take place at the crematorium, instead of in front of the black wall, on account of the great number of the condemned. A covered van backed out from the opened gate. Lockets and other cherished mementos, thrown away by the condemned shortly before their death,[46] lay scattered on the ground, a symbol of their final farewell to the world. Nobody thought of resisting anymore. With the prospect of death before them, all were busy with thoughts about their past life and relatives that had to be left behind. The van made its journey several times. As many people as possible were crowded into it every time.

Mildner's big, blue car was already standing in front of the crematorium. The old Auschwitz crematorium stood at a distance of approximately 100 metres from the camp.[47] It was said to have originally been a storehouse for turnips.[48] The stone building was surrounded on three sides by earthen embankments on which grass, young trees and beautiful flowers were planted. A level concrete

---

[46] Hardly. They were rather snatched away from them.

[47] Broad is referring here to crematorium I in the base camp of Auschwitz.

[48] This hall was originally a vegetable store of the Polish Army, until September 1939. The camp authorities adapted the place to serve as a crematorium and gas chamber.

block served as its roof. The area in front of the crematorium was closed in by a high wall with two large gates, the entrance and the exit. Thus when wagons loaded with corpses, brought from the mortuary of Block 28,[49] arrived of an evening to be unloaded, the whole place was hidden from the eyes of unwanted onlookers. A stranger would not so easily have guessed that the rectangular mound planted with many-coloured flowers, was in reality the crematorium—unless he noticed the thick metal pipe bent at right angles, which projected from the roof and emitted a monotonous humming. But even then he would hardly know that this was the ventilation pipe, which made the air in the mortuary at least a little more bearable. The square chimney, which stood some metres away and was connected by underground flues with the four ovens, also had quite an ordinary appearance. But the smoke did not always rise above the chimney in transparent, bluish clouds. It was sometimes pressed down to the ground by the wind. And then one could notice the unmistakable, penetrating stench of burnt hair and burnt flesh, a stench that spread over many kilometres. When the ovens, in which four to six bodies could be burnt at the same time, were stoked up and dense, pitch-black smoke coiled upwards from the chimney, or when at night the tall flame issuing from the chimney was visible from afar, then there was no doubt as to the purpose of the mound. On the side farthest from the road one could notice gaps in the earthen embankment, where windows with iron bars provided the crematorium furnace with fresh air.

Weird noises were heard in that dark space. They were produced by the steel bars and shovels with which coke was shovelled into the ovens, and with which corpses were pushed into the flames. The interior of the crematorium consisted of the furnace, a hall, and a spacious mortuary in the roof of which, besides the ventilation pipe, six covered air-shafts were built. The condemned men and women stood in the yard before the crematorium. A wrought-iron lantern hanging above the entrance door gave a cosy impression, as if it hung over the door of a home. This was a sight full of irony, if one remembered that countless people had entered through that door without ever returning, and that day after day, whole wagon-loads of corpses were tugged in over its threshold.

The prisoners of the Summary Court were conducted into the hall in groups of forty. They had to undress there. An SS guard stood at the door to the mortuary, where the execution was to take place. He led in ten people at a time. The shots and the thudding of heads when they hit the cement floor were audible in the hall. One could witness nerve-racking scenes: mothers saying goodbye to their daughters; men, former officers judging by their military carriage, shaking hands with their fellows for the last time; some people saying their last prayers.

The mass murder, more vile than could be imagined, was meanwhile going on in the mortuary. Ten prisoners went naked into the mortuary. The walls were stained with blood, and in the background there lay the corpses of those already

---

[49] The mortuary where the corpses of prisoners—dead or murdered—were deposited, was located in the cellars of this block. Corpses of prisoners hanged or shot at executions were not kept in the mortuary.

shot. A wide stream of blood was flowing towards the drain in the middle of the hall. The victims were obliged to step quite close to the corpses and formed a line. Their feet were stained with blood; they stood in puddles of it. Some cried out when recognizing a near relative, the father perhaps, among those lying on the floor and still groaning.

The right-hand man of the camp leader, *SS-Hauptscharführer* Palitzsch, did the shooting. He killed one person after another with a practised shot in the back of the neck. The mortuary was getting more and more packed with corpses. Mildner, who was there together with his staff, watched, with cold eyes, the executioner at his work. The corpses lay all around him too.

The SS guard finally shouted from the hall that no one was left outside. Then Palitzsch, stepping over the corpses, shot those who were still moving or groaning. He put down his gun at last, turned to his master and stood at attention to signify that he had done his duty. Mildner looked at him with a significant, fiendish smile and then slowly raised his arm in the Nazi salute, remaining in that position for several seconds. Thus he acknowledged the services of his hangman. Mildner turned to go. Raising his arm again and again to salute the SS-men on his right and left, smiling jovially he reached the door, stepping over the corpses on his way out.

The clerks of Section II were then kept busy writing the records of the executions. Cause of death—several shots through the chest, of these one through the heart and two through the lungs . . . thus ran the records. It is better to be cautious, and even in such confidential papers it would never do to put down in writing that shooting in the back of the neck[50] was practised in Nazi Germany, a claim so successfully exploited by foreign propaganda.

Such was the end of those whom *SS-Obersturmbannführer* Dr. Mildner had sentenced to death. Many executions were, however, performed by hanging. In the yard of Block 11 there were 12 trap-door gallows.[51] They could be pushed into the ground, the holes were concealed with wooden covers. Just like exercise bars in a gymnasium. There was much inventiveness in Auschwitz, as far as killing people was concerned.

A public execution of thirteen Polish engineers took place one day.[52] They were hanged " in retaliation " for the escape attempt of a prisoner working in the building section.[53] At this execution, which was performed in front of the prisoners' kitchen in the presence of other prisoners, Aumeier behaved with the most repulsive brutality. An iron rail was placed on two posts. The ropes, with which the prisoners were to be hanged, proved to be too short. Quick death by breaking the neck was therefore impossible. The stools were removed from

---

50 *Genickschuss*.

51 Two transportable gallows and several posts were to be seen in the yard of Block 11. The posts were used when the punishment known as " hanging from the stake " was ordered.

52 Twelve prisoners were hanged during evening roll-call on July 19, 1943. They were: Zbigniew Foltański, Józef Gancarz, Mieczysław Kulikowski, Czesław Marcisz, Bugusław Ohrt, Leon Rajzer, Tadeusz Rapacz, Edmund Sikorski, Janusz Skrzetuski-Pogonowski, Stanisław Stawiński, Józef Wojtyga and Jerzy Woźniak.

53 This escape took place on May 20, 1943. Three prisoners from the surveyors' squad (*Vermessungskommando*) made their escape on that day. They were Stanisław Chybiński, Kazimierz Jarzębowski and Józef Rotter.

under the feet of the victims, and several minutes later their bodies were still writhing convulsively. Although Aumeier thought they could be "left struggling for a while yet," even he found this had lasted long enough. The execution squad got its order: "Cling to them!" The prisoners who were standing nearby secretly clenched their fists. The sight of the "retaliation measures" and of the martyrdom of innocent people brought tears of rage to their eyes.

After the executions in the crematorium or in Block 11, the dead were still not left alone. An SS doctor, usually *SS-Hauptsturmführer* Kitt or *SS-Obersturmführer* Dr. Weber, pounced upon the still warm corpses and cut pieces of flesh from the thighs or buttocks. They were used for growing bacteriological cultures in the Institute of Hygiene.[54] The Institute was located at some distance from the camp on the road leading to Rajsko, and *SS-Obersturmführer* Dr. Weber was its head. Weber was above all a bacteriologist. The only thing generally known about the Institute was that prisoners who were experts in chemistry and bacteriology were employed in its numerous laboratories. Block 10 of the base camp belonged to the Institute. Several hundred Jewish women were kept in Block 10 and served as experimental guinea-pigs. The block was completely isolated from the rest of the camp. Laboratories and wards with beds lodged on the ground floor. The first floor had no partition walls and was full of three-tiered bunks for those of the "experimental subjects" who were not bedridden. The prisoners who could walk were sometimes led for a walk in the camp, always under surveillance. The greatest care was taken not to let them come into touch with other prisoners; the secret goings-on in Block 10 had to be safeguarded as much as possible. Professor Clauberg and Lieutenant Dr. Schumann conducted research work in typhus, sterilization by radiation and in artificial insemination. They were helped by some Jewish prisoners, themselves scientists. The experiments in sterilization resulted in the loss of a great many lives. The attempts at artificial insemination involved exceedingly painful operations, and the "patients" were not anaesthetized. Not one of the SS doctors felt that the experiments in Block 10 were in fact bestially criminal. The experimental guinea-pigs were Jews, outlawed and with no right to live!

[REVOLT AT BUDY]

Budy was a poor village, some four kilometres from the Auschwitz concentration camp. It consisted only of a few wretched peasant huts. Most of these were not inhabited and had gone to ruin. Some of the Polish inhabitants had reported "of their own free will" for work in Germany, while others were detained in concentration camps, because they were supposed to have somehow sabotaged "the peaceful reconstruction of the East."[55]. A sub-camp belonging to Auschwitz was established there, to facilitate work in the fields which then

---

[54] The *Hygiene-Bakteriologische Untersuchungsstelle der Waffen-SS* at Rajsko.

[55] In actual fact Poles were simply deported from the areas adjacent to the camp. Some of them were sent to the so-called *Generalgouvernement* (Tarnów and Gorlice), others were taken to the Sudeten region, or to work inside the Third Reich.

formed part of the camp activity zone.[56] The school, situated away from the road, and a large hut served as living quarters for the prisoners. The fact that at night the single barbed-wire fence was neither charged with electricity nor brightly illuminated suggested that the prisoners there were less dangerous.

It was a camp for women. The ground floor of the school was occupied by the block and camp seniors, both of whom were citizens of the Reich and former prostitutes. There was also a kitchen and an infirmary. Several German women prisoners with special duties in the camp, and a considerable number of Jewish women, slept in the attic which had two windows.

But the majority of women prisoners lived in the wooden building. Among them were Jewish, Ukrainian and Polish women, 300 to 400 altogether. The landscape around the camp, with its meadows, fields, woods and lakes, was so lovely that it was difficult to imagine that starvation, brutality and despair were reigning in the place. But these unavoidable by-products of all concentration camps had entered this idyllic spot of the earth with the arrival of the sub-camp.

Grabner's deputy, Criminal Office assistant Wesnitza, a criminal investigator and two clerks were told one morning in the autumn of 1942 to pack quickly their typewriters and writing materials and get into the roomy car, waiting in front of the commandant's office. Nobody knew what had happened, but judging by Grabner's expression the event must have been out of the ordinary. The car quickly drove in the direction of Budy. A few metres from the camp it was stopped by a sentry. But on recognizing Grabner the guard apologized and explained that according to the commandant's orders he was not to let any unauthorized persons pass through. The car proceeded to the camp where Grabner made everybody get out. During the drive he had already hinted that a revolt had broken out at Budy.[57]

It was with a feeling of curiosity that the employees of Section II passed the gate of the camp. The guard saluted them. They heard a peculiar buzzing and humming in the air. Then they saw a sight so horrible that some minutes passed before they could take it in properly. The square behind and beside the school was covered with dozens of female corpses, mutilated and bloody, lying in complete chaos. All were covered only with threadbare prisoners' undergarments. Half-dead women were writhing among the corpses. Their groaning mixed with the buzzing of immense swarms of flies, which circled round the sticky pools of blood and the smashed skulls. That was the origin of the strange humming sound which the newcomers had found so peculiar on their arrival. Some corpses hung in a twisted position on the barbed-wire fence. Others had evidently been thrown out from an attic window which was still open.

Grabner gave the order to find some women among those lying on the

---

[56] At first prisoners' squads worked on the abandoned farms, later one of the Auschwitz sub-camps was organized here.

[57] This incident probably occurred in the first days of October 1942. During his interrogation Höss gave the following account of it: "The action took place late at night; after being informed of it I immediately went to the camp and found that the Frenchwomen had been killed with poles and axes; the heads of some of them had been completely severed and some had died after being thrown out of the windows on the first floor." (Trial of Rudolf Höss, former commandant of the Auschwitz concentration camp, heard by the Supreme National Tribunal in Warsaw, vol. 21, c. 43.)

ground who could be interrogated, to obtain their evidence as to what had happened. Wesnitza stepped around the corpses and tried in vain to find among the victims somebody who could talk. But he failed and so took as witnesses some of the less mutilated prisoners, who were just washing their wounds at the well. Their evidence was as follows:

The SS-men, who acted as guards in the camp, used to get the German women prisoners to maltreat the Jewish women. If the former did not comply, they were threatened with being driven through the chain of sentries and "shot while escaping." The bestial SS-men regarded it as a pleasant pastime to look at the sufferings of the maltreated Jewesses. The result of this unbearable situation was that the German women always were in a state of fear lest the tormented Jewish women take vengeance on them for their terrible lot. But the Jewish women, who mostly belonged to intellectual circles (e.g. some had formerly been students of the Sorbonne, or artists) never even thought of stooping to the level of the vulgar German prostitutes and of planning revenge, though it would have been understandable if they had done.

The evening before, one Jewess was returning from the lavatory and was on her way upstairs to the sleeping quarters. A German woman thought she held a stone in her hand, but that, of course, was only her hysterical imagination. At the gate below, a sentry was standing guard. As everybody knew, he was that woman's lover. Leaning out from the window, she cried for help, saying she had been hit by the Jewess. All guards on duty immediately ran upstairs and together with the depraved German women prisoners they began to hit the Jewish women indiscriminately. They threw some women down the winding stairs, so that they fell in a heap, one upon the other. Some were thrown out of the window and fell to their deaths. The guards also drove the Jewish women from the barracks into the yard. The German woman, who had instigated the butchering, stayed behind in the bedroom with her lover. This may have been what she originally intended. The "rebellion" was meanwhile mastered with bludgeons, gun butts and shots. Even an axe had been used as a weapon by one of the female capos. In their mortal fear a few Jewish women tried to creep under the wire fence in order to escape the butchering. They got stuck and were soon killed. Even when all the women lay on the ground, the fiends, drunk with blood, kept hitting the helpless victims again and again. They wanted, above all, to kill everybody, so as to destroy all witnesses of their atrocities.

At about five a.m. the commandant was notified of the so-called rebellion, which had been successfully overcome. He drove to Budy and inspected the traces of the bloody orgy. A few wounded women, who had hidden among the corpses, then rose and thought they were saved. But *SS-Sturmbannführer* Höss soon left the camp, after a short inspection. As soon as he left, the wounded women were shot.

The SS investigators and SS medical orderlies came later next morning "to give medical help to the injured." Some less seriously wounded women had managed to hide at the beginning of the tragic incident and not leave their hiding places so soon. They were interrogated and then "looked after" by the orderlies. The criminal investigators did a lot of photographing of the scene. Only one copy of each photograph was later developed in the dark room, under strict supervision. The plates had to be destroyed in the presence of the commandant and the photos were put at his disposal. In an empty room the orderlies did their work. One after another the victims with some traces of life still left in them were pulled into the room. A practised hold was applied and the syringe was inserted under the left breast. The patient collapsed and died some seconds after this "treatment." Two cubic centimetres of phenol,[58] a cheap disinfectant, were injected into the heart.

Outside, on the stairs, cowered an elderly woman. She had been in concentration camps for years owing to her religious convictions. She was to be re-educated according to the Nazi dogmas and made to reject "the false teaching of the International Bible Students' Association." She was unable to forget what she had witnessed. The rest of the women looked on with terror as the half-dead as well as the living were pushed inside, while corpses were carried out by another door and thrown on a wooden cart.

Six German women prisoners, who to a greater or lesser degree had participated in the atrocities, were taken to Block 11 together with the "Axe Queen" Elfriede Schmidt, the favourite of the SS butchers. After the interrogation and confession of their guilt they lay, silenced forever, in the mortuary of the crematorium. Only small, barely visible red dots under their left breasts betrayed the cause of their deaths. Their parents, as usual, received properly worded letters of condolence from the commandant. They were informed that their daughters had been on such and such day admitted to the prisoners' hospital, suffering from such and such a disease to which they succumbed "in spite of the best medical care and treatment." An unspeakably cynical note sounded in the close of these conventionally worded letters, namely that the deceased had not voiced any last wish and the commandant was sincerely with them "in their painful loss." Even an urn with the ashes would be sent on request. Those who were acquainted with the cremation methods in Auschwitz, where several corpses were simultaneously cremated in one oven, could not but shudder at this farce. The dossiers of the six murdered women were closed with the medical report on the course of their "disease," and the circumstances which had led to the demise. The SS camp doctor[59] signed the reports. They were written by a medically trained prisoner, whose job in the hospital was to concoct such reports for each prisoner who had died in camp, whatever the cause. All the countless victims—those with "penal report 2" who had been shot in Block 11, the sick who had had phenol injected into their hearts, the victims of starvation or of tortures—all had regrettably lost their lives, according to the Deaths' Book, by succumbing to some ordinary disease; death was inevitable, since the disease had taken a turn for the worse.

By the deaths of the six special prisoners the crimes at Budy were sufficiently expiated, in the opinion of the camp authorities. The guard in question got a reprimand, and in future guards were not allowed to enter the camp. The number of prisoners rose again to normal; after all, Jews were arriving daily!

---

[58] See Kremer's Diary, p. 169, entry dated October 24, 1942.

[59] The *Lagerartzt*, a member of the SS, was the senior physician over all the SS doctors in the camp.

[MASSACRE OF SOVIET P.O.W.'S]

Some 12,000 Russian prisoners of war were brought to Auschwitz in the winter of 1941—1942.[60] Barely six months later only 150 were still alive, according to the hard facts as supplied by the registration office. The SS-men and particularly the camp authorities had somehow got to trust the remaining 150, and they were detailed to work squads, where survival was possible. They were trusted to such an extent that in time they used to be assigned to the search *kommandos*,[61] when a prisoner escaped from the area of the large sentry chain. Nobody seemed to notice that they somehow always failed to locate the fugitives, who then managed to disappear under cover of darkness. It was a shock to the camp authorities to learn that 90 Russians had broken through the large sentry chain while looking for fugitives, and had escaped themselves.[62] A search *kommando* with all available soldiers immediately set to work with tracker dogs, but without any results worth mentioning.

How few, however, were those who had managed to escape alive from the Birkenau camp, as compared to the thousands who had starved to death or had been murdered.

The Russians were, however, just as unimportant as the Jews. Besides those 12,000, other Russians and Ukrainians were often sent to the camp, either by commandants of various p.o.w. camps, who thought them politically too active and refractory, or from military formations which consisted of Russians fighting side by side with the Germans. Those Russians were sent to Auschwitz because of "political unreliability" or because they were suspected of having formerly been Soviet commissars. Before they could fully understand where they had come, they were, as a rule, shot in Block 11.

So also were those Russians, Cossacks and Caucasians, who served in formations organized by the SD for political reasons behind the Russian front-lines. Any one of them, if he made an unfavourable impression on the Germans, quickly landed in Auschwitz. They often drove into the camp by car, without having the slightest suspicion. They got their greatest shock when the driver, a German SD-man, told them they had to remain there, while he drove away. Many Russians from the so-called "Zeppelin" *Kommando*,[63] formed close to Auschwitz as an intelligence service unit by an *SS-Untersturmführer*, met with a similar fate. Nobody knew anything of their whereabouts, least of all their former comrades.

Russian forced labourers often left their places of work, driven eastwards by hunger or homesickness. If recaptured, they were sent to protective custody in Auschwitz.[64] The cause of their detention was concisely called "breach of

[60] The first mass transport of Soviet prisoners of war came to *KL Auschwitz* on October 7, 1941. See also p. 48, note 57.

[61] *Suchkommando*.

[62] This occurred on November 6, 1942. See p. 48, note 58.

[63] The full name was *Sonderkommando Zeppelin*.

[64] I.e. to the camp.

contract," and a red stamp was affixed across the first page of their dossiers, with the words, "*Vereinfachtes Verfahren! Sowjetische Arbeitskraft!*"[65]. That meant that their release was not essential; nor was it important whether they were guilty or not. They were only "Soviet workers." There were plenty of them and it did not matter in the least if a few thousands of them perished.

The Russians, brought to Auschwitz in 1941—1942, came to the sub-camp Birkenau, which was then in the process of construction.[66] Their misery here was incredible. People lost their reason owing to starvation. They would greedily hurl themselves on any kind of food. Whole wagon-loads of corpses drove to the Auschwitz crematorium every evening. Half-dead men, unable to bear their torments any longer, crept of their own free will into the wagons and were bestially murdered there.

One Russian lay one day on the heap of corpses in the open wagon. He was only just alive. His head was helplessly dangling over one of the side bars of the wagon. An SS-man seized a bludgeon and hit the dangling head with all his strength. The Russian was thrown back for a moment, but he soon fell forward, his head dangling again, this time below the bar. Another blow sent the head of the man, who was dead by then, over the bar again. The SS-man seemed to think it a huge joke. Although the unhappy prisoner was no longer alive, the SS-man continued to hit the head till it became a formless, bloody pulp.

Another SS-man enjoyed stepping on the bodies of the men dying on the ground, and crushing their throats or necks with the butt of his gun.

The camp authorities finally decided to put an end to the Russians' plight, using their own methods. Thousands of p.o.w.'s were shot in a wood near Birkenau and were buried in large collective graves, one layer of corpses lying on another. The graves were some 50 to 60 metres long, 4 metres deep and their width was probably 4 metres too. The camp authorities had thus solved the Russian problem to their utmost satisfaction!

But then came the time when Katyń hit the headlines in all German newspapers. The authorities were unpleasantly reminded of the mass graves in their own camp. At the same time there were complaints from the fisheries that fish had perished in the large lakes around Birkenau, e.g. near Harmense. Experts maintained that this was due to cadaveric poison in the ground waters. That was not all. The sun was very hot that summer in Birkenau, so the bodies, which had only partially decomposed, began to fester and dark red matter seeped out from gaps in the ground. The resulting stench was indescribable.

Something had to be done about it and quickly. In view of Katyń the presence of mass graves was most compromising, particularly mass graves in which corpses evidently could not decompose properly, but came into sight.

SS-Hauptscharführer (later *Obersturmführer*) Franz Hössler, who was arrested in Belsen in 1945, was ordered to open the graves and burn the corpses,

---

[65] Simplified procedure. Soviet worker.

[66] The camp at Birkenau was constructed at the end of 1941 and the beginning of 1942. Soviet prisoners of war, who worked there, perished in great numbers due to starvation and hard labour. See Autobiography of Rudolf Höss, p. 47.

maintaining the utmost secrecy about his job. He found 20 to 30 particularly reliable SS-men for the job and made them sign a pledge, that in the event of their betraying the trust put in them, or mentioning in any way the nature of their task, they would be put to death. These SS-men were, of course, not expected to put their hands to the shovels and themselves remove the traces of the atrocities. There were plenty of prisoners to do this. Hössler's special squad[67] consisted of several hundred Jews from all the countries occupied by the Germans. They worked in two shifts. Many prisoners refused to do the work and were liquidated with pistol shots. The SS-men, who supervised the opening of the mass graves and the cremation of the decomposing but still quite well preserved corpses, got special food rations from the SS mess. Every evening they received 1 litre of milk, sausage, cigarettes and, of course, vodka.

The prisoners working in the special squad lived in the Birkenau camp, in barracks which were separated from the other buildings by wooden board fencing. In the countryside not far from the camp (an area, by the way, which was less marshy and very lovely), one could, for long weeks, see dense whitish smoke clouds rising towards the sky from several spots. Nobody was allowed to come near these places without a special pass, but the stench betrayed the truth about which people around Birkenau began to whisper.

Severe punishment awaited the SS-men if they let any prisoner from that bloody squad run away. At night the wind drove the unbearable stinking smoke low to the ground. No guard could bear to stay there. This was exploited by two prisoners who knew they had nothing to lose by escaping—even if they gained nothing—and so they made their get-away under cover of the smoke and ran into a nearby wood. They were missed only two hours later, at roll-call. Several prisoners were questioned and a large scale search was conducted, but in vain. The fugitives were not found. The commandant was furious. How would they inform the *Reichsführer*[68] of the fact? What would happen if the fugitives, one a French and the other a Greek Jew, managed to get abroad or started to tell the German population about the happenings at Birkenau? It was unthinkable! The guards responsible for the get-away were sent for many months to Matzkau, a penal camp for the SS near Gdańsk.

Another incident occurred when a guard became sleepy, due to the heat and the stifling smell of the smoke. Two prisoners then ran away in different directions. The guard, *SS-Schütze* Strutz was so surprised that he could not, at first, make up his mind whom to shoot at. Before he came to a decision, both fugitives had disappeared into the wood. The guard would certainly have gone to Matzkau for a long stretch too; he sat, frightened, in Section II being interrogated, when an incoming report saved him. The two poor devils had lost their way in the wood, they had run in circles and finally fallen asleep, exhausted and hungry, in a barn near Auschwitz where they were found and recaptured. A thorough interrogation followed. Its object was, above all, to

[67] *Sonderkommando*. The *Sonderkommando* at the time numbered about 400 prisoners. When the action of cremating corpses came to an end, they were all gassed on December 3, 1942, in crematorium I at *KL Auschwitz*.

[68] Himmler.

obtain information whether other prisoners of the special squad had also planned to escape. The questioning disclosed a veritable abyss of human despair. The fugitives were brought to Block 11 from which there was no return for them. The *SS-Schütze* Strutz felt relieved when he took up his duties again with the determination to be more careful in the future.

SS-Hauptscharführer Moll was a zealous helper of Hössler in the work at Birkenau. Moll and Palitzsch were perhaps the greatest butchers of the last war. The career of Palitzsch ended in Matzkau. The mass murders which he, of course, only committed to serve Great Germany, and because of his deep ideological and racial convictions, did not prevent him from entering into close relations with enemies of the state, including Jews, provided they were female, young and pretty. He used to threaten them afterwards that he would finish them off, should they "squeal," but that did not avert his fate. His love affair with a Jewess remained, luckily for him, undiscovered. But his affair with the Latvian prisoner Vera Lukans, as well as his custom (widely popular with SS-men in Auschwitz) of keeping for himself valuable objects, taken from prisoners on their arrival in camp, in order to provide for his old age, resulted in his being sentenced to several terms in prison.

SS-Hauptscharführer Moll received the Cross of War Merit, First Class, for his meritorious activities in Birkenau. Hössler was the proud owner of the same decoration: KVK.[69] After the escapes of the special squad prisoners, Grabner and the commandant seriously considered whether they should not let them all have "the special treatment"[70], that being the official term for murder. But at that moment they thought it unnecessary; the special squad did after all work well. Besides, they were dying off due to cadaveric poisoning, and then new prisoners, Jews exclusively, would replace them. After several weeks of work all traces of the butchering of Russians in Birkenau were finally obliterated.[71]

But the special squad was not allowed to rest.[72]

In Block 11 there were cells with one tiny window, through which one could not look outside, as the windows lay below ground level; still, some air was available thanks to them. But there were also windowless dark cells. A narrow vent, ending in the mysterious iron baskets affixed to the outer wall, allowed so little air that breathing was very difficult. One day forty Russians suffocated in such a cell. They were forcibly crowded into the cell and literally could not move there at all.[73]

Apart from those dark cells, which at any rate measured eight square metres in area, the devices for torturing men, which existed in that building, were completed by four standing cells. The dark cells were little more than half a square metre in area, and many prisoners were doomed to spend there,

---

[69] *Kriegsverdienstkreuz*—Cross of War Merit.

[70] *Sonderbehandlung*—cryptonym denoting that the prisoner was to die in the gas chamber.

[71] This *Sonderkommando*, which was employed in removing and burning corpses from the mass graves, was then liquidated itself.

[72] Broad means here the new *Sonderkommando* organized in December 1942.

[73] The date of the incident described by Broad is not known. We do, however, know that in March 1942, 39 prisoners were put into cell 20 in the cellars of Block 11, and that 24 out of that number died.

naturally without a single ray of light, terrible hours or even weeks. It was out of the question to sit down. The prisoners cowered in the darkness. When the cold in winter was severe, it was impossible to get warm by moving about, which made a stay in the "standing bunker"[74] particularly distressing. Prisoners, who were to be "made ripe" for interrogation, were consigned to standing bunkers. Together with the dark cells, these also served as punishments. Mediaeval means to torture were often used to extract confessions. In the garret of the terrible Block 11, victims used to be hung by their wrists, which were tied behind their backs. Their feet were also bound by rope so that the body, when hanging by the arms and twisted backwards, could be racked. But those who were thus tortured at "the stake" usually fainted after a quarter of an hour, and therefore after the introduction of the "swings" the latter became the only means of extracting confessions.

[GAS]

One day corpses of Russian p.o.w.'s were dragged out of a dark cell. As they lay in the yard, they looked strangely bloated and had a bluish tinge, though they were relatively fresh. Several older prisoners who had been through World War I remembered seeing corpses like that. Suddenly they understood . . . gas!

The first attempt at the greatest crime, which Hitler and his helpers planned and committed in a frightening way, never to be expiated, was successful.[75] The greatest tragedy could then begin, a tragedy to which millions of happy people, innocently enjoying their lives, finally succumbed.

From the first company of the *SS-Totenkopfsturmbannes*, stationed in the Auschwitz concentration camp, *SS-Hauptscharführer* Vaupel selected six particularly trustworthy men. Among them were those who had been members of the black General SS for years. They had to report to *SS-Hauptscharführer* Hössler. After their arrival Hössler cautioned them to preserve the utmost secrecy as to what they would see in the next few minutes. Otherwise death would be their lot.

The task of the six men was to keep all roads and streets completely closed around an area near the Auschwitz crematorium. Nobody should be allowed to pass there, regardless of rank. The offices in the building from which the crematorium was visible were evacuated. No inmate of the SS garrison hospital was allowed to come near the windows of the first floor which looked onto the roof of the nearby crematorium and the yard of that gloomy place.

Everything was made ready and Hössler himself made sure that no uncalled-for persons would enter the closed area. Then a sad procession walked along the streets of the camp. It had started at the railway siding, located between the

---

[74] *Stehbunker*.

[75] Broad is referring here to the first attempt to use Cyclon B, fully reported by Höss. See pp. 70—71.

SS-Obersturmbannführer Rudolf Höss (right) with *Reichsführer* SS Heinrich Himmler during one of the latter's visits to *KL Auschwitz*. Photo taken by an SS-man, year unknown

Rudolf Höss at the moment of his extradition to Polish authorities. Photo taken in 1946

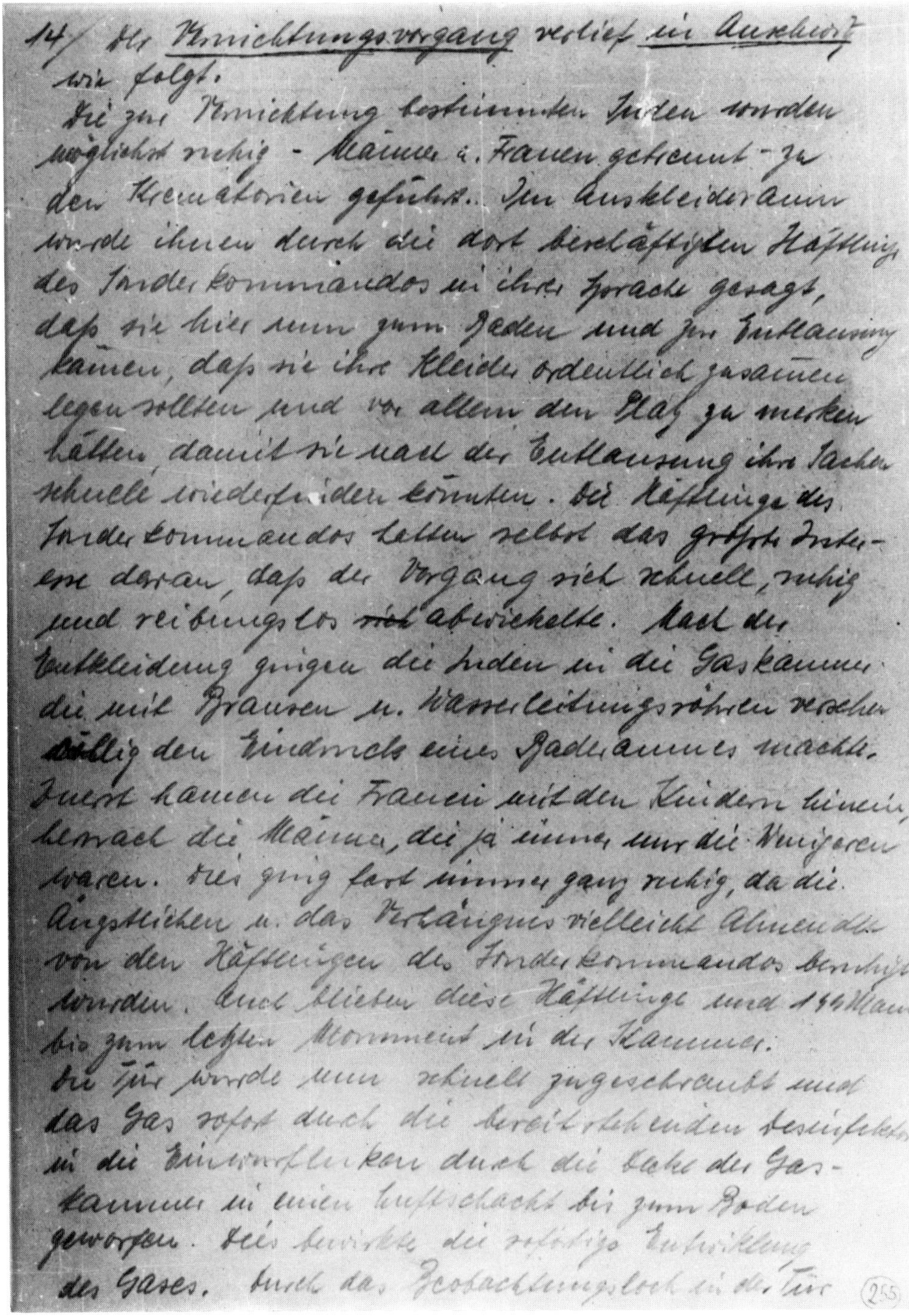

14/ Der Vernichtungsvorgang verlief in Auschwitz
wie folgt.
Die zur Vernichtung bestimmten Juden wurden
möglichst ruhig – Männer u. Frauen getrennt – zu
den Krematorien geführt. Im Auskleideraum
wurde ihnen durch die dort beschäftigten Häftlinge
des Sonderkommandos in ihrer Sprache gesagt,
daß sie hier nun zum Baden und zur Entlausung
kämen, daß sie ihre Kleider ordentlich zusammen
legen sollten und vor allem den Platz zu merken
hätten, damit sie nach der Entlausung ihre Sachen
schnell wiederfinden könnten. Die Häftlinge des
Sonderkommandos hatten selbst das größte Inter-
esse daran, daß der Vorgang sich schnell, ruhig
und reibungslos ~~sich~~ abwickelte. Nach der
Entkleidung gingen die Juden in die Gaskammer,
die mit Brausen u. Wasserleitungsröhren versehen
völlig den Eindruck eines Baderaumes machte.
Zuerst kamen die Frauen mit den Kindern hinein,
hernach die Männer, die ja immer nur die Wenigeren
waren. Dies ging fast immer ganz ruhig, da die
Ängstlichen u. das Verhängnis vielleicht Ahnenden
von den Häftlingen des Sonderkommandos beruhigt
wurden. Auch blieben diese Häftlinge und ein SS-Mann
bis zum letzten Moment in der Kammer.
Die Tür wurde nun schnell zugeschraubt und
das Gas sofort durch die bereitstehenden Desinfektoren
in die Einwurfluken durch die Decke der Gas-
kammer in einen Luftschacht bis zum Boden
geworfen. Dies bewirkte die sofortige Entwicklung
des Gases. Durch das Beobachtungsloch in der Tür

(255)

Pages from Rudolf Höss's manuscript with a description of the mass extermination of Jews at *KL Auschwitz*

konnte man sehen, daß die dem Einwurfschacht am nächsten Stehenden sofort tot umfielen. Man kann sagen, daß ungefähr 1/3 sofort tot war. Die anderen fingen an zu taumeln, zu schreien und nach Luft zu ringen. Das Schreien ging aber bald in ein Röcheln über und in wenigen Minuten lagen alle. Nach spätestens 20 Minuten regte sich keiner mehr. Je nach Witterung, feucht oder trocken, kalt oder warm, weiter je nach Beschaffenheit des Gases – das nicht immer gleich war – nach Zusammensetzung des Transportes, viel Gesunde, Alte oder Kranke, Kinder, dauerte die Wirkung des Gases 5–10 Minuten. Die Bewußtlosigkeit trat schon nach wenigen Minuten ein, je nach Entfernung von dem Einwurfschacht. Schreiende, Ältere, Kranke, Schwächliche und Kinder fielen schneller als die Gesunden u. Jüngeren.

Eine halbe Stunde nach dem Einwurf des Gases wurde die Tür geöffnet und die Entlüftungsanlage eingeschaltet. Es wurde sofort mit dem Herausziehen der Leichen begonnen. Eine körperliche Veränderung konnte man nicht feststellen, weder Verkrampfung noch Verfärbung, erst nach längerem Liegen, also nach mehreren Stunden zeigten sich an den Liegestellen die üblichen Totenflecken. Auch waren Verunreinigungen durch Kot selten. Verletzungen irgendwelcher Art wurden nicht festgestellt. Die Gesichter zeigten keinerlei Verzerrung.

Den Leichen wurden nun durch das Sonderkommando die Goldzähne entfernt und den Frauen die Haare abgeschnitten.

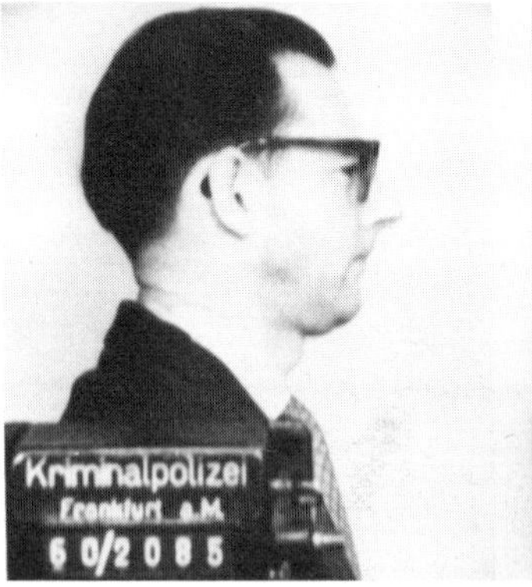

SS-Unterscharführer Pery Broad, an employee of the Political Section in the camp

SS-Oberscharführer Josef Klehr, an SS sanitary orderly

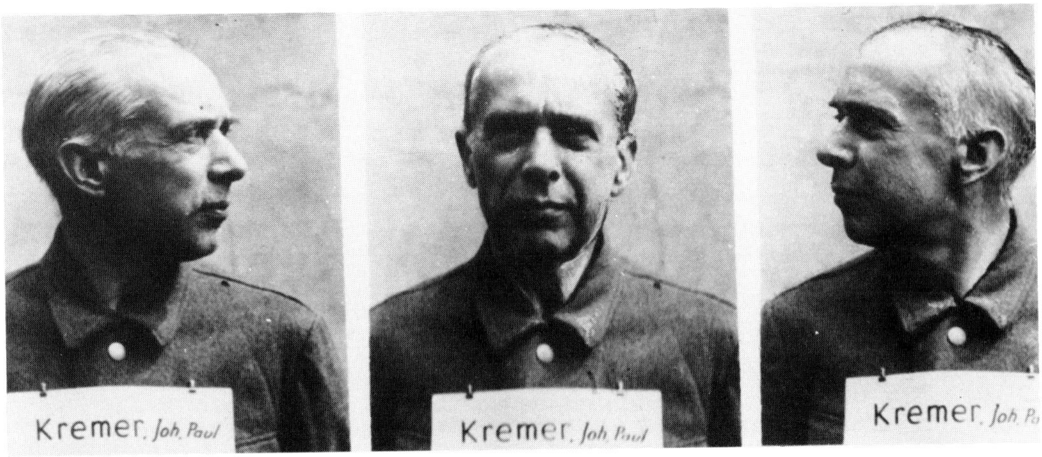

SS-Obersturmführer Johann Paul Kremer, an SS camp physician

One of the notebooks used by Kremer to write his diary

One page of Kremer's diary with a list of documents during his service at *KL Auschwitz* and description of a *Sonderaktion* (special action) in which he took part →

Herrn aus Breslau sei, mit dem ich eine ganz unglaubliche Ähnlichkeit habe. Er sei mit diesem Herrn im 1. Weltkriege im Felde zusammen gewesen. Wie viele Doppelgänger habe ich eigentlich in der Welt?! Abends bei einer Sonderaktion zugegen (4. Mal).

Morgens bei einer Sonderaktion zugegen (5. Mal). 10. September 1942

Heute Obersturmbannführer Lolling im Lager, bei dessen Vorstellung ich erst erfuhr, dass ich Hauptsturmführer Kitt vertrete, der jetzt zur Erholung auf dem Obersalzberg sich befindet. 11. September 1942

Zum 2. Male die Auschwitzer Krankheit. Temperatur 37,8. Heute die 3. und damit letzte Spritze gegen Fleckfieber erhalten. 14. September 1942.

In Berlin bei der Kleiderkasse Allwettermantel bestellt nach Schneidermaßen: Bis Taille 48, Ganze Länge 133, Halber Rücken 22, Bis Ellenbogen 51, Ganze Ärmellänge 81, Oberweite 104, Taillenweite 100, Gesäß 124. Uniformbezugschein dafür beigegeben, d.h. für einen Uniform-Wetterschutzmantel. Heute mit Dr. Meyer das Frauenlager Birkenau besucht. 17. September 1942

Heute Sonntagnachmittag von 3–6 Uhr Konzert der Häftlingskapelle in herrlichem Sonnenschein angehört: Kapellmeister Dirigent der Warschauer Staatsoper. 80 Musiker. Mittags gab's Schweinebraten, abends gebackene Schleie. 20. September 1942.

Wegen Otto an das Polizeipräsidium Köln (Abt. Kriminalpolizei) geschrieben. Abends Entenklein. Dr. Meyer erzählt mir von einer Vererbung eines Traumas (Nase) in der Familie seines Schwiegervaters. 21. September 1942

Heute Nacht bei der 6. und 7. Sonderaktion. Morgens ist Obergruppenführer Pohl mit Gefolge im Haus der Waffen-SS eingetroffen. Vor der Tür steht ein Posten, welcher als erster seinen Präsentiergriff vor mir macht. Abends 23. September 1942

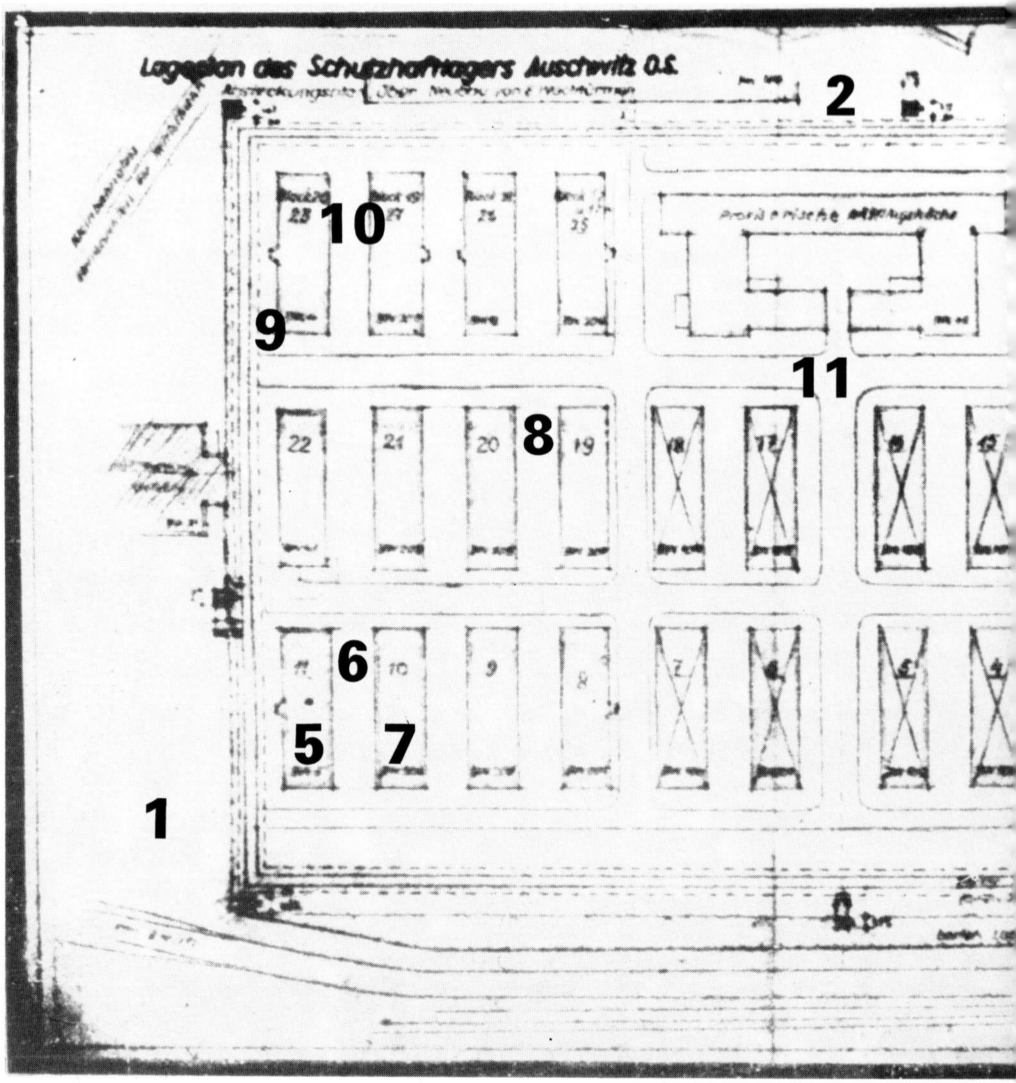

INSTALLATIONS AND SITES OF MASS EXTERMINATION AT *KL AUSCHWITZ (STAMMLAGER)*

1. Gravel pits — *Kiesgrube* — where executions by shooting were held
2. Gravel pits
3. Gravel pits
4. Crematorium I
5. Block 11 („Block of Death")
6. Yard of Block 11
7. Experimenting station in Block 10
8. Place where prisoners were killed with phenol injections through the heart
9. Place where prisoners were killed with phenol injections through the heart
10. Mortuary in the cellars of Block 28
11. Collective gallows

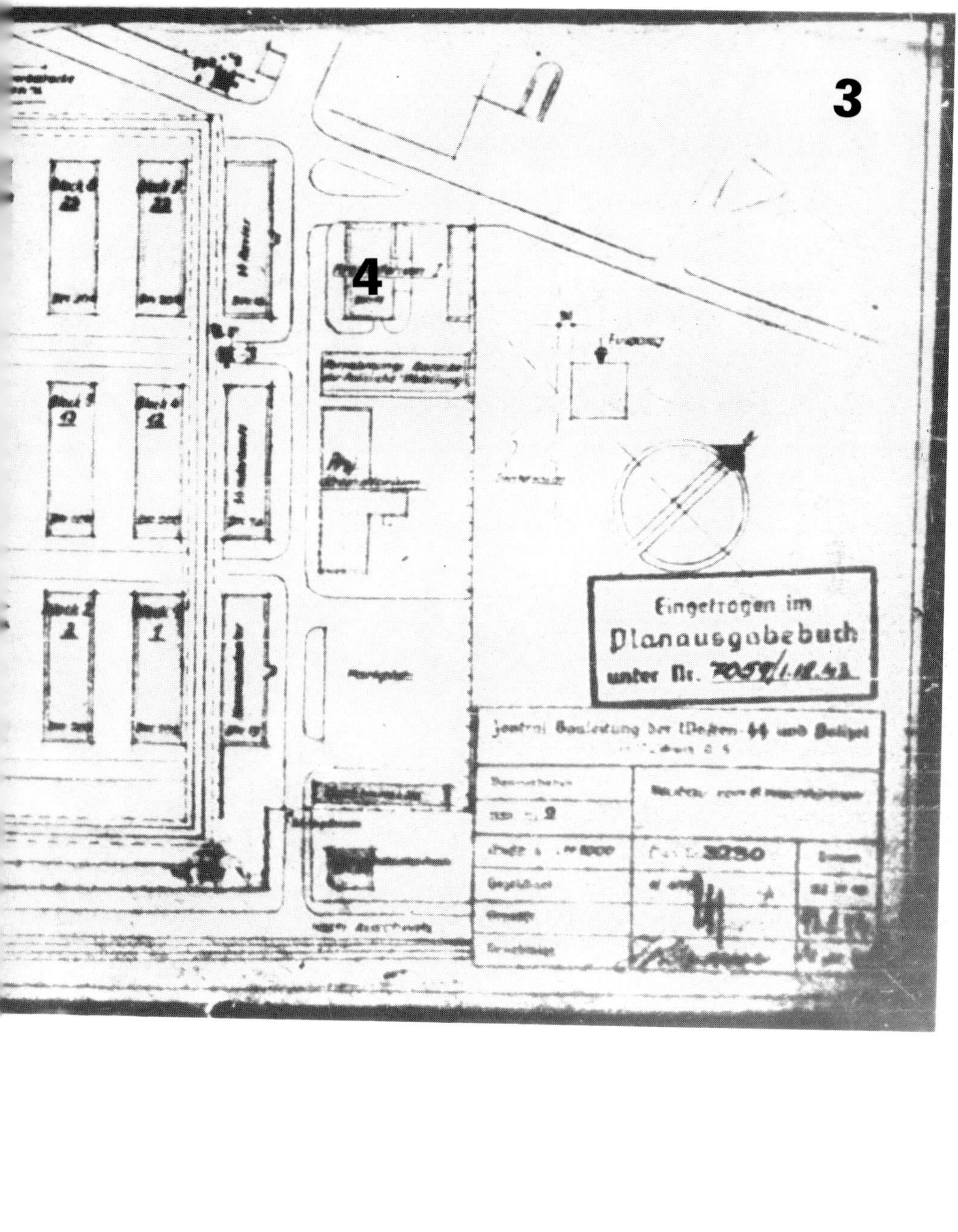
3
4
Eingetragen im
Planausgabebuch

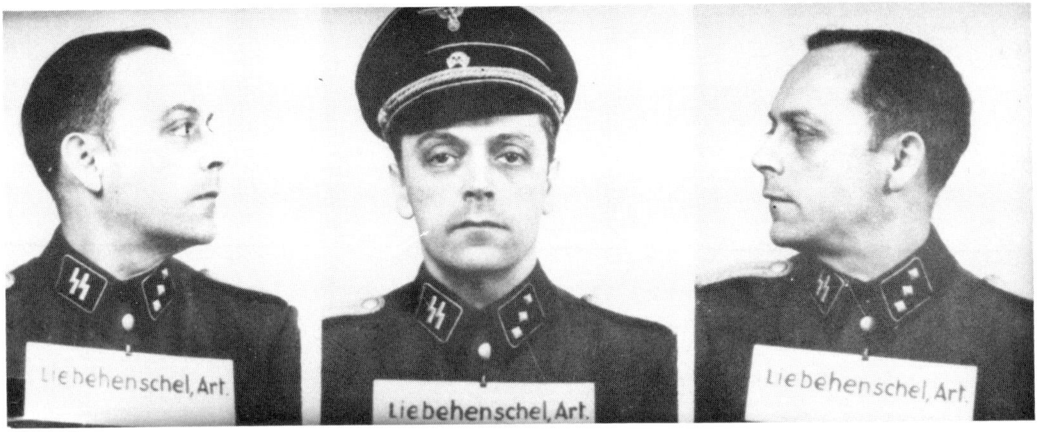

SS-Obersturmbannführer Arthur Liebehenschel, the second commandant of *KL Auschwitz*

SS-Hauptsturmführer Hans Aumeier, leader of the base camp *KL Auschwitz I*

SS-Sturmbannführer Richard Baer, the third and last commandant of *KL Auschwitz*

SS-Hauptscharführer Gerhard Palitzsch, *Rapportführer* in the base camp, notorious for his cruelty

Members of the Auschwitz SS garrison in the dock in Cracow. Photo taken in 1947

Part of the dock in the trial of members of the SS garrison at Auschwitz-Birkenau before the Supreme National Tribunal in Cracow. Sitting in the front row from the left: Arthur Liebehenschel, Marie Mandel and Hans Aumeier. Photo taken in 1947

Auschwitz. SS-men from the garrison of *KL Auschwitz*

Auschwitz. Entrance gate to *KL Auschwitz* with the inscription *Arbeit macht frei* (Work gives freedom) over the gate. Photo taken by Stanisław Łuczko after the liberation of the camp in 1945

Auschwitz. The base camp *KL Auschwitz I*. Photo taken by Henryk Makarewicz after the liberation of the camp in 1945

Auschwitz. *SS-Oberscharführer* Ludwig Plagge, *Rapportführer* (first from the roght) and Rudolf Höss (in the centre), probably during a visit of *Gauleiter* Bracht. Photo taken by an ss-man, year unknown

Rudolf Höss (first from the right) during a visit of *Reichsführer SS* Heinrich Himmler (first from the left) and other high SS officials from Berlin at *KL Auschwitz*. Photo taken by an SS-man, year unknown

Monowitz near Auschwitz. *Reichsführer SS* Heinrich Himmler (first from the left in the first row), engineer Faust (second from the left, wearing civilian clothes) and Rudolf Höss (in the foreground) inspecting the construction of IG-Farbenindustrie buildings. Photo taken by an SS-man in 1942

Birkenau. Camp sector B II of *KL Auschwitz II — Birkenau* with wooden barracks. Photos taken by an SS-man in 1943—44

Birkenau. Interior of a barrack. Photo taken after the liberation of the camp in 1945

Birkenau. Prisoners' latrine. Photo taken after the liberation of the camp in 1945

Monowitz near Auschwitz. View of the Buna-Werke plant which used cheap prisoner labour. Still from *The Chronicle of the Liberation of the Camp* shot by Red Army cameramen in 1945

Rajsko near Auschwitz. Prisoners employed at the construction of a sub-camp where rubber-yielding plants were experimentally grown. Photo taken by an SS-man, year unknown

Auschwitz. Distribution of meals. Photo taken an SS-man, year unknown

Auschwitz. Laying the foundations of an hospital. Photo taken by an SS-man, ye unknown

Birkenau. Prisoners at earthworks. Photos taken by SS-man Kamann in 1942 or 1943

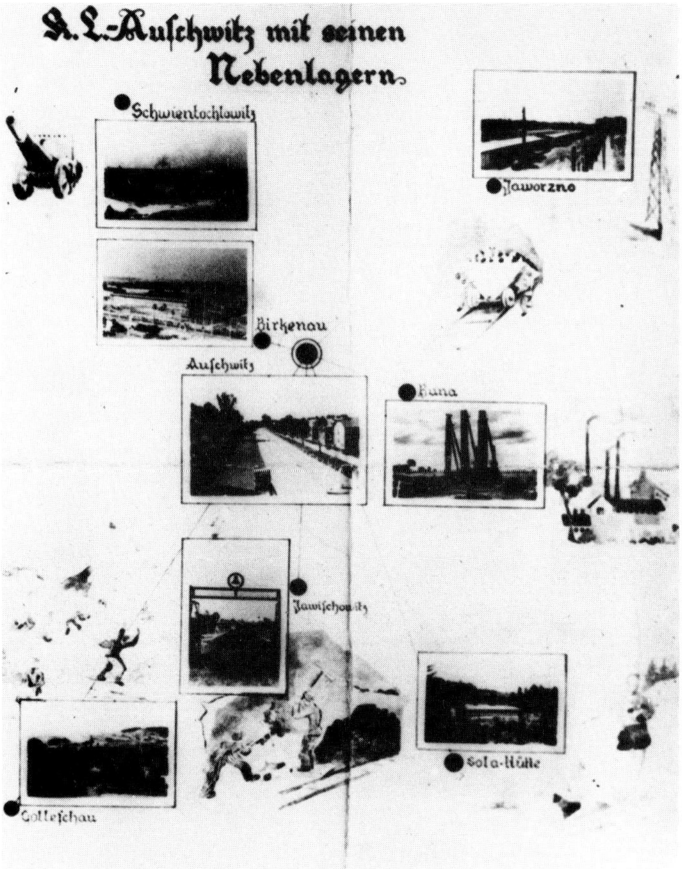

Plan made in the camp showing several of the over forty Auschwitz sub-camps

Budy near Auschwitz. School building where the women's penal company was housed. Photo taken after the liberation of the camp

Auschwitz. Block 11, known as Block of Death, and the gate leading into its courtyard, as they are today. Photo taken by Tadeusz Kinowski

Auschwitz. Room in Block 11 where the Summary Court held its sittings, as it is today. Photo taken by Lidia Foryciarz

Auschwitz. Execution or Death Wall where prisoners were shot, as it is today. Photo taken by Andrzej Piotrowski

Auschwitz. Entrance to one of the hospital blocks (Block 20), as it is today. In the first room on the left (marked with an „x") SS-men used to kill prisoners with phenol injections. Photo taken by Tadeusz Kinowski

Birkenau. Main camp gate with the unloading ramp where transports of deportees arrived. Photo taken after the liberation of the camp

Birkenau. Arrival of a transport of Hungarian Jews condemned to death. Photos taken by an SS-man in 1944

Birkenau. Before a selection. Photos taken by an SS-man in 1944

Birkenau. Camp physician *SS-Obersturmführer Heinz* Thilo (marked with an „x") during the selection of a newly arrived Jewish transport. Photo taken by an SS-man in 1944

Birkenau. After a selection, awaiting death in the gas chamber. Photo taken by an SS-man in 1944

Cyclon B

Birkenau. Women driven into the gas chamber. Photo taken secretly by a member of the camp Resistance Movement in 1944→

Birkenau. Construction of crematorium III. Photos taken by SS-man Kamann in 1942 or 1943

Birkenau. Crematorium ovens. Photo taken by an SS-man in 1943

← Birkenau. Crematorium IV. Photos taken by SS-man Kamann in 1942 or 1943

Birkenau. Burning of corpses on pyres. Photo taken secretly by a member of the camp Resistance Movement in 1944

Birkenau. View of a pyre. Photo taken after the liberation of the camp in 1945

irkenau. Unloading ramp
ith personal effects of the
urdered victims. Photo ta-
en by an SS-man in 1944

irkenau. Sorting of the per-
nal effects of the murdered
ctims. Photos taken by an
S-man in 1944

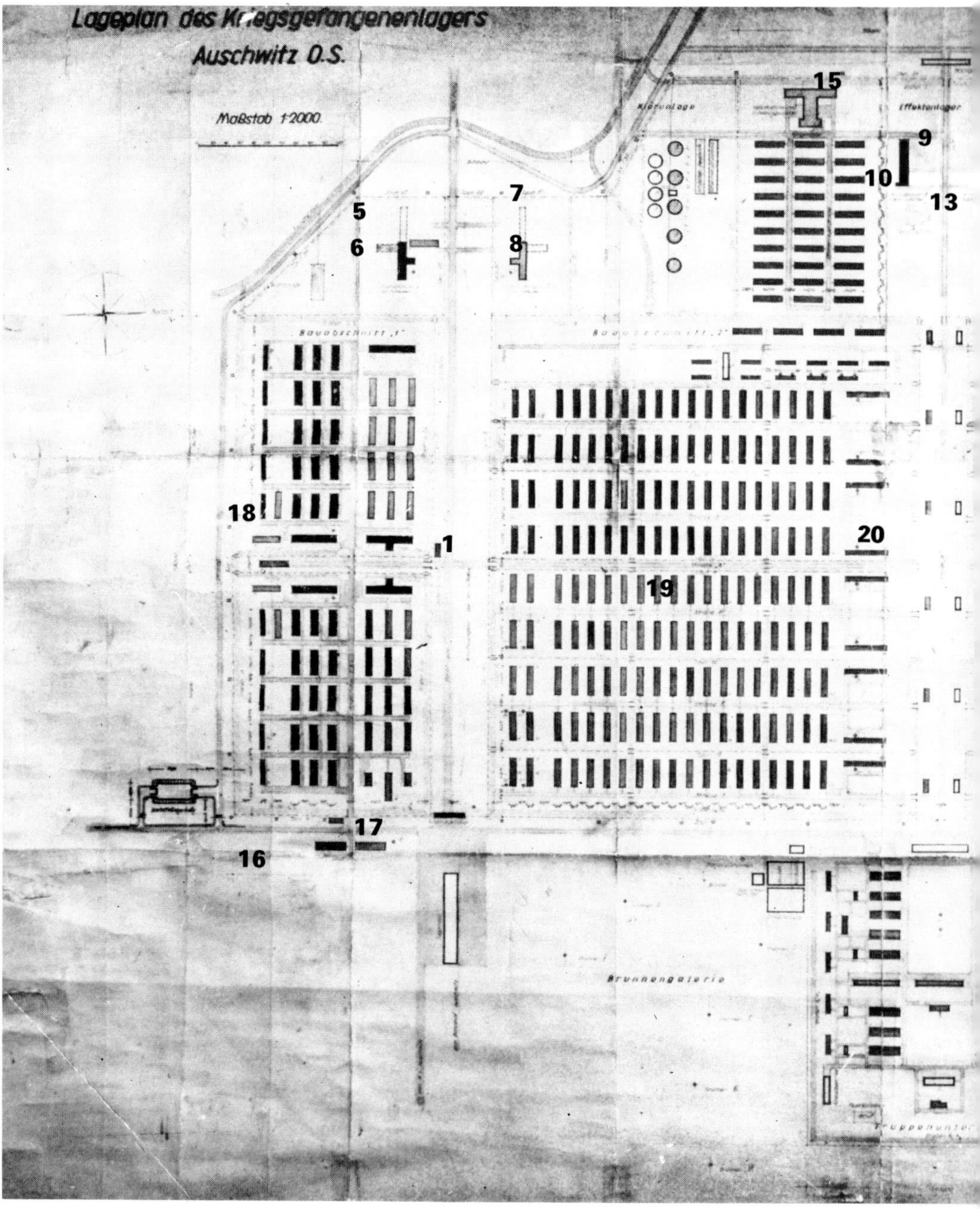

Lageplan des Kriegsgefangenenlagers
Auschwitz O.S.
Maßstab 1:2000
Effektenlager
Brunnengalerie
15
9
10
13
7
5
6
8
18
1
20
19
17
16

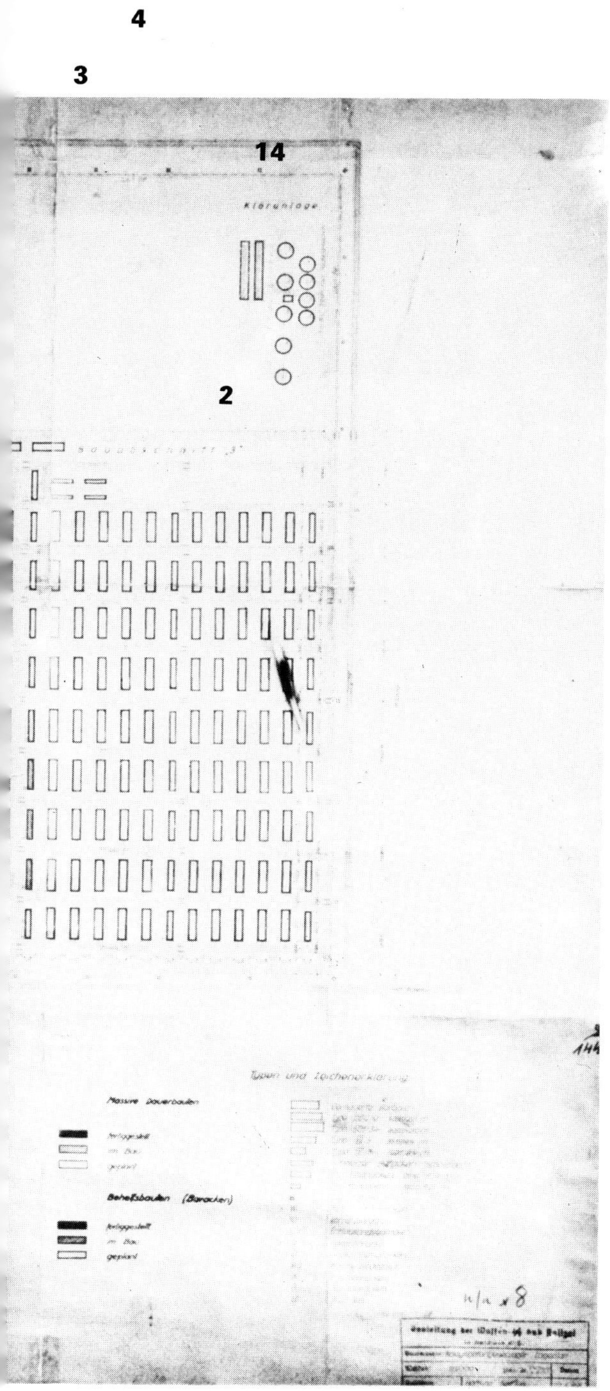

INSTALLATIONS AND SITES OF MASS EXTERMINATION AT *KL AUSCHWITZ II (BIRKENAU)*

1. Railway ramp
2. Bunker 1, the first gas chamber
3. Bunker 2, the second gas chamber
4. Pyres for burning corpses
5. Gas chamber and crematorium II
6. Sites where ashes from crematorium II were buried
7. Gas chamber and crematorium III
8. Site where ashes from crematorium III were buried
9. Gas chamber and crematorium IV
10. Site where ashes from crematorium IV were buried
11. Gas chamber and crematorium V
12. Site of cremating pits
13. Pond into which ashes from crematoria IV and V were dumped
14. Site where corpses of prisoners and Soviet POW's, murdered in the camp, were buried
15. Sauna
16. Block 25 ("Block of Death")
17. Experimenting station of Dr. Horst Schumann
18. Block 2: men's penal company
19. Blocks of the men's penal company and the *Sonderkommando*
20. Site where executions by hanging took place

Auschwitz. Rudolf Höss's villa as it is today. Photo taken by Tadeusz Kinowski

Auschwitz. SS mess room in the so-called *Haus der Waffen-SS*. Photo taken by an SS-man, year unknown

Auschwitz. Interior of one of the SS offices. Photo taken by an SS-man, year unknown

Auschwitz. SS barracks. Photo taken by an SS-man, year unknown

Auschwitz. SS stables. Photos taken by an SS-man, year unknown

garrison storehouse[76] and the German Armaments Factory[77] (the siding branched off from the main railway line, which led to the camp). There, at the ramp, cattle vans were being unloaded, and people who had arrived in them were slowly marching towards their unknown destination. All of them had large, yellow Jewish stars on their miserable clothes. Their worn faces showed that they had suffered many a hardship. The majority were elderly people. From their conversation one could gather that up to their unexpected transportation they had been employed in factories, that they were willing to go on working and to be as useful as they could. A few guards without guns, but with pistols well hidden in their pockets, escorted the procession to the crematorium. The SS-men promised the people, who were beginning to feel more hopeful, that they would be employed at suitable work, according to their occupations. Explicit instructions how to behave were given to the SS-men by Hössler. Previously the guards had always treated new arrivals very roughly, trying with blows to make them stand in ranks "at arm's length," but there were no uncivil words just now! The more fiendish the whole plan!

Both sides of the big entrance gate to the crematorium were wide open. Suspecting nothing the column marched in, in lines of five persons, and stood in the yard. There were three or four hundred of them. Somewhat nervously the SS guard at the entrance waited for the last man to enter the yard. Quickly he shut the gate and bolted it. Grabner and Hössler were standing on the roof of the crematorium. Grabner spoke to the Jews, who unsuspectingly awaited their fate, "You will now bathe and be disinfected, we don't want any epidemics in the camp. Then you will be brought to your barracks, where you'll get some hot soup. You will be employed in accordance with your professional qualifications. Now undress and put your clothes in front of you on the ground."

They willingly followed these instructions, given them in a friendly, warm-hearted voice. Some looked forward to the soup, others were glad that the nerve-racking uncertainty as to their immediate future was over and that their worst expectations were not realized. All felt relieved after their days full of anxiety.

Grabner and Hössler continued from the roof to give friendly advice, which had a calming effect upon the people, "Put your shoes close to your clothes bundle, so that you can find them after the bath." "Is the water warm? Of course, warm showers." "What is your trade? A shoemaker? We need them urgently. Report to me immediately after!"

Such words dispelled any last doubts or lingering suspicions. The first lines entered the mortuary through the hall. Everything was extremely tidy. But the special smell made some of them uneasy. They looked in vain for showers or water pipes fixed to the ceiling. The hall meanwhile was getting packed. Several SS-men had entered with them, full of jokes and small talk. They unobtrusively kept their eyes on the entrance. As soon as the last person had entered, they disappeared without much ado. Suddenly the door was closed. It had been made tight with rubber and secured with iron fittings. Those inside

---

[76] *Truppenwirtschaftslager.*

[77] *Deutsche Ausrüstungswerke* (DAW).

heard the heavy bolts being secured. They were screwed to with screws, making the door air-tight. A deadly, paralyzing terror spread among the victims. They started to beat upon the door, in helpless rage and despair they hammered on it with their fists. Derisive laughter was the only reply. Somebody shouted through the door, "Don't get burnt, while you make your bath!" Several victims noticed that covers had been removed from the six holes in the ceiling. They uttered a loud cry of terror when they saw a head in a gas-mask at one opening. The "disinfectors" were at work. One of them was *SS-Unterscharführer* Teuer, decorated with the Cross of War Merit. With a chisel and a hammer they opened a few innocuous-looking tins which bore the inscription "Cyclon, to be used against vermin. Attention, poison! To be opened by trained personnel only!" The tins were filled to the brim with blue granules the size of peas.

Immediately after opening the tins, their contents was thrown into the holes which were quickly covered.

Meanwhile Grabner gave a sign to the driver of a lorry, which had stopped close to the crematorium. The driver started the engine and its deafening noise was louder than the death cries of the hundreds of people inside, being gassed to death. Grabner looked with the interest of a scientist at the second hand of his wrist watch. Cyclon acted swiftly. It consists of hydrocyanic acid in solid form. As soon as the tin was emptied, the prussic acid escaped from the granules. One of the men, who participated in the bestial gassing, could not refrain from lifting, for the fraction of a second, the cover of one of the vents and from spitting into the hall. Some two minutes later the screams became less loud and only an indistinct groaning was heard. The majority of the victims had already lost consciousness. Two minutes more and Grabner stopped looking at his watch.

It was over. There was complete silence. The lorry had driven away. The guards were called off, and the cleaning squad started to sort out the clothes, so tidily put down in the yard of the crematorium.

Busy SS-men and civilians working in the camp were again passing the mound, on whose artificial slopes young trees swayed peacefully in the wind. Very few knew what terrible event had taken place there only a few minutes before and what sight the mortuary below the greenery would present.

Some time later, when the ventilators had extracted the gas, the prisoners working in the crematorium opened the door to the mortuary. The corpses, their mouths wide open, were leaning on one another. They were especially closely packed near to the door, where in their deadly fright they had crowded to force it. The prisoners of the crematorium squad worked like robots, apathetically and without a trace of emotion. It was difficult to tug the corpses from the mortuary, as their twisted limbs had grown stiff with the gas. Thick smoke clouds poured from the chimney.—This is how it began in 1942!

Transport after transport vanished in the Auschwitz crematorium. Day after day! Victims began arriving in ever greater numbers and the murdering had to be organized on a grand scale. The mortuary proved too small for such quantities. The cremation took too long. And Hitler was impatiently awaiting the extermination of millions of Jews from France, Belgium, Holland, Germany, Poland, Greece, Italy, Czechoslovakia and Hungary. Jews kept coming in cattle vans from transit camps, such as Verne near Paris, Westerbork in Holland, Theresienstadt in Czechoslovakia, Antwerp, Warsaw, Salonika, Cracow, Berlin, later also Budapest, etc. So Birkenau had to be enlarged! A year later things had already changed.

[THE TWO LITTLE FARMHOUSES]

At some distance from the Birkenau camp, which was growing at an incredible rate, there stood, amidst pleasant scenery, two pretty and tidy-looking farmhouses, separated from one another by a grove. They were dazzlingly whitewashed, cosily thatched and surrounded with fruit trees of the kind that usually grew there. Such was the first hasty impression! Nobody would have thought it credible that in those insignificant little houses as many people had perished as would have filled a city. The attentive spectator might have noticed signs in many languages on the houses. The signs read: "To disinfection." Then he might observe that the houses were windowless, but had a disproportionate number of remarkably strong doors, made air-tight with rubber and secured with screwed-down bolts, while small wooden flaps were fixed near the bolts. Near the small houses there were several incongruously large stables, such as were used in Birkenau to accommodate prisoners. The roads leading to them bore the tracks of many heavily loaded vans. If the visitor discovered, in addition, that from the back doors there led a railway track to some pits hidden by brushwood fences, then he would certainly guess that the houses served some special purpose.

The N.O.C. on duty crashed his way through the buildings occupied by the commandant's staff. A whistle sharply shrilled through the silent night. "A transport has arrived!" Tired and cursing the SS-men jumped from their beds, covered with the finest eiderdowns. These were the drivers, employees of the section receiving new transports and of the prisoners' property stores, the camp leaders and disinfectors, all who were on duty that night to receive new transports. "*Verdammt nochmal;*[78] these transports keep on arriving all the time, not a moment's rest, where does this one come from?" "I think it's from Paris. But there is one from Westerbork already in the station, we must push it quickly to the ramp. A big transport from Theresienstadt has been reported, due to arrive early in the morning." "Hell! That lot in Lublin[79] don't work any more, it seems. Everything comes to us. Well, let's hope the Frenchmen have at least brought plenty of sardines with them!"

They had meanwhile dressed. Motorcycles were being started up in front of the barracks and were driving away. Six large lorries had left the garages and were driving towards the transport ramp in Birkenau. The medical orderlies were driving in an ambulance. Driving through the rutted roads made some tins loose. They bounced on the floor of the ambulance. Their labels read: "Cyclon."

---

[78] Damnation!

[79] Broad is thinking here of the concentration camp at Majdanek.

The sleepy disinfectors cowered on the side benches. Round gas-mask containers, which hung above their heads, noisily struck one another. *SS-Oberscharführer* Klehr was sitting in front beside the driver. His steady work with arriving transports had won him a KVK. The ambulance proceeded straight to the innocuous looking farmhouses, the "bunkers" as those gas chambers were generally called. Meanwhile the lorries and motorcycles had come up to the ramp. A long train consisting of closed freight-cars was standing at one siding of the shunting-yard. The doors of the cars were fastened with wire. Flood-lights threw a glaring light on the train and the ramp. Anxious faces were visible in the small hatches, which were barred with barbed wire. The sentries had taken their positions around the train and at the ramp. Their commander reported to the SS leader, responsible for the reception of the transport, that all sentries were on guard. The cars could be unloaded. The commander of the escort squad which had guarded the train on its journey, usually a police officer, handed over the transport list to an SS-man of the receiving squad. The list contained the name of the place where the transport had come from, the number of the train, and the names, surnames and dates of birth of the Jews brought to Auschwitz. The SS-men of the camp garrison had meanwhile made the newcomers get off the train. A pell-mell of all colours could be seen on the ramp. There were smart Frenchwomen in fur-coats and silk stockings, helpless old men, children, their heads in curls, old grannies, men in their prime, some wearing fashionable suits, others in workmen's clothes. Mothers with infants in their arms were alighting together with sick persons, who had to be carried by helpful people.

First of all the men and women had to be separated, amidst heart-breaking scenes of farewell. Husbands were separated from their wives, mothers waved goodbye to their sons for the last time.

Both columns were made to stand on the ramp in ranks of fives, several metres apart from one another. If someone, unable to restrain his pain at the separation from his beloved, once again ran over to the other column to press the hand of, or to say a few consoling words to his dearest, an SS-man would brutally hit him and make him go back to his column. The SS doctor then began to segregate those fit for work from those he considered unfit. Mothers with babies were unfit as a rule, just as those who had impressed him as being weak or sickly. Portable wooden step-ladders were brought to the rear of the lorries and those whom the SS doctor found to be unfit for work climbed in. The SS-men of the receiving squad counted all who climbed in. They also counted the persons fit to work, who then had to march on to the camp for men, or for women. The entire luggage was to be left on the ramp. The prisoners were told it would be brought later by vans. This was true, but the prisoners would never see their property again. All their belongings would be sent to safes, stores and canteens of the SS administration. Smaller bags with personal things as well as their clothes would be taken from them on entry into the camp.

These poor victims of the frenzied drive to destroy presented a picture of unspeakable misery after they had left the camp sauna.[80] Once fashionable

[80] Bath-house.

and lively women and girls, they now had their heads shorn and a prisoner's number tattooed on their left forearms; and they were clothed in sack-like, blue and white striped smocks. The majority of them soon broke down, unable to bear the hardships of their fate.

The lorries with all those, who were not to be used for work in camp, had meanwhile departed. The SS-men were asked what the big fires, visible from afar, were for. Their replies were not very reassuring. Most of them took little pains to keep the prisoners in the dark as to their future. The continuous radio messages from abroad, telling about conditions in Germany, meant that the unhappy people partly foresaw what was in store for them at Auschwitz. But many of them could not bring themselves to believe, not till their last moments, that the Germans who liked to represent themselves as a nation of philosophers and poets to the world could be capable of such barbarous deeds.

The prisoners' squad was now busy at the ramp loading the scattered trunks and boxes into lorries. The engine driver, instead of taking the empty train from the siding, tried to stay on at the ramp as long as possible. He kept hammering around the locomotive, watching for a favourable opportunity to snatch some food or valuables scattered on the ramp. In a business-like way the SS-men of the receiving squad compared their total of the arrivals with the number on the list. A small difference would be of no importance A small note would be put next morning under the glass top of Grabner's desk. It was quite laconic: Arrivals on ... with transport No... 4,722; fit to work: 612, unfit to work: 4,110. Each SS-man then got a slip for his special ration and vodka.[81] One fifth of a litre for every transport. No wonder that alcohol was freely flowing in the commandant's staff mess. The higher camp officials, the prominent SS leaders, got special ration cards too, even if they had nothing to do with a transport. The ramp was soon deserted and empty, except for the wooden step-ladders which hundreds of thousands of people had mounted, people whose lives were shortly to end, in a matter of minutes only.

The lorries had been driving back and forth several times in order to bring all those who were condemned to die to the bunkers. The people had to undress in the stables and were then crowded into the gas chambers. The inscriptions pointing to "disinfection," the talk of the SS-men and, above all, the pleasant appearance of the little farmhouses had many times made those who were about to die feel hopeful. They expected to be employed at some less heavy work, suited to their physical condition. But it also occurred that whole transports were fully aware of their impending fate. The murderers had to be very careful in such cases. Otherwise they could be shot with their own pistols, as had happened in the case of *SS-Unterscharführer* Schillinger.[82]

[81] Compare Kremer's Diary, pp. 162—163, entry dated September 5, 1942.

[82] Broad refers here to an event which occurred on October 24, 1943. An RSHA transport from *KL Bergen-Belsen* brought 1,700 Jews, citizens of various countries. They had been told they would go to Switzerland. On the unloading ramp at Birkenau they learnt that they had been deceived, as they found themselves in an extermination camp. One of the women then snatched a revolver from an SS-man, shot *SS-Oberscharführer* Schillinger and wounded *SS-Unterscharführer* Emmerich. Other women jumped bare-handed on the SS-men, who called for help. When help came, some of the prisoners were shot or killed with grenades and the rest were killed in the gas chamber of crematorium III. Their bodies were cremated in crematoria II and III.

From the moment when everybody had been locked in the gas chambers and the doors bolted, the task of the majority of the SS-men was over. Just as in the old Auschwitz crematorium, the "disinfector" now had to do his job. Only the sound of lorries was not considered necessary here. The SS authorities in question probably did not realize that the inhabitants of the small village Wohlau,[83] situated not far from there across the Vistula, had often witnessed the scenes of terror at night. Thanks to the bright flames from the pits, where corpses were continually burnt, they could see processions of naked people marching from the barracks, where they had undressed, to the gas chambers. They heard the cries of people, brutally beaten because they did not want to enter the chambers of death; they also heard the shots which finished off those who could not be squeezed into the gas chambers, which were not roomy enough. In the daytime Polish civilian workers were busy building big new crematoria, in the vicinity of the farmhouses used as gas chambers. They worked within the camp area, at a distance of several hundred metres from the farmhouses, so they were able to see prisoners tugging objects from the doors, loading wagons and driving them to the pits, over which clouds of smoke were forever hovering. Specialists in this kind of work laid a thousand or more corpses, layer upon layer, in the pits. Layers of timber were placed between the corpses, and then the "open air theatre" [*Freilichtbühne*] was set on fire with methanol.

The SS-men in Auschwitz murdered systematically and with pleasure, but they were just as eager to fill their pockets. When a gas chamber had been opened and ventilated, and the corpses dragged outside by the prisoners who were forced to perform this horrible job, then one of the latter, detailed to the gruesome task, began to extract gold teeth from the jaws of the corpses, using a special tool. He collected them in a pot. Even the hair, shorn in the *sauna* from the heads of new arrivals, was converted into money!

If one asked an SS-man, pointing to the corpses of men and women lying on the ground, together with the children who lay as if asleep, why those people had to be exterminated, then as a rule one got the answer, "It must be so!" And that answer seemed, in his opinion, to be quite conclusive. Such was the influence of propaganda, which found with them an only too eager acceptance, due to their sadistic tendencies, to their megalomania and their intellectual limitations. These creatures, who hardly deserved to be called men, considered themselves the representatives of a highly developed race fully entitled to deprive members of another race of the right to live, more, to exterminate them by all possible means. They did not regard Jews as human beings. The proverb "*Des einen Tod ist des anderen Brot*"[84], was never better illustrated than in the extermination camp of Auschwitz. The thugs of Auschwitz enjoyed a life of comfort and pleasure till January 17, 1945, when the advancing Soviet Army put an end to their gruesome deeds.

Himmler was dissatisfied with the extermination methods in Auschwitz. First of all they were too slow. On the other hand, the great pyres were spreading

[83] In Polish, Wola.

[84] One man's death is another's bread.

such a stench that the whole countryside for miles around had been infected. At night, the red sky above Auschwitz was visible from far away. But it would have been impossible to do away with the immense quantities of corpses, both of those who had died in the camp and of those who had perished in the gas chambers, without the huge pyres. The chimney of the Auschwitz crematorium showed dangerous clefts due to overheating. Sentries were punished for gossiping; they were supposed to be guilty of betraying the secrets, but it was by reason of the unmistakable sweet smell and the nightly flames that the neighbourhood of Auschwitz learnt about the goings-on in the camp of death. Railwaymen used to tell the civilian population how thousands were being brought to Auschwitz every day, and yet the camp was not growing larger at a corresponding rate. The same information was supplied by the police escorts of the transports. The result was that a party speaker, when making his speech in the town of Auschwitz, had to retreat as most of the audience was hostile.

In the camp itself many SS-men read the indignant outcries of the German press about Katyń with a smile. The comparison with their own ethic and morals in conducting the war struck them as a huge joke, and was enjoyed as such. The guard corps had too much insight into the gassings, although only the special *Kommando* was supposed to be in the know. *SS-Oberscharführer* Knittel, the head of Section VI, was responsible for the education of the soldiers and for inculcating them with the proper outlook. On account of his theatrical mannerisms he was called "the army saviour" by scornful soldiers. He had the greatest difficulties with his lectures as the general feeling was against him. Simple soldiers on guard duty were often heard saying that they could not imagine being discharged and becoming free men again. To guard the guilty secrets they would probably have to march into the gas chambers themselves in the end, so some of them thought. It was characteristic that everyone considered that Himmler was sufficiently unprincipled and brutal to conceive such a plan. The general feeling grew worse when it was announced that nobody would be given leave from the camp for nearly a year on account, as they said, of epidemics.[85] But it was common knowledge that the real reason was to keep so many people who were "in the know" from mixing with the civilian population.

[MUTINY OF THE UKRAINIAN SS]

There was a company of Ukrainian soldiers on guard duty in Auschwitz, who were particularly prone to the belief that they would be liquidated one day even if no one else was, because they were foreigners. The first signs of unrest became evident when they were ordered into the bath-house to be deloused. They refused to enter the bath-house and did so only when a German *SS-Unterscharführer* had gone in first. The mistrust and hostile attitude of the Ukrainian company towards the Germans steadily increased. One night it came to a head.

[85] So-called *Lagersperre*, meaning that all leaves and passes of the SS-men were cancelled.

Some 20 Ukrainians fled, armed with rifles, machine-guns and ammunition.[86] All available troops were mobilized and dispatched after them. When they reached the fugitives they found them barricaded in a quarry in a good strategic position. The fight which lasted one whole day ended with the SS having two and the Ukrainians seven casualties. Six Ukrainians committed suicide to escape being taken prisoner. One slightly wounded man was captured and the rest escaped. The wounded man and three alleged accessaries were executed, but the camp authorities in Auschwitz, afraid of renewed conspiracies, transferred all Ukrainian guards to the Buchenwald concentration camp.

[THE DEATH FACTORY]

All these incidents showed that it was high time to abolish the public pyres and to conduct the extermination of Jews, which was now planned on an even larger scale, in the utmost secrecy. The building of four new crematoria was speeded up. Two of them had underground gas chambers, in each of which 4,000 people could be killed at the same time. The other two smaller crematoria had two gas chambers partitioned into three sections, built on the ground floors. In each of these death factories there was an immense hall where " evacuees " had to undress. The halls of crematoria I [II] and II [III] were also underground. Stone stairs, about two metres wide, led down to them. But before all four crematoria were finished, a chimney in one of them, which had already been in use, burst due to over-exploitation and was in need of repairs. Crematoria I [II] and II [III] had fifteen ovens each, and each oven was equipped to hold four or five corpses. The building section[87] of the Auschwitz concentration camp was so proud of their achievements that they placed a series of pictures of the crematoria in the hall of their main building for everybody to see. They had overlooked the fact that the civilians, coming and going there, would be less impressed with the technological achievements of the building section; on seeing the enlarged photos of fifteen ovens, neatly arranged side by side, they would, instead, be rather apt to ponder on the somewhat strange inventions of the Third Reich. Grabner soon took care to quash the bizarre publicity. But he could not prevent the numerous civilian workers, employed by the building section to construct the crematoria, from talking to outsiders about the construction plans, with which they were naturally thoroughly acquainted.

Auschwitz reached its climax in the spring of 1944. Long trains from Hungary arrived incessantly at the Birkenau sub-camp. All Hungarian Jews were to be exterminated in one sweep. The former commandant of Auschwitz, *SS-Sturmbannführer* Höss, now head of Office DI in the SS Economic and Administrative Head Office in Berlin, was responsible for the operation. *SS-Hauptsturmführer*

---

[86] In the night of July 3/4, 1943, sixteen Ukrainian SS-men escaped from the guard company, taking with them weapons and ammunition. In the course of the pursuit, eight of these were killed and one was captured. On the German side, *SS-Scharführer* Karl Rainicke and *SS-Schütze* Stephan Rachberger were killed. The fight took place in the vicinity of Chełm Wielki (now Chełm Śląski) near Bieruń.

[87] *Zentralbauleitung der Waffen-SS und Polizei in Auschwitz O/S.*

Kramer, who later became notorious for his excesses in Belsen, was then the commandant of Birkenau. A new railway siding, with three lines leading to the new crematoria, made it possible to have one train unloaded while another was arriving.

An average of 10,000 people came to Birkenau every day. The percentage of those doomed to "separate detention"[88], as it was now termed instead of *Sonderbehandlung* [special treatment], was especially high in these transports. Many went mad with thirst and mental depression during the journey.

The reputation of Auschwitz was widespread at that time. When the people, squeezed into the cattle vans, noticed the sign with the name Auschwitz on the railway station through which they were passing, they could no longer be told any tales.

The four crematoria were exploited to the utmost. Because of over-use, the ovens were constantly in need of repair. Then only crematorium III [IV] would remain in working order. There was no help for it—the pyres had to be used again to dispose of the thousands of corpses lying in big heaps behind the crematoria. The gas chambers were hurriedly opened to be ventilated, as soon as the last groans had stopped. The streets in the camp were again jammed with endless columns of new victims. The special squads got reinforcements and worked feverishly to empty the gas chambers again and again.[89] One of the white farmhouses had to be used again. It was designated as bunker 5, and there Moll plied his bloody trade. *SS-Oberscharführer* Muhsfeld, who had already acquired experience in mass murder at Lublin, directed crematoria I [II] and II [III]. *SS-Oberscharführer* Voss was entrusted with the gassing and cremating in crematoria III [IV] and IV [V]. There were no breaks.

The last corpse had hardly been taken from the gas chambers, dragged through the square and brought behind the crematorium to the pit filled with corpses, when the next consignment for gassing were undressing in the hall. It was next to impossible to remove the countless clothes from the undressing room fast enough. A child's thin wailing was sometimes heard from under a bundle of clothing, forgotten in the hurry. The child would then be lifted, held aloft and shot through the head by some utterly bestial hangman. Höss urged the SS-men, who were mostly drunk while on duty at the five extermination centres, to hurry as much as possible.

The Russians had already occupied the entire eastern part of Hungary. There was no time to lose. Lublin, the notorious twin establishment of Auschwitz, was already in the hands of the Russians and its gas chambers could be used no more. There was talk that Höss was very close to decoration with the Knight's Cross of War Merit.

If the number of those who perished in the course of those few weeks were calculated at half a million, then the calculation would be rather too low than too high. Meanwhile regular transports from Poland, Theresienstadt, etc. still kept arriving.

---

[88] *Gesonderte Unterbringung* denoted death in the gas chamber.

[89] As soon as the extermination of Hungarian Jews had begun the number of prisoners working in the *Sonderkommando* was increased to a thousand persons.

The feelings of the prisoners of all nationalities in the camp, faced with the mass murdering, were feelings of utter despair. They could not help being completely cast down by the constant and dreadful dying, which even Auschwitz had not witnessed before to such an extent. Many had lost the last of their relatives, those who till then had managed to survive in Hungary, where up to 1944 conditions had been better than in Slovakia or in Poland. The German prisoners from the Reich were forced to witness the atrocities with helpless rage and shame. They knew that the ignominy, which had dishonoured German culture, would imprint an indelible stigma on German history.

The weeks of the Hungarian action constituted the craziest climax—but they were also a turning point in the history of the extermination camp. Some time elapsed, and the gassing of Jews had to be stopped. The Germans were being pushed out from all the occupied territories. This was no longer a time when prisoners were hopelessly looking into a bleak future. They knew the day of their liberation was not so distant and this conviction made them hold out with their utmost strength. The SS-men also felt some slight misgivings, when finishing the remains of Greek figs or Hungarian sausage at their meals. Inwardly they began to curse the tattoo on the inner side of their arms. They even became gentler with the prisoners. But they could not undo what had been done. All papers dealing with "special treatment" or "separate detention" were removed from the dossiers. The same was done, by order of the Reich Main Security Office in Berlin, with papers in which punishment by flogging was mentioned.

[THE REVOLT OF THE *SONDERKOMMANDO*]

Another terrible massacre occurred in Birkenau in the autumn of 1944.[90] The special squads in the crematoria were no longer wanted, and their number was to be reduced. Several hundred workers were to be sent in "a transport to Gleiwitz." They knew what this meant! They would be driven in lorries once around the Birkenau camp, to make the other prisoners believe they really were departing, and then they would be brought to the gas chambers.

Prisoners[91] made shell fuses in the *Weichsel-Union-Werke*,[92] and the members of the special squads—resolved to take desperate measures—managed somehow to get from them explosives, with which they made primitive hand-grenades. A simultaneous outbreak was planned in all of the crematoria. The fire started in crematorium III [IV] was to be the signal. Although the desperate action failed, crematorium III [IV] was burnt down, and about eighty prisoners succeeded in escaping from crematorium I [II] through the barbed-wire fences around it; but both this eighty and several hundred others from the other crematoria, particularly from crematorium III [IV], lay shot by the evening of

[90] This happened on October 7, 1944.

[91] More accurately, women prisoners.

[92] In 1943, inside the large sentry chain, prisoners built an armaments factory which at first belonged to *Krupp*; it was later taken over by *Union-Werke*.

that unlucky day in front of the charred ruins. Those who were not shot while breaking out of the burning crematorium III [IV], were driven into the gas chamber which was undamaged. In tens they were let out and ordered to lie down in the yard on their bellies. There they were shot in the back of their heads. "The transport to Gleiwitz" was thus dispatched.

Several days later five SS-men were seen walking about, very proud of their newly received Iron Crosses [*Eisernes Kreuz*]. The commandant of Auschwitz, *SS-Sturmbannführer* Beer,[93] pointed out in his speech to the soldiers that this was the first time that troops in a concentration camp were decorated by the *Reichsführer* with Iron Crosses, for "their heroic conduct in suppressing a mass outbreak."

[LIQUIDATION OF THE GYPSIES]

The extermination programme of the Third Reich included not only Jews and the people of the East, but also Gypsies who "had to be removed from Europe as an inferior race." In February 1943 the commandant of the Auschwitz concentration camp received a telegramme from Office V [Reich Criminal Police Office] of the Reich Main Security Office, announcing the arrival of several thousand Gypsies. The telegramme stressed that "Gypsies should not be treated like Jews, for the time being." A motley crowd of French, Hungarian, Czech, Polish and German Gypsies came to the camp in the course of the next few weeks. They came with their children and their personal possessions.

They were brought to a separate sector of Birkenau, called the Gypsy camp. Then, in March, express letters arrived with red margins, containing further orders. According to these, by order of the *Reichsführer* all Gypsies "regardless of whether or not they were of mixed blood" should be sent to work in the concentration camps. The exceptions were to be Gypsies and half-breeds who had stable abodes, were socially well adjusted and were holding steady jobs. This clause was a mere formality and was never observed. It was precisely the settled Gypsies who were the easiest prey, and so they formed the largest percentage of the camp inmates. Girls who had worked in army offices as typists, workmen in the OT [Organisation Todt], students of music schools, and others with a solid background of steady and efficient work, suddenly found themselves in a concentration camp as prisoners with shaved heads and in blue-white prison clothes, their prison number tattooed on their arms. That was not all, the madness went further. Hundreds of soldiers, who had not the slightest idea that they were half-breeds, were transferred from the front lines, deprived of their uniforms and sent to the concentration camp, just because they happened to have twelve or even less per cent of Gypsy blood. Those decorated with the Iron Cross and other medals for bravery were overnight sent behind the barbed-wire fences of Auschwitz as "anti-socials"[94]. According to secret orders, this should not have happened. Half-breeds, who had

---

[93] Baer.

[94] The so-called *Asoziale*, marked with black triangles.

distinguished themselves as soldiers during the war, should have been exempted from the general rule, on condition that they consented to be sterilized. But the majority of them were never asked to consent, they were simply arrested. All were promised they would be brought to a Gypsy settlement. The documents dealing with the Gypsy problem were sent by the Criminal Police Office of the Reich and by the Reich Central Office for Combatting Gypsies,[95] and were signed by Criminal Councillor Otto, Dr. Ritter and Böhlhoff.

About 16,000 Gypsies were transported to Auschwitz.[96] After a few months, more than one third of them had already succumbed to a typhus epidemic. Berlin wanted to exterminate the Gypsies, but it seemed that Berlin was afraid to go to extremes, and so procrastinated for a considerable time before coming to a final decision. The die was cast in July 1944. Himmler ordered those fit for work to be kept in camps, while the rest were to be gassed.[97] Families were forcibly separated. The half-breeds chosen for work never saw or heard of their parents or children again.

Even some of the Auschwitz SS-men were fed up with the Gypsy action. They met acquaintances from their home towns among them and could not understand why reliable and brave soldiers should be arrested, not because they committed any crimes, but because of their race. And there was no hope of discharge for those who were detained. In some particularly unjust cases, when the decrees were being openly violated, petitions for release were sent to the Reich Central Office and the accompanying letters, though carefully worded, stressed the contradiction existing between decree and practice. The Criminal Police sought in every way to deny this, and withheld their consent to the applicants. They maintained that the applications of the Gypsies were based on lies. Their investigations, they said, had clearly shown that the petitioners had never been awarded the decorations they mentioned. Trite remarks followed, e.g. that the applicant had been universally known in his home town as an unruly character, and that frequent thefts, the culprit of which could not be traced, had stopped when the Gypsy in question was arrested. Such phrasing was supposed to justify the refusal. The Reich Central Office was well aware of the determination of the *Reichsführer* to make all Gypsies disappear from the face of the earth, if only they could be captured. The clauses about exceptions were just paper decorations on the extermination decrees. Those who wanted to help Gypsies could easily lose favour, because of their softness. Criminal Councillor Otto would then write to Auschwitz saying he hoped "they would take care not to forward such petitions in the future."

Individual bearers of distinguished decorations were, however, discharged from camp on condition that they agreed to be sterilized. But hardly anyone could be persuaded to undergo sterilization, as the methods of the Hygiene Institute were only too well known. It transpired that there had been innumerable cases of death among those subjected to the experiments. Some Gypsies actually refused to be discharged because their wives and children were to

---

95 *Reichszentrale zur Bekämpfung des Zigeunerunwesens.*

96 See p. 50, note 64.

97 See p. 51, note 69.

be kept in the camp, or because they found—shortly after receiving their discharge—that their families, free until then, had just arrived in the camp.

A drastic case was that of the Gypsy family of Tikulitsch-Todorowitsch. The nine members of that family were Croatian citizens. The Croatian embassy had used its influence in the Criminal Police Office of the Reich to secure the discharge of the family. The entire property of Gypsies used to be confiscated and "taken over by the Reich," just as was the case with Jewish property, therefore protracted negotiations were necessary to restore their property to them. In the summer of 1943 the family was finally to be sent back to Croatia. Grabner found he could not reconcile this fact with his concern for the interests of the state. The harmless Gypsies might, in his opinion, disturb Croatia's friendly relations with Germany by their tales about conditions in Auschwitz. So he simply procrastinated by sending reports to Berlin that the family in question was in quarantine before being released and could not leave it on account of a typhus epidemic in camp. Meanwhile one member of the family after another succumbed to the hard conditions of camp life. Finally only a small boy of four survived, who was the darling of all the prisoners and was looked after by all. But nobody was troubled any more whether he was released or not. When the Gypsy camp was finally liquidated and those fit to work were transferred to the concentration camps of Buchenwald, Mittelbau and Ravensbrück, the boy followed the weak, the children and the old people into the gas chamber.

["ABANDON ALL HOPE"]

It often happened that a few hours after the reception of a transport in Auschwitz, urgent inquiries arrived from the Reich Main Security Office or from the SS Economic and Administrative Head Office. They were signed by *SS-Sturmbannführer* Eichmann or *SS-Obersturmbannführer* Liebehenschel, who was later the commandant of Auschwitz, and eventually by Berlin. The messages were sent because it had transpired, while the transports were already on their way to Birkenau, that some person in a transport was Aryan, or that for various other reasons he should not have been sent with the RSHA transport to the extermination camp; it had turned out due to the intervention of the foreign press of a friendly or allied country or as result of their own investigation. The list of a transport contained names of all its members, and the leader of the transport handed the list to the section receiving the newcomers. It was kept in the office of that section.

Those who were sent to work in camp were registered in the registration office of Section II. Such persons had their individual dossiers, or at least personal cards for filing. Below the heading: "cause of detention," one read: "in accordance with RSHA order No. . . ." The number depended on the country from which the transport had come. Newcomers were noted in the list of arrivals in the order of their camp numbers. The person, about whose whereabouts the telegrammes inquired, was first looked for in the list of arrivals. If not found there, then it was too late. A check of the transport list in the receiving section showed that the person in question had arrived with the transport, but had been doomed to "special treatment" as unfit to work. One should not imagine that those unfit to work were solely the crippled, the old and the seriously ill. When the doctor on duty selected people on the crowded ramp, he did it in a rather arbitrary fashion. At the most 10 to 15 per cent in every transport were declared fit to work. In spite of lamentations that maintenance of manpower was of the utmost importance, one considered it one's foremost duty to do away with as many "enemies of the state" in the camp as possible. Otherwise wagon-loads of sausage and meat, which were intended for the scanty prisoners' rations, would hardly have rolled daily from the prisoners' kitchen stores, superintended by *SS-Unterscharführer* Egersdörfer, to find their way into the SS mess. The food in the SS mess grew distinctly worse when Egersdörfer started a quarrel with the chef of the SS kitchen, *SS-Oberscharführer* Scheffler, as a result of which the "extra rations" were discontinued. The lack of logic, visible in the contradictory objectives of achieving maximum manpower and productivity, while at the same time making the living conditions of prisoners in every way unbearable and thereby destroying healthy men by the thousands, was typical of the state of affairs in the concentration camps.

When information was requested by the Reich Main Security Office concerning a past transport, as a rule nothing could be ascertained. Former transport lists were destroyed. Nobody could learn anything in Auschwitz about the fate of a given person. The person asked for "is not and never has been detained in camp," or "he is not in the files"—these were the usual formulas given in reply... At present, after the evacuation of Auschwitz and the burning of all papers and records, the fate of millions of people is completely obscure. No transport or arrival lists are in existence any more.[98]

The RSHA transports were solely and exclusively aimed at exterminating Jews from all the European countries then under German occupation. Detention[99] on political charges or preventive custody[100] on criminal charges was ordered by the Secret State Police for certain persons, or by the Criminal Police in all other cases. The whole system was created by the Nazi regime in order to make unwanted Germans and foreigners, who were under suspicion and considered dangerous, disappear. They could be made to vanish for any period of time or forever, without much fuss and without trial in a court.

Apart from the extremely small percentage of criminal offenders, no concentration camp inmates were detained in accordance with the statutes of German law. Pure, unrestrained lawlessness was given full play. In countless instances the prisoner had no idea at all why he had been arrested. In the case of terror reprisals in the occupied countries, there were daily occurrences whereby some unfounded suspicion or personal dislike on the part of Gestapo officers was the only cause why people, who were not conscious of any guilt, were brought to concentration camps.

---

[98] A small number of transport lists and lists of newcomers to the camp is at present in the possession of the State Museum at Oświęcim.

[99] *Schutzhaft.*

[100] *Vorbeugungshaft.*

The case of Koch is but one example of how the private interests of higher Police and SS leaders could get people to a concentration camp. The engineer Koch from Breslau was sent to Auschwitz supposedly as a "war-time spiv." The evidence against him was, of course, insufficient for a regular court trial, and so he was detained in custody "until further notice." After several months the Gestapo from Breslau, which had sent Koch to Auschwitz, notified the commandant of Auschwitz, that a lawyer by the name of Horawa would arrive there, and that he should be allowed to have a meeting with Koch. The prisoner was conducted into a room in the commandant's office, where Horawa told him that an SS general[101] wished to buy his estate, valued at one million Reichsmark. Koch refused saying he had bought the estate for his son who had been disabled in the war and whom he planned to give the training indispensable for a landowner. In a persistent and unmistakably threatening way, Horawa pointed out that the refusal would displease the highly influential general, a fact which could prove ominous for a prisoner in custody. Koch knew he was at the mercy of the blackmailer and had to surrender unconditionally being completely helpless in face of this open pressure. So finally he declared his readiness to sell, provided that his son consented too. Horawa left, sure of his victory. He was convinced that the son, who was worried about his father being in danger, would readily consent, especially after a skilfully dropped hint concerning the father's dependence on the favour of the SS.

From time to time the Police Office which had sent a prisoner would fix the date for checking the necessity of his further imprisonment, but as little attention was paid to such dates as to the treatment of prisoners according to camp status 1, 2 or 3. This division of prisoners existed on paper only. In reality the guiltless got the worst treatment and had to work hardest, while prisoners with special duties in the camp, so-called capos, were convicts with several prison terms behind them and known for their brutality.

Should one of the Police Offices have the rare idea of wanting the discharge of a prisoner, they would request the commandant of the concentration camp to send them a report on the prisoner's behaviour, his work in camp, on his character and political opinions. The request for a report would first reach Grabner. He would ask for the prisoner's dossier and then give his opinion as a police officer. If the prisoner belonged to the intelligentsia, he could not hope for a favourable report. And if in addition he happened to be a foreigner, his case was virtually hopeless. Grabner's hatred of the intelligentsia, to which he could not be said to belong even by the greatest optimist, was limitless. Otherwise he was interested in why the prisoner had been detained, and what punishment in camp had been given in his case. According to these data he drew with a red pencil a 1, a 1/2 or a 2 on the request for information, and signed it with a large elaborate Gr. 1 meant that the report was favourable. This happened above all in the case of capos from the leather factory, the munitions plant, the slaughter-house, dairy and the gardening establishment, from whom Grabner derived profit in the form of furniture, various utensils and food. The numeral

---

[101] *Brigadeführer.*

1/2 meant: still negative that time, but the next inquiry was to have a positive answer. The numeral 2 meant that the report was unfavourable. Afterwards the letter was forwarded to the authorities of the camp. Grabner's will was respected in all cases. If a 2 was written on the papers, the report would inform the police office that the prisoner was lazy, rebellious and politically still very unsound, even if the man in question had done all he possibly could to give satisfaction to his superiors. The reports on a prisoner's behaviour often ended with, "This stay in camp has still not re-educated him sufficiently to make a decent man of him. So that he may be of value to his community. I therefore refuse to discharge him. The Commandant."

And Grabner almost always wrote—2.

If an inquiry was made by the police office which had arrested the prisoner, and if the camp authorities—Grabner above all—favoured him, then he had some prospects of being released after some time. But the two factors coincided in an extremely small percentage of cases.

The police might inquire very often, but if reports on a prisoner's behaviour were negative, no petition for discharge could be brought to the Reich Main Security Office. And very often there were no inquiries.

A small number of Poles with remarkably low camp numbers could be seen at Auschwitz. They were the few survivors from the transports which had come to Auschwitz at the very beginning of the camp, sent there by the Gestapo of Cracow and of nearby places. They were absolutely guiltless. They were arrested as hostages, were victims of street round-ups or were suspected of having read a leaflet of the Polish Resistance Movement without handing it over. The majority of them had already succumbed to camp life. Not one person from these transports was discharged. There were no inquiries and their petitions were left without an answer. It was a known fact in Auschwitz that the Gestapo in Cracow had lost the dossiers of the unfortunate creatures, but would not admit it; they simply waited for the last of them to be reported dead.

Grabner had a fixed idea, which approached a persecution mania, that the Polish intelligentsia in camp had formed resistance organizations and was preparing an armed revolt. Every trifle was for him an act of sabotage, endangering the state. His inordinate megalomania made him conceive an idea, the enormity of which he was unable to grasp fully. He ordered an investigation of the Poles' dossiers in order to find out who in any way belonged to the intelligentsia. On the cover of such dossiers the letter S was written, which meant *Sonderpole*.[102] There were about 5,000 of them altogether. He intended to have these prisoners successively shot in Block 11. But he was no longer able to put his plan into action. Fate forced him to pay for his deeds by bringing him into a similar situation to that into which he had put thousands of prisoners, namely to be waiting for his own death sentence.[103]

---

[102] Special Pole.

[103] The case of Grabner was brought to the SS court. He was charged with exceeding his powers and was sentenced to 12 years in prison.

[AN SS MAN'S HONOUR]

Hitler's plan to exterminate the Jews had in view not only the ideological aim of "cleaning Europe," but it also helped to a great extent to finance and support Germany's war economy. Millions in German and foreign currency were acquired in Auschwitz merely by seizing them as the transports arrived. Diamonds, thousands of gold rings, chains and watches, heaps of furs, clothes and objects of every kind could be seen in the store-rooms of the sections responsible for confiscated money and valuables and in the big sorting and storing barracks of the Auschwitz SS garrison. Clothes and articles of daily use were sent by the train-load to the *Volksdeutsche Mittelstelle.*[104] Despite all efforts, the organiztion set up for the purpose could not cope with the sudden influx of things. Piles of costly underwear, as high as a house, were ruined, as they were left lying about in the open for weeks. Jewellery, paper money and bullion were dragged by the trunkful to the cellars of the administration building, for nobody was able to inspect or count the valuables quickly enough. A whole staff was employed at the job to count, day after day, immense sums of money. Guards with machine-guns were used to watch over the vans, in which the treasure was sent to Berlin.

Many might have wondered how it came about that the SS who at the beginning of the war were hardly able to purchase the equipment they needed, a few years later were in a position to buy out whole streets with impressive administration buildings.

Tens of thousands literally lay in the streets of Birkenau, carelessly thrown away by prisoners marching from the ramp to the camp, or dropped from the lorries during their drive to the gas chambers. Most of the guards, when making such finds, could not resist the strong temptation, and in spite of the danger of being severely punished did not return everything to the section for valuables, or even kept the whole amount for themselves.

At the railway station obscure railwaymen and profiteers could sell you any quantity of vodka. The black marketeers made huge profits. They could get rid of their goods for gold dollars, roubles or Reichsmark. Their customers had plenty of different kinds of currency.

This became known in Berlin, where they were shocked by the corruption and immorality. Himmler sent a special commission which was to act with severity, and above all, to put an end to the unwelcome drain on the resources. Dr. Morgan was at the head of the commission. In Auschwitz *Obersturmführer* Reimers, *Hauptsturmführer* Barth[105] and *Hauptsturmführer* Dr. Drescher were particularly active. All of them were members of the Gestapo. The situation here was so alarming that there was even a burglary in one of the money stores of the section which looked after the valuables. Considering the immense amount of coffers containing uncounted money, it proved to be quite impossible to tell how many of these had been taken, and even less possible to find out what amount of money had been stolen by the burglar.

---

[104] *Reichskommisariat für die Festigung des deutschen Volkstums.*

[105] Bartsch.

The Polish Resistance Movement was meanwhile unceasingly active, attempting to uncover the secrets of Auschwitz and to let the world know about the atrocities committed there. Escaped prisoners and letters, secretly sent outside with the help of civilian workmen employed in the camp area, had provided much material. A pamphlet was compiled under the title "The Camp of Death." Outsiders probably thought it was exaggerated horror propaganda, but in fact it contained only a fraction of the truth. With a "request to state their opinion," the commandant's office in Auschwitz received a copy of the pamphlet from the Reich Main Security Office in Berlin. They raged in Berlin and wanted to know how that much could have leaked out. The Poles also knew about murders in Block 11!

Some time afterwards it was said that the radio station Daventry issued death verdicts against some important SS leaders at Auschwitz for their war crimes, the victims of which had been, besides Germans, also French, Polish and Russian citizens. Himmler then lost his patience. He charged the special commission to attend, above all, to these things and to conduct investigations concerning all those to whom the responsibility belonged. He himself was not responsible for things done "without his knowledge or without his order" in concentration camps, where decisions were made "as to the life or death of enemies of the state." Such decisions were his privilege alone, and no one besides himself was entitled to condemn prisoners, particularly non-Jews.

It would cost all the overzealous accomplices their heads, for they must take the blame for the murders upon themselves. He and his close associates would then again enjoy full blamelessness, and be known for their respect of the law. Grabner was arrested. It did not help when he pointed out that the commandant and Mildner had been informed about the executions and had approved them. Mildner had meanwhile been nominated inspector of the Security Police and the SD in Denmark, so he was too far to be reached. The commandant found a way out of this quandary by committing perjury. The same could be said of the behaviour of Aumeier and of those SS leaders, who had had their say in the "clearing out" operations in Block 11, for example, *SS-Hauptsturmführer* Schwarz, who was later commandant of the Auschwitz camp in Monowitz, or *SS-Obersturmführer* Hoffmann,[106] who had for some time been commandant of the Auschwitz concentration camp. But the death sentence planned for Grabner could not be pronounced without loss of face, as there was a strong feeling of indignation among wide circles of the SS against the cowardly attitude of the SS leaders. The trial was forever being put off. Grabner was physically and mentally broken, a crushed man, when after endless months of Gestapo arrest he was sentenced to a twelve-years' prison term. The advancing Russian army finally put an end to that farce of a trial. The goings-on of which "the *Reichsführer* most sharply disapproved" came to an end in a way he certainly would not have approved of!

In the middle of January 1945, Auschwitz was evacuated in wild panic. All prisoners who were able to walk were dragged off to concentration camps situated deep inside Germany, from which most were liberated several months

---

[106] Hofmann.

later.[107] Those who were ill were left behind to their fate, both in Auschwitz and in the sub-camps. They would have been shot at the last moment, but all the SS leaders were scared and did not dare to give the order.[108]

In front of all the administration buildings in Auschwitz piles of personal documents were set on fire and those buildings, in which the greatest mass murders had been committed, the greatest in the history of mankind, were blown up. Somewhere among the ruins there lay a tin bowl from which some prisoner had probably eaten his watery soup. He had awkwardly scratched on it a boat floating at the mercy of a raging sea. Above there was an inscription: "Don't forget the forlorn man"[109]. On the back of the bowl an aeroplane was seen with the American star on its wings and in the act of letting a bomb fall. The inscription above that picture was "*Vox dei!*"[110]

---

[107] About 60,000 men and women prisoners took part in the evacuation on foot, which led them into the interior of Germany. The majority of them perished due to exhaustion on the way, after arriving in other concentration camps, or during the successive evacuation in April of the camps located inside the Reich.

[108] Weak and sick prisoners, who were left in the Auschwitz camps and sub-camps, were to be shot by special SS detachments whose task it was to obliterate all traces of crimes. That order was carried out in part at Birkenau, where on January 25, 1945, 350 Jewish prisoners, men and women, were shot, while on January 27, 1945, over 200 prisoners were shot or burnt alive in the sub-camp Fürstengrube. The SS special detachments were unable to carry out the order fully, as they were threatened with encirclement by the army of the First Ukrainian Front which liberated about 7,650 prisoners (men and women) from Auschwitz on January 27, 1945.

[109] Broad uses English here.

[110] The Voice of God.

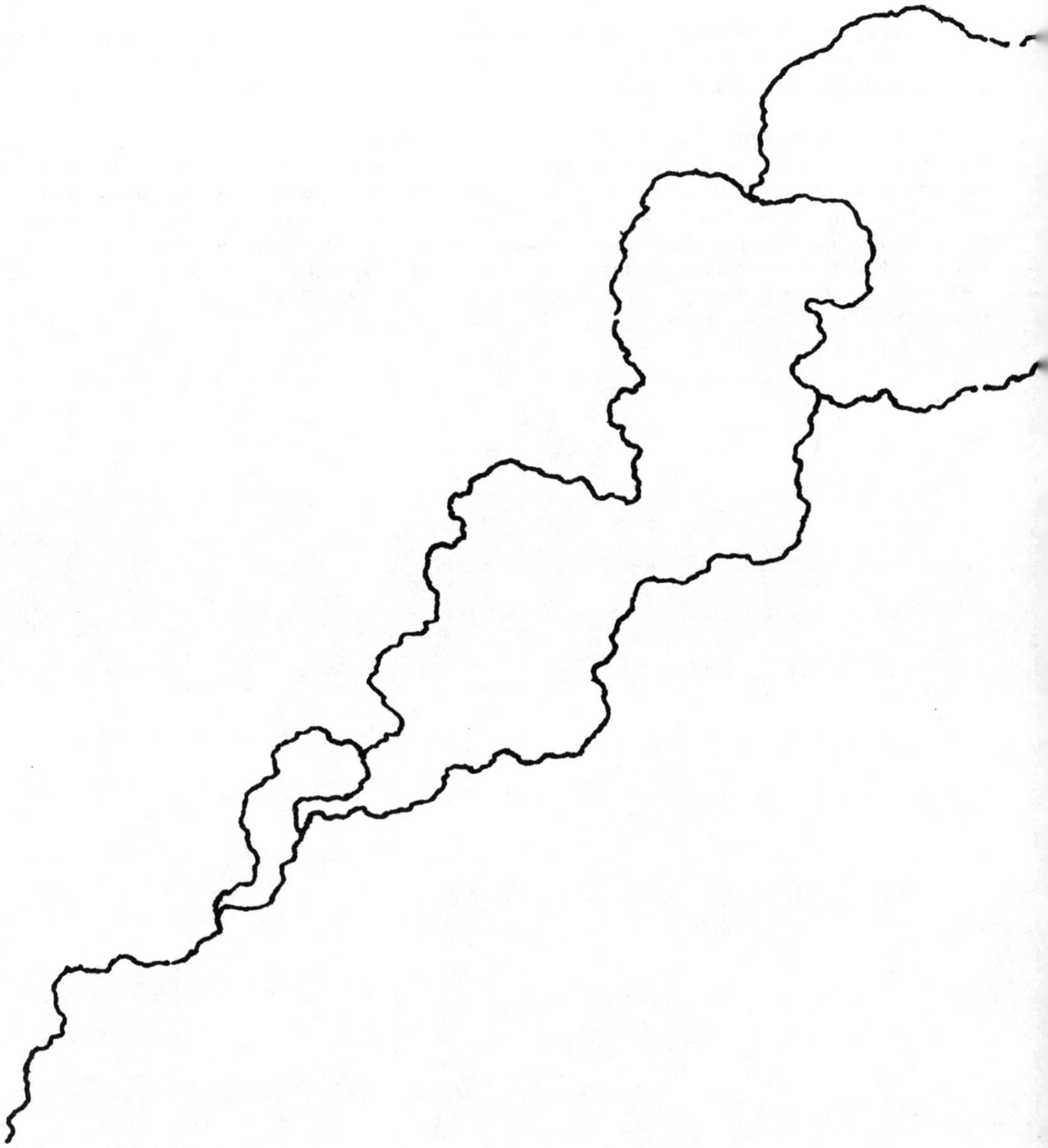

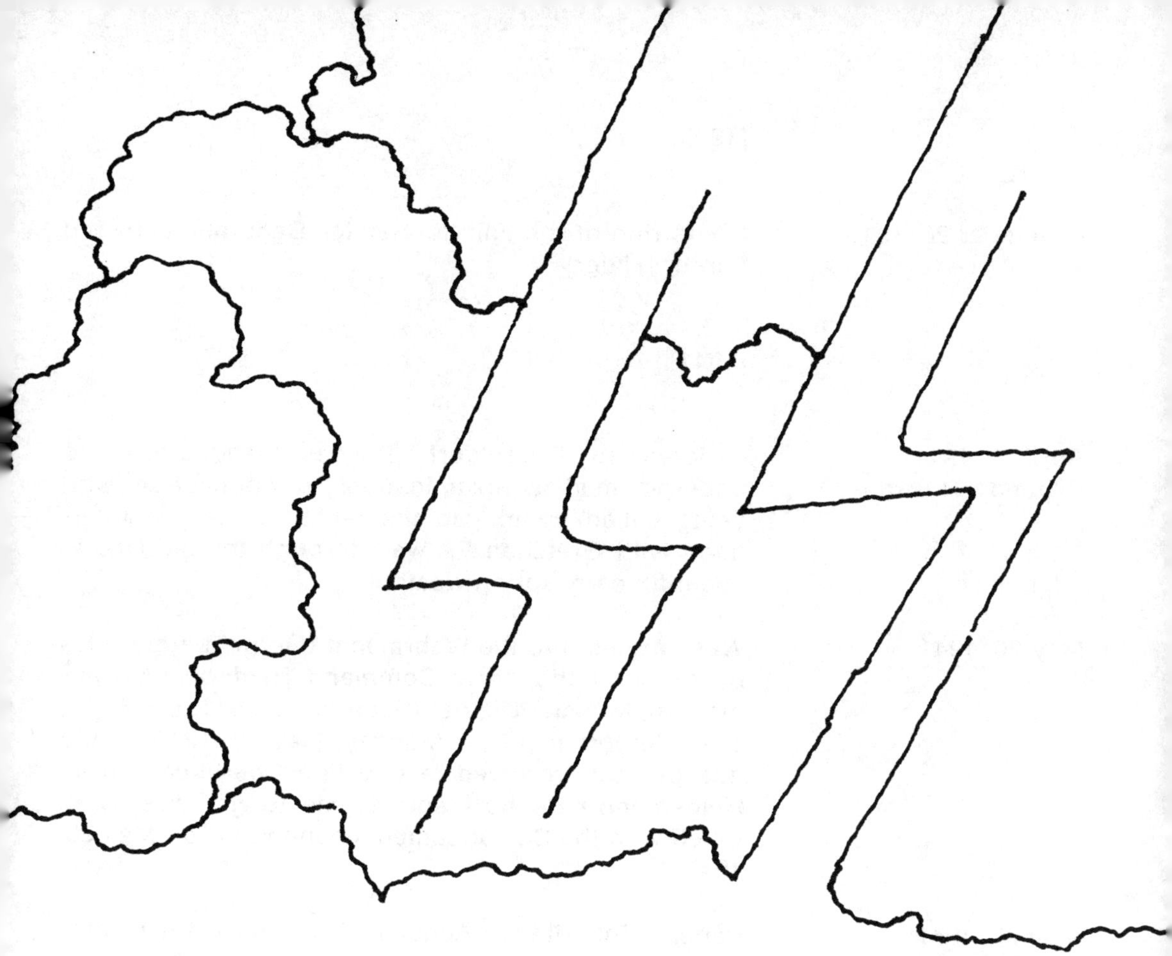

DIARY
of Johann Paul Kremer

[1940][1]

. . . .

November 26, 1940 — Conferring of the Faithful Service Decoration[2] by the Führer [Hitler].

. . . .

[1941]

. . . .

April 10, 1941 (Maundy Thursday) — Ordered to Düsseldorf (Police Headquarters) to undergo medical examination, in connection with being called up to join the ranks of the SS. Afternoon with Gretchen.[3] A walk through the gardens in beautiful early spring weather.

May 20, 1941 — Was entered into the Wehrmacht [German army] files by order of the Army Command [*Wehrbezirkskommando*], Münster District (Section IIb, 3671) on May 9, 1941. Appointment for Monday, May 12, 1941. Could not get the reserved occupation[4] certificate from Heinemann.[5] Becher[6] advises me to get directly in touch with the SS. Documents handed in [on May 20, 1941].

May 30, 1941 — Paper: " Inherited or Acquired ? A Noteworthy Contribution to the Problem of the Hereditary Nature of Traumatic Deformations " sent today to Professor Dr. G. Just, Berlin-Dahlem, to be published in the journal for the science of human constitution and heredity.

May 31, 1941 — Paper: " New Elements of Cell and Tissue Research " sent today to the editor of *Mikrokosmos*, G. Stehli, Ph.D., Stuttgart-O, Pfizerstrasse 5—7. The editors had asked me to send them a suitable paper.

. . . .

---

1 The text published below is only a part of Kremer's diary written in 1899—1945. We have chosen only excerpts describing how the author found himself in Auschwitz, the entire section dealing with his service at *KL Auschwitz* and fragments concerned with the period following his return to Münster.

2 No exact description of this decoration appears in the diary.

3 The author of the diary omitted the surname of this person.

4 *UK-Schein*—abbreviation used in the army, of the word *unabkömmlich* meaning unavailable, i.e. in reserved occupation.

5 No data as to the position of this person. Probably an employee of the university.

6 From the entries of December 4, 1942, and December 26, 1943, we know that Becher was the Dean of the Faculty of Medicine.

June 3, 1941

Went to Stelberg[7] in the afternoon and saw a young, completely tailless cat belonging to Wurth.[8] Many salamanders and toad larvae in the pond. Took a snapshot of the new horse. Then to Maria[9] in Oberfeld; she is shortly expecting her 3rd child. Supper there. Back to Hartegasse through Stelberg, where Albert[10] brought "Peter"[11] in a sack and basket to be inspected. Rudolf[12] had a giddy turn.

. . . .

June 14, 1941

Ordered to report at the SS Sanitary Office, Berlin W 15, Knesebeckstrasse 43—44, on June 18, 1941, at 2 p.m.

June 18/19, 1941

Left Münster 10.29 p.m. Air-raid warning in Hamm. Arrival at Berlin—Friedrichstrasse at 7.08 a.m. Shaved, had my shoes shined, then by a no. 1 bus to Knesebeckstrasse. Great surprise there! "Now, really! Even professors are now being called up!" Presented myself to the Divisional Surgeon. Was accepted with the rank of *Hauptscharführer* as member of the SS Military Force and got leave to return to Münster till recalled. Filling in of forms and curriculum vitae. Then to dinner at Aschinger's and after that back to Kaiserallee by 57 bus for the medical examination. Then again to Knesebeckstrasse to the Sanitary Office, and after a long wait finally permission to leave. Supper at the Lindenrestaurant. After a short walk around, departure at 9.48 p.m. in a crowded long-distance train. Stood in the corridor the whole time. Again air-raid warning beginning from Hanover. Arrival in Münster at 6.15. Had to wait outside as I had no key. The Witzemanns'[13] Irmgard finally let me in, but could not manage to open the room door upstairs.

---

[7] Place in the vicinity of Münster.

[8] No data concerning this person. It may have been a member of Kremer's family on the maternal side, as his mother's maiden name was Wurthe.

[9] No definite data are to be found in the diary about Maria.

[10] Probably the Christian name of the above-mentioned Wurth.

[11] Cat's name.

[12] Probably a cousin, as the entry of April 15, 1905, states: "my cousin Rudolf was born at Stelberg."

[13] Name of Kremer's neighbours. Kremer spelt this as Wizemann in his subsequent entries. Wizemann was a *Hauptstellenleiter* in the National-Socialist German Workers' Party (*Nationalsozialistische Deutsche Arbeiterpartei*—NSDAP).

Then to Miss Glaser,[14] Kinderhauserstrasse 16, to get the key and the canary. Then to the Anatomy [Building][15] and in the after[noon] took a short nap after spending 2 days and 2 nights in my clothes.

June 30, 1941

Just had returned the paper "Inherited or Acquired" asking me to shorten it by half and to stick to the facts.

. . . .

August 16, 1941 (Saturday)

A telephone call to the Anatomy from the Sanitary Office Berlin, that I am to apply immediately for a military train ticket and to leave for the SS military hospital Munich-Dachau.[16] The call was taken by Havixbeck,[17] who then tried in vain to reach me.

August 18, 1941 (Monday)

As I was going out, Mrs. Lücke[18] told me that somebody had tried to get in touch with me on Saturday, as I had been "called up." I went to the District Army Command, but nobody there knew anything about this. I went to town once again in the afternoon, as I wanted to begin my holiday in Marburg the day after tomorrow. In front of the Anatomy I ran into Havixbeck, who finally told me about the call-up order, while Edom—whom I had asked that same morning—had known nothing about it. In short, I immediately went to the District Army Command and got my ticket to Munich-Dachau.

August 19, 1941 (Tuesday)

After reporting my departure at the Garrison Headquarters I left at 7.32 p.m., headed for Munich, via Dortmund, Essen, Köln, Mainz, Mannheim, Heidelberg, Stuttgart, Augsburg, Ulm.

August 20, 1941

Arrival Munich 11 a.m. Continued journey to Dachau at 12.10 and arrived there at about 1.15 p.m. Presented myself to the Chief Surgeon, *Sturmbannführer* Rossmann, who assigned me to the Sur[gery] Dep[artment].

---

[14] Probably the daughter of Kremer's housekeeper.

[15] The Institute of Anatomy where Kremer worked.

[16] Presumably a training centre for SS physicians, selected to work in concentration camps, existed at the concentration camp in Dachau.

[17] Nothing definite is known of this person. Probably an employee of the university.

[18] One of Kremer's neighbours.

Uniform and room allocation in Room 17 in the Sanitary Barracks. The room quite new and not previously used.

August 21, 1941
Ustf. Wolfbauer
Ustf. Zeidler

Introduced myself at the Surg[ery] Depar[tment] to the Chief, *Hauptsturmführer* Morawe. Spent the afternoon in the polyclinic with him; at the same time had opportunity to meet his wife. Morawe is surgeon in Haspe, his wife is from Duisburg. They have three children.

August 22, 1941
(Friday)

Present at several operations: *Hydrozele funiculi spermatici*,[19] *appendicitis*,[20] extraction of shell splinter with Evipan anaesthesia with strong tremor (lowering of blood pressure).

August 23, 1941
(Saturday)
A Youth.[21]

Studied books. The first Sunday without rain at last. Walked in the afternoon to Mariabrunn, with a delightful view of Munich and the Alps. Edam cheese sandwiches without coupons. Good beer. Back to Dachau through game-preserve with beautiful scenery. At 8 o'clock in the evening went to the charming SS cinema, chiefly to see the weekly news from Russia.

August 24, 1941
(Sunday)

Strong stormy showers again at night. Cloudy and cool. Weather cleared in the daytime. Stayed in camp, packed a parcel and read surgical text-books. Did some writing (Springer, *Mikrokosmos*). Showers again in the evening.

August 25, 1941
(Monday)

3—4 lecture for participants of san[itary] courses (fainting, loss of consciousness, apparent death, chilblains, etc.).

. . . .

August 29, 1941
(Friday)

Have chosen X-ray photos for the lectures in Münster from those of *Hstuf.* Köster from Gelsenkirchen.

August 30, 1941
(Saturday)

Took leave for Saturday and Sunday. Went to Munich in the afternoon and visited Hellabrunn Zoo with its unique pavilion of anthropoidal apes, which Sobotta[22] and his wife were also visiting at

---

[19] Water cyst of the seminal cord.

[20] Appendicitis.

[21] *Ein Junge* in German.

[22] Nothing is known about this person.

the time. The feeding of the young apes was most interesting, with their well-mannered behaviour at table.

August 31, 1941 (Sunday)

Cold rainy weather. In the Soldiers' Cinema in the evening. *Submarines Westwards*.[23]

September 1, 1941 (Monday)

Opening of the new mess-room in the doctors' barracks. On duty in the military hospital for the first time.

September 2, 1941 (Tuesday)

Ustf. Ludwig (ears, nose and throat) called up as a substitute for Schnabel.

. . . .

September 4, 1941 (Thursday)

Coupon for riding-boots. Got 4 cakes of soap and 1 packet of soap flakes. Parcel with cigars arrived from Münster. For breakfast first-class real coffee, fresh bread with plenty of butter, honey and apricot jam. Sandwiches for elevenses. After supper went for a delightful walk with the *Sturmbannführer* through the environs of Dachau. Evening at Ziegler's in the Ludwig-Thoma-Stübel.[24] Wonderful weather.

September 5, 1941 (Friday)

Operated together with *Hstuf.* Morawe. Removed shell splinters from r.[ight] elbow and near r.[ight] groin, also appendectomy.

September 6, 1941 (Saturday)

Was surgeon on duty Saturday and Sunday. A young man with high temperature brought in in the evening to be operated on. Later drinks in the mess-room till 1.30 a.m.

September 20, 1941 (Saturday)

Left for Oberstdorf. Departure Saturday, Sept. 20, at 12.40 p.m. Changed trains in Munich at 3.25 p.m. Here coffee in Rheinischer Hof (beer-house), walk with *Utsf.* Kersten and snapshots with pigeons in front of the Feldherrenhalle in Odeonsplatz. Arrival at Oberstdorf at 8.20 in the evening. Spent the night in Hotel and Café Baur, together with merchant Dewner from Ziegenhain. Cost: 3.50 [RM], breakfast 1.10 [RM]. Lively atmosphere in the evening at the

---

23 *U-Boote westwärts* in German.

24 A restaurant.

concert in the café. Cost of ticket from Dachau to Oberstdorf 2.90 RM.

. . . .

September 23, 1941 — *Ustf.* Ludwig left again for Berlin.

September 24, 1941 — Instruction at the San[itary] School of the SS Military Formations[25] began with a lecture on injuries. Corrected paper sent again to Springer.

September 25, 1941 — *Brigadeführer* Grawitz[26] came to the SS Military Hospital, visited the wards, took his meals in the mess-room together with the surgeons and spent the evening with us, staying till late.

He made interesting disclosures about the future political, economic and ideological state of things. Farewell on Friday morning.

October 7, 1941 — Went to Bayrischzell to stand in for the senior surgeon N. Pankow of the *Waffen-SS* sanatorium[27] (Alpenrose), who was obliged to go to Berlin. First-class food but the weather foggy.

October 8, 1941 — Ride in official car to Berghof (Mrs. Theato) and visit to this beautifully situated and tastefully furnished home. Then proceeded to the Police Home and saw some patients. Splendid sunny weather and very good visibility.

. . . .

October 10, 1941 — Return of Dr. Pankow, and soon after dinner departure via Munich for Dachau. In Munich went to get the *Polyphot* pictures and ordered enlargements.

. . . .

October 13, 1941 — Collected riding-boots from the military clothes store[28] in concentration camp Dachau for 84 RM. I was advised to use linseed oil for the soles and light or yellow leather oil for the upper leather, if boots not in

---

[25] *Sanitäts-Schule der Waffen-SS.*

[26] Senior Surgeon of the SS and Police (*Reichsarzt SS und Polizei*) and Head of the Chief Sanitary Office of the SS.

[27] *Genesungsheim der Waffen-SS.*

[28] Kremer used the undecipherable abbreviation *Unertl.* in his diary. It probably means *Unterkunftslager.* (military clothes store).

use for some time. Evening in the Soldiers' Cinema: *Mrs. Luna.*[29]

October 14, 1941 — Information from Berlin that I am again granted leave till recalled, beginning from tomorrow, to go to Münster. During the night of 14/15 disturbing noise in the mess-room, made chiefly by Wolfbauer, Kersten, Pfister, Metzmacher and others, who forcibly tried to enter my bedroom. They broke the window, threw water, bread and pieces of iron inside, tried to pick the lock, making an unbelievable racket.

October 15, 1941 — Reported the night's occurrences, on the advice of Plötner, Pauli and Morawe, to Dep[uty] Chief Surgeon Köster. Then farewells in the mess-room at noon. In the afternoon return of the remaining items of uniform to the store and at 8 o'clock departure with 2 pharmacists for the station, where I had already deposited my trunk in the morning, in the rain. Departure from Munich at 6.40 p.m. through Augsburg, Stuttgart, Mannheim, Köln, Düsseldorf and arrival at Münster at 9.32 in the morning. Mrs. Deppe[30] at once prepared dinner for me.

. . . .

November 9, 1941 (Sunday) — Appointed *Unterscharführer* of the *Waffen-SS*.

. . . .

[1942]

January 14, 1942 (Wednesday) — Have just received news through the Chief Surgeon of the SS Garrison Hospital in Dachau, that I was promoted on Nov.[ember] 9, 1941, from *SS-Reserveführer* to *SS-Untersturmführer*.

January 16, 1942 — Lieutenant Helmut Cremer from Hörde killed in the East.

---

[29] *Frau Luna* in German.

[30] One of Kremer's neighbours.

January 21, 1942 (Wednesday)

Things have begun to move.[31] My publication: "A Noteworthy Contribution to the Problem of the Hereditary Nature of in Traumatic Deformations" seems to have been printed, as Prof. Dr. Hofmeier, University Clinic, Strassburg (Citizens' Hospital) is the first to ask me for an impression.

January 27, 1942 (Tuesday)

Sanitary Inspector Dr. M. Schiller, M.[unicipal] Sanitary Office, Stuttgart W. Rotebühlstrasse 43, informed me, in connection with my above mentioned publication, that a scar on one of her ears is related to an injury of her father's. She further thought that the corneous inside surface of palms and soles in the case of one family might be linked with visual influence during pregnancy. The paper in question has also appeared in the journal for problems of human heredity (1942, no. 2). She would be very glad to have the impressions of hands relating to my case.

January 30, 1942 (Friday)

I received the following letter from Prof. Hans Weinert, Director of the Institute of Anthropology at the University of Kiel, Hospitalstrasse 20: "Dear Professor,—I am certainly not the only one who wants to contact you after reading your sensational treatise on the possible hereditary nature of traumatic deformations. Your communication is of immense importance and the fact that it was not publicised before speaks in its favour. Your thorough investigations have solved many problems simultaneously.—Would it be possible to let me have the original photos of the hands (also X-ray pictures) ? I would use them only for my lectures. I am always ready to reciprocate.

Heil Hitler![32]
Respectfully yours,
Signed Hans Weinert."

January 31, 1942 (Saturday)

Today, on the hundredth birthday of my late father,[33] I saw for the first time the volume with the above mentioned paper in the univ[ersity] library here. But so far I have not received any copies of it.

---

[31] In the German original *Die Puppen sind am Tanzen*.

[32] The Nazi greeting, also used in correspondence at the end of letters.

[33] Wilhelm Kremer—the father of Johann Paul—was a miller who later farmed an estate of 70 morgs. He died in 1900 at the age of 58. The author's mother (Elisabeth née Wurthe) died in 1910, aged 69. The family consisted of four sons and one daughter.

I wrote long letters to my sister, to Hermann and Gretchen[34] about the 100th birthday of my father.

. . . .

March 17, 1942 Treated the canary with "Nebelord" for mites, which had bothered it considerably.

March 22, 1942 Party Group Leader[35] Sprenger has asked for an opinion about me.

March 23, 1942 Hännschen[36] ceased to suffer at 2 p.m. I was extremely sorry, as I had been so used to this poor little fellow, always so lively. Cremation. Party Group Leader Sprenger came in the evening and issued a political reference about me, which he allegedly has been asked for by somebody outside. [The last sentence crossed out in the original—Editor's note].

. . . .

May 5, 1942 Mrs. Thiemann and Miss Rebbe came visiting here last week. The latter left today and Mrs. Thiemann returned home on Sunday. Bought today a fire-proof porcelain pot at the Kepa for 4.25 RM. Have just received a postcard from Otto, who announces that he will be visiting me as an "air-raid victim." Immediately answered that I could not possibly put him up here and so was forced to disappoint him under the present difficult conditions. A swelling has suddenly appeared on my left eye; I hope it is not an orbital sarcoma [*Orbitalsarkom*]!

May 6, 1942 Otto arrived after all at about 11 p.m. He said he had first gone to Clieve near Anrichts where he had been at military school some 38 years ago. He seemed rather depressed and left shortly before midnight for the station, where he thought he would get a night's lodging by showing his certificate of having been bombed out. He intended to go to Gretchen the next morning, to Düsseldorf, where he had already invited himself to dinner.

. . . .

---

34 Probably Kremer's sister and brother-in-law (compare entry of August 11, 1945).

35 *Zellenleiter*—District Official of the NSDAP party group.

36 Name of canary.

May 9, 1942

Today (Saturday) Agnes arrived from Köln and wants to stay till tomorrow evening. Again she brought all sorts of delicacies (ham, bacon, sausage).

. . . .

May 19, 1942

H. Weinert's reply to my paper arrived today: chance has by chance coincided with another chance.

. . . .

June 20, 1942

This morning handed the documents dealing with my former divorce proceedings, together with the marriage certificate,[37] to Professor Hallermann, in order to have the divorce proceedings resumed. He reiterated, as he had done time and again, that after a separation of 20 years a marriage is bound to be dissolved; but I would not escape paying alimony. I then signed the papers giving him power of attorney at the hearing.—The starlings are sitting on eggs for the second time. Ordered today vegetables from a stall keeper in the market.

. . . .

July 25, 1942

Today, Saturday, rode by bicycle to the allotment of Fritz Steinkamp, who let me have as many currants as I could gather, free. I returned with blackcurrants, lovage[38] and cherries as well. There I had the opportunity to practise again my youthful prank of climbing the tree without the help of a ladder.
With the consent of the Chairman of the Court of Honour of the N[ational] S[ocialist] G[erman] Medical Society[39] in Munich, I was appointed as from today assessor of the disciplinary tribunal for the district of Westphalia-North by its President Dr. Fenner.

August 4, 1942

Queued today in a downpour for 2 hours to get 2 herrings. Then presented myself to the district President (Pg) [*Parteigenosse*] Dr. Fenner, Eisenbahnstrasse 10 II, District Office for National Socialist Workers' Party, N.S. Medical Society, Münster in Westphalia.[40] Was made most cordially welcome!

. . . .

[37] Kremer was married in 1920 and after some months separated from his wife. He did not obtain a formal divorce until 1942 (compare entry of September 9, 1942).

[38] *Liebstöckel* in German—herb used as ingredient for sauces and soups.

[39] *Nationalsozialistischer Deutscher Ärztebund*—National Socialistic German Medical Society. The District Court of Honour was called *Gau-Disziplinargericht. Organisationsbuch der NSDAP*, München 1943, Zentralverlag der NSDAP, Franz Eher Nachf., p. 235.

[40] *Gauamtsleitung für Volksgesundheit der NSDAP.*

August 8, 1942	Ordered to join the SS Military Hospital in Prague as of August 15, 1945, till the end of term holidays.
August 14, 1942 (Friday)	Departure for Prague: Münster—8.40 p.m., Osnabrück—0.57, Dresden: Arrival—10.12 a.m., departure —11.22 a.m. Arrival in Prague—3.15 p.m.
August 15, 1942	Beginning from Dresden, beautiful sunny weather. Went from station by tram to the SS Military Hospital Podol and introduced myself to the superintendent, *Sturmbannführer* Dr. Fietsch. Accommodation in a patient's room on 3rd floor (no. 344). Surgeons, etc. Aide-de-camp: *Hstf.* Koebel, pharmacist; Head of the Administration: *Stubf.* Dorn; Surgery: *Stubf.* Winne from Danzig, Liek's pupil; Internal [Diseases]: *Stubf.* Leppel from Köln; Skin: *Obstuf.* In den from Düsseldorf; Eyes: *Obscharf.* Frederking from Langendreer; X-rays: *Obstuf.* Jung from Aachen; Neurology: *Obstuf.* Janzen.
August 16, 1942 (Sunday)	A half hour's trip through town to see the sights with *Oschf.* Frederking and wife from Langendreer. Later a cup of mocha coffee in a café (1.50 RM).
August 20, 1942	Evening in the mess-room with wine from old supplies, surgeon on duty at the same time.
August 21, 1942	Ordered an SS officer's cap from the Office for Distribution of Clothes of the SS[41] in Berlin by messenger who, however, did not succeed in getting it.
August 24, 1942	Bought paper, spectacles and a belt. My room-mate (patient) *Ustuf.* Fritz Joachim from St. Andrä, Postal District St. Rupprecht near Villach (Carinthia), was today transferred to Hohenlychen. Room no. 464.
August 27, 1942	*Brigadeführer* Gentzken[42] visited the hospital on his

[41] *Reichskelderkasse der Schutzstaffeln.*

[42] The person in question was probably the Head of the Sanitary Service of the SS (*Chef des Sanitätswesens der Waffen-SS*) Dr. Karl Genzken, whose name Kremer misspelt.

way to Carlsbad. He spoke of the repudiation of intellectualism, particularly by Goebbels,[43] of the gradual deterioration of the universities and of the Ministry for Population Policy.[44]

August 28, 1942 — Was sent to Berlin to buy the cap. On leaving I was informed that the officer on duty wanted to speak to me. He told me, on behalf of *Ustuf.* Koebel, that I was not to go to Berlin.

August 29, 1942 — Ordered according to F.S.[45] USSZ 2150 Aug. 28, 42, 1833, no. 1565 to Concentration Camp Auschwitz to replace a surgeon there who had been taken sick.

August 30, 1942
Stabsscharführer Wilhelmy.[47] Vide Virchow Director 1936! — Departure from Prague 8.15 a.m. through Böhmisch Trübau, Olmütz, Prerau, Oderberg. Arrival at Concentration Camp Auschwitz 5.36 p.m. Quarantine in camp on account of numerous contagious diseases (typhus, malaria, dysentery). Received top secret order through the garrison physician *Hauptsturmführer* Uhlenbrock[46] and accommodation in a room (no. 26) in the *Waffen-SS* club-house [Home].[48]

August 31, 1942 — Tropical climate with 28° Centigrade in the shade, dust and innumerable flies! Excellent food in the Home. This evening, for instance, we had sour duck livers for 0.40 RM, with stuffed tomatoes, tomato salad, etc. Water is infected, so we drink seltzer-water which is served free (Mattoni). First inoculation against typhus. Had photo taken for the camp identity card.

September 1, 1942 — Have ordered SS officer's cap, sword-belt and braces from Berlin by letter. In the afternoon was present at the gassing of a block with Cyclon B against lice.

---

[43] Dr. Josef Goebbels, Minister for Propaganda in the Third Reich.

[44] *Ministerium für Bevölkerungspolitik*.

[45] This is probably the order transferring Kremer to the concentration camp of Auschwitz.

[46] *SS-Sturmbannführer* Kurt Uhlenbrock was garrison physician (*Standortärzt*) in the concentration camp of Auschwitz.

[47] *SS-Oberscharführer* Anton Wilhelmy held the position of company chief, under the SS garrison surgeon (*Spiess bei der Dienststelle SS Standortärzt*) in *KL Auschwitz*.

[48] *Haus der Waffen-SS*—hotel building situated near the railway station in the town of Oświęcim (Auschwitz).

September 2, 1942	Was present for first time at a special action[49] at 3 a.m. By comparison Dante's Inferno seems almost a comedy.[50] Auschwitz is justly called an extermination camp!
September 3, 1942	Was for the first time taken ill with the diarrhoea which attacks everybody in the camp here. Vomiting and colic-like paroxysmal pains. Water did not cause it as I had not drunk any. Neither was it the bread. People who take white bread only (diet) also fall ill. Most probably it is the unhealthy continental climate, very dry and tropically hot, with clouds of dust and insects (flies).
September 4, 1942	Against diarrhoea—for 1 day gruel and mint tea, then on diet for a week. Took charcoal tablets and tannalbin. On the way to recovery.
September 5, 1942	At noon was present at a special action in the

---

[49] 957 Jews from the camp at Drancy (France) were brought that day to *KL Auschwitz*. Only 12 men and 27 women out of that number were sent to the camp, the rest were gassed in gas chambers. All data concerning transports are quoted after the Kalendarium der Ereignisse im Konzentrationslager Auschwitz-Birkenau compiled by Danuta Czech and published in *Hefte von Auschwitz*, nos. 2—7.

[50] Kremer was one of the defendants at the trial of the Auschwitz camp garrison. The trial took place before the Supreme National Tribunal in Cracow in the period from November 24 to December 22, 1947. During the interrogation Kremer was repeatedly questioned. It was then that he offered detailed information on the meaning of some of the entries in his diary. Excerpts from his explanations are quoted in this publication under the respective dates. In the official record of the interrogation of August 18, 1947, in Cracow, Kremer stated as follows: "By September 2, 1942, at 3 a.m. I had already been assigned to take part in the action of gassing people. These mass murders took place in small cottages situated outside the Birkenau camp in a wood. The cottages were called 'bunkers' [*Bunker*] in the SS-men's slang. All SS physicians on duty in the camp took turns to participate in the gassings, which were called *Sonderaktion* [special action]. My part as physician at the gassing consisted in remaining in readiness near the bunker. I was brought there by car. I sat in front with the driver and an SS hospital orderly [*SDG*] sat in the back of the car with oxygen apparatus to revive SS-men, employed in the gassing, in case any of them should succumb to the poisonous fumes. When the transport with people who were destined to be gassed, arrived at the railway ramp, the SS officers selected from among the new arrivals persons fit to work, while the rest—old people, all children, women with children in their arms and other persons not deemed fit to work—were loaded onto lorries and driven to the gas chambers. I used to follow behind the transport till we reached the bunker. There people were driven into the barrack huts where the victims undressed and then went naked to the gas chambers. Very often no incidents occurred, as the SS-men kept people quiet, maintaining that they were to bathe and be deloused. After driving all of them into the gas chamber the door was closed and an SS-man in a gas mask threw the contents of a Cyclon tin through an opening in the side wall. The shouting and screaming of the victims could be heard through that opening and it was clear that they were fighting for their lives [*Lebenskampf*]. These shouts were heard for a very short while. I should say for some minutes, but I am unable to give the exact length of time."

women's camp[51] (Moslems)[52]—the most horrible of all horrors. *Hschf.* Thilo,[53] military surgeon, was right when he said to me today that we are located here in the *anus mundi* [anus of the world]. In the evening at about 8 p.m. another special action with a draft from Holland.[54] Men compete to take part in such actions as they get additional rations—1/5 litre vodka, 5 cigarettes, 100 grammes of sausage and bread. Today and tomorrow (Sunday) on duty.

September 6, 1942

Today an excellent Sunday dinner: tomato soup, one half chicken with potatoes and red cabbage (20 grammes of fat), dessert and magnificent vanilla ice-cream. After dinner we welcomed the new garrison doctor, *Obersturmführer* Wirths[55] from Waldbröl. *Sturmbannführer* Fietsch in Prague had been his regimental surgeon.

It has been a week since I came to camp and still I have not been able to get rid of fleas in my room

---

[51] A selection took place that day in the women's camp at Birkenau, resulting in the killing in gas chambers of about 800 women prisoners. In the formal record of the interrogation of July 18, 1947 (Cracow) Kremer explained this entry as follows: "The action of gassing emaciated women from the women's camp was particularly unpleasant. Such individuals were generally called *Muselmänner* [Moslems]. I remember taking part in the gassing of such women in daylight. I am unable to state how numerous that group was. When I came to the bunker they sat clothed on the ground. As the clothes were in fact worn out camp clothes, they were not let into the undressing barracks but undressed in the open. I could deduce from the behaviour of these women that they realized what was awaiting them. They begged the SS-men to be allowed to live, they wept, but all of them were driven into the gas chamber and gassed. Being an anatomist I had seen many horrors, had dealt with corpses, but what I then saw was not to be compared with anything ever seen before. It was under the influence of these impressions that I noted in my diary, under the date of September 5, 1942: 'The most horrible of all horrors. *Hauptsturmführer* Thilo was right when he said to me today that we were located here in the *anus mundi*.' I used this expression because I could not imagine anything more sickening and more horrible."

[52] Prisoners in a state of acute starvation were called Moslems in camp slang. A Moslem was like a walking skeleton. The bones were barely covered with skin, the eyes had a far-away look. Apathy and somnolence were typical symptoms of starvation disease. Complete psychological exhaustion went together with general physicial emaciation.

[53] *SS-Obersturmführer* Heinz Thilo, Doctor of Medicine, was a camp physician in *KL Auschwitz*.

[54] 714 Jews were brought in a draft from Westerbork (Holland) to *KL Auschwitz*. Only 53 women were sent to the camp, the rest were killed in gas chambers. In the official record of the interrogation of July 18, 1947 (Cracow) Kremer explained: "An SS physician was always present at such gassings. The physicians took turns in being on duty. Among the physicians of the period when I was in the camp I remember the following names: Thilo, Kitt, Uhlenbrock, Wirths, Meyer, Entress. The special actions mentioned in my diary were only part of the actions, which were taking place during the time covered by my diary. There were, of course, many more, only other physicians participated in these."

[55] *SS-Sturmbannführer* Eduard Wirths, Doctor of Medicine, was a camp physician at *KL Auschwitz*.

in spite of using all kinds of insecticides, such as Flit (*Cuprex*) etc.

I got a refreshing impression after visiting the commandant's aide-de-camp for the first time. Above his room I saw a big inscription on paper, "Cyclists, dismount!"[56] We have also verses worthy of notice hanging in the office of our SS hospital:

"If you make a thousand lucky hits,
People see them, they nod and pass,
But even the smallest yelping dog
Will never forget, should you miss but once!"[57]

In the evening at 8 o'clock attended another special action outdoors.[58]

September 7, 1942

The second inoculation against typhus. Rainy and cool weather today.

September 9,1942

I see light again; the black curtain hanging over my life has been lifted!

This morning I received most welcome news from my solicitor Professor Dr. Hallermann in Münster, that I was divorced from my wife from the 1st of this month. Later was present as physician at the flogging of 8 camp inmates[59] and at one execution by shooting with a small-calibre gun. Got soap flakes and 2 cakes of soap. At noon a civilian jumped out of the blue at my bicycle, just like an assassin, ran alongside and begged me to tell him whether I was State Councillor Heuner from Breslau to whom I bore a remarkable resemblance. He had fought in World War I side by side with that gentleman. How many doubles have I, then,

[56] In the original *Radfahrer absteigen*, an ironical allusion to persons who bow their heads (a cyclist's position) in front of their superiors, while treading (the movement when pedalling) on their inferiors.

[57] The text in the original is as follows:

Has Du im Leben tausend Treffer,
Man sieht's, man nickt, man geht vorbei,
Doch nie vergisst der kleinste Kläffer,
Schiesst du ein einzig Mal vorbei.

[58] That day 981 Jews were brought from the camp at Drancy (France) to *KL Auschwitz*. 16 men and 38 women out of this number were admitted to the camp as prisoners. The rest were killed in gas chambers.

[59] In the printed form of a punishment order (*Strafvergügung*) there was the notice that a prisoner sentenced to be flogged should be examined by the SS doctor before the punishment. The doctor was also to be present at the punishment. The doctor signed the form, thus recording his examination and his presence. But this was a mere formality. SS doctors never examined prisoners sentenced to be flogged nor was there ever a case recorded of a doctor opposing the inflicting of that punishment. Henryk Kuszaj: Strafen, die von der SS an Häftlingen des Konzentrationslagers Auschwitz vollzogen wurden. *Hefte von Auschwitz*, Oświęcim 1960, no. 3, pp. 14, 40 and 41.

	running about in this world ?[60] In the evening present at a special action (4th time).[61]
September 10, 1942	In the morning was present at a special action (5th time).[62]
September 11, 1942	*Obersturmbannführer* Lolling[63] came to camp today, and when presented to him I learned only then that I was standing in for *Hauptscharführer* Kitt,[64] who was now convalescing in Obersalzberg.
September 14, 1942	Again relapsed into the Auschwitz illness ; temperature 37.8° Centigrade. Today given the third and final inoculation against typhus.
September 17, 1942	Have ordered a casual coat from the Clothes Distribution Office [*Kleiderkasse*] in Berlin. Tailor's measurements : down to the waist 48, whole length 133, half of the back 22, down to the elbow 51, whole length of sleeve 81, chest measurement 107, waist 100, seat 124. Have enclosed coupons for the coat, as part of my uniform. Together with Dr. Meyer[65] today visited the women's camp in Birkenau.
September 20, 1942	This Sunday afternoon from 3 p.m. till 6 p.m. I listened to a concert of the prisoners' orchestra in glorious sunshine ; the Kappelmeister was a conductor of the Warsaw State Opera. 80 musicians. Roast pork for dinner, baked tench for supper.
September 21, 1942	Wrote to the Police Head Office in Köln (Criminal Dep[artment]) in connection with Otto. Duck for supper. Dr. Meyer told me about the hereditary nature of a trauma (nose) in the family of his father-in-law.

---

60 This question is asked by Kremer in connection with the entry of April 14, 1942, when he related a similar occurrence.

61 That evening 893 Jews were brought to *KL Auschwitz* in a transport from Westerbork (Holland). 59 men and 52 women were sent to the camp as prisoners, the rest were killed in gas chambers.

62 That day 1,001 Jews were brought to *KL Auschwitz* from the camp at Malines (Belgium). 21 men and 64 women were sent to the camp, the rest were killed in gas chambers.

63 *SS-Standartenführer* Enno Lolling, Doctor of Medicine, was the Head of the Sanitary Office in the SS Economic and Administrative Head Office.

64 *SS-Obersturmführer* Bruno Kitt, Doctor of Medicine, was Senior Physician of the women's hospital at Birkenau.

65 *SS-Obersturmführer* Georg Franz Meyer, Doctor of Medicine, was a camp physician at *KL Auschwitz*.

September 23, 1942 — This night was present at the 6th and 7th special actions.[66] *Obergruppenführer* Pohl[67] with suite arrived at the *Waffen-SS* club-house in the morning. The sentry at the door presented arms before me for the first time. At 8 o'clock in the evening supper in the Home with *Obergruppenführer* Pohl, a truly festive meal. We had baked pike, as much of it as we wanted, real coffee, excellent beer and sandwiches.

September 25, 1942 — *Gruppenführer* Grawitz visited the hospital and the camp. During the visit he asked me what a physician should, first of all, prescribe in all cases of infectious diseases. I really could not give an answer as it is not possible to generalize in such cases. And what was it he had in mind? Listen and be surprised—a laxative! As if a physician should prescribe a laxative for every cold, sore throat, diphtheria, not to mention typhoid! Medical knowledge cannot be schematized like that, not to mention the fact that a young, inexperienced doctor in the hospital had just a few days ago lost his patient by carelessly prescribing castor oil in the case of a freshly perforated gastric ulcer.

September 27, 1942 — This Sunday afternoon, from 4 till 8, a party in the club with supper, free beer and cigarettes. Speech by Commandant Höss and a musical and theatrical programme.

September 30, 1942 — This night was present at the 8th special action.[68] *Hstuf.* Aumeier[69] told me, when I asked for information, that *KL Auschwitz* was over 12 kilometres in length and 8 kilometres wide. Its area covered 22,000 morgs [1 morg—5,600 m^2], including 12,000 morgs of arable and 2,000 morgs of fish ponds.[70]

---

[66] A transport of Jews from Slovakia was brought that day, and after the selection 294 men and 67 women were admitted to the camp. On the same day a transport of Jews arrived from the camp at Drancy (France), from which 65 men and 144 women were sent to the camp. The rest of both transports were gassed.

[67] *SS-Obergruppenführer* Oswald Pohl, Head of the Economic and Administrative Head Office.

[68] On that day 617 Jews were brought to *KL Auschwitz*. 37 men and 119 women were admitted to the camp as prisoners, the rest were killed in gas chambers.

[69] *SS-Hauptsturmführer* Hans Aumeier was one of the *Lagerführers* of the Auschwitz camp.

[70] The activity zone (*Interessengebiet*) of *KL Auschwitz*. See p. 121, note 56.

October 3, 1942	Today I preserved fresh material from the human liver, spleen and pancreas,[71] also lice from persons infected with typhus, in pure alcohol. Whole streets at Auschwitz are down with typhus. I therefore took the first inoculation against abdominal typhus. *Obersturmbannführer* Schwarz[72] ill with typhus!
October 6, 1942	*Obersturmführer* Entress[73] met with an accident on his motorcycle; I dressed his injuries; Commandant Höss fell from his horse; *Obersturmführer* Wirths still absent.
October 7, 1942	Present at the 9th special action (new arrivals and women Moslems).[74] Wirths finally back. Am acting for Entress in the men's camp (introducing doctors, etc.).
October 9, 1942	Parcel with 9 lb. soft soap, value 200 RM, sent to Münster. Rainy weather.

---

[71] In the official record of the interrogation of July 30, 1947 (Cracow) Kremer offered the following explanation in connection with this matter: "In my diary I mentioned in several entries the taking, for research purposes, of fresh human material. It was like this: I had been for an extensive period of time interested in investigating the changes developing in the human organism as a result of starvation. At Auschwitz I mentioned this to Wirths who said that I would be able to get completely fresh material for my research from those prisoners who were killed by phenol injections. To choose suitable specimens I used to visit the last block on the right [Block 28], where sick prisoners from the camp came for medical examination. During the examination the prisoners who acted as doctors presented the patients to the SS physician and described the illness of the patient. The SS physician decided then—taking into consideration the prisoner's chances of recovery—whether he should be treated in the hospital, perhaps as an outpatient, or be liquidated. Those placed by the SS physician in the latter group were led away by the SS orderlies. The SS physician primarily designated for liquidation those prisoners whose diagnosis was *Allgemeine Körperschwäche* [general bodily exhaustion]. I used to observe such prisoners and if one of them aroused my interest, owing to his advanced state of emaciation, I asked the orderly to reserve the given patient for me and let me know when he would be killed with an injection. At the time fixed by the orderly the patients selected by me were again brought to the last block, and were put into a room on the other side of the corridor opposite the room where the examinations, during which the patient had been selected, had taken place. The patient was put upon the dissecting table while he was still alive. I then approached the table and put several questions to the man as to such details which pertained to my research. For instance, I asked what his weight had been before the arrest, how much weight he had lost since then, whether he took any medicines, etc. When I had collected my information the orderly approached the patient and killed him with an injection in the vicinity of the heart. As far as I knew only phenol injections were used. Death was instantaneous after the injection. I myself never made any lethal injections."

[72] *SS-Hauptsturmführer* Heinrich Schwarz was the head of the Prisoners' Employment Section (*Arbeitseinsatz*).

[73] *SS-Obersturmführer* Friedrich Karl Hermann Entress, Doctor of Medicine, was a camp physician at *KL Auschwitz*.

[74] On that day 2,012 Jews were brought to *KL Auschwitz* from Westerbork. 40 men and 58 women were sent to the camp as prisoners. The rest were killed in gas chambers.

October 10, 1942 — Fresh material from liver, spleen and pancreas taken and preserved. Had a stamp with facsimile of my signature made for me by prisoners. Had heat in my room for the first time. Cases of typhus and typhoid still occurring. Camp still closed.[75]

October 11, 1942 — For Sunday dinner roast hare, a whole fat haunch, with dumplings and red cabbage, for 1.25 RM.

October 12, 1942 (Hössler!)[76] — The second inoculation against typhus; strong reaction in the evening (fever). In spite of this was present at night at another special action with a draft from Holland (1,600 persons). Horrible scene in front of the last bunker! This was the 10th special action.[77]

October 13, 1942 — Arrival of *Ustuf.* Vetter.[78] *Stubaf.* Cäsar[79] also ill with typhus, after his wife died of it a few days ago. Was present at a punishment and then at the execution of 7 Polish civilians.[80]

October 14, 1942 — Got the overcoat (size 52) from Berlin, price 50 RM. Following the suggestion of the Sanitary Office, I have

---

[75] On account of an epidemic of spotted fever in the camp and cases of the disease noted among the SS, Höss ordered a temporary closing of the camp (*Lagersperre*) on July 10, 1942, and its complete isolation on July 23, 1942. On October 7, 1942, these restrictions were partly lifted, though the camp continued not to accept new transports. The temporary regulations included, for example, a ban on leaving the camp by the SS-men and their families (without valid passes), restrictions as to their movement within the camp and a ban on visits to the town of Auschwitz. *Cf.* Danuta Czech: Rola męskiego obozu szpitalnego w KL Auschwitz II. *Zeszyty Oświęcimskie*, Oświęcim 1974, no. 15, pp. 23—34.

[76] *SS-Obersturmbannführer* Hössler was the *Schutzhaftlagerführer* in the women's camp at Birkenau.

[77] On that day 1,703 Jews from Holland were brought to *KL Auschwitz*. 244 men and 108 women were sent to the camp as prisoners. The rest were killed in gas chambers. In the official record of the investigation of July 18, 1947 (Cracow), Kremer gave the following explanation for this entry: "In connection with the gassing described by me in my diary under the date of October 12, 1942, I have to explain that around 1,600 Dutchmen were then gassed. This is an approximate figure which I noted down after hearing it mentioned by others. This action was conducted by the SS officer Hössler. I remember how he tried to drive the whole group into one bunker. He was successful except for one man, whom it was not possible by any means to squeeze inside the bunker. This man was killed by Hössler with a pistol shot. I therefore wrote in my diary about horrible scenes in front of the last bunker, and I mentioned Hössler's name in connection with this incident."

[78] *SS-Obersturmführer* Helmuth Vetter, Doctor of Medicine, was a camp physician at *KL Auschwitz*.

[79] *SS-Obersturmführer* Dr. Joachim Caesar was head of the agricultural units connected with *KL Auschwitz*.

[80] The civilians mentioned here were probably those brought from the prison at Myslowitz and kept in Block 11 (Block of Death), who remained at the disposal of the Summary Police Court. Sessions of this "court" took place once every few months at *KL Auschwitz*. Its president was Dr. Rudolf Mildner, head of the Gestapo in Kattowitz, and later Dr. Thümmler.

	asked about the beginning of the winter term in Münster.
October 15, 1942	First frost this night, the afternoon again sunny and warm. Fresh material of liver, spleen and pancreas taken from an abnormal individual.
October 16, 1942 Soap, soap flakes, foodstuffs	This afternoon I sent the second parcel, value 300 RM, to Mrs. Wizemann, to be kept for me. Had a photo taken of a syndactylous Jew in camp (father and uncle had the same affliction).
October 17, 1942	Was present at a punishment and 11 executions. Have taken fresh liver, spleen and pancreas material after an injection of pilocarpine. Drove to Mikołów with Wirths, who had told me earlier that I would have to stay on longer.[81]
October 18, 1942	In wet and cold weather was on this Sunday morning present at the 11th special action (from Holland). Terrible scenes when 3 women begged merely to have their lives spared.[82]
October 19, 1942	Went to Kattowitz with *Ostuf.* Wirths and Mrs. Höss[83] to buy shoulder-straps for the overcoat. Got back through Mikołów.
October 24, 1942	6 women from the Budy[84] mutiny got the needle[85] [phenol injections] (Klehr).[86]

---

[81] i.e. in *KL Auschwitz*.

[82] On that day 1,710 Jews from Holland were brought to *KL Auschwitz*. 116 women were directed to the camp as prisoners. The rest were killed in gas chambers. In the official record of the interrogation of July 18, 1947 (Cracow) Kremer made the following statement in connection with this entry: "During the special action, described by me in my diary under the date of October 18, 1942, three women from Holland refused to enter the gas chamber and begged for their lives. They were young and healthy women, but their begging was to no avail. The SS-men, taking part in the action, shot them on the spot."

[83] Hedwig Höss, née Hensel; the commandant of the Auschwitz camp married her on August 17, 1929. They had five children, born in the years 1930—1943 (two sons and three daughters).

[84] *Cf.* Broad's reminiscences, pp. 120—123, and Höss's diary, p. 59.

[85] In the official record of the interrogation of July 30, 1947 (Cracow) Kremer explained this entry as follows: "I was present once again at a killing with a phenol injection, this time of one of the six women from the group who were sentenced to death as a result of the so-called mutiny at Budy. The execution was performed by Klehr, in the dissecting room of the last block on the right at Auschwitz [Block 28]. All these women were healthy, of German origin, I think. They were killed by Klehr in a sitting position. I was detached to be present at the execution in order to certify death. I looked on while the first of these women was killed and then left."

[86] *SS-Oberscharführer* Josef Klehr was then SS orderly (*SS Sanitätsdienstgrad*) in the camp hospital, where he used to kill prisoners with phenol injections through the heart.

October 25, 1942

Today, Sunday, took a bicycle trip via Rajsko to Budy in wonderful autumn weather. Wilhelmy back from his trip to Croatia (plum brandy).

October 31, 1942

Very beautiful autumn weather for the last 14 days, so that every day one has the opportunity of sunbathing in the garden of the *Waffen-SS* club-house. Even the clear nights are relatively mild. As Thilo and Meyer are home on leave I took over the duties of military physician. On account of an official trip to my military authorities I asked for 5 days' leave to go to the SS military hospital in Prague.

November 1, 1942

Today, Sunday, after duty in the hospital, chiefly collecting blood samples from venulae, at 1.01 p.m. departure from Auschwitz by long-distance train to Prague. Rain on the way; the train was overcrowded. Arrival in Prague at 10.30 in the evening. In utter darkness I finally got to the SS military hospital, using several trams, and there a nurse I knew put me up for the night on an "ottoman" in Dr. Schreiber's office.

November 2, 1942

Was very early awakened from my dreams by Dr. Schreiber and had to leave my primitive bed with its horsecloth. After breakfast in the SS Home kitchen I mailed the 3rd parcel with boots and apple compote (value 300 RM) to Münster. Then reported to the Chief, *Stubaf.* Fietsch, and later food at Deutsches Haus (Graben). Afterwards I got my riding-boots (32 RM) in Gerstengasse and returned to the SS officers' mess at 5.30 p.m. for a first-class meal of one course with lots of meat. In the evening I visited *Hstuf.* Rüttner in his room. He described his new technique of operating on tonsils and also told me the latest jokes in Berlin (*Odab—o du arme Landwirtschaft*—oh, you poor agriculture; England is situated farthest from Europe;[87] What would you do if I acted like Hess?[88] Hermann:[89] Führer, we'll follow you! Goebbels: Führer,[90] we thank you; etc.).

---

[87] The point of the joke is that the Nazi army had not invaded England in spite of several years of warfare.

[88] Rudolf Hess, Hitler's deputy in the NSDAP, escaped by plane to Great Britain on April 5, 1941, and was interned there till the end of the war.

[89] Hermann Göring, Marshal of the Reich.

[90] Adolf Hitler is meant here. He held the title of *Führer* (leader of the party).

November 3, 1942

After breakfast I took tram no. 17 to the market where I managed to buy some press-studs and, most important, a very smart potato grater. Then back again to the town centre, where I ordered reading glasses at a price of 14.50 RM, and finally had dinner at the Deutsches Haus. I went to the Victoria Cinema at 3 p.m. and saw the picture *Andreas Schlütter*. I was quite surprised to see the most luxurious and tasteful furnishings of the place, and I must confess I have never before visited a cinema of such elegance. The production of the film had cost fabulous sums, and Heinrich George was its star performer. It presented the situation of an independent, creative man who failed to get the recognition he deserved from his fellow men and who was finally ruined by intrigues and persecution. Owing to my own experiences I felt the final words very deeply: "Life passes but deeds are eternal."

November 4, 1942

Early this morning I tried above all to take some pictures of Prague Castle as seen from the Oberlandrat Building and from the Manes Bridge. The sunlight was very capricious. Then I proceeded to the Old Town to do some shopping. In the vicinity of Altstätter-Ring I bought a fountain pen for 7.50 RM and a lady's handbag for 14.35 RM. Then back to the hospital to a one-course dinner at 12.30 p.m. Here I learned that I should vacate my room as an *Ostubaf.* was to occupy it. The man in question was a patient of IIb in the emergency ward. I now had to take my suitcases to his room. He was, however, sufficiently careful to have a brief look at my room first. After that he changed his mind, so I could carry my suitcases back again to my room upstairs. He was *Ostubaf.* Deutsch and he told me that *Stubaf.* Fietsch had been his regimental surgeon. When I asked him about *Ostuf.* Wirths he told me he knew him well and asked me to convey his regards. He explained that Wirths was rather soft and had all sorts of trouble with his wife and children.—After dinner I went again to town, took pictures of the Wenzelplatz as seen from the Landesmuseum, and of the Teinkirche, too. Then I fetched my glasses and went to see Willy Forst's *Operetta*, which had been an immense success and had been on at the Astra in Wenzelplatz for two weeks. The heroine was most adequately played by

Maria Holst. I was fired with enthusiasm when leaving this most exquisitely furnished cinema; one thing only is possible—to love or to work; both at the same time are impossible.—If one has been successful, one is like a mountain climber who has reached the summit. The work is done and one is quite lonely. I was, at any rate, utterly enthusiastic about the film with its Makart style, its Strauss operettas and its sophisticated, gorgeous revues.

November 5, 1942

In the morning I forwarded the 4th parcel, value 300 RM, to Mrs. Wizemann. Contents: lady's handbag with fountain pen, glasses, etc., riding-boots, note-paper, brown shirts,[91] potato grater, etc. Then some shopping in town and dinner at the Deutsches Haus. The weather cloudy and wet. In the evening packing to be ready for next morning's departure and at 8 p.m. party in the mess-room. I drank a whole litre of a wonderful Bulgarian wine which put me into the right frame of mind. It was already past midnight when I went to bed.

November 6, 1942

The nurse woke me at 6 in the morning, and soon after I was at the station (trams nos. 21 and 7), where I got into the express for Mährisch Ostrau at 8.10. In Prerau I changed trains and boarded the Vienna—Cracow express. I had hardly entered the second class compartment, when a major-general started a conversation and was my companion for the rest of the journey. We were almost the only two occupants of the compartment. He told me about his experiences at the front and shook hands with me at the end of the journey. The whole trip Prague—Auschwitz took over 9 hours. Having reached my destination I immediately set off to the SS officers' mess, where at last I had the chance to eat as much as I wanted.

November 8, 1942

Took part this night in 2 special actions in rainy and murky weather (12th and 13th).[92] In the morning I welcomed *Hschaf.* Kitt, a pupil of mine from Essen, at the hospital. Another special action in the afternoon,

---

[91] Brown shirts were worn by the Nazi storm troops (*SA-Sturmabteilungen*).

[92] Jews from the concentration camp at Lublin (Majdanek) were brought on that day. 25 men were sent to the camp as prisoners. The rest (number unknown) were directed to gas chambers.

the 14th in which I had participated[93] so far. In the evening a cosy gathering to which I was invited by *Hstuf*. Wirths, now present in camp. We had Bulgarian red wine and plum brandy from Croatia.

November 10, 1942 — First light snowfall today and frost at night.

November 13, 1942 — Fresh material (liver, spleen and pancreas) from a Jewish prisoner of 18, extremely atrophic,[94] who had been photographed before. As usual, the liver and spleen were preserved in Carnoy, and the pancreas in Zenker[95] (prisoner no. 68030).[96]

November 14, 1942 — Today, Saturday, a variety theatre performance in the mess-room (quite grand!). The dancing dogs excited great enthusiasm and so did the bantam cocks which crowed in unison, the packaged man and the group of cyclists.

November 15, 1942 — Was present at a punishment in the morning.

November 16, 1942 — Sent a parcel of soft soap (circa 12 lb.,) value 300 RM, to Mia and Gretchen.

November 17, 1942 (14 kg!) — Sent a small trunk to Mrs. Wizemann (the 5th parcel). Value 300 RM. Contents: 2 bottles of brandy from the canteen, vitamins and tonics, razor blades, toilet soap and shaving soap, thermometer, nail clippers, bottles of iodine, laboratory preparations in 96% alcohol, X-ray photos, cod-liver oil, stationery, envelopes, scent, darning wool, needles, tooth-powder, etc., etc.[97] Snowfall in the evening which turned the

---

[93] This transport was presumably the 990 Jews from the camp at Drancy (France). 145 men and 82 women were sent to the camp as prisoners. The rest were killed in gas chambers.

[94] Undernourished, emaciated.

[95] Names of various substances.

[96] The prisoner with the camp number 68030 arrived at *KL Auschwitz* on October 14, 1942, with a transport from Holland. His name was de Yong (or de Gong, but the latter is less probable), Hans, born February 18, 1924, in Frankfurt. He perished on November 13, 1942.

[97] In the official record of the interrogation of July 30, 1947 (Cracow) Kremer commented on the parcels sent by him from the camp: "In the attic of the building where the dissecting was done, remedies, various instruments and all kinds of objects of everyday use were sorted. These things were brought to Auschwitz by people who directly upon arrival were sent to the gas chambers. Prisoners let me have various things from among these objects, such as soap, tooth-paste, thread, darning thread, needles, thermometers, nail-scissors and suchlike, necessary for everyday use. I packed them into parcels and sent them to my friends."

streets into marsh and mire. Made ready for tomorrow's departure for Prague. In the hospital : Gambor,[98] Brauner,[99] Biedermann,[100] Wilks,[101] and in the wards : Klehr and Scherpe,[102] all of them "old barbed-wire fighters" and "concentration camp sly foxes"[103] [*KL-Hasen*]. *Stabsscharführer* Ontl[104] wangled a coupon for a pair of breeches from me. The pharmacist, *Hauptsturmführer* Krömer,[105] was always very helpful in preparing the necessary reagents : Sauther,[106] the dentist, has been transferred to Minsk.

November 18, 1942 — Today at 1.20 p.m. departure for Prague via Oderberg, Mährisch Ostrau (change trains), Prerau, Olmütz. Arrival in Prague at 10.11 p.m. Here I caught a good connection to the military hospital. Sister Anna, on night duty, saw to it that I got my former room.

November 19, 1942 — I reported to the Chief Physician and had breakfast, then got my trunk from the station and had dinner at the Deutsches Haus. In the afternoon I returned some pieces of uniform, which had been lent to me, to the Clothes Office and packed my suitcases.

November 20, 1942 — Breakfast, then took leave of the deputy garrison physician Himstedt from Hameln, *Stubaf.* Matz from Stettin, *Stubaf.* Küttner, *Hschf.* Fredeking, *Ustuf.* Fasching, *Hstuf.* Koerber and others. *Ustuf.* Jung, the radiologist, promised to supply me with some very good X-ray photos for my lectures. After I received the railway ticket my personal luggage was taken to

---

[98] *SS-Unterscharführer* Eduard Gambor worked in the office of the SS garrison physician at *KL Auschwitz.*

[99] *SS-Unterscharführer* Ferdinand Brauner was also employed in the office of the SS garrison physician at *KL Auschwitz* (*Schreibstube SS Standortarzt*).

[100] No definite data concerning this SS-man are held in the Archive of the State Museum at Oświęcim.

[101] *SS-Unterscharführer* Martin Wilks was head of the accounts department connected with the SS garrison physician (*Reichnungsführer bei der Dienststelle SS Standortarzt*).

[102] *SS-Oberscharführer* Herbert Scherpe was then SS orderly in the hospital of *KL Auschwitz I.*

[103] In the original *KZ-Hasen*—meaning someone who knows all the camp tricks.

[104] *SS-Oberscharführer* Friedrich Ontl was then supervisor of the stores of the SS hospital at *KL Auschwitz.*

[105] *SS-Sturmbannführer* Dr. Krömer (pharmacist) was manager of the SS pharmacy at *KL Auschwitz.* Kremer has misspelt his name.

[106] Dr. Erich Sauther was employed in the dentistry ward of the SS hospital at *KL Auschwitz.*

Hiberner Station. Departure at 4.13 p.m. via Dresden, Leipzig, Hanover, Osnabrück. Arrival in Münster at 6.38 a.m.

November 24, 1942 — For the first time in the new anatomy barracks in Westring.[107]

November 29, 1942 — Saw Becher in the Anatomy, and he officially informed me that a chair of the biology (of heredity)[108] was soon to be created. Thus I would lose my lecture on the subject of heredity in human beings. I gave him to understand that I had counted on this chair, what with my training both as a biologist and a medical man, and that I had been led to believe, when getting my leave to lecture, that I should be a candidate for it. But he seemed not to know a thing about this and was very evasive. And so, among other excuses, he told me I was not looked upon as being "fully qualified" and that I had tried to serve two masters, although he must have known very well that my biological studies had been conducted according to all the rules and quite independently of my medical course. I had not studied medicine first, in order then to take some convenient doctoral thesis from a connected field as a philosophical dissertation, which was the case with him and with Quast from Bonn. When he then mentioned that the party was greatly interested in the nomination, I replied that I had been the first *Dozent* of Münster University to join the party.

December 1,1942 — Today I paid my respects to the new District Health Officer, Dr. Fenner, who welcomed me most cordially and appointed me to be chairman of the District Honorary Court. I took the opportunity to repeat what Becher had told me the day before yesterday, and he promised to speak for me as strongly as he could.

December 3, 1942 — I talked today with Rector Mevius about the matter. He reproached me for having published my work "A Noteworthy Contribution to the Problem of the Hereditary Nature in Traumatic Deformations," which had

[107] The former building, in which the Institute of Anatomy had been located, was bombed in the course of military operations.

[108] In the original—*Erbbiologie*.

been a grave error, he said. He had been asked God knows how many questions from all sides about it. Among others the Secret State Police [*Gestapo*] was interested in the problem. In fact he prevaricated a lot and made no binding promise.

December 4, 1942

Went to see Dean Becher again this morning; he was much more polite this time. I spoke again of the matter and repeated to him my conversation with Mevius. He said he had not paid much attention to the publishing of my work on heredity. He mentioned that he had even spoken for me when the question of my getting the professorship had been brought up during the conference. I said I had been most grateful to him at the time. Then I spoke at length about my philological studies,[109] about my experiences in surgery (deformations),[110] and about the fact that Jost[111] had stipulated I should not take sides when I published my work on hereditariness. Finally I begged him not to refuse me his support, as he had given it to me many times before. I was in a much more optimistic mood when I left him.

December 16, 1942

Hermann and Albert[112] arrived today quite unexpectedly from Berlin. Albert had been at Hermann's for a brief visit, then Hermann had naturally taken a quick home leave till the 30th. Hermann still looked well-fed and Albert told me that the stumpy-tailed tomcat in Stelberg had disappeared late last summer and after several months, when it was getting colder, reappeared again looking quite fat. At Voss's in Oberbrisdam [?] and at Theo Baltiefen's in Unterbüschen some stump-tailed cats had been born recently. Hermann was in a hurry to get to the station, as he wanted to visit Gretchen in Düsseldorf (*où est la femme?*)

December 22, 1942

Was nominated Chairman of the District Honorary Court.

. . . .

---

109 Kremer must have made a mistake here, as besides his medical degree he obtained a degree from the Faculty of Philosophy.

110 *Missbildungen*.

111 Kremer spelt this name Just earlier in the text (*cf.* entry of May 30, 1941). The person referred to is the same.

112 Kremer's relatives.

. . . .

January 13, 1943

Mrs. Glaser left for Krefeld today. I heard from Gülker at the Sanitary Office for National Health that Fenner had put in a good word for me at the District Office—concerning the chair of heredity biology—but that they had told him I would not be taken into consideration on account of my Driburg work—A Noteworthy Contribution to the Problem of the Hereditary Nature of Deformations.—They had nothing else against my person. There we have the much praised freedom of scholarship! It is difficult to imagine a greater gagging of it! Science with a blindfold over its eyes is and remains only a farce. And so I have really become a victim of my sincere belief in scientific ideals and in the unlimited freedom of research, as I had never even dreamt there existed anything like "a gagged science." By such manoeuvres science has received a mortal blow and has been banished from the country! The situation in Germany today is no better than in the times when Galileo was forced to recant and when science was threatened by tortures and the stake. Where, for Heaven's sake, is this situation going to lead us in the twentieth century!!! I could almost feel ashamed to be a German. And so I shall have to end my days as a victim of science and a fanatic of truth.

There is no Aryan, Negroid, Mongoloid or Jewish science, only or true or false science!

. . . .

January 27, 1943

Today I went to see Becher who now freely admitted that I had been disqualified on account of my work. I should have taken a stand, for or against—this was his opinion even now, probably borrowed from Mevius. I showed him my correspondence with v[on] Verschuer [?]. From his words I got the impression that I should have been against the hereditariness of acquired characteristics, but he did not dare to say so openly.

When I asked Becher for the opportunity to continue my work I was again refused by him; he gave me all kinds of evasive answers!

January 30, 1943

Was nominated reserve *SS-Obersturmführer*.

. . . .

March 1, 1943

Went today to shoemaker Grevsmühl to be registered, and saw there a leaflet sent him from Kattowitz by the Soc[ialist] Party of Germany.[113] The leaflet

[113] The leaflet was, of course, illegal, because the Socialist Party of Germany was banned.

stated that we had already liquidated 2 million Jews, by shooting or gassing.

. . . .

March 5, 1943

I had to walk round today with a collection box for the war winter aid. People in town found the collecting a nuisance, to say the least. I finally had extraordinary success at the District Office for National Health, where thanks to Mr. Gülker the box was simply snatched from my hands and there was even a 10 mark note in the collection. Mr. Gülker took this opportunity to tell me that Fenner had again spoken on my behalf at the District Office but the University (Mevius and Becher) had been stubborn in their opposition. Then he proposed I should ask for work in a hospital to escape the vexations. This proposal had, I am sure, its origin at the University which would then have the chance to get rid of me in the simplest way. He repeatedly stressed the fact that there would be no difficulties in the present situation for a specialist in surgery like me. I could, for instance, get the job of head surgeon at the District Hospital in Harford. I immediately sensed that my scientific achievements and my active work of long standing in the party annoyed the gentlemen from the University. Their guilty conscience made them wish to escape further responsibility by simply shoving me aside, and later they would wash their hands of me saying that this was what I myself had wanted. No—I shall consider the matter carefully—but I do not intend to let them get rid of me, the oldest party member among the Münster *Dozents*. By their treatment of me these important persons have unequivocally proved that services to the party, about which they are always talking, are of no value to them.—Mr. Gülker further told me that he had inquired at the Gestapo, and that they knew of nothing which could have tipped the scales against me. It seems that all these intrigues have again originated from Mevius.

. . . .

April 28, 1943

Persuaded by my sister Hilde Burgmer, I decided to pay them a visit at Brenn, and went there by the 3.30 bus. But nobody there knew that Hilde had been expecting me, as she had gone to Köln that very day to see Agnes. I was, nevertheless, most hospitably received, as always, by Alois, Maria and Thea. We had Berg waffles with cream, ham, cakes and then a very good moselle wine in the evening. Maria promised me " something " in addition and told me Hilde would bring it with her. Agnes had got a book for me, *The Hero of Ommerbron* [*Der Held von Ommerbron*] by Osenthal. It was a wonderfully cosy evening, full of care for the guest, a care that was not far from self-sacrifice, and their hospitality made them bring the best and the last from kitchen and cellar in a most cordial and sumptuous way—and yet they were no relatives of mine!

April 29, 1943

This shameless yelping cur, who even demanded 125 gramme butter coupons from me for the few days I spent there, had the cheek to maintain that the poor soldiers at the front had no outstanding merit and therefore were not entitled later to get better positions in the state. One is forced to spit on people with such a way of thinking!

And by the way, if he should prefer another doctor to me, as I had no medical knowledge at all, this would only show how far above his narrow horizon I had managed to rise, and how little he was able to be a judge of my achievements

He would not let the bombed-out family, living in their house, have a latch key on principle, and my sick sister was

A glaring contrast to this reception was, alas, experienced by me next day at the hands of my brother-in-law in Hartegasse. Even earlier there had been repeated squabbles between us due to his quite impossible political views, but at dinner matters were brought to a head when he refused to admit that our soldiers at the front felt any love for our country, were heroes and full of sacrifice. He maintained they were driven forward into enemy lines by their superiors who used sheer force. Those who failed to march on were simply shot. When I asked him where he had got such information and whether he had witnessed such proceedings, he replied he had not been born yesterday and so could freely express his opinions. I then felt wholly justified in refuting his words, saying that I had more experience of life than he. It was then that he attacked me personally, maintaining that he had a wider experience and much more knowledge than I ever had. What I had learnt was nothing compared with his knowledge. My medical knowledge was so poor that he would never trust himself to my care. I had done so many silly things and finally—and this was the last straw—I had let my relatives " support " me. My sister listened to this altercation without a word and finally remarked ; " Now, you two have had it out for all times."

But my attitude to my brother-in-law had now definitely changed and I told him I was honoured to be judged by him in this way. By this I wanted to allude to his bats in the belfry, coupled with his brutal lack of consideration, his lack of family sense, his insatiable greed, his lack of any feeling for our country, his obsession for contradicting all and sundry and his compulsion to be

obliged to get up at night and repeatedly open the front door while he quietly stayed in bed, showing no concern whatever for anything

quarrelsome. Very typical of him was also the fact that he openly admitted he was for the establishing of a Rheineland republic. It is obvious that such a man, bent on destruction, should not be part of our family circle. I have therefore arrived at my irrevocable decision to cut him out of my will and not to be present at his funeral if he dies.

A strange coincidence! In Harnisch my father had often opposed his father's incredible lack of moral and political reliability, a lack which made me, too, an opponent of the thoroughly depraved kindred of my brother-in-law. This quarrelsome and dogmatic brawler, this freebooter without a country, this miser who had never worn a uniform, had the cheek to tell me, a soldier of nearly sixty, when I defended the honour of German soldiers, that I should report for service at the front. Therefore, by openly severing relations with him, I think I have done my duty towards the honour of my family and, last but not least, the honour of my poor, tormented sister.

The afternoon of that wretched day in Stelberg and Oberfeld brought back my inner composure. Again and again I noticed how all the family were trying to avoid my so-called brother-in-law and how they wanted to have no truck with him. And Otto told me that immediately after my mother's funeral this moral and political rascal had demanded to get his slice, but my eldest brother, who had quickly come to know the swine's true worth, had shown him the door. My mother was barely in her grave when the skinflint already tried to gather his profits, regardless of everything. Fie! one can only spit upon such a low mentality, unworthy of man.

Gerda in Stelberg baked a delicious plum cake, we also had ham and fresh eggs. Some photos were taken. Towards the evening Anna, Otto and myself went to see Maria in Oberfeld, where we were met by Fritz and the children. Here we had the special Berg dish: fried cakes with slices of bacon and cooked rice. Finally Maria let me have a piece of cured bacon to take with me. She was in advanced pregnancy as was Anna, who arrived later on from Wipperfürth. Otto accompanied me to Hartegasse.

. . . .

May 2, 1943

Today, Sunday, I got the news from the Sanitary

Head Office, Berlin, Knesebeckstrasse, that as of January 30th I was promoted to the rank of *SS-Obersturmführer*, reserve officer. 30 copies of *Mikrokosmos* arrived at the same time, price 25.30 [RM]. Sum remaining after this deduction from my royalities: 44.35—25.30 = 19.05 RM only.

May 22, 1943

By letter from the Head of the District Personnel Office,[114] Dr. Grässner, I was asked to a conference organized by the District Management Westphalia-North. I made an appointment for 11 a.m.

May 24, 1943

Today a conference in the District [Party] Building with Dr. Grässner, not on the subject of the Driburg case, as I had supposed, but because they wanted my cooperation as lecturer in the district propaganda machine (population policy, race hygiene). He proposed I should first attend a course dealing with such essential problems, taking place in Berlin-Babelsberg. I accepted this proposal with joy, if only to look for some beetles in Berlin. It may only have been the result, among many other motives, of the desire to stop my scientific work. If only people could see behind the scenes of the scheming university flunkeys who are my ill-wishers. I have always been a thorn in their flesh because of my work and of the fact that I was the first to join the party. Let's wait and see!

. . . .

June 10, 1943

Today I saw the film *Paracelsus* which I liked very much indeed. "He who is his own master should not be the servant of another man." "Test the pride of your heart, to see if it can give up honours and wealth, then follow me!" This film could have been made to depict the university cliques of today, who suppress everyone who has his own opinions. And when their poor victims are dead, they misuse their names to foster their own unlimited arrogance as much as they can, and celebrate their memory as belonging to their circle, even erecting monuments to them. Shame to those scientific eunuchs who can only grasp the babbling of their own teacher, which they hand down from generation to generation. I do not belong to their circle, and I forbid anyone to

---

[114] *Gaupersonalamtsleiter.*

honour me with the gown worn by those stupidly prattling castrates.

. . . .

June 20, 1943 (Sunday)

Departed at 11.40—travelling via Osnabrück, Hanover, Stendal, Spandau, Berlin-Zoo—and arrived at the Reich School of the Race Policy Office in Potsdam-Babelsberg 2, Griebnitzstrasse 4 (which, as I learnt, had once been General Schleicher's[115] villa) at about 7.30 p.m. There are about 50 participants, called up from all the Districts. Room and board are good, the intellectual claims poor. Most of the time is spent in recreation and conversation without constraint. The director of the studies is *Reichshauptstellenleiter* Dr. Erich Oppermann, a zoologist, who had received his doctor's degree in Rostock with Paul Schultze. The only interesting lectures were those of the former Cath[olic] theologian from Eichstadt, Father Fernkorn ; of the resident physician, Dr. L. Vellguth ; and of the specialist in hygiene, Dr. Dahr from the Reich Health Office[116] (*Beringinstitute*). The latter determined my blood group on June 25, 43. It was blood group A, quite clearly recognizable in my case. Last Wednesday (June 23) I was visited in the afternoon by Hermann from Jüterbog. He told me that Albert was already in Russia and gave his address: Private Albert Kremer, Army Postal Service no. 36759. B. We sat for some time in the Babelsberg park and then in a tavern. Next day, on Thursday, I went to Finkenkrug in the afternoon to look for some beetles which were of particular interest to me (*Galeruca Dahli*). But the entire tract of land, once rich in fauna, had become quite dry and its earlier life was now destroyed. I saw there only some scanty willows with sporadic *Melosoma 20 punctatum*. Our course also included some very pleasant morning runs in the woods, and a joint beer-drinking excursion to Nicolskoe. The picturesque landscape re-

---

[115] Kurt von Schleicher (born April 7, 1882), German right-wing politician and general. He occupied high positions in the Reichswehr and advocated a policy of rapprochement between Germany and the USSR. In 1929 he became secretary general of the Reichswehr Ministry. He attempted to cause a split in the NSDAP by making use of the antagonism between Hitler on the one hand and Gregor Strasser and Ernst Röhm on the other. Hitler considered him to be a dangerous adversary and so he was killed, together with his wife (June 30, 1934) during the " night of the long knives " (Röhm's coup d'état).

[116] *Reichsgesundheitsamt.*

minded one of Russia. We also visited the most interesting castle of Babelsberg, with its reminders of the old Emperor Wilhelm and his times full of impressive unaffectedness and simplicity. Particularly noteworthy was the stick which Wilhelm I had cut himself and which he had always used, discarding all others offered to him. On the last day of our course Dr. Groos from the Race Policy Office was the speaker in the morning. But together with some others, I had to leave quietly before the lecture ended in order to catch the long-distance train, which left from Schlesischer Bahnhof in Berlin at 12.05, going west. I was fortunate enough, this time too, to get a nice seat by the window in a second class compartment, and the journey as far as Osnabrück was not dull thanks to a conversation with a pleasant lady-traveller.

August 26, 1943

Everybody takes notice, with wordless bitterness and almost with despair, of the heavy bombing raids by the English and the Americans and all are waiting and waiting for retaliation. Everyone is conscious of the fact that something is bound to happen, for it cannot go on like this. Those who attack the achievements of culture wage war against all civilized mankind and not only against us. Today the party group leader[117] came and asked party members whether anyone owned a pistol. We could not find out the reason for his questions.

. . . .

September 12, 1943

I was notified today by my solicitor Dr. Hallermann that the solicitor of my divorced wife had forwarded him the following letter: "In the case Kremer-Winterseel Versus Kremer I received your letter of September 6, 1943, from which I gathered with regret that your client does not intend to change his offer of alimony which, in my opinion, is insufficient and does not correspond to the income level of both parties. — As my client wishes to avoid going to law in the matter of alimony she is forced to accept the offer of your client."

I paid 153 RM before the divorce and now I am paying 50 RM only. Thus the problem of alimony has been solved for the time being.

. . . .

117 *Blockleiter.*

September 22, 1943

Solictor Dr. Hallermann told me on October 26, 1943, that he had seen the official accusation with his own eyes. It stated that the rector of Münster University had received ham originating from a pig slaughtered on the black market.

Albert got 16 days' convalescence leave and is now on his way home (since yesterday). His new address, according to Hermann, is: *Grenadier* Albert Kremer, Reserve Battalion 82, Göttingen, Convalescents' Company. Today I went with Steinkamp to look for mushrooms in Berdel, situated between Wolbeck and Telgde, but the result was far from satisfactory. Mevius has been removed from the office of rector. The most incredible rumours are afloat in Münster. I learnt from a certain source that he had got meat on the black market through the notorious black marketeer Baxmann in Bielefeld, a dentist who had been sentenced to a term in prison and who committed suicide there by hanging. And so he [Mevius] had to leave in dishonour, a slur affecting the whole university. It is better to reach a venerable old age than to be driven away from the rector's office in disgrace. The worthlessness of this man, whom I saw through at once, has at last been recognized. He had played the star role, together with Heiderich and Walter, in the intrigues directed against my person. In spite of all this we see "the honest rector" walking in the streets, untroubled and with his head raised high, as if he had only suffered from dyspepsia after having eaten a piece of meat.

November 5, 1943

A notice in today's paper informs us that the pathologist, Professor Siegmund, had been promoted to the office of rector. At 2 o'clock in the afternoon, in brilliant sunshine, another air-raid over Münster. This time it was chiefly the district with the clinics which was hit by incendiary bombs. Farmer Elvering completely burned out. The barrack for contagious diseases of the children's clinic and the former students' dormitory, established by Paul Krause, are in flames, too. Great clouds of smoke are also visible behind the clinics, above the lake (Aasee), in the direction of Nienberge and behind the surgical clinic.

November 6, 1943

People were most indignant this morning when not a single line about yesterday's horrors appeared in the morning paper. And, as far as I could learn, about 30 farms were destroyed in the vicinity of Gievenbeck, not to speak of the neighbourhood of Roxel and Mecklenbeck. Apart from this raid we had another air-raid warning again this morning, when I was shopping at the butcher's.

. . . .

November 20, 1943

Box collecting for winter aid, organized by military units. Mrs. Wizemann gave as much as 0.20 RM, Mrs. Deppe about 3 RM. People gave money in plenty at the District Health Office, which has been transferred to Erphostrasse on account of its total destruction by bombing. Here Gülker told me that Professor Erich Becher from Frankfurt had been given the St. Clement Hospital by the Senior Mayor, although Professor Arneth had wished to continue working there. The contract had already been signed. Quite by accident, however, the District Health Office[118] came to know that Becher had been treated several times at Haus Kammen for depression. Gülker showed the diagnostic card to me and it pointed to a severe psychosis with tendencies towards suicide and sexual murder. His paternal grandfather had been a master builder and a heavy drinker;[119] his father had been the university rector, a man with a violent temper leading to attacks of fury. Becher once tried to commit suicide by taking Adalin and using a razor. At the Sackmann Cold Water Treatment Institute he had on one occasion spent hours immersed in cold water in order to get pneumonia. While in the Institute he contemplated the rape and murder of the nurse who attended him. He himself stated that these disturbances were the results of his troubles with the faculty members and of his love affairs. Gülker then sent me, with his greetings, to the deputy district pharmacist,[120] Dr. Krausser, Piusallee 8, who also contributed most handsomely to the collection. I spent the afternoon in Steinkamp's garden. He told me he had a sieve for my kitchen. It was frightfully cold outdoors.

. . . .

December 26, 1943
(Sunday)

Today I read the following lines in the Christmas issue of the *Münsterschen Zeitung*: "Professor Dr. Johann Kremer is 60 years old. On December 26, Professor Kremer (science of human heredity), of

---

[118] *Gaugesundheitsamt.*

[119] Kremer used the Latin word *potator* in the original.

[120] *Gauapothekerführer.*

Münster University, doctor of medicine, doctor of philosophy, celebrates his 60th birthday. Born at Stelberg near Köln, he studied in Heidelberg, Strasbourg and Berlin, first philosophy, mathematics and natural sciences, later medicine. In 1914 he received the degree of doctor of philosophy in Berlin and in 1919 the degree of doctor of medicine, and was for a considerable time assistant surgeon at the Charité surgical clinic of the university, at the ward of internal diseases of the Municipal Hospital Berlin-Neukölln and the surgical clinic of the University of Köln; he was also prosector in the Institutes of Anatomy in Bonn and Münster. In 1929 he became *Dozent* of anatomy in Münster and was there promoted in 1936 to assistant professor. He became full professor in 1939. At the same time he was commissioned to lecture on the science of human heredity."

Not a word about my scientific works, let alone an evaluation! The representatives of orthodox science, the bookish scholars are not bold or capable enough to pass judgment on my works. Those who think their own thoughts are excluded from their ranks. Only mechanical factory products from the conveyor belt are esteemed by them. Herein lies the explanation why I was continuously impeded in my scientific work. They want and preach their own science only, and maintain it is the only right one. This dogmatic attitude crushes any spiritual individuality and blacklists all achievements that do not conform to their traditional views. And so I was refused work in the Institute of Anatomy, in spite of many good words in my favour addressed to the dean of the med[ical] faculty, to Becher. My scientific work had to be completely discontinued. I am therefore thinking of establishing a small laboratory of my own out of my modest means, once the war is over. Basically, I only need badly a microtome, since I have brought materials from Auschwitz which absolutely must be worked on. And I had an idea this morning. I shall put my thoughts in a book, perhaps under the title, *Retrogression of Tissues*[121] or *Histolysis*, and so my views shall at least be preserved. They are correct and will remain so, even if the whole of orthodox science should rise in arms against them.

121 *"Gewebliche Rückbildung" oder "Gewebsrückbildung"* in the original.

The latter has so far taken into consideration only one half of human life and speaks about histogenesis, but omits the integrating factor of histolysis. Scientists have produced books on human evolution but they have forgotten the other, equally important aspect, the science of human retrogression of which the approach of old age forms an essential part. In my opinion we are dealing not only with the history of evolution, but also with the history of retrogression.

Words fail me trying to express how the bookish scientists have got themselves into a blind alley by accepting the concepts of leucocytes and phagocytes; they will never be able to escape from their impasse without the radical interference of an outsider. I am going to write about the histology of retrogression, and I hope to be done with it by my 65th birthday. The essential thing is that I shall demonstrate in my book that the cells which are officially known as leucocytes or phagocytes are in reality genuine tissue cells, which have separated from the tissues, have more or less suffered decay or are still laden with remnants of decaying tissues. With the help of the pigmentary cells of liver I have already been able to prove that such tissue cells get into the circulation and thereby partly into other organs, finally undergoing complete disintegration.

A festive meal today—half a pound of roast veal with mushrooms.

. . . .

[1944]

January 28, 1944

Today sent the following letter to the Rectory, Pützerlin, Post Office Mulkenthin, Ad[ministrative] District Stettin:

"My dear Rector, You will be surprised, I am sure, on receiving my letter which deals with quite a special matter, not at all connected with your professional duties. The problem in question has to do with the science of heredity, and as I am not acquainted with any other educated person in the place you live in, I feel encouraged to ask you for accurate information on the subject of interest to me.

Under these circumstances you will forgive me, I hope,

if I take up your time which is sufficiently occupied with your daily duties.—The matter is as follows: several years ago I was presented by a police officer I knew (Erdmann from Pützerlin), with a small, stumpy-tailed kitten, which I then gave to some relatives in the Rhineland and which, I must admit, had plenty of progeny with the same characteristics. As you can imagine, many people would wish to know something about the origin, heredity, etc. of these stumpy-tailed cats. But unfortunately the above-mentioned police officer has disappeared in our present times of war, so I am unable to obtain the desired information through him. Thanks to your extensive familiarity with the inhabitants of your locality you could, perhaps, gratify my curiosity and that of others. To be candid, I will confess that I represent the subject of human heredity at the University of Münster and so am particularly interested in the case.—I should like to receive your replies to the following essential questions: (1) Can any people at Pützerlin recall the approximate time when stumpy--tailed cats first appeared there or where they had come from? (2) What is the opinion of people as to the cause of this particular deformation? (3) Was the opinion, among others, current that the phenomenon occured when a cat had acquired a stumpy tail through some accident (having been run over, etc.) and then had handed the deformity down to posterity? (4) Is the ratio of stumpy-tailed to normal kittens born there approximately equal? (5) Has any other kind of deformity of a more grave nature than stumpy tails ever been observed among the cats there? (6) Are the coats of stumpy-tailed cats always of the same colour, i.e. black with white spots, or are they grey, ginger or completely white or black? (7) Is it possible to find any evidence in oral accounts that the stumpy-tailed cats were introduced there from some other place; if so, what place, and particularly, is there any connection with the tailless cats of the Isle of Man (*Manxcats*?) (8) Do the local inhabitants ascribe any special positive traits to the stumpy-tailed cats (being better mousers, etc.) and what is the proportion of the local normal cats to the deformed cats in approximate numbers? I should be most gratified and obliged to you if you would be kind enough, dear Rector, to answer all these questions conscientiously and, of course, without any obligation.—In the hope that you will meet my request with full understanding, I remain yours . . .[122]

February 24, 1944[123]

Today, at 11 o'clock a.m., I received the extremely sad news that my elder brother, Josef Kremer, died suddenly and unexpectedly on Monday evening, February 21, in Monheim on the Rhine. His funeral will take place tomorrow, Friday, February 25, at 9.30 a.m. from St. Joseph's Hospital in Monheim. It is Thursday noon at the moment and twice this morning we have had an air-raid warning, so under the present circumstances it is quite impossible for me to attend the funeral. And on top of everything I have a lecture tomorrow at 11.45. I am very sorry I cannot pay my last respects to the poor fellow, but will at once send a telegram with my condolences. The telegram, which I just sent at 4.12 p.m., was worded as follows:

"Deeply shaken by departure of my unforgettable brother. Sincerely condole with all who mourn at his coffin." I was informed that it was not possible under present circumstances to send a wreath. What a pity that I was not informed earlier of his death, by telegram, then I could have arranged matters more suitably.

Josef's measurements, taken by me in 1927: height—165; skull—14.5; 19, index—76, blood pressure—140

It is a strange coincidence that I heard of his death today, February 24, for my eldest brother Wilhelm died on just the same day, February 24, 1933, eleven years ago in Stelberg, and so both of them died at Shrovetide exactly. Josef was born on October 11, 1874, at Odenhohlermühle. He was of slender build and was the only one in the family to have my father's black hair and brown eyes. He did not get on as well as the others in elementary school, but was very conscientious, and later, after my father's death, kept the accounts of the Stelberg farm. He wore small hats so his brain does not seem to have developed to a normal size. In youth Josef suffered from dizzy spells whenever he mounted any heights. I remember that he twice had falls, due to dizziness;

[122] Kremer does not give the rest of the letter. What followed were probably the usual polite expressions.

[123] Entries dealing with events after February 9, 1944, come from the second volume of Kremer's diary.

once he fell from a pear tree growing below the house, and another time from the dove-cote which father had let him make for his pigeons. The greatest blunder of Josef's life was his marriage to our dairymaid Maria Krämer, daughter of the *Kalverkrämer* who was widely known as a man of ill repute, while she herself, when a child, used to come begging for bread to my mother. She was also known to be morally below the mark. The family was unanimous in trying to dissuade him from marrying her, and I personally even asked the minister to intervene in this matter. It was solely due to her that my brother lost the small, model estate of Moitzfeld near Bensberg, which he had bought, so he ended his life in Monheim, living on charity. And on top of everything this woman has betrayed him all along. Two children, Maria and Otto, were the fruit of the marriage, but neither was Josef's child. All Bensberg was acquainted with this fact. Maria was a daughter of an English prisoner of war from the time of World War I. He had been employed as a farm-hand at Moitzfeld. Otto's father was a neighbour, a forester in Dölitz *, who supervised the kettler hunting-grounds. He was a short, thick-set and athletic man with a pointed beard, and used to be seen in the kitchen in company with Josef's wife day in, day out, thus deceiving his already silver-haired wife most abominably. Old Goher, who lived in Josef's house, told me that he had seen them sinning together under gooseberry bushes, and that they had also been seen in the woods on specially prepared beds.

(The place Dölitz is situated in East Pomerania, in the vicinity of Stargard.)

I could not even begin to relate all the gossip going round Bensberg at the time on the subject of Josef's wife. But he would not listen to any such remarks and gave his name to these children of sin. I must therefore once again stress the fact that Josef had no children of his own, as both Maria and Otto were fathered by other men. They have nothing to do with our family. All this gives an idea of how badly fate had treated Josef.

March 2, 1944

Today I was again commanded by the local group as member of the military formations,[124] to take part

[124] *Kampfverbände.*

in the street collection. The task was to sell 100 badges, delightful little china figurines representing characters from fairy-tales, for which people in the district Sanitary Office in Erphostrasse fairly scrambled, taking nearly all of them as soon as I offered them. The rest were left for the pharmacists and some chosen passers-by in the streets. I also secured a series of them for myself, and *Hans in Glück* [Lucky Hans] with the pig in his arms could not, of course, fail to be among them. In the afternoon I first went to the Wizemanns with my box. This time it was Wizemann himself who appeared at the door, and when I offered him the box he behaved in an extraordinarily impolite manner, so that it was immediately evident he did not wish to have anything to do with the collection. He rudely gave all sorts of evasive replies, saying he had visitors, that Mr. So-and-so was there, but he could not, after all, say no to me, so he reached for his wallet and put some small coins into the box. While doing so he suddenly flared up, saying most angrily that a fifty bit had accidentally found its way into the box!

At any rate this experience was a most unpleasant one for me, considering that I was dealing with a party official of high standing who always boasted everywhere of his party membership. But quite adequate compensation for his rudeness was my meeting with Mrs. Deppe, who again put 2—3 RM into my box.

March 6, 1944

And a characteristic anticlimax to the story: Mrs. Wizemann, whom I met today on the stairs, told me, her eyes shining, that her husband had been awarded the Cross of War Merit, First Class. During World War I men who skulked at home, although barely 45 years old and fit, were sent to the front. Today they rest on their laurels and receive War Crosses of Merit. Mrs. Wizemann informed me with great pride that her husband had already, years ago, received the Cross of War Merit Second Class. Nobody seems to pay attention to people like me who: firstly, am fully active in my profession; secondly, have volunteered for the army in spite of being 60 years old; and thirdly, am without any help at home, as my housekeeper[125] was called up to join the Red Cross.

---

125 Kremer has probably his housekeeper Mrs. Glaser in mind.

March 7, 1944 — I had a reply to my letter of January 28 of this year from the vicar of Pützerlin. After some wandering my letter had reached him, and he promised to investigate the matter of the stumpy-tailed cats thoroughly. It was evident from the letter that he himself was quite interested in the problem. His address is: E. Röker, 4 Priemhausen, via Stargard, in Pomerania.

. . . .

March 18, 1944 — I made my first spring excursion today, walking over Gievenbeck. Beautiful early spring weather! I was deeply shocked in the evening when, listening to the air-raid warnings on the radio, I could hear at the same time the news in German, on the same wave-length. It must have been the enemy's transmitter. They said that Winitza, where the *Führer* had until recently had his headquarters, had fallen. The main railway junction in the middle of the Eastern Front was lost, so that our troops there were cut off from any possibility of retreat. The troops retreating from the Crimea were likewise held back in Odessa, as the Romanian ships were taking only Romanian soldiers on board. Our soldiers were already "grumbling" because of this. Public feeling in Romania was also said to be critical towards us. Because of the destruction of the Messerschmidt, Dornier and Zeppelin[126] plants we no longer had a sufficient amount of planes at our disposal. Furthermore, transports of our reinforcements in the Baltic Sea were under continual bombardment by the Russians. The speaker of the warning service later on admitted that a foreign propaganda transmitter had broadcast completely false reports on the same wave-length.

March 20, 1944 — The fall of Winitza was finally made known today.

. . . .

May 9, 1944 — Trust in God has become extremely weak! Yesterday morning I was passing St. Joseph's Church in Hammerstrasse, when an air-raid warning was sounded. How the old monks, aunts, hobbling old geezers, grannies, nuns and worshippers of both sexes rushed headlong out of the church, as if driven by some

[126] All industrial plants mentioned here belonged to the aircraft industry.

force! As quickly as their legs could take them they stormed into the air-raid shelter; it was great fun to observe them! Right in the middle of mass they took to their heels and not one among them thought of facing the danger in the presence of the Maker of our destinies.—I then went to the air-raid shelter myself, and found it very much overcrowded at that time.—We had considerable frost in the night; the meadows were quite white early this morning. But we shall have a change of weather, it seems. The wind has changed and seems to be blowing from the east.

. . . .

May 25, 1944

Alois Burgmer sen[ior] came unexpectedly this afternoon for a short visit. This was a surprise indeed! He had been discussing with the military authorities the transfer of his severely wounded son Josef from Russia to his home-town hospital at Lindlar, and it looked as though his efforts would be successful. He stayed with me till the next morning and had to put up with a night's rest on the sofa. We had the opportunity for a long talk, about the maniacal quarrelsomeness of my brother-in-law, for instance. Alois had just come from Havixbeck, where he had spent several days. Mrs. Glaser immediately became nervous because she feared she would have to part with some of her coffee beans. So I had to sacrifice some of my own for Alois. When Mrs. Glaser noticed, she could not refrain from grumbling in front of Alois, saying that I kept my coffee for myself and would not share it with anyone. I have not acquired a single coffee bean from the black market, while Mrs. Glaser has her coffee every afternoon, obtaining it from questionable sources, but never thinks of letting me have even a sip of it. But such is life; some people do not rest until they have used up all their rations, and then demand that others, who know how to save, share with them.

. . . .

June 21, 1944

Today I was caught in town by an air-raid warning, and so hurried to the shelter near St. Anthony's Church. The dear pastors and nuns were in a great hurry indeed, showing little trust in God as it was their own persons which were concerned. But the nuns lacked sports training, they had forgotten how to run. One of them tried to help another nun, who had stopped and kept asserting that she was unable to go on. They were middle-aged women about 30—35 years old, but one could see that the long years of inactivity had made their extremities so weak, that thay could not by any means keep pace with other passers-by. This is an example of what happens if one systematically neglects one's body. I even thought, as I rushed past, that one of the nuns had had a stroke. Tailor Hülsmann finally sent me today, after many years, the jacket of my new suit.

. . . .

September 13, 1944

The damage caused by yesterday's air-raid is quite considerable and all are of the opinion that it is more serious than that of October 10, last year. This time it was the whole southern quarter, beginning with Wolbeckerstrasse as far as Kappenbergerdamm, that was hit, and so seriously that houses which remained intact were indeed a rarity. The neighbourhood of the main railway station, Marienplatz and Josefsviertel (Augustastrasse, Dahlweg) are completely devastated. The railway station is a heap of ruins, as is St. Anthony's Church, and St. Joseph's Church had lost both its domes. One house only was left standing in Augustastrasse (Ahlhorn), the rest are all burnt out. Mainly incendiary bombs were dropped, but numerous explosive devices were also among them. There are two yawning bomb craters again in the Domplatz also in Saltzstrasse. The post-office had been squarely hit again. The Kaiserhof, Continental Hotel, Küpper-Fechtrup, are all completely burnt out. The entire Weselerstrasse and Scharnhornststrasse, beginning from the St. Clara Convent, are non-existent. The Baugewerkschule [Technical School of Building] is a heap of ruins, as is the Neuer Krug. Several farms behind the clinics have again fallen victim to the attacks of these gangsters. Hardly a house fit to live in remains in Hammerstrasse. The Landesbauernschaft [County Farmers' Union] in Ludgeriplatz and the Ländliche Spar- und Darlehnkasse [County Savings and Credit Bank] had been severely hit and have to be evacuated. Several explosive bombs fell on Breul and one of them damaged the Germania Monument in the gardens there. The Landesbahnhof [railway station] has again been badly hit. Today the whole town is enveloped in clouds of smoke, and in many spots fire-engines are trying to put out smouldering fires. Soldiers and posted everywhere. The " big " newspaper is being published in diminished size, for their offices have also been destroyed. It is impossible to relate all the heavy blows of fate which have fallen upon many families, for example the Jellentrup family living in my neighbourhood, in Hüfferstrasse. Their only daughter, a lively sportswoman, did war-time work at the parcel post-office near the railway station. Somebody brought her bicycle and bag to the parents, but there was no trace left of their daughter. The old father asked in vain far into the night at all the hospitals, whether his daughter had been taken in, but finally he was forced to give up when they told him, " Your daughter doesn't matter now." This morning I saw the poor woman trying to find not only her daughter, but her husband, too. He returned soon after, luckily, but there was no trace of their daughter anywhere. The greatest horror, however, happened next day when they were informed that their only son, and their only child, had fallen on an Italian battlefield. I now rode my bicycle to Venne in the afternoon to get my permit to collect berries. Besides red berries I found a spot where there were plenty of bilberries, all in " bunches," obviously a second crop, due to the favourable weather of the season. I brought a pound of them home, to be used in pancakes. While at Venne I observed hundreds of four-engine enemy bombers again approaching the industrial region.

September 15, 1944

A walk through the town to see the frightful damage with my own eyes. It surpasses everything seen up till now. In the afternoon I walked over the meadows behind Gievenbeck, where I found many champignons, particularly in Merten's pasture. I brought home a whole bag of them, all perfect specimens, almost without maggots; they had grown very abundantly in spite of the drought and the cold weather. Besides a large meal I had a lot of them to dry for the winter. Once again it was rather warm outside, but the sky gradually clouded over. There is still no water and no electricity. Today I read in the paper that Auschwitz[127] had suffered a vicious

---

[127] The air-raid by American aircraft, described by Kremer, did in fact take place. The planes dropped bombs on the factories of IG Farbenindustrie at Dwory near the town of Auschwitz and considerably damaged part of the industrial equipment. At *Auschwitz I* two

air-raid on September 13, and that members of parliament Breitscheid[128] and Thälmann[129] had been killed in the Buchenwald concentration camp near Weimar during another air attack on August 28.

. . . .

October 5, 1944
(Thursday)

Today, just before noon, when the sky was slightly clouded, one of the most shattering air-raids upon Münster that I had ever experienced took place. Its duration, also the shattering effect of the screaming engines and the detonations, were exceptional. I had gone to the cellar shortly before and there I had to endure this horror alone with the three "children of spring"[130]. Here I had the opportunity to grasp what the fear of death really means. It would not and would not end, and with every fresh approach of the enemy's bombers one believed one's last moment had come. Tortured, shocked and exhausted, one could only press into a corner of the cellar to await the end of that hell. Smoke came over the town, driven from the east, and covered it with a thick black mantle. The town had again suffered dreadfully. Especially hard hit were the Mauritz quarter and Warendorferstrasse, including the St. Francis Hospital. The railway crossing at Bohlweg is no more, so that trains from Warendorf cannot reach the station. On the other side passengers travelling in the direction of Hamm are obliged to get in and out of trains at Stille, as the main railway station can no longer be used. The situation of the Westphalia railway is

---

buildings, the living quarters of the SS, were destroyed. Fifteen SS-men were killed and 28 were wounded. A barrack in which clothing workshops were housed was destroyed and 40 prisoners were killed, 65 severely injured and 13 remained buried under the ruins. Two bombs fell on *Auschwitz II*. One of them damaged the railway track leading to the crematoria. The other demolished an air-raid shelter situated between the railway tracks, killing around 30 civilian workers.

128 Rudolf Breitscheid (born November 2, 1874), German politician and social-democratic leader. Since 1912 member of the Socialist Party of German (SPD). In the years 1918—1919, Prussian minister of home affairs, in 1920—1923, member of the Reichstag. One of the chief leaders of the SPD. In 1933 emigrated to France. Arrested by the Gestapo in 1940, died at *KL Buchenwald* in 1944.

129 Ernst Thälmann (born April 16, 1886, in Hamburg), leader of the German and international workers' movement, one of the leaders of the Communist Party of Germany (KPD). After Hitler took over in Germany, Thälman (together with other leaders of the KPD) was imprisoned on March 5, 1933, and killed eleven years later at *KL Buchewald* (August 18, 1944). In the eyes of the world Thälmann had been a symbol of the resistance of progressive German forces against Nazism.

130 The meaning of the words *mit den drei Frühlingskindern* is obscure.

similar; the trains get only as far as Graumendorf, for the railway tracks along Loddenheide are completely ruined. The Landesbahnhof has again ceased to exist. Many soldiers have lost their lives in the covered trench in Fürstenbergerstrasse (County Archive). The entire harbour district was in flames. The Domplatz and Überwasserkirchplatz look like fields full of bomb craters. The organ loft of the Uberwasserkirche had a direct hit and nothing is left of it. The Spiekerhof is impassable on account of the ruins of the houses in it. The staircase of the University had a direct hit and is completely ruined. And only fragments are left of the backs of the old college buildings, so that a continuation of studies in Münster is now not possible, if only for that reason. The university library has not been damaged very much, having only a broken roof and windows; I met the head librarian as he personally swept the debris from the pavement with a broom. Opposite, the Landesversicherungsanstalt [County Insurance Company] has been badly hit again, while in Pferdegasse several houses have been completely razed to the ground. In Ägidiistrasse there is a huge, gaping bomb crater in front of Kolpinghaus and the street is therefore closed to traffic. However, the arch has suffered most. After a bomb had dislodged great quantities of earth from the front of the Stadtweinhaus, both the balcony and the decorations of that building for the most part disappeared. The old City Hall has immense cracks in its walls, and two angels have fallen from its top. Kluxen*, not far from St. Lambert's Church, was obliterated during the attack, and so was the third house beyond the City Hall at the corner of a small street (a hat shop). The former Englischer Hof, now Petzold, had its left façade substantially damaged, while nearby Stuhlmacher is now quite ruined. On the other side of the arch one can see the exteriors of houses with historical gables, but one can look through most of them as the back parts of them have been extensively ruined by the bombs which fell on the Domplatz. The photographer Heinkele has lost his entire laboratory. The old historic café Mädendorf (Rombergkaffee)* is destroyed; the region of the clinics was again spared this time. The nearest bombs fell into the mounds of rubble in Hindenburgplatz and onto the back of the Landgerichtes [Law Courts], tearing away a huge

My former lodgings, Schützenstrasse 47/51, where I lived during my military service in Münster 1907/1908, are completely destroyed.

* Which had previously been destroyed

* This had happened on September 30, 1944

part of the building. Right in front of my tailor's (Hülsmann) there is a tremendous bomb crater. His flat was, of course, very heavily damaged. But my overcoat, which I had taken there to be repaired, luckily remained intact. We are again without water and there has been no electricity since September 12.

. . . .

November 16, 1944

First snow fell today. The sound of the big guns at the front can now be heard quite distinctly and people remark on it with worried faces. We are still without gas and water. Wizemann managed, a few days ago, to have his mechanic connect our house with the electric supply next door. Mr. Hatting, whom I knew through Miss Althoff from Darfeld, came towards evening in a soldier's uniform. He told me he had learned from a foreign radio station that Professor Esch had been dismissed from his office, because he had published an article in a medical journal opposing the calling up of women to work. The information was said to have come from Sweden.

November 18, 1944
(Saturday)

This was again a day of horror for Münster. At about 3 p.m. the terrorist airmen destroyed irreplaceable works of culture and innumerable human lives. They came so suddenly that they immediately followed the air-raid warning. I packed my things and left my house, taking my bicycle in order to get to the Gievenbeck shelter as quickly as possible. But I had hardly reached Coesfelderkreuz when I heard behind me the bombs hitting the town, and near the garrison hospital the threatening roar of the engines was already above my head. I was lucky enough to reach the shelter in a great hurry. Soon after we heard detonations in our immediate vicinity. Men rushed breathlessly into the shelter, and we saw that they had just thrown themselves into the mud of the street to avoid the danger. I met Mrs. Hünnebeck and her daughter in the shelter; I told them about the attacks by enemy pilots dive-bombing our country. The all-clear was finally sounded and as we left the air-raid shelter we noticed the awful results of the raid. The second house from the shelter, in the direction of the town, was a confused heap of ruins. And I had put my bicycle just by its hedge. Luckily it was still intact, though it presented a sorry sight.

My wire donkey[131] had become chalk white, as if terribly frightened. The dust from the ruins had given it a new coat of paint. I was very glad to be able to mount it again and to take to my heels. On the left I soon saw the damage caused by an air-mine to the eastern section of the garrison hospital. On account of two huge bomb craters right in the middle of the street, I had to dismount my bicycle twice and finally saw innumerable damaged windows and roofs in Hittorfstrasse. The Botany Institute in the Palace Garden was on fire and the flames were visible from afar. My flat was, thanks heaven, quite intact. Only about half a dozen tiles were dislodged in the front part of the roof. We had an air-raid warning again in the evening, and our fellow-sufferers in the cellar soon told us more about the damage done. The Schutzenhof shelter had been hit and did not withstand the impact. Innumerable corpses lay under its ruins, and in Hüfferstift they had not yet finished operating on the seriously wounded, who included Professor Coenen. The bomb, said to be of a new type, hit the roof of the shelter and exploded. Its core had then broken through to the floor of the shelter. I was told by people who had been in the shelter that they had not even noticed the hit. All sorts of rumours are afloat and are repeated again and again, their aim evidently being to calm people. The newspaper reported that the bomb had chanced upon the weakest spot of the shelter. But others maintained that the shelter was unsuitable : instead of cement some inferior material had been used, etc., etc. The number of those killed was said to amount to about 86. In one cellar vault in Münsterstrasse, which was always much frequented, circa 60 people were killed (I mean the old beer-house). The wing of the staff headquarters in Roxelerstrasse, below which an air-raid shelter was situated, was also hit. The panic there was negligible. The devastation of residential districts was again enormous. For example, the middle of Roxelerstrasse, where Werning lived, and particularly the corner of Roxeler- and Wilhelmstrasse. The huge Hotel "Westend" is a heap of ruins, which continues as far as Neutor. My baker's shop, Mrs. Büsche's, is also in ruins. At Neutor the left wing of the general

The front part of the old Überwasser cemetery—

[131] In the original, *wie sah mein Drahtesel aus ?* This, of course, means Kremer's bicycle.

with the tomb of Hamann, the " wizard of the North "—is destroyed.

headquarters was swept away and there is very considerable damage in Jüdefelderstrasse—the Essen butcher's shop was again hit. There is damage in Brink, too. The sight of Frauenstrasse is overwhelming. A heap of ruins, nearly as high as a house, blocks the street. Brüning, Wilmsens, etc. are completely demolished and so, again, is Hüfferstrasse where, in the neighbourhood of the Palace Garden, not a single house is habitable. The two men in Münster who lost their legs, solicitor Holtkötter and tobacconist Lammerding in Droste-Hülshoff Avenue, have both been deprived of their nice little houses. The remaining fragments of the Agidii military barracks in town, where I did my voluntary military service in 1907/1908, are now quite burnt out. I saw them still in flames on Wednesday, November 22. The Kreuz district was again badly hit, including Professor Rosemann's house in Studtplatz. Indeed, when looking at the neighbourhood of the Holy Cross Church (Studtstrasse, Gertrudenstrasse and Finkenstrasse, etc., etc.), one inevitably comes to the conclusion that this time the Kreuz district suffered most severely.

. . . .

[1945]

. . . .

January 27, 1945
(Saturday)

Went to the market today in deep snow, to look for some meat. There were only half dozen butchers' stalls. As I looked round at the first stall (of butcher Koch) Mrs. Koch, a stout bespectacled woman in her thirties, was serving a customer, refusing to sell her bacon for meat fat coupons. From time to time she would shout to her girl, " Be with you in a minute ! " As I did not find anything worth buying I moved on to the other stalls but soon returned empty-handed, having decided to go home past the Cathedral. On my way home I had an experience and saw a sight, which reminded me of the well-known realistic pictures of country life as painted by the Dutchman Breughel.[132] I was just passing Koch's stall when I noticed Mrs. Koch, who in the familiar posture, showing her

[132] The famous family of Dutch painters. Pieter the Elder (c. 1525—1569) painted mainly—with a great sense of humour—scenes of rural festivities and pastimes. He was a pupil of Pieter Coeck van Aelst.

backside, was relieving herself. Her fat, naked bottom, spanned tightly by her garters, was turned right in my direction and she was by no means disturbed by my presence.—This was also a chapter of war history, happening in Münster, in the middle of the Domplatz.
I went to Steinkamp's garden in the afternoon to gather the winter kale still in it. At the entrance to the allotments I noticed a woman with a sledge on which she had piled up all sorts of useless things. She asked me whether I also had a plot there and then told me that things got stolen in a dreadful way. Somebody had stolen her five hens and a cockerel after having made away with her dog. Since she was bombed out she had kept preserves, a store of sugar etc. in the gardens, and now she has lost everything. Nothing was left except the cut-off heads of her hens, broken glass jars and a big " heap " in front of the door.
Steinkamp's summer house had again had its door torn away from the lock ! This time I was unable to put it right. I returned home with a bag full of kale.

. . . .

February 21, 1945

There has been plenty of fish to be bought everywhere in Münster since last week. I queued today at Hambrock for smoked cod for 6 RM and ate it all in one day. We also have fresh cod, fish marinade and fish paste everywhere, so that one gets rather tired of it. Wizemann grumbled that he would have to join in the mass mobilization[133] on Sunday, but that he had so far managed to get himself into the second wave. He kept boasting that " a great strike," prepared by our side, will take place in the middle of March, while everyone knows that our fate is sealed. I made a bet with him, staking everything I owned that there is not a grain of truth in that rumour, but he in turn would bet only what he had on him. The air-raid alarms are so maddening that one cannot help wondering whether anything is done to prevent the raids or whether utter passivity is the general practice. I got a very nice modern luggage basket for my old bicycle at Döbbeler's today.

[133] In the original *Volkssturm*—mass levy of recruits. In the final stages of World War II the Germans called up older men no longer fit to serve.

February 23, 1945

It is worth recording what Wizemann said this evening, as he was going to the garrison: "The outcome of the war will be decided by the beginning of March, and it will be in our favour!"

March 14, 1945

Listening to the enemy transmitter from the occupied regions I heard today that the Anglo-Americans assured the population of complete religious freedom as their first gift; in this way they want to make people submissive, and patient.

. . . .

March 30, 1945

The thunder from the approaching front is becoming more and more threatening. I am still busy repairing the roof of my house and working in the garden. The weather is very cloudy, cool and rainy. At about 10 o'clock in the evening numerous heavy detonations were to be heard in the north of the town. Apparently this was our soldiers blasting the munition stores near Greven. People thought Münster was under fire and fled to the cellars of the clinics.

March 31, 1945

There was nothing to be had at the market today. I only managed to get a bottle of apple-juice, at Niemer's in Salzstrasse. There were long queues in front of the baker's and the butcher's. We have no electricity and the maddest rumours are rampant. People say the enemy has by-passed Münster and has already advanced through Reihne[134] and Greven. We are kept guessing as to whether Münster will be declared an open town, or be defended. It seems that the enemy has encircled us and the entire industrial region, so that we are completely cut off from the rest of Germany. In the afternoon people came from Hittorfstrasse with whole joints of beef. The meat was given free at Vennemann's down in Hammerstrasse. It was frozen meat for the front, which could no longer be sent. It was quite a sight to see men and women plodding along with a whole front joint of beef slung across their bicycles. The old butcher, Hessing, vouched that the meat was perfect. He and his wife told me, among other things, that Dortmund and Hamm had already surrendered. Havixbeck had defended itself and was razed to the ground. Mrs.

[134] Proper spelling *Rheine*.

Glaser came shortly after from the Konerings, bringing vegetables and three bottles of liquor; the latter she had got free at the Hölscher distillery, located in the direction of Nienberge. One could take away as much of it as one wished. The farmers had already filled their milk cans with it, and Mrs. Konering immediately sent Mrs. Glaser off with several bottles. Things were in an unbelievable state there, with both soldiers and civilians drunk. The whole place had swum in spirits, and the tipsy conscript soldiers had jokingly pointed their rifles at the crowd. There was no supervision, everyone could take as much as he wanted. Mrs. Glaser also told us that one could get any quantity of coal one wished from the commissariat in Steinfurterstrasse. Horse carts, push-carts, etc., were on their way there in their hundreds, and came back with coal. The shops near the military barracks and in Steinfurterstrasse were selling tinned meat for household coupons. I mounted my bicycle at once to get at least a sample of this. Going there was like moving in a procession. People were rushing there on horse, bicycle, with push-cart, knapsack, rucksack or bag, eager to snatch what they could. A long queue had already formed in front of the door and I immediately took my place at the end of it. It lasted an immeasurable time as the soldiers repeatedly crowded in at the front. Finally another fully loaded wagon came from the barracks opposite, and was unloaded through the window. The friendly soldier on the box told us he would gladly give everyone of us a crate of tins, they had so many of them they did not know what to do with them. Shortly afterwards one of those standing nearby removed a crate from the wagon without being stopped from doing so by the members of the convoy. When the crowd noticed this all of them, men and women alike, rushed at the wagon, pushing and pulling off one crate after another, despite the fact that the wagon was already moving away, and so stole everything. Each crate contained 16 tins. It was a horrible spectacle to see the human pack storming the wagon and wildly grabbing everything within reach with boundless greed. A gentleman at my side remarked that even in 1918 things had not been as bad as this. Now the door of the shop was bolted and we were told that everything had been sold, and that no new transports of goods were expected. I had my bicycle already in my hand to return home empty-handed, when someone suddenly announced that the shop opposite would now sell things. Everybody rushed there at once. As I had to lock my bicycle first, I again found my place at the end of the queue. After some time we were again told that the first shop across the street would get one more wagon after all. When I heard this I quickly returned there, to find only 2—3 persons in front of me. And I stubbornly remained there although the shopkeeper repeatedly stated she would not get any more goods. But it soon became known that another transport would arrive. The waiting, however, was very painful, because it was only after 2 hours at least that the hoped-for wagon with 100 crates made its appearance. At last I was able to get the tinned meat I wanted (a layer of lard on top and pork underneath). Each person got 4 tins at 1.60 RM a tin, for one household coupon. I therefore got 8 heavy tins for myself and Mrs. Glaser, and I had great difficulty in cramming them into my bag. To get them I had stood about 4 hours in the wintry cold. I had ample opportunity to watch, among other things, the drunks comining staggering home from Nienberge. Among them there was a grey-haired old man who was unable to hold himself upright and who kept reeling from one side of the road to the other like a tight-rope walker. All at once he collapsed in the street, his legs straddled, hitting the back of his head hard upon the pavement. A soldier quickly ran up and finally set him on his feet, but as he did so he took an empty bottle out of the drunk's pocket, threw it away, then took out a full bottle and speedily transferred it to his own pocket, to the joy of the onlookers. On my way back I was stopped by 2 policemen before I reached the town, and, was told to do some war work. All of us, men, priests, boys, girls, etc. had to move pieces of iron, rails and twisted wires, carrying them or transporting them in carts, to form a barricade across the street. After taking a turn of work I was able to proceed home. Mrs. Glaser was already waiting for me and the ration card, then left at once, although night was setting in, to hurry to Schweitzer's in Hufferstrasse where rice was being distributed. Not long after, she returned with 4 pounds of the best rice per person. As I had also got plenty of full-cream milk at Konerding's, since the milk deliveries have been stopped, we immediately set about preparing a delicious Easter rice pudding. Finally the neighbours came round with plenty of the beef which had been distributed earlier, so at Eastertide 1945 nobody in fact had to endure hunger in Münster. It was a condemned man's last meal because the enemy, said to have taken up positions in Albachten, Nienberge and Roxel, continued with the thundering of heavy guns in a frightful way. Particularly after 10 p.m. there seemed to be heavy fighting going on to the south-west. On my way home from the military barracks I had already seen several policemen, driving from the direction of Nienberge with an American prisoner. But people hardly noticed them in the crazy turmoil.

April 1, 1945
(Easter Sunday)

Stormy and rainy weather, wet, cold and cloudy. The night passed quietly, without any serious disturbances. There are no air-raids any more. Only the thundering of artillery is heard from time to time, whereupon it ceases for a number of hours. We do not know how things stand as there has been no electricity since yesterday, and so we cannot make use of the wireless set. We had a magnificent dinner today. Delicious beef broth with noodles, beans with bacon, potatoes, apple-sauce and red berries. For breakfast we had cold ham, bread and butter with real coffee and plenty of full-cream milk. At 4 p.m. the bell rang and Mrs. Hessing, who lives across the street, came to tell us hurriedly that all sorts of fine things could be had free from the storehouse of the military barracks in the Univ-Sportplatz, such as peas, biscuits, noodles, etc. It took me only a moment to mount my bicycle and rush there. I saw with joy the delicious golden-yellow peas in the hall and I got to work filling with them two big air-raid-shelter paper bags which I had brought, when a captain behind me ordered us to clear the hall as the military barracks were within range of the artillery fire. However two women helped me to tip the contents of the paper bags into a half-empty sack, which I was able to take away. Mrs. Glaser appeared at that moment and took care of it, while I managed to get a large box of biscuits and 6 packages of crackers outside. Mrs. Glaser had already taken 2 large cartons of bread and 2 paper bags of noodles. The captain's orders to leave the hall were getting more and more pressing, but I dared to enter once more and secured for myself 2 large paper bags filled with green peas. The hall presented an awful spectacle: peas were strewn all over the place in layers as thick as a thumb and were stamped upon by people, who had come here in great numbers to get the supplies with which they loaded bicycles, push-carts, hand-carts and horse carts. The entire area in front of the storehouse, where people arrived and departed, was paved with peas, noodles, etc. Mrs. Glaser and I managed to take our supplies home on our bicycles without any loss. Altogether there was about 50 pounds of shelled yellow peas, 20 pounds of green peas, 8 pounds of noodles and around 70 pounds of biscuits and crackers, a store which could last almost for years.

April 3, 1945
(Tuesday after Easter)

Events happen precipitately! The weather is rainy and windy, the barometer predicts unsettled weather! People in the streets have been showing their uneasiness since early morning. I went upstairs to the kitchen window at about 7 o'clock, on hearing a heavy, hollow rolling. And what did I see? In the rain tanks were approaching from Coesfelderkreuz via Westring, flanked on both sides by troops on foot. People began to stir in Hittorfstrasse, that is the few who were not in the cellars of the clinics or in the air-raid shelters. It is hard to believe, but people began hanging sheets of white curtains out of the windows as white flags. Some made do with white kerchiefs, which they spread over the window sills (Gerdemann, the parish accountant, people living over Wucherpfennig, etc.). Soon after, the first Americans appeared with their guns ready to fire and in their clay-coloured uniforms. They patrolled the streets, entering the houses in search of our stray soldiers, who had been left in the lurch by their officers. I watched from my window as about 30 men were led from the cellar of the house of Loos, Hittorfstrasse 13. The poor boys had to put their hands up: they were shouted at and were taken away as quickly as possible, marching in double file. Some time later I met my first American, when he was talking to Miss Fröhling and Mrs. Glaser by the front door. He impressed me as a quiet, reasonable man and even shared his cigarettes with me and the ladies.

Mrs. Glaser, returning with the milk from the Konerdings, had already brought an army breakfast package with her, containing biscuits, dried fruits, chewing-gum, cigarettes, sugar and coffee with milk. She had found it in the street, lying in the rain. We looked in wonder at the American soldiers who were playing at being soldiers, under umbrellas in fact. They were of generally medium height, young well-fed men, some of them evidently of mixed race. Their uniforms and equipment were of prime quality. I had a really incredible adventure at 4.00 p.m. when Mrs. Glaser left, and I was on my way down to the cellar to take some things there. Quite unexpectedly I bumped into two weird figures on the lowest step of our cellar staircase. The wavering light of a candle-end suddenly shone on me. One of these fellows had got into the cellar through the window and had his back turned towards me, while the other stood in the entrance to the cellar and lit his way with the candle. At first I thought they were burglars, American soldiers who were trying to steal our provisions. But when I spoke to them I soon understood that they were looking for hiding-places, weapons, munitions, etc. However I kept treading on their heels and talking to them, thus managing to divert their attention and to show them, after a while, to the door without giving them opportunity to enter the upper part of the house. I heard later that the same two fellows had broken into the ground-floor window at Lücke's; after ransacking the flat they had gone to the cellar, trying to spy out everything there. Meanwhile Professor Lenhartz had his still usable car commandeered from his garage behind the house. Towards the evening the sun broke through the clouds from time to time, and in the abating rain I saw a wonderful rainbow over the town of Münster, a rainbow of such magnificence as I have rarely seen in my lifetime. But the war continued in spite of everything, the big guns thundered on with unabating force and masses of war vehicles were rushing through the town. Wild rumours of draconian orders were being put about.

. . . .

April 6, 1945

Early this morning Mrs. Glaser and I took a brief-case and a hand-cart, and brought them home filled with small coal briquettes and 2 sacks of coal from army supplies in Grevenerstrasse. I wanted to repeat the performance but Mrs. Glaser refused, as she felt tired. So I mounted my bicycle and rode once more to the warehouse of the Einem military barracks, from where I brought a considerable load (around 30 pounds of green peas, 50 pounds of yellow shelled peas and a lot of crackers). Mrs. Glaser in turn went off to the artillery depot and returned with great quantities of toilet paper, electric bulbs, pails, soap, brushes, leather grease and packages of crackers. This afternoon the Lückes' house was again used as a billet (military police). They broke in the front door at the Lückes' and later I was asked whether we had the key to the connecting door. The conversation was conducted in a very friendly tone, and after the officer had taken leave the soldier who stayed behind spoke to us in German and treated us, Mrs. Glaser and me, to cigarettes.

. . . .

April 15, 1945 (Sunday)

Today is a calm, cool and rainy Sunday. We do not see much of the Americans so far. Hittorfstrasse is still free, so there is always the temptation to bring some things from over there (the owl, oil paintings, kitchen things, preserves, etc.). We still hear rumours that we shall not be allowed to remain in our new flat[135] for long. What would happen in such a case is difficult to imagine, considering the enormous quantity of our possessions. Moreover one can hardly forget that a robbing and plundering mob of foreigners is continually roaming the streets in broad daylight. They disturb the inhabitants, force their way into cellars and appropriate the few remaining things saved by our distressingly poor people, who have lost everything. One is completely defenceless and left at the mercy of this rabble. There is no peace anywhere, the martyrdom of our poor nation seems to have no end.

April 18, 1945

This night I suffered badly from indigestion caused by fresh bread. In the afternoon I went to the garden again to plant potatoes. The weather is oppressive and sultry. I was told by Mrs. Glaser that my house in Hüfferstrasse 62 has been requisitioned by the

---

[135] Kremer was forced to leave his former flat on April 8, 1945, because it was commandeered by soldiers of the American army.

Housing Office for 2 families; she heard this from the female upstairs.

April 19, 1945 — Our former flat was completely ransacked again in the night, the bookcase was broken open and the Deppe Mende wireless set from our room was stolen. In accordance with the order of the military authorities, I registered my radio set in Münzstrasse. Nobody could tell me what was likely to happen to it. In the afternoon I finished planting the potatoes on the allotment. On the return journey I brought home a wall-clock, which the foreigners had dragged there from somewhere, also the Agethens' quilt cover and a swastika flag. The clock seems to be in perfect order, its chimes have a marvellous tone and I hope to have gained in it a companion for my future days when it will tell me its story. I derived great satisfaction on my way back, noticing how an idiot boy, known to me, repeatedly greeted the Americans with great fervour. I have not, until now, noticed this kind of behaviour in the case of the other people.

. . . .

May 4, 1945 — The weather continues very cold and rainy, with sporadic thunderstorms. The wind is still blowing from the west. Wizemann suddenly made his appearance before noon; he said he wanted to go to his office. He is staying with a friend in Eupenerweg, and is trying to trace the provisions stolen from him (brandy, eggs, preserves, etc.). He has suddenly started saying that he had no connection with the party; he had been chief staff leader in the Farmers' Union,[136] but not in the party. He is no longer a director and has no idea what is going to happen to him.

. . . .

May 22, 1945 — The Americans have removed most of their signboards from the houses in Hittorfstrasse[137] and are getting ready to depart and make room for the English. It is quite probable that the English will continue with the billeting. I brought home heads of angels and old glass from St. Peter's Church behind the University (great value as antiquities!).

---

[136] *Bauernschaft.*

[137] Kremer had lived in this street, at number 17, before he was evicted by the American army.

The garden is completely overrun by snails, owing to the wet and cold weather. Have once more sown carrots and peas.

. . . .

June 10, 1945 (Sunday)

The weather is still dull and cool, warm summer days are slow in coming. The Americans are still masters of the town. It is shameful to observe how mothers sell their daughters only for a sip of coffee from the Americans. I observe the latter daily, as they slip into Mrs. Müller's flat next door. She launders their uniforms and uses her young daughter Else as enticement, all to get some coffee. There are coffee parties there every other day, to which Mrs. Fröhling sends her daughter Waltraud to catch an American for herself. And to think that a German officer was barely good enough for these people, whose daughters throw themselves away on American privates, with their parents' blessing. Mrs. Hünnebeck is also endeavouring to enter that match-making society, as she seems very much to want an American millionaire for her daughter Elisabeth. They have not a word to spare for our poor front-line soldiers, who are now returning home. Plundering continues in the allotments. The cherry tree has become almost entirely bare after having been beaten with poles and all kinds of sharp garden tools. We also hear disturbing news of another sort. Russians are said to have broken into the bishop's house, and the indignant farmers told us that the pastor at Gievenbeck had been soundly beaten by the Americans.

June 11, 1945

Pastor Gründner came to see me this evening, hoping to swindle me out of my car. On account of his extensively scattered congregation a car was an absolute necessity to him, and the military authorities had promised him one. He had been given a requisitioned car, but it was a closed one. He had "accidentally" seen my open car in the garage and wanted to know whether I would sell it. He could not stand the sticky atmosphere in a closed car in summer, and anyway as he had been told, all cars would shortly be requisitioned. This sly, red fox of an evangelist was the first to arrive with a hand-cart wherever there was anything to be had free from our soldiers, for example peas, tinned meat, coal, etc. He was of no help to his evangelistical sisters (the

Salkowskis), except in getting their furniture into security. When the Americans arrived he instantly made himself known to them as the so-called vicar of the garrison hospital, and after the American fashion he affixed a large signboard with a flag to the door of his house, saying that Luth[eran] rel-[igious] services would be held there in the chapel. That creature lost no time in trying to get a car from the Americans, cycling being evidently beneath his dignity, and in view of the attitude of the authorities in occupation, full of chicanery, he was instantly promised one. Not satisfied with this success he was using it as a stepping-stone to having a car of his own, by tricking his fellow-man in distress into selling for a pittance. He considered my open car, which is still in very good condition, to be quite suitable for his needs. In any case the car would soon be requisitioned, so he came to save me from that misadventure by offering me an undoubtedly better price. I would be rid of my trouble and would have good money, the value of which would increase, in my pocket! Naturally I was not to be had by that swindling servant of the evangelical religious community. I have simply taken note of the more than shabby behaviour and guile of this servant of God.

. . . .

July 10, 1945

Mrs. Rebbe and daughter left today with a big box of things which they had come by illegally. They had contributed only 1/4 pound butter towards their keep. I have filled in the questionnaire sent in by the military authorities. On a special sheet of paper I wrote in paragraph D: "No speeches or publications; only one publication is to be mentioned, for which I have had to bear the responsibility, namely: ,A Noteworthy Contribution to the Problem of the Hereditary Nature of Acquired Qualities'." A certain Mr. Schmidt from the Street Traffic Office came in the evening and presented me with a document, according to which my Opel car was requisitioned. Under Paragraph 15 of the Reich Service Law I was obliged to surrender my car at once with all its accessories to the Senior Mayor, Street Traffic Office—such was the wording used. The party interested, Doctor Humpe, has so far not been seen.

. . . .

July 20, 1945

I was told by Mrs. Hessing today that people are talking about the further advance of the Russians into Westphalia and the Rhineland. Have sent the first post-cards to Stelberg, Hartegasse, and Marburg. Mr. and Mrs. Lücke told us yesterday that Mrs. Fröhling had been informed last week of the death of her husband who, being a major, had had to defend Hilversum.

July 23, 1945

This morning I ran into Mr. Sauermann of Hüfferstrasse at the entrance to the Savings Bank. It was with some difficulty that I recognized him, he looked so miserable and down at heel. Because of his former employment he had been ordered to do some work (shovelling in Preussensportplatz)[138] for which, as he supposed, he had his friends Doctor Reichling and Tocke to thank. And this man had been a civil servant for 34 years and had lost his only son, a young medical student, in the war. The post-card to Marburg has been returned. Mrs. Deppe downstairs keeps the death of her mother a secret from everybody (she buried her mother recently in Telgte). She does not wear mourning and does not mention her mother at all, a sign of the moral downfall of that female who nevertheless hurries to church every Sunday and receives Holy Communion in a most sanctimonious pose.

July 26, 1945

The weather is still very hot and dry. The corn ripens before its time, gnats are pestering us more than ever, and Russians, Poles and Italians still harass the starving, needy and homeless inhabitants. People are crowded into goods trains like cattle and carried hither and thither, while at night they try to find shelter in the stench of dirty, verminous bunkers. Quite indescribable is the fate of these poor refugees, driven into uncertainty by death, hunger and despair. Kurt came this morning and in his aggressive way wanted to make me go with him tomorrow to gather red whortleberries. But I refused this invitation in spite of his indignant airs, because the Venne bridge has been destroyed, the Russians are still besieging the roads and he had intended to go the considerable distance to Venner Moor on foot. I give here a list

[138] The work probably entailed filling up the anti-air-craft and anti-tank ditches.

of important objects stolen by the Americans from the house in Hittorfstrasse 17,[139] according to estimats:

1. Deppe: 1 carpet (2.5 by 3.5), 3 upholstered chairs, 2 little bed-side cupboards, 2 blue quilts, 3 down pillows, 1 feather-bed, 1 car.
2. Wizemann: 1 couch, 1 upholstered chair, heavy courtains for 2 windows, boy's bicycle, alcohol.
3. Lücke: 1 couch, 2 bed-side cupboards, 1 lady's bicycle, 1 sewing box, tools.
4. Mrs. Glaser: 1 wall-clock, 1 armchair, 1 handwoven cover, 1 hair-drier, 1 Agfa-Box, several large kitchen spoons.
5. Professor Kremer: portable gramophone, cigars and alcohol.

July 28, 1945

In accordance with the valuation sent by the municipal authorities, I was obliged today, with heavy heart, to deliver my beautiful green open Opel car for the trifling sum of 530,00 RM. The buyer of the car is the specialist in nervous diseases, Dr. Humpe, Münster, Prioreistrasse 34. The entire garage rent during the war years would have been higher than the price I am now getting for the car. One should also add the many beautiful memories, which I was obliged to give away together with the car.

July 31, 1945

Former party officials are ordered, on pain of a penalty, to present themselves in the city hall. I therefore went there today, obeying the summons on the last day, to set all minds at rest. Today I received a card from Hermann, informing me of his safe return home to Stelberg.

August 2, 1945

A messenger from Essen brought a letter today from Miss Schmitz, which I was to pass on to the intruders in my house. In it they were summoned to pay the monthly rent of 175 RM to me, including the arrears from May till August (700 RM). Mrs. Glaser personally handed over the letter to one of the people in question, who said she would visit me "at once." She appeared in pyjamas, just like a brothel madam.

. . . .

---

[139] The house where Kremer used to live.

August 6, 1945

Yesterday and during the night I had severe pain in the region of the bladder, the right kidney and the right urethra, which, in my opinion, point to the passage of a urinary stone. Today I received an order to do shovelling work from Zuhorn, the officiating Senior Mayor. Work begins tomorrow at 7 p.m. in Servatiiplatz. One has to put up with things like this because one was an SS physician. No one considers the fact that I lost my position through the NSDAP, since I dealt the party one of the heaviest blows in the ideological sense by publishing my work on the hereditary nature of acquired qualities.

. . . .

August 10, 1945

Was today interrogated for the record by the military authorities in Warendorferstrasse in connection with my SS membership. I was obliged to wait there for hours in spite of my serious illness. Finally I was informed I should have to appear before the Englishmen in Wülnerstrasse on Sunday at 9 a.m. Vossholt was also present; he told me he had got a certificate of ill health from the official physician at Borchardstrasse. So I went there, too. The official physician, a former student of mine, at once gave me the certificate on the basis of which I was exempted from shovelling during the month of August. He thought that my skin rash was caused by herpes zoster. On my return home my colleague, Wucherpfennig, the local specialist in skin diseases, confirmed the diagnosis saying that all my health problems were due to this disease. So at least I had the consolation that my fears of a serious kidney complaint were unfounded. He prescribed dry treatment with powder for the rash.

August 11, 1945

Mrs. Glaser handed in the SS dagger in answer to the call by the authorities. There is a change for the better in the state of my health, but my appetite is still very poor. I had to take sleeping pills in the night to ease the pain. My fears that the things I had left with my sister at Hartegasse were stolen by the *Amis* have, alas, been justified. Today I received simultaneously letters from my brother-in-law and from Gretchen, telling me that my possessions had, except for a few things—some shirts and papers—fallen into the hands of the troops marching through there. These included valuables of immense worth: 2 gold watches, 4 large rings with diamonds, jewels, lapis lazuli and pearls, also the new field-glasses.[140]

---

[140] Here the diary comes to an abrupt end.

EPILOGUE BY MIECZYSŁAW KIETA *

We have put offered Readers three unusual reports on KL Auschwitz, *the camp whose name has entered the history of mankind for ever. Its name has become in all the languages of the world the most tragic and most expressive symbol of the times when Nazi Germany raised lawlessness to the rank of law, brute force and ruthlessness to the rank of civil virtues—thus making crime the basis of ethics and morality.*

I think that after closing the book, having read the memoirs of Rudolf Höss, the diary of Johann Paul Kremer—doctor of medicine and philosophy—or the report of Pery Broad, we should begin to ponder deeply over what we have learned.

*It was not by chance that the State Museum at Oświęcim has chosen this time to publish a joint selection of documents, written by three SS-men who differed so widely as to their position in the camp hierarchy and also as to their responsibility, age, profession and intellectual level. In spite of such differences, in spite of the different periods of time when the reports were written, in spite of the dissimilar motives and circumstances in which they were written, they are bound together by the unique subject—*KL Auschwitz*—meaning the series of events in which they themselves participated, which they themselves created, which they themselves observed.*

A quarter of a century has elapsed since those times. New generations have grown to maturity, both in our country and in Europe, generations that are fortunate enough not to have known war or not to remember it. They depend on historical sources or historical myths when looking for information and truth concerning the epoch of crematoria, gas chambers and the extermination of millions of human lives, conducted on an industrial scale.

The search for this truth is not only of historical, scientific and cognitive value. It also comprises a deeply human, moral and political sense. Such inquiry moulds our consciousness, stimulates thought and reflection, helps us to formulate appraisals and conclusions.

The documents contained in this publication contribute to our knowledge of the truth about the position of Auschwitz in the system of Nazi genocide. And—let us add—this time the documents were not written by the victims of the crimes, but by their perpetrators.

Twenty-five years after the liberation of Auschwitz our knowlege of its life is very extensive, and the truth about it has been fully confirmed by documentary

* Mieczysław Kieta (1920—1984), in 1942—1944 prisoner of *KL Auschwitz*, then of *KL Gross-Rosen* and *KL Flossenbürg-Leitmeritz*, from which he escaped in April 1945. After the war, journalist, author of many articles about Auschwitz; active in many associations and organizations, acting, for example,as Secretary General of the International Auschwitz Committee and member of the Main Commission for the Investigation of Nazi Crimes in Poland. This Epilogue was written in 1970 to the first edition of *KL Auschwitz Seen by the SS*.

evidence. Our knowledge is based not only on a wealth of diaries, reminiscences and creative works—much of this written by former Auschwitz prisoners—but also on the scientific research, monographs and, last but not least, on the records of the trial of Rudolf Höss, former commandant of KL Auschwitz, *heard by the Supreme National Tribunal (1946), or of the trials of 40 members of the SS garrison, heard by the Supreme National Tribunal in Cracow (1947), as well as on reports from the three Auschwitz trials in Frankfurt am Main (1963—1967).*

But records of court proceedings are of necessity only concise statements of facts and circumstances, indispensable in law. The results of scientific investigations and research provide an objective compilation and evaluation of facts. The reminiscences and reports of former prisoners are the total of their observations, experiences and impressions which may be of an entirely private nature, but may also contain things known to them from hearsay. They are naturally very emotional, subjective and therefore in a sense one-sided; however their authenticity and subjectivity possess qualities which are worthy of respect.

Time, however, is inexorable. Each passing year makes the handful of former prisoners of KL Auschwitz, *who directly witnessed the Auschwitz crimes, smaller and smaller. Soon there will be none left. Only written reports, documents and books will remain. Only history will remain and history tends to become lifeless with the passing of time, becomes more and more distant, hard to reconstruct and fails to arouse the imagination. Such are the laws of life.*

Nobody and nothing will then be able to recall the horrifying, and shattering immensity of the Auschwitz atrocities when in times to come its last witnesses have departed. These are matters which go beyond the limits of human imagination; they are unimaginable. Just like the four million KL Auschwitz *victims. The figure is an empty, dehumanized concept for contemporary man who did not participate in the Auschwitz reality, who did not pass through its horror. The figure denotes only a certain quantity, nothing more. And what about the generations of the next century, for whom events of the forties of our century will be more and more hidden under the dust of history, under the layers of more recent happenings, beyond the barrier of passing time.*

And yet—this figure denotes not only millions of persons converted into ashes—it also denotes millions of individualities already formed or meant to be formed by life. These individualities represent personal human fates, filled with joy and drama, with experiences, emotions, plans for the future and with hope. All that was blown away together with the smoke of the crematoria and pyres, set alight by the Nazi murderers.

Such is the basic truth about KL Auschwitz. *It was shared both by its prisoners and by their slaughterers. Both were familiar with it through personal experience. The prisoners however were the objects of this truth; they came to know its sting, which was turned against mankind, humanity and against their very selves. They had suffered its consequences.*

The SS-men—from the highest camp authorities down to the warders of lowest rank—were those who had planned, organized and achieved the truth about Auschwitz, each one in his own sector and according to his function, competence and range of responsibility. This fact makes the autobiography of Höss, the diary of Kremer or the reminiscences of Broad of value, not only as historical documents or as corroboration of the paralysing truth, remembered by former prisoners in all its fullness of shape and contour. They are also indicative of the mentality and character of Auschwitz criminals, of their perverted moral criteria, of their thought processes.

It is worth while, even necessary, to reflect upon one fact. Men created the Auschwitz inferno for other men. Men turning against other men, against whole nations, transformed crime into the crime of genocide.

We must not forget this. Whatever happened once, may happen again. But also—according to the wording of the Auschwitz Appeal at the 20th anniversary of the liberation of Auschwitz in 1965—whatever was once terminated by human heroism and selfless effort may be prevented from happening again in the future. It is within the power of man to prevent the rebirth of the ideology and practices of Höss, Kremer, Broad—namely, the philosophy of fascism and the crime of genocide.

APPENDICES

DEPOSITION OF STANISŁAW DUBIEL
REPORT OF JANINA SZCZUREK
SS RANKS AND THEIR WEHRMACHT EQUIVALENTS
BIOGRAPHICAL NOTES
BIBLIOGRAPHY

DEPOSITION OF STANISŁAW DUBIEL

Oświęcim, August 7, 1946. The district investigating magistrate Jan Sehn, acting in accordance with the Decree of November 1945 (Official Gazette of Current Legislation of the Polish Republic, no. 51, item 293) concerning the Central and District Commissions for the Investigation of German Crimes in Poland, being himself member of the Central Commission, questioned—in accordance with Article 255 and in connection with Articles 107 and 115 of the Penal Code—the above mentioned person, who submitted the following statement:

> My name is Stanisław Dubiel; born November 13, 1910, at Chorzów; son of Klemens and Anna née Pietrzok; Roman Catholic; Polish nationality and citizenship; resident at Chorzów I, ul. Powstańców 49.

I spent the period from November 6, 1940, until January 18, 1945, in the concentration camp at Auschwitz. My camp number was 6059. Almost from the beginning I worked as a gardener, first with *Lagerführer* Fritzsch who held this position till the end of 1941, then with his successor *Lagerführer* Aumeier, who became *Lagerführer* in January 1942 after Fritzsch had been transferred to Flossenbürg. On April 6, 1942, I was assigned as gardener to the house of the camp commandant Rudolf Höss. I continued to work there until Höss left the camp, or even longer, till the departure of his family from Auschwitz. Höss was transferred from Auschwitz to the Head Office in the autumn of 1943. His family left Auschwitz in the summer of 1944. While working in the garden and in Höss's household I had the opportunity for close and direct observation of both Höss and his family. Höss used to come to his house very frequently during the day, he often rode on horseback or drove about the camp, using all means of transport, looked into all corners and was interested in all camp matters. He never stayed long in his office. Official papers needing his signature were brought to his house and he signed them there. He often received SS dignitaries as guests in his house, including Himmler who visited him twice. During the first visit Himmler conversed most cordially with Höss and Mrs. Höss.[1]

[1] What Dubiel refers to as Himmler's first visit in Höss's home was in fact his second visit

Himmler held Höss's children on his lap and they called him "*Onkel Heini*" [uncle Heini]. Such scenes were commemorated by photos, enlargements of which hung on the walls of Höss's home. During Himmler's second visit to Auschwitz,[2] shortly before Höss ceased to be the camp commandant, Himmler stated in a conversation held in the garden that [Höss] had to leave Auschwitz because the British radio had had too much to say about the extermination of prisoners at Auschwitz. There ensued a discussion during which Höss said that he was convinced that by his activities at Auschwitz he had served his country well. He said so immediately after Himmler had broached the subject of gassing people. I heard part of the discussion myself, the rest I heard from the women prisoners, readers of the [Holy] Writ [Jehovah's Witnesses] who were employed in Höss's household. They were two German women, vehement opponents of the Hitlerite system. One of them, Sophie Stipel, came from Höss's home town, i.e. from Mannheim-Ludwigshafen, and had known him since his childhood, as they used to live in the same street. She told me that during the second conversation with Himmler Höss's exact words had been: "*Ich dachte, ich werde meinem Vaterlande damit einem Dienst erweisen*" [I thought I should thus be of service to my country]. I presume that Sophie Stipel is now living with her daughter in Heidelberg. Both Stipel and her friend always told us everything about the conversations, concerning camp matters, which they had heard. They always notified us whenever we had to be particularly careful because there was danger of a bad break. It was thanks to their help that we were often able to avert disaster. The inspector of concentration camps, *SS-Obergruppenführer* Schmauser,[3] was also a frequent guest in Höss's household. Several times, I think five altogether, Höss received the head of the *Wirtschafts- und Verwaltungshauptamt* [Economic and Administrative Head Office], *SS-Obergruppenführer* Pohl. There was a very cordial atmosphere during those visits. It was evident that Höss and Pohl were friends. We got the impression that Höss gave Pohl some gifts. During all those visits the Höss's entertained their guests with lavish hospitality. The food needed for the receptions had to be "organized" by me, by order of Mrs. Höss. Before every reception Mrs. Höss told me what was needed or she would tell me to ask Sophie, the cook. Mrs. Höss never gave me any money or coupons which were ordinarily needed to buy food. I managed in the following way: Through my friend, Adolf Maciejewski, who was capo in the prisoners' food store, I got in touch with the manager, *SS-Unterscharführer* Schebeck, whom I visited every week to take the rations for the women prisoners employed in Höss's household. In a conversation I had with Schebeck I mentioned a conversation I had overheard, in which Höss spoke about Schebeck's promotion. Schebeck was most anxious to be promoted, so he

---

on July 17 and 18, 1942. Dubiel could not have witnessed Himmler's former visit, which took place on March 1, 1941, as he was then employed as gardener by *Lagerführer* Fritzsch.

[2] This was Himmler's third visit to *KL Auschwitz*. Its date is not known. Höss did not mention it in his Autobiography, perhaps because of the topic of their conversation (as remembered by Dubiel).

[3] The post of the Inspector of Concentration Camps was held by *SS-Gruppenführer* Richard Glücks. Schmauser, mentioned here, was commandant of the South-Eastern SS District in Wrocław and Higher SS and Police Leader of that district.

asked me whether I did not require anything for Höss's household and in this way our relationship was established. When collecting the food rations for the women prisoners I always brought back provisions for the Hösses as well. I could easily carry the things to the house because Schebeck always helped me. In this way I took 3 bags of sugar, each containing 85 kilos, in the course of just one year. Mrs. Höss always stressed that no SS-men should hear of these transactions. I assured her that I had settled everything with my friend. I also arranged the matter with Schebeck, who was to act as if he did not know a thing about the transactions, of which Höss, as I told him, had no knowledge. Finally I told him the truth, saying that I was organizing the food with Höss's knowledge, but that any disclosure of this fact would surely have very sad consequences for both of us, as Höss would be certain to deny everything. I told Schebeck this so that he would realize that we need not fear anything from Höss, so long as we used discretion. I made use of this situation to help my fellow prisoners by getting more goods out of Schebeck, part of which I then smuggled into the camp to feed those prisoners who needed it most, particularly the sick prisoners. I used to carry provisions in a basket first, but later I would bring them in a push-cart. The food store was well supplied at the time as provisions taken from the Jews—who came to Auschwitz in mass transports and were then in the majority of cases directed straight to the gas chambers—were kept there. I took the following items from the store for the private use of the Höss household: sugar, flour, margarine, various baking powders, condiments for soup, macaroni, oat-flakes, cocoa, cinnamon, semolina, peas and other food-stuffs. Mrs. Höss was never satisfied; she would always start talking about what she needed for her household, thus letting me know what I should supply her with. The food was not only for her own use, she sent part of it to her relatives in Germany. I also supplied Höss's kitchen with meat from the butcher's and always with milk. I must state that Höss and his family were entitled to get one and a quarter litres of milk, according to his milk coupons. Day after day I would take 5 litres of milk for Höss's kitchen from the camp dairy. Mrs. Höss often demanded cream as well. The dairy was paid for 1¼ litres only. Höss never paid for the provisions taken from the prisoners' food stores or from the camp butcher's, which were used in his own household and kitchen. Another caterer for Höss's household was the manager of the canteen and at the same time the manager of the camp slaughter-house, Engelbrecht, who was promoted from the rank of *SS-Oberscharführer*, to that of *SS-Obersturmführer* during his stay at Auschwitz. He supplied Höss with meat, sausage and cigarettes from the canteen. I saw chests, each containing 10,000 Yugoslav Ibar cigarettes, stored in the house of Höss. These cigarettes could only be had from the prisoners' canteen. Mrs. Höss would treat me to them; she also used them to pay the prisoners for work done on the quiet (*Schwarzarbeiten*) which they were forced to do, although they were exposed to the danger of the most severe punishments if caught. It is characteristic that Höss himself issued the order forbidding this kind of work. He did not observe this rule in the case of his own household. I maintain that he was well aware of my deliveries to his household. It often happened that he found me in the kitchen unpacking the things I had just brought. He also saw the provisions piling up in the pantry and larder of his house. He made use of them for himself and for his guests at the parties. That he was provident in household matters was also shown by the fact that during his trips to Hungary, where he used to go when he was no longer commandant of the camp, he would send whole cratefuls of wine. He made trips to Hungary as the special plenipotentiary for exterminating Jews in Europe (*Sonderbeauftragter für die Judenvernichtung in Europa*), as his wife called him officially. She stated in a conversation with me that the enemies of Höss had not succeeded in ruining him, on the contrary, he had been promoted and was entrusted with an even more important mission. I should like to stress once more that I had to organize for Höss even the most trifling objects of daily domestic use, such as shoe polish or shoe brushes. It was characteristic that Mrs. Höss often exchanged the underwear which was sent for the women prisoners who worked in her household. This was underwear from the "Canada" storehouses, looted from the Jewesses who were sent to the gas chambers and occasionally supplied to the domestic servants. The equipment and furniture of Höss's home were of similar origin. Everything was made by prisoners from camp materials. The rooms were furnished with the most magnificent pieces, the desk drawers were lined with leather from the warehouses of the leather factory (*Lederfabrik*) where there were stores of leather goods looted from the Jewish mass transports. A former prisoner and criminal by profession, Erich Grönke, used to supply Höss with leather and leather goods. Höss managed to obtain Grönke's release and then employed him as manager of the leather factory. Grönke daily drove to the Höss home and brought leather products of all kinds, shoes for men, women and children. All the clothes for the commandant and his sons were made in Grönke's leather factory. The best tailors were employed to make them, first Poles, later Jews from France, Belgium and other countries, craftsmen known all over the world. Two Jewish dressmakers were employed in the Höss home for about a year and six months. They made dresses for Mrs. Höss and her daughters, using materials supplied by Grönke from the stores taken from the Jews. I want to point out that clothes and other Jewish property in the warehouses of the tannery (*Lederfabrik*) were checked for hidden valuables, above all gold, currency of high value and diamonds. Grönke himself told me that great quantities of such valuables used to be found. My friend Stanisław Jarosz, who worked in the tannery, confirmed this. They worked in a special, locked room. When they found valuables, they handed them to Grönke, without any receipt. I suppose that Grönke, and through him Höss also, took advantage of these valuables. It was characteristic that Mrs. Höss, for whom I grew rare flowers in the garden and in the hothouses, was never satisfied with what I could do and grow, using the means available in the camp. She would send SS-men to the house of my fellow prisoner, Roman Kwiatkowski from Będzin (Łąki no. 1), who also worked with me, and from there they used to fetch the seeds and plants which she had ordered. Plants were also brought by Kwiatkowski's sons, acting on the instructions of Mrs. Höss's agents. I should not like to omit here a certain fact, which I had the opportunity to observe myself. Höss instructed a prisoner working in the slaughter-house to prepare for him some tinned pork meat. The pork was not properly processed and was spoiled. When Höss found this out he ordered the tins which had gone bad to be sent to the prisoners' kitchen and in their place, he drew from Engelbrecht fresh meat from the slaughter-house. Making use of the prisoners' work and the camp supplies for his own needs, Höss settled down in such a well-equipped, magnificent home that his wife remarked "*hier will ich leben und sterben*" [I want to live here till I die]. They lacked nothing in their household and nothing could be lacking, considering the immense quantities of all kinds of possessions accumulated in the camp. Besides the above mentioned caterers to Höss's household, *SS-Rottenführer* Hartung should not be forgotten. He held a post in the horticular enterprise at Rajsko. Without the knowledge of Caesar, the head of agriculture in the camp, he supplied Höss with thousands of pots, seeds and plants, and in autumn with vegetables for winter storage. Every winter I had to "organize," with the help of my contacts, of course, 70 tons of coke to heat the house and, above all, the hothouses. Höss could not help seeing all these things piling up in his household, he knew that I used to supply him with them but he never asked where I got them from and how they were paid for. Little wonder, then, that Mr. and Mrs. Höss, being so provident, accumulated in the so-called *Haus Höss* [Höss Home] such quantities of goods, that four freight-cars were required to take them away when Höss was recalled from Auschwitz.

From the comments of Mrs. Höss I gathered that Höss was very keen on remaining at Auschwitz. Being transferred to the Head Office of the *Wirtschafts- und Verwaltungshauptamt* did not suit his purpose, and he considered this to be the result of intriguing on the part of the Head of Agricultural Economy in the camp, Dr. Joachim Caesar, with whom he had been on bad terms. Höss was on friendly terms with the Head of the Camp Building Section, Bischoff. That the Political Section and particularly its Head, Grabner, was subordinated to the camp commandant is seen from the fact that I had been released from a bunker, and my name crossed out from the list of persons designated by the Political Section to be shot. As I had been arrested on the charge of belonging to a secret Polish organization, a fact which must have been noted in my dossier kept by the Political Section, this section put my name on the list of persons to be shot three times. The first time this happened was on June 12, 1942, when I was taken together with 172 other men from the block and from the *Schreibstube* [office]. Like them, I was to have been led to the yard of Block 11.[4] Höss then requested my release and my return to work; his request was obeyed. In the afternoon of the same day Grabner came to Höss's garden, accompanied by the aide-de-camp of Höss and by Hössler, demanding that I be delivered to be shot. Höss, and particularly Mrs. Höss, categorically opposed their demand, and they had their way. I again found myself on the list of persons to be shot in July or August 1942,[5] and for the last time on October 28, 1942. In this last

[4] The year 1942 at *KL Auschwitz* was marked by an exceptional reign of terror. Mass executions, conducted by functionaries of the *Politische Abteilung*, constituted reprisals against defenceless prisoners for the activities of the underground organizations within the country against the invader. On June 12, 1942, 60 Polish political prisoners were shot in the yard of Block 11, at the wall of death. They had been brought in transports from Silesia and Cracow-Tarnów in 1940 and 1941. *Cf.* Danuta Czech: Kalendarium der im Konzentrationslager Auschwitz-Birkenau, Oświęcim, *Hefte von Auschwitz*, 3, 1960, p. 64.

[5] On July 14, 1942, about 200 Polish political prisoners were shot in the yard of Block 11, at the wall of death. They had been brought to the camp in transports from Silesia, Cracow, Lublin, Łódź, Radom and Warsaw in 1940 and 1941. *Ibid.*, p. 71.

instance I was to have been shot together with a group of 280 prisoners from the Lublin region.[6] This time, too, Höss objected. Mrs. Höss often reminded me of this fact, thereby wishing to make me more eager to render the services which I have briefly described above. I must stress that neither Höss nor Mrs. Höss interceded on my behalf out of idealistic motives. They were both bitter enemies of the Poles and Jews. They hated everything Polish. Mrs. Höss often said to me: "*Die Polen müssen alle zusammen für die Greueltaten in Bromberg bezahlen.*[7] *Sie sind nur dazu, um zu arbeiten bis zum Verrecken*" [The Poles must all of them pay for the atrocities in Bydgoszcz. They exist only to work until they perish].

She said about the Jews that they must disappear from the face of the earth to the last man, and that at the proper time the end of even the English Jews would come.

REPORT OF JANINA SZCZUREK

On January 13, 1963, Mrs. Janina Szczurek, maiden name Przybyła, born November 24, 1909, at present resident in Oświęcim, ul. Górnickiego 9, made the following report concerning the help she gave to the prisoners, and conditions in the household of Höss:

I do not remember the exact month or day when the wife of the concentration camp commandant, Hedwig Höss, came to my flat with the offer of employing me as dressmaker at her home. I do not know from whom she had got my address, perhaps from the labour exchange where I was registered as a dressmaker.

I did dressmaking at home with the help of some apprentices. I could not refuse and so accepted the offer, not knowing at that time that I was dealing with the wife of the concentration camp commandant at Auschwitz.

On the appointed day I went on foot to the address given me and only then did I find out where I was to work.

---

[6] The approximately 280 Polish political prisoners shot on October 28, 1942, included mainly prisoners sent by the Security Police and SD from Lublin and Radom. *Ibid.*, p. 97.

[7] On September 3, 1939, German infiltrators made a provocatory attempt at an armed seizure of Bydgoszcz. This attempt had been prepared by the SS with the cooperation of the NSDAP. Its aims included provoking the Polish civilian population to an armed uprising and thus "justifying" the policy of extermination adopted towards the Polish nation. Polish troops, then stationed in the town, took part in the fighting together with national defence patrols, including Boy Scouts and pupils of grammar schools. By September 5, that is until the moment when Hitler's army entered Bydgoszcz, about 50 Nazi agents were killed in battle or shot after being sentenced in court, approximately 700 were arrested (the majority of them later released). The Poles lost about 240 soldiers. In retaliation for the suppression of the operation and for the alleged persecution of the German minority, the Nazis, after entering the town, began the first shootings and on September 9 and 10, 1939, conducted mass executions in the course of which approximately 1,500 Poles perished. Altogether, as a result of further extermination by the Nazis, the casualties of the Polish population in Bydgoszcz during the occupation amounted to 36,500 inhabitants. Falsifying the events in Bydgoszcz on September 3 and 4, 1939, the Nazi propaganda called them the "bloody Sunday" and started a defamatory campaign against alleged Polish atrocities and murders committed against the German minority. *Wielka Encyklopedia Powszechna PWN*, Warszawa 1970, vol. 13, p. 74.

At first I felt afraid to go there alone, so I used to take my apprentice with me to feel safe. Her name was Bronka Urbańczyk, now Mrs. Ciepła, from Stare Stawy.

I met camp prisoners for the first time at Höss's home. I remember the names of prisoners: Bronek Jaroń from Cracow, Wilhelm Kmak from Grybów near Tarnów and the prisoner Kwiatkowski, whose first name I do not remember. Jaroń and Kwiatkowski worked in the garden of Höss, and they often came to the house where they did the heavier work. Jaroń always cleaned shoes. He asked me to get in touch with Mrs. Stankiewicz and her daughter, Helena Kwiatkowska. The latter's father-in-law was the owner of a drugstore in Oświęcim [town]. Here I used to obtain injections, vitamins and mercury ointment, which I brought to Höss's house. The medicines were taken from me by the prisoners themselves or by the domestic help of Mrs. Höss, Angela—Aniela Bednarska, a resident of Oświęcim. Angela used to cache the parcels in the garden, adding some food "organized" from Höss's kitchen. Very frequently Angela would give me money from her wages, which I then spent on medicines for the prisoners. After some days I stopped going to work. I was hungry as I used to get only one dish for my meal (*Eintopf*) and 3 marks as wages. I could earn much more working at home. Then Mrs. Höss sent Angela to make me come again. She raised my wages to 10 marks and I got better food. I used to share the food with the hungry prisoners who would search the dustbins for peelings, though they were beaten for doing so by the capos.

The prisoner Kmak stayed in Höss's house all the time. He used to paint the walls. He did his work slowly and he asked us not to prevent the children drawing on the walls. Staying there was his only contact with the civilian world.[1]

When I wanted to speak to the prisoners I pretended that my sewing-machine was out of order. When nobody was nearby I would inform the prisoners about the situation in the world.

I used to sew for Mrs. Höss very often, and she would even make me come to do her ironing. When I was returning home Angela, on Mrs. Höss's orders, used to pick a bunch of flowers in the garden for me to take home. It was then that she could cache food [in the garden] while I stood watch at the gate, in case any SS-men were approaching. It was safest to hide the food in the evenings when the Höss couple left for the theatre or the cinema. We stood in greatest fear of the governess of Höss's children, a German woman, Elfriede from Hameln.

Mrs. Höss was loyal to us. She kept no strict watch on us when the prisoners

---

[1] Wilhelm Kmak, born January 24, 1904, at Grybów, varnisher by trade, sent to camp on August 30, 1940, camp number 3456, worked in the camp workshops as a painter. On August 31, 1943, he was put in the bunker of Block 11 together with two fellow prisoners, charged with illegally taking camp meat and sausage from the slaughter-house to the camp. During the inquiry, conducted by the Political Section, he mentioned the names of SS-men for whom he also had "organized" sausage. To hush up the matter and to get rid of the witnesses, all three were executed by firing squad on September 4, 1943.

were working in her house. The Hösses' children, with the exception of Klaus the eldest, did not wrong the prisoners working there either. They used to run about in the garden and watch the prisoners work. One day they came to me and asked me to sew them arm-bands with badges such as the prisoners had. I did not realize what the consequences would be of this request. Klaus put on the arm-band of a capo, and for the other children I sewed triangles of different colours on their clothes. The children were pleased, but as they ran about the garden they met their father, who tore off their badges and took them inside. I was not punished but only warned not to do such things.

I sewed in the Hösses' household until a sewing room was established in the camp. From that time my work was done by women prisoners, Jewesses.

SS RANKS AND THEIR WEHRMACHT EQUIVALENTS

SS rank	Wehrmacht equivalent	Rough English translation
SS-Bewerber		candidate
SS-Mann	*Soldat*	private
SS-Sturmmann	*Gefreiter*	lance-corporal
SS-Rottenführer	*Obergefreiter*	senior lance-corporal
SS-Unterscharführer	*Unteroffizier*	corporal
SS-Scharführer	*Unterfeldwebel*	junior sergeant
SS-Oberscharführer	*Feldwebel*	sergeant
SS-Hauptscharführer	*Oberfeldwebel*	sergeant-major
SS-Stabsscharführer	*Stabsfeldwebel*	staff sergeant-major
SS-Sturmscharführer	*Hauptfeldwebel*	
SS-Untersturmführer	*Leutnant*	second-lieutenant
SS-Obersturmführer	*Oberleutnant*	lieutenant
SS-Hauptsturmführer	*Hauptmann*	captain
SS-Sturmbannführer	*Major*	major
SS-Obersturmbannführer	*Oberstleutnant*	lieutenant-colonel
SS-Standartenführer	*Oberst*	colonel
SS-Oberführer	*Brigadekommandeur*	brigadier-general
SS-Brigadeführer	*Generalmajor*	major-general
SS-Gruppenführer	*Generalleutnant*	lieutenant-general
SS-Obergruppenführer	*General*	general
SS-Oberstgruppenführer	*Generaloberst*	colonel-general
Reichsführer SS—Himmler's personal title as head of the SS	no equivalent	

BIBLIOGRAPHICAL NOTES

Aumeier, Hans,
SS-Hauptsturmführer
(born August 20, 1906)

Member of the NSDAP (no. 164755) and the SS (no. 2700). Since the establishment of the camp at Dachau, he served in the following camps: *KL Dachau*, *KL Esterwegen*, *KL Lichtenburg*, *KL Buchenwald* and *KL Flössenbürg*. He was transferred to *KL Auschwitz* in January 1942, where he succeeded Karl Fritzsch as senior *Lagerführer*. While holding this post he was found guilty of corrupt practices, as a result of which he was transferred, upon Höss's suggestion, on August 18, 1943, to be commandant of the camp at Vaivara in Estonia. After the liquidation of camps in the Baltic countries Aumeier was entrusted with the labour camps near Landsberg. In January 1945 he was put in charge of the newly established *KL Grini* near Oslo in Norway. The Supreme National Tribunal in Cracow sentenced him to death on December 22, 1947, in the trial of members of the SS garrison of Auschwitz-Birkenau.The sentence was carried out.

Baer, Richard,
SS-Sturmbannführer
(born September 9, 1911)

Member of the NSDAP (no. 454991) and the SS (no. 44225). He began his service in concentration camps in 1933 as a member of the guard company at *KL Dachau*. In 1939 he was transferred to the Death's Head Formations. After sustaining an injury in 1942, he was assigned to be aide-de-camp at *KL-Neuengamme* and then, in 1943, at *KL Auschwitz*. After three days he was recalled to the *WVHA*, to be Pohl's aide-de-camp, and in November 1943 he took over the function of Head of Office DI (Political Department) in the Inspectorate of Concentration Camps. He became commandant of *KL Auschwitz* on May 11, 1944, and commander of the garrison on July 27 of the same year. After the evacuation of the Auschwitz camp he was appointed commandant of *KL Mittelbau*. Because of an injury to his leg he left for Styria (Austria) before the capitulation. He went into hiding and under an assumed name worked as a woodsman in the vicinity of Hamburg until December 1960. In July 1963 he died suddenly in prison, pending investigation, in Frankfurt am Main.

Baretzki, Stefan,
SS-Rottenführer
(born in 1919)

As a *Volksdeutsch* he was deported to Germany after the outbreak of the war. He was called up to serve in the *Waffen-SS* at Auschwitz in the autumn of 1942. Till January 1945 he was *Blockführer* in the men's camp at Birkenau. The Court of Jury in Frankfurt am Main sentenced him to life imprisonment on August 19, 1965.

Bartsch (Barth), Helmut,
SS-Hauptsturmführer

SS judge, member of the special commission investigating corrupt practices in the SS.

Becher, Kurt,
SS-Standartenführer
(born in 1909)

Until 1942, an employee of a wheat dealing firm. In the summer of 1942 he was appointed head of a commission for the purchase of arms for the SS. He conducted negotiations concerning the take-over of the famous stud-farm Schlenderhahn from Baron von Oppenheim, who in return was allowed to emigrate. In the years 1944—1945 he acted as Himmler's plenipotentiary in negotiations with representatives of Jewish financiers, the aim of which was to spare, for high reimbursement, some Slovakian and Hungarian Jews from extermination. Becher appeared as a witness at the trial of the chief war criminals before the International Military Tribunal in Nuremberg.

Bischoff, Karl,
SS-Sturmbannführer

From October 1, 1941, to the autumn of 1944, he was the second successive manager of construction work at the Auschwitz concentration camp. Subsequently he was promoted to head of the building inspectorate of the *Waffen-SS* and Police for the region of Silesia, based at Kochłowice near Kattowitz.

Blobel, Paul,
SS-Standartenführer
(born August 13, 1894)

Member of the NSDAP (no. 844662) and the SS (no. 2910). From June 1941 to January 1942 he was commandant of *Sonderkommando 4a* (belonging to *Einsatzgruppe C*) which was active in the Soviet Union (Kiev, Poltava). In June 1942, on orders from Heinrich Müller, he commenced the operation of obliterating all traces of mass extermination in Poland and the USSR. He was arrested after the war and charged with the murder of 60,000 people. The American Military Tribunal No. II in Nuremberg sentenced him to death on April 8, 1948, in the trial of the *Einsatzgruppen* (Case IX). He was executed by hanging on June 8, 1951.

Boger, Wilhelm,
SS-Oberscharführer
(born December 19, 1906)

Member of the NSDAP (no. 153652) and the SS (no. 2779). Called up in 1933 as a member of the SS to the auxiliary police; in 1937 promoted to the rank of criminal police officer and in 1939 transferred to the Gestapo in Ciechanów. On December 1, 1942, he was detailed to *KL Auschwitz*, where he remained till the liquidation of the camp, as a functionary of the Political Section. He worked in the same section at *KL Mittelbau* from February to March 1945. He was arrested by the American Military Police in June 1945. In November 1946 he escaped from the extradition transport heading for Poland. At first he went into hiding, then he worked as trade clerk in Stuttgart. The Court of Jury in Frankfurt am Main sentenced him to life imprisonment on August 10, 1965, depriving him of civil rights for ever.

Bracht, Fritz,
SS-Brigadeführer
(born January 18, 1899)

Member of the NSDAP. In 1935 he was appointed the deputy *Gauleiter* and in 1941 the *Gauleiter* and *Oberpräsident* of Upper Silesia.

Brandl, Therese
(born February 1, 1909)

Member of the DAF (*Die Deutsche Arbeitsfront*) from 1934 and the NSDAP from 1943. She began her service at *KL Ravensbrück* in September 1940. Between April 1942 and December 1944 she was a wardress (*Aufseherin*) in the women's camp at *KL Auschwitz-Birkenau*. The Supreme National Tribunal in Cracow sentenced her to death on December 22, 1947, in the trial of members of the SS garrison of Auschwitz-Birkenau. The sentence was carried out.

Brauner, Ferdinand,
SS-Unterscharführer
(born April 24, 1911)

From 1942 till the evacuation of *KL Auschwitz* he was employed in the office of the garrison physician.

Broad, Pery,
SS-Unterscharführer
(born April 25, 1911)

Joined the *Hitlerjugend* in 1931. In 1941 volunteered for the SS. In April 1942 he was detailed to *KL Auschwitz* where he was first a guard and then a functionary of the Political Section. On May 6, 1945, he was taken prisoner by the British. He was released in 1947. On April 30, he was arrested in connection with Auschwitz investigations. The Court of Jury in Frankfurt am Main sentenced him to four years' close confinement on August 19, 1965.

Caesar, Joachim,
SS-Obersturmbannführer
(born May 30, 1901)

Doctor of Agronomy. Member of the NSDAP (no. 626589) and the SS (no. 74704). After Hitler came to power he became mayor of Holstein; from

1934 he was a full-time employee of the Training Office of the SS, later its head. He came to *KL Auschwitz* in February 1942. On March 12, he became head of the agricultural department. He supervised farms, stock-farms and the experimental plant-growing station at Rajsko. He has not so far been brought to justice. He lives in the Federal Republic of Germany.

Clauberg, Carl, honorary *SS-Brigadeführer* (born September 28, 1898)

Doctor and Professor of Medicine, gynaecologist. At Himmler's orders he conducted at *KL Auschwitz* criminal experiments aimed at finding a new method of sterilization of women. After the war he was a prisoner of war in the Soviet Union. On his release in 1956 he returned to Kiel. Shortly after he was detained and died in prison on August 9, 1957, before judicial proceedings had begun.

Danz, Luise (born December 11, 1917)

She began service in the women's camp at *KL Ravensbrück* in February 1943. In 1944 she was a wardress in women's camps at *KL Lublin* (Majdanek) *KL Płaszów* and *KL Auschwitz-Birkenau*. From January till the end of April 1945 she was a wardress in the women's camp at Malhof. The Supreme National Tribunal in Cracow sentenced her to life imprisonment on December 22, 1947, in the trial of members of the SS garrison of Auschwitz-Birkenau.

Dejaco, Walter, *SS-Obersturmführer* (born 1909)

Member of the NSDAP and the SS. Between 1941 and 1944 he was at *KL Auschwitz*, first as head of the planning department and then deputy head of the *Zentral Bauleitung der Waffen-SS* responsible for the expansion of the Auschwitz camp and its mass extermination installations. The charge preferred by the Court of Jury in Vienna in 1972 was later dropped since the majority of the jurymen adjudged that he had simply carried out orders and could not be called to account.

Egersdörfer, Karl, *SS-Unterscharführer* (born July 20, 1902)

Member of the NSDAP since 1934 and the SS (no. 289457). He was detailed to serve in the SS garrison of *KL Auschwitz* on March 31, 1941. He was in charge of the prisoners' kitchen in the base camp from July 1941 onwards. He was pronounced not guilty by the British Military Tribunal in Lüneburg on November 17, 1945, in the trial of members of the SS garrison at *KL Bergen-Belsen*.

Eichmann, Adolf,
SS-Sturmbannführer
(born March 19, 1906)

Member of the NSDAP (no. 899895) and the SS (no. 45326). He had entered his full-time career in the SS in September 1933, and a year later was transferred, with the rank of *SS-Scharführer*, to the staff of *Reichsführer SS* Himmler in the Main Security Office (*Sicherheitsdienst*), where he was an official in the department dealing with matters of race and resettlement (*SS-Rassen- und Siedlungsamt*), in section II 112 which was responsible for matters of denominations, freemasonry, Marxism and Jewish affairs. From 1937 onwards he dealt with problems connected with the emigration of Jews from the territory of the Third Reich. In 1938, after the annexation of Austria by the Third Reich, he was detailed to Vienna to occupy the position of Head of the Central Office for Jewish Emigration (*Reichszentralstelle für jüdische Auswanderung*). When Hitler occupied Czechoslovakia, Eichmann was sent there in the second half of 1939 as an expert in matters of Jewish resettlement, in order to organize the "emigration" of Jews from Czechoslovakia. In December 1939 Himmler appointed him to a special post in the Reich Main Security Office, concerned with deporting the Polish population from territories annexed by the Third Reich. This department was designated as IV D4. This designation was changed several times in connection with the constant reorganization of the Reich Main Security Office, but it was always supervised by department IV, which had as its aim the identification and combatting of opponents (*Gegner-Erforschung und Bekämpfung*), that is, by the former Gestapo. Following another reorganization in 1941 Eichmann's department was called IV B4.

In mid-1941, the leaders of the Third Reich took the decision concerning the so-called final solution of the Jewish question. The organizing of this operation was entrusted to the Reich Main Security Office, or more precisely to the section designated IV B4, that is to Eichmann's department. After receiving his orders Eichmann devised a plan for "resettling the Jewish population of the occupied countries to the East."

Conscious of his responsibility for the crimes committed, Eichmann went into hiding in Germany after the capitulation of the Third Reich. Later he managed to reach Italy, then the Middle East and finally Argentine. On May 11, 1960, he was captured in Buenos Aires by a group of Jewish volunteers and abducted to Israel. Eichmann's trial in Jerusalem lasted from April 11 to December 15, 1961. He was sentenced to death and he was hanged on June 1, 1962. His remains were cremated and the ashes scattered on the high seas.

Eicke, Theodor,
SS-Obergruppenführer
(born October 17, 1892)

Member of the NSDAP (no. 114901) and the SS (no. 2921). He was the founder of the concentration camps (with the exception of Dachau), which were given their specific character by him. In 1933 Himmler appointed him commandant of *KL Dachau*. One year later he became the first inspector of concentration camps and paid particular attention to reinforcing the guard companies in the camps. As a result of his efforts Hitler approved the plan to form 25 guard companies in the concentration camps; this led to the development of the so-called Death's Head Formations (*Totenkopfverbände*). After the campaign in Poland, in which several formations of the 4th Death's Head Regiment had participated, Eicke received Hitler's order to form a Death's Head Division as soon as possible, and was promoted to the rank of *Generalleutnant*. He was succeeded as inspector of concentration camps by Richard Glücks. Eicke was killed on the eastern front in March 1943, during a reconnaissance flight near Kharkov.

Entress, Friedrich Karl Hermann,
SS-Hauptsturmführer
(born December 8, 1914)

Doctor of Medicine. He was camp physician at *KL Gross-Rosen* from January 3 to December 10, 1941. On December 11, 1941, he took over a similar post at *KL Auschwitz*, where he stayed till October 20, 1943. He conducted selections among sick prisoners in the camp and also in the RSHA transports. From October 21, 1943, to July 25, 1944, he was garrison physician and at the same time senior camp physician at *KL Mauthausen*. Subsequently, from August 3, 1944, to early 1945 he was senior camp physician at *KL Gross-Rosen*. He was sentenced to death by the American Military Tribunal at Dachau in 1946, in the so-called Mauthausen trial. The execution took place on May 28, 1947, at Landsberg.

Fischer,
SS-Hauptsturmführer

Doctor of Laws, member of the special commission investigating corrupt practices in the SS at *KL Auschwitz*; official of the Gestapo.

Fritzsch, Karl,
SS-Hauptsturmführer
(born July 10, 1903)

Member of the SS (no. 7287). In May 1940 he was brought from *KL Dachau* to occupy the position of the first *Schutzhaftlagerführer* at *KL Auschwitz*, then newly established. In January 1942 he was transferred to *KL Flossenbürg*, and then to one of the sub-camps of *KL Mittelbau*. He died in May 1945.

Gebhardt,
SS-Sturmbannführer

Commandant of the SS garrison at *KL Auschwitz* until 1942.

Genzken, Karl,
SS-Gruppenführer
and *Generalleutnant*
of *Waffen-SS*

Doctor of Medicine. Member of the NSDAP and the SS. In 1940 he was chief physician of the SS hospital in Berlin and supervisor of the medical personnel in the concentration camps. From May 1940 he was head of the Sanitary Office of the *Waffen-SS*. In 1942 he was appointed head of the sanitary service of the *Waffen-SS* in the office group D of the RSHA. He was responsible for conducting experiments with sulphamides and typhus on concentration camp inmates. The American Military Tribunal No. I in Nuremberg sentenced him to life imprisonment on August 29, 1947, at the trial of SS physicians.

Globocnik, Odilo,
SS-Gruppenführer
(born April 21, 1904)

Member of the NSDAP (no. 429939) and the SS (no. 292776). In 1933 he received a prison sentence for his part in the murder of a Jewish jeweller in Vienna. After his release from prison he took active part in operations connected with the annexation of Austria (*Anschluss*) by the Third Reich. He was appointed the second *Gauleiter* of Vienna, but several months later, in January 1939, he was removed from this position for speculating in illegal foreign exchange. In November of the same year Himmler appointed him Higher SS and Police Leader for the Lublin district in the so-called *Generalgouvernement*. He held this office until September 1943, when he was appointed Higher SS and Police Leader in Trieste, where he apparently committed suicide on May 31, 1945.

Glücks, Richard,
SS-Gruppenführer
(born April 22, 1889)

Member of the NSDAP (no. 214855) and the SS (no. 58703). In 1936 he took over the function of staff officer (*Stabsführer*) in the Inspectorate of Concentration Camps in Oranienburg. When World War II broke out and Theodor Eicke was appointed commander of the Death's Head Division, he succeeded the latter as inspector of concentration camps. His subsequent fate is unknown.

Goebbels, Josef
(born October 29, 1897)

Doctor of Laws. Member of the NSDAP. From 1926 *Gauleiter* of Berlin and from 1928 member of the Reichstag, also responsible for party propaganda. From 1933 Minister for Propaganda and Education. In July 1944, he became Plenipotentiary for Total War. A few days before the capitulation of the Third Reich, on May 1, 1945, he committed suicide together with his wife, having previously administered poison to his six children.

Göring, Hermann,
Marshal of the Reich
(born January 12, 1893)

One of the chief Nazi leaders, marshal of the Reich. He joined the NSDAP in 1922 and soon became chief of the SA. From 1928 a member and from 1932 chairman of the Reichstag. From 1933 Air Minister of the Reich and Prime Minister of Prussia. He was the organizer of the Gestapo and initiator of the concentration camps. In 1935 he became commander in chief of the Luftwaffe. In 1936 he was appointed Plenipotentiary for the Four-Year Plan and was responsible for the war economy of the Third Reich. In 1937 he became the chairman of an immense state concern (coal, iron and steel) "Hermann Göring," which during the war took over industrial plants in Austria, Czechoslovakia and Poland. He was one of Hitler's oldest and closest associates and was named by Hitler himself as his successor. His influence began to wane in 1943, after the unsuccessful attempts of the Luftwaffe to defeat the Allied Air Force.

In 1945, not long before the capitulation of the Third Reich, he attempted, unsuccessfully, to seize power. He was expelled from the party by Hitler, degraded and divested of all functions. Sentenced to death by the International Military Tribunal in Nuremberg on October 1, 1946 (at the trial of the chief war criminals), he committed suicide in his cell on October 15, 1946.

Grabner, Maximilian,
SS-Untersturmführer
(born October 2, 1905)

Member of the NSDAP (no. 1214137), secretary of the Criminal Police. He worked in Kattowitz, in the State Police Office. Transferred after the establishment of *KL Auschwitz* to be head of the camp's Political Section. He held this post until December 1, 1943, when, in connection with numerous corrupt practices, he was removed from his duties and arrested. The special SS court sentenced him to 12 years in prison in 1944.

The Supreme National Tribunal in Cracow sentenced him to death on December 22, 1947, in the trial of members of the SS garrison of Auschwitz-Birkenau. The sentence was carried out.

Grawitz, Ernst Robert von,
SS-Obergruppenführer
(born June 8, 1899)

Professor and Doctor of Medicine. Member of the NSDAP (no. 1102844) and the SS (no. 27483). He was Head Physician of the SS (*Reichsarzt SS*) and Chief of the SS Main Sanitary Office (*SS Sanitätshauptamt*). He committed suicide in April 1945.

Günther, Hans,
SS-Hauptsturmführer

From July 22, 1939, he was deputy to the Head of the Jewish Department in the Reich Main Security Office, in charge of deportations of Czechoslovakian Jews. As far as we know he was killed in Prague in May 1945.

Hartjenstein, Fritz,
SS-Obersturmbannführer
(born July 3, 1905)

Member of the NSDAP and the SS. He did service in the SS Military Formations from 1938, first as commander of a platoon and then in a company of the guard garrison of *KL Sachsenhausen*. In 1939 he was for some time *Lagerführer* of the labour camp of Niedernhagen-Wawelburg. In 1940—1942 he served in the Death's Head Division. In 1942 he was appointed commander of the SS garrison at *KL Auschwitz*; subsequently, from November 1943 to May 1944, he was commandant of *KL Auschwitz II*, later transferred to the post of commandant of *KL Natzweiler* and its sub-camps. He was sentenced to death for the first time by the British Court in Wuppertal on June 5, 1946, and then again by the French Court in Metz on July 2, 1954. He was not charged with his criminal activities at *KL Auschwitz*. He died in prison.

Hess, Rudolf
(born April 26, 1894)

He joined the NSDAP in 1920. From 1925 onwards he was Hitler's personal secretary and his closest associate. In 1933 he was appointed minister without portfolio and Hitler's deputy as the leader of the NSDAP. He was a member of the Privy Cabinet Council and the Defence Ministers' Council. In 1939 Hitler appointed him his second successor (after Göring). On May 10, 1941, Hess flew to Great Britain in order to put peace proposals before the British Government. He was interned in Scotland until the end of the war. In the trial of the chief war criminals the International Military Tribunal sentenced him to life imprisonment on October 1, 1946. He died in the Spandau prison in West Berlin in 1988.

Himmler, Heinrich,
Reichsführer SS
(born October 7, 1900)

One of Hitler's most important associates. After World War I he served in the nationalist volunteer detachments (*Freikorps*). He joined the NSDAP (no. 14303) in 1922 and the SS (no. 168) in 1925. He was appointed *Reichsführer der Schutzstaffeln* (SS) on January 6, 1929. From January 31, 1933, he was Chief of the Bavarian Police and from the autumn of that year Commissary Chief of the Political Police in Mecklenburg, Lübeck, Baden, Hessen-Anhalt and Bremen. He succeeded Hermann Göring as Chief of the Gestapo in 1934.

On February 10, 1936, he was appointed Chief of the entire German police (*Reichsführer SS und Chef der deutschen Polizei*) in the Reich's Ministry of Internal Affairs and from August 1943 he was also Minister of Internal Affairs. Moreover on October 7, 1938, he acquired the post of Reich Commissioner for the Strengthening of German Folkdom (*Reichskommissar für die Festigung des Deutschen Volkstums*). In 1943 he was given general responsibility for matters of administration of the Reich. In July 1944 Hitler appointed him commander in chief of the Replacement Army and in December 1944 commander in chief of the Rhine army group and in January 1945 commander in chief of the Rhine-Vistula army group. Thus a great many powers were concentrated in his hands. This enabled him to create a formidable force, namely the SS, to reorganize the police and unite it with the SS. He was the chief initiator of the mass murders of political opponents and Jews, and masterminded the exploitation of the slave labour which citizens of the occupied countries were forced to carry out. To reach this objective he ordered the establishment of concentration and extermination camps.

In the last days of World War II, owing to his failure to check the progress of the Soviet armies by the Rhine-Vistula army group, and also because of his attempts to get in touch with the Western Allies in order to conclude an armistice, he was excluded from the party by Hitler and stripped of all functions. Arrested by the British on May 21, 1945, he was exposed and on the following day was taken to the Headquarters of the Second British Army in Lüneburg, where he committed suicide during interrogation.

Hitler, Adolf
(born April 20, 1889)

From 1921 leader (*Führer*) of the NSDAP. In 1922 he organized party storm (terrorist) troops, *Sturm-Abteilungen* (SA). In November 1923 he led an unsuccessful coup d'état in Munich, as a result of which he was sentenced (in 1924) to five years in prison. While in prison in Landsberg he wrote the book *Mein Kampf*, in which he formulated his chauvinistic and racialist programme of German supremacy in Europe. At the end of 1924, when he was released from prison, he reorganized and developed the NSDAP and founded the guard detachments (*Schutzstaffeln*; SS), which in time became the most criminal Nazi organization. In 1932 he put forward his own candidacy for the office of President of the Reich, achieving 36.8% of votes in the election. On January 30, 1933, thanks to the backing of big business, he was appointed Chancellor by Paul Hindenburg, President of the Reich. On April 30, 1934, with the help of Hermann Göring and Heinrich Himmler, he disposed, during "the night of long knives," of his opponents within the SA leadership—above all Ernst Röhm—as well as other political adversaries. After Hindenburg's death on August 2, 1934, Hitler took both offices (of president and chancellor) for himself; then began his reign of increasing terror and political blackmail. Carrying out his programme of German hegemony in Europe, as set forth in *Mein Kampf*, Hitler was the initiator of the annexation of Austria (*Anschluss*) in 1938, of the occupation of Czechoslovakia in 1939, and, after the renunciation of the Polish-German non-aggression pact in April of the same year, of the invasion of Poland on September 1, 1939, which was the beginning of World War II. He was the initiator of mass murders of many millions of people during the war, particularly Poles and citizens of the USSR. He was the initiator of the extermination of Jews in the occupied and dependent countries. His will sanctioned crimes and formed the framework for all the doings of the governors of the occupied countries. When all plans had failed and the defeat of the Third Reich became inevitable, Hitler, who had been responsible for all the atrocities, legalized his union with Eva Braun, on April 29,

1945, and together with her committed suicide on the following day, i.e. April 30, 1945, in the underground bunker of the Reich Chancellery in Berlin.

Hofmann, Franz-Johann,
SS-Obersturmführer
(born 1906)

Member of the NSDAP. He served in a guard unit at *KL Dachau* from 1933, and in December 1942 was transferred to *KL Auschwitz*. At first he was second *Lagerführer* of the base camp, then *Lagerführer* of the Gypsy camp at Birkenau. In December 1943 he took over the post of *Lagerführer* of the base camp. He took part in selection of RSHA transports at Birkenau. In the summer of 1944 he was transferred to *KL Natzweiler*. For his activity at *KL Dachau* the Court of Jury in Munich II gave him life sentence on December 19, 1961. He found himself in dock again in Frankfurt am Main where the Jury sentenced him to life imprisonment, on August 19, 1965, this time for his criminal activity at *KL Auschwitz*.

Höfle, Hans,
SS-Hauptsturmführer
(born June 19, 1911)

Member of the NSDAP and the SS (no. 307469). He was staff officer with *SS-Gruppenführer* Globocnik in Lublin and Resettlement Commissioner for the Warsaw ghetto.

Höss, Rudolf,
SS-Obersturmbannführer
(born November 25, 1900)

Member of the NSDAP (no. 3240) and the SS (no. 193616). He began his service in concentration camps on December 1, 1934, at Dachau, in the rank of *SS-Unterscharführer*. On April 1, 1935, he took over the position of *Blockführer* and a year later that of *Rapportführer*. On August 1, 1938, he was transferred to *KL Sachsenchausen* where he was first an aide-de-camp and from Septemter 11, 1939, *Schutzhaftlagerführer*. During these four years of service in concentration camps he was promoted to *SS-Hauptsturmführer*. On May 4, 1940, he was appointed commandant of *KL Auschwitz*. While holding this position he was promoted first to *SS-Sturmbannführer* on January 30, 1941, and then to *SS-Obersturmbannführer* on July 18, 1942. He was recalled from the position of commandant of *KL Auschwitz* in November 1943. On November 10, 1943, he became commissary head of DI office in the D group of offices of the SS-WVHA, and on May 1, 1944, he was officially appointed to this position. After the defeat of the Third Reich he was hiding under the name of Franz Lang. Arrested on March 11, 1946, near Flensburg, on the basis of an extradition decision he was handed over to the Polish authoritiea. He was brought to Warsaw on May 25, 1946, and transferred to a prison in Cracow on July 30, where preliminary investigations were conducted. On April 2, 1947, the Supreme National Tribunal in Warsaw sentenced him to death. He was hanged at Oświęcim on April 16, 1947.

Hössler, Franz,
SS-Hauptsturmführer
(born February 4, 1906)

Member of the NSDAP and the SS (no. 41940). In 1940—1941 he was manager of the camp kitchen at *KL Auschwitz* and for a short time *Rapportführer*. In 1942 he was in charge of a prisoners' squad engaged on the construction of an SS rest home (*Sola-Hütte*) at Międzybrodzie near Żywiec. In late 1942 and early 1943 he commanded various prisoners' squads at Birkenau, including the *Sonderkommando*, and then worked in the Employment Section. From August 27, 1943, to January 1944, he was *Lagerführer* in the women's camp at Birkenau (*Auschwitz II—Frauenlager*). Transferred to *KL Dachau*, he was in charge of a prisoners' squad in one of its sub-camps till June 1944, when he returned to *KL Auschwitz* as *Lagerführer* of the base camp until evacuation. In 1945 he was a member of the garrison of *KL Mittelbau Dora*. After the evacuation of this camp in April 1945 he moved to *KL Bergen-Belsen*. He was sentenced to death on November 17, 1945, by the British Military Court at Lüneburg, in the trial of the SS garrison at *KL Bergen-Belsen*. He was executed on December 13, 1945, at Hameln.

Jambor, Eduard,
SS-Unterscharführer
(born July 13, 1900)

Worked as clerk with the SS garrison surgeon at *KL Auschwitz*. He was transferred to Berlin after the evacuation. He died on July 24, 1945.

Kaduk, Oswald,
SS-Unterscharführer
(born August 26, 1906)

Joined the SS in 1940. From 1942 to January 1945 he served at *KL Auschwitz* where he was first a *Blockführer* and then *Rapportführer*. He took part in the selections of prisoners in the hospital of the base camp and at Birkenau. He actively participated in executions. On March 24, 1947, the Soviet Military Tribunal charged him with being a member of the SS and sentenced him to 25 years of penal servitude. He was put in jail at Bautzen from which he was released in 1956. The Court of Jury in Frankfurt am Main sentenced him to life imprisonment on August 19, 1965, and deprived him of civil rights *in perpetuum*.

Kitt, Bruno,
SS-Obersturmführer
(born August 9, 1906)

Doctor of Medicine, head physician of the women's hospital at *KL Auschwitz II* (Birkenau) where he used to select sick patients to be sent to the gas chamber. He was also a physician at *KL Neuengamme*. At the trial of the garrison of the latter camp the British Military Court passed the death sentence on him. The execution took place on October 8, 1946, at Hameln.

Klehr, Josef,
SS-Oberscharführer
(born October 17, 1904)

In August 1938 he was called up to the SS and detailed to guard service at *KL Buchenwald*. In 1940 he became a sanitary orderly, first in the prisoners' and the SS hospitals at *KL Dachau* and from early 1941 in the prisoners' hospital at *KL Auschwitz*. In the spring of 1943 he was put in charge of the disinfection section and he conducted mass killings of prisoners with gas. In July 1944 he was appointed head of the camp hospital in the sub-camp *Gleiwitz I*. He was also responsible for sanitary matters in the sub-camps *Gleiwitz I—IV*. As a sanitary orderly he participated in the selections of RSHA transports and in the camp hospitals. He also killed prisoners with phenol injections through the heart. The Court of Jury in Frankfurt am Main sentenced him to life imprisonment on August 19, 1965, and deprived him of civil rights *in perpetuum*.

Knittel, Kurt,
SS-Oberscharführer
(born September 23, 1910)

He was head of Section VI (*Kulturabteilung*) in the *Kommandantur* of *KL Auschwitz*, where he was responsible for the training and political education of the SS guard garrison. After the liquidation of *KL Auschwitz* he was transferred to *KL Mittelbau*.

Koch, Karl Otto,
SS-Standartenführer
(born August 2, 1897)

Member of the NSDAP (no. 475586) and the SS (no. 14830). In 1935 he was commander of the guard garrison at *KL Esterwegen* and *KL Columbia-Haus* in Berlin ; in 1936 he was appointed commandant of the camp at Esterwegen. On August 1, 1937, already as *SS-Standartenführer*, he took over as commandant of *KL Buchenwald* where he remained until December 1941. He was removed from this post for misappropriating funds and introducing inhuman terror in the camp, inhuman even by the SS standards. Arrested towards the end of 1941, he was released thanks to Himmler's intercession and appointed commandant of *KL Lublin* (Majdanek). From here he was transferred to postal guards duty in August 1942. In December 1943 he was again arrested and sentenced to death by the SS court. He was executed at the beginning of 1945.

Kramer, Josef,
SS-Hauptsturmführer
(born November 10, 1906)

Joined the NSDAP in December 1931 (no. 733597) and the SS in January 1932 (no. 32217). From 1934 worked in concentration camps: at *KL Dachau* in 1936, *KL Sachsenhausen* in 1937 and then at *KL Mauthausen* where he held the post of aide-de-camp. Between May and November 1940 he was aide-de-camp at *KL Auschwitz* and then was appointed *Lagerführer* at *KL Dachau*. In April 1941 he was appointed *Lagerführer* and in October 1942 commandant of *KL Natzweiler*. He returned to *KL Auschwitz* and between May 8 and November 1944 was commandant of *KL Auschwitz II*, then of *KL Bergen-Belsen*. The British Military Court in Lüneburg sentenced him to death on November 17, 1945, in the trial of members of the SS garrison at *KL Bergen-Belsen*. He was executed on December 13, 1945, at Hameln.

Kremer, Johann,
SS-Obersturmführer
(born December 26, 1883)

Doctor of Medicine and Philosophy, *dozent* at the University of Münster. Joined the NSDAP in July 1932 and the SS in 1935. Between August 30 and November 17, 1942, he was an SS camp physician at *KL Auschwitz*. On December 22, 1947, in the trial of members of the SS garrison at Auschwitz-Birkenau, the Supreme National Tribunal in Cracow sentenced him to death. Reprieved due to old age, he was released after serving ten years and on January 10, 1958, returned to Germany. In 1960 he was again charged, in Münster, and sentenced to ten years in prison, with the ten years in Polish prison counted towards the sentence. The University of Münster stripped him of his doctor's degree. He died in the 1960's.

Krömer,
SS-Sturmbannführer

Doctor of Pharmacy, manager of the SS pharmacy at *KL Auschwitz*. Died on February 18, 1944.

Langefeld, Joanna

Was wardress at the first women's camp at Nohringen (*Kreis Nordheim*). From 1941 to April 1942 she was the head supervisor (*Oberaufseherin*) of *KL Ravensbrück*. Between April and October 1942 she was in charge of the women's camp at Auschwitz and between October 1942 and April 1943 she held the same post at *KL Ravensbrück*.

Lächert, Marthe Luise Hildegard (born March 19, 1920)

In April 1942 the SS employed her in the women's camp of *KL Ravensbrück*. From October 1942 till August 1943 she was a wardress at *KL Lublin* (Majdanek) and between April and July 1944 at *KL Auschwitz-Birkenau*, in the sub-camps at Rajsko and Budy. On December 22, 1947, the Supreme National Tribunal in Cracow sentenced her to 15 years in prison in the trial of members of the SS garrison of Auschwitz-Birkenau.

Liebehenschel, Arthur, *SS-Obersturmbannführer* (born November 25, 1901)

Member of the NSDAP (no. 932760) and the SS (no. 39254). He was aide-de-camp at *KL Lichtenburg* in 1934 and worked in the Inspectorate of Concentration Camps in Berlin in 1936. He was employed in the political department of which he later became head (later designated Office DI). In November 1943 he was transferred to *KL Auschwitz*, where he was given the post of commandant of the base camp (*KL Auschwitz I*) and commander of the garrison (*Standortälteste*). In May 1944 he was appointed commandant of *KL Lublin* and after the evacuation of the camp in July 1944 he was transferred to Trieste, to the office of the Higher SS and Police Leader Globocnik. On December 22, 1947, the Supreme National Tribunal in Cracow pronounced the death sentence in his case, at the trial of members of the SS garrison of Auschwitz-Birkenau. The sentence was carried out.

Lolling, Enno, *SS-Standartenführer* (born July 19, 1888)

Doctor of Medicine. Member of the NSDAP (no. 4691483) and the SS (no. 179765). Called up to the SS military formations during the war, he was at first camp physician at *KL Dachau*, next chief physician in the Inspectorate of Concentration Camps. After reorganization he was appointed head of the Sanitary Office (DIII) in the Economic and Administrative Head Office of the SS (WVHA-SS). He committed suicide in 1945.

Loritz, Hans, *SS-Oberführer* (born December 21, 1895)

Member of the NSDAP (no. 298668) and the SS (no. 4165). Until April 1936 he was commandant of *KL Esterwegen*, then of *KL Dachau*, and, from the beginning of 1940 until August 31, 1942, of *KL Sachsenhausen*. He committed suicide.

Maier, Franz Xaver,
SS-Untersturmführer

Member of the SS (no. 69600) detailed from the SS Death's Head Division Buchenwald (*SS-Totenkopfdivision Buchenwald*) to the newly established concentration camp at Auschwitz to the position of second *Lagerführer*. He held this post for a few months only. Charged with corrupt practices he was court-martialled.

(In the footnotes to the Polish edition of Rudolf Höss's autobiography, edited by Professor Jan Sehn and published in 1965, his first name is wrongly mentioned as Max and the surname erroneously spelled as Meyer, the author probably confusing him with the head of the camp administration, *SS-Untersturmführer* Max Meyer.)

Mandel, Maria
(born January 10, 1912)

Joined the *NS-Frauenschaft* in 1941 and the NSDAP in 1942, decorated with the War Cross of Merit (*Kriegsverdienstkreuz*) second class. Volunteered for service in concentration camps in 1938. She first served at *KL Lichtenburg*. Between May 1939 and October 1942 she was at *KL Ravensbrück*, first as a wardress (*Aufseherin*) and then main wardress (*Oberaufseherin*). From October 1942 to November 1944 she was *Oberaufseherin* and then commandant (*Lagerführerin*) in the women's camp at *KL Auschwitz-Birkenau*. She was sentenced to death by the Supreme National Tribunal in Cracow on December 22, 1947, in the trial of members of the SS garrison of Auschwitz-Birkenau. The sentence was carried out.

Maurer, Gerhard,
SS-Standartenführer
(born December 9, 1907)

Member of the NSDAP (no. 387103) and the SS (no. 12129). From 1934 he worked together with Pohl, who employed him first in the Inspection Department and then at establishing the Central Board of SS Enterprises. When in 1941 the Inspectorate of Concentration Camps had been incorporated with the WVHA as group D under Pohl's supervision, he was appointed Head of Office DII (employment of prisoners) which he considerably enlarged. He appointed a responsible head of the Employment Section (*Arbeitseinsatz*) in each camp to deal with the problems of employing prisoners in the armaments industry. In 1943 he became deputy to Glücks (Inspector of Concentration Camps) who in fact began handing over to him all important matters. The Voivodship Court in Cracow sentenced him to death on December 6, 1951. The sentence was carried out.

Mengele, Josef,
SS-Hauptsturmführer
(born March 16, 1911)

Doctor of Medicine and Philosophy. In the spring of 1943, he suffered injury on the eastern front. Between May 1943 and August 1944 he was a doctor in the Gypsy family camp (BIIe) at Birkenau and between August and December 1944 in the men's prison hospital (BIIf) at Birkenau. At the same time he worked in the clinics of BIIa, BIIb and BIId camps at Birkenau as chief physician (*Oberarzt*). Between December 1944 and January 17, 1945, he was a physician in the SS hospital at Birkenau. He had a laboratory in the Gypsy camp (BIIe) where he conducted pseudomedical experiments on twins, physiology and pathology of dwarfism and the causes and methods of treatment of noma (*noma faciei*). He conducted his experiments on children and young people whom he later killed. He evaded arrest and sought refuge in various South American countries. Charged with crimes committed at *KL Auschwitz*, he is still at large.

Meyer, Georg Franz,
SS-Obersturmführer
(born September 5, 1917)

Doctor of Medicine. He was camp physician at *KL Auschwitz*. He now lives in Vienna where he has a practice.

Meyer, Max,
SS-Untersturmführer

Member of the SS (no. 289455). He was transferred from the Inspectorate of Concentration Camps to *KL Auschwitz* in 1940, to be head of the camp administration (*Verwaltungsführer*).

Mildner, Rudolf,
SS-Standartenführer
(born July 10, 1900)

Doctor of Laws. Member of the NSDAP (no. 614080) and the SS (no. 275741). High State Councillor (*Oberregierungsrat*), Chief of the State Police in Kattowitz. He was chairman of the special commission which conducted selections among Soviet prisoners of war in November 1941. He was also presiding judge of the Summary Court (*Standgericht*), the sittings of which took place in the base camp at Auschwitz.

Moll, Otto,
SS-Hauptscharführer
(born March 4, 1915)

He began his service at *KL Auschwitz* on May 2, 1941. At first he supervised agricultural work, then was in charge of a penal company (*Strafkompanie*), and, until the crematoria at Birkenau were ready for action, commander of the *Sonderkommando* which cremated corpses in pits near Bunkers 1 and 2. For his criminal activities he was awarded by the *Führer* the War Cross of Merit, first class, with Swords on April 30, 1943. Between September 1943 and March 1944 he was in charge of the Auschwitz sub-camp *Fürstengrube*, and between March and May 1944 of the newly established sub-camp *Gleiwitz I*. In May 1944 he was recalled from Gleiwitz to *KL Auschwitz* by the plenipotentiary for the extermination of Hungarian Jews, former commandant Rudolf Höss, to take the post of chief head of crematoria at Birkenau, his responsibility being the cremating of corpses in the open air. Moll was the author of the plan for liquidating the Auschwitz camp by bombing (so-called Moll's Plan). When the operation of the extermination of Hungarian Jews had been over, he returned to the sub-camp *Gleiwitz I* to his former position. In January 1945 he superintended the evacuation of prisoners from Gleiwitz sub-camps. He was sentenced to death by the American Military Court at Dachau on December 13, 1945. The sentence was carried out on May 28, 1946.

Morgen, Konrad,
SS-Sturmbannführer
(born June 8, 1908)

Doctor of Laws, judge of the SS court, head of the special SS commission investigating corrupt practices in concentration camps. Between July 1943 and mid-1944 he conducted investigations against SS garrison members at *KL Buchenwald*, *Lublin*, *Auschwitz*, *Oranienburg*, *Herzogenbusch*, *Dachau*, in Warsaw and Cracow-Płaszów. After the war he appeared as witness at the trial of the chief war criminals before the International Military Tribunal in Nuremberg, at the trial of the WVHA-SS functionaries before the American Military Tribunal No. IV in Nuremberg, and at the trial of Mulka and others before the Court of Jury at Frankfurt am Main.

Muhsfeldt, Erich,
SS-Oberscharführer
(born February 18, 1913)

After joining the SS in 1940 he underwent the proper training and was detailed to the Auschwitz camp in August 1940 where he first supervised a prisoners' squad and was then a *Blockführer*. He was transferred to *KL Lublin* (Majdanek) where he was put in charge of the squad which buried the bodies of prisoners who had died or had been murdered. When the crematorium at Majdanek was put in action, in June 1942, he supervised its operation. He took part in major executions. Transferred again to *KL Auschwitz* in June 1944, he supervised the *Sonderkommando* in crematoria II and III and later was put in charge of all crematoria. After the war the American Military Court passed the life sentence on him on January 23, 1947, for the crimes he had committed at *KL Flossenbürg*. Subsequently he was extradited to Poland where on December 22, 1947, he was sentenced to death by the Supreme National Tribunal in Cracow in the trial of members of the SS garrison at Auschwitz-Birkenau. The sentence was carried out.

Müller, Heinrich, *SS-Gruppenführer* (born April 28, 1900)

Member of the NSDAP (no. 453199) and the SS (no. 107043). He was Head of Office IV (Gestapo) in the RSHA and deputy Head of the Security Police and Security Service. Fate unknown.

Nebe, Arthur, *SS-Gruppenführer*

In 1933—1945 he was the organizer and then Head of the Criminal Police in the Reich Main Security Office. Till November 1941 he commanded " Action Group B " (*Einsatzgruppe B*) in White Russia. He was hanged before the end of the war for his participation in the conspiracy against Hitler, organized on July 20, 1944.

Ontl, Friedrich, *SS-Oberscharführer* (born August 25, 1909)

He was in charge of the store in the SS hospital at *KL Auschwitz*. In September 1942 he became chief clerk in the garrison surgeon's office. In July 1943 he held the post of SS sanitary orderly in the Auschwitz sub-camp *Neu Dachs* at Jaworzno.

Orlowski, Alice (born September 30, 1903)

She was a wardress in the women's camps at *KL Lublin* (Majdanek) from July 1943 to April 1944, *KL Płaszów* from April 1944 to October 1944 and the sub-camp Budy of *KL Auschwitz-Birkenau* from October 1944 to January 1945. The Supreme National Tribunal in Cracow sentenced her to 15 years' imprisonment on December 22, 1947, in the trial of members of the SS garrison of Auschwitz-Birkenau.

Palitzsch, Gerhard Arno Max, *SS-Hauptscharführer* (born June 17, 1913)

Member of the NSDAP (no. 1965727) and the SS (no. 79466), and of the Death's Head Formations. He did guard duty at *KL Lichtenburg*, *KL Buchenwald* and *KL Sachsenhausen*, where he began as *Blockführer* and was then *Rapportführer*. Transferred to *KL Auschwitz* in May 1940, he was *Rapportführer* there and since November 11, 1941, he used to shoot prisoners with small-calibre weapons at the wall of death in the yard of Block 11. When the Gypsy camp was established at Birkenau he became its *Lagerführer*.

Palitzsch used to inspire the prisoners with particular terror as he proved to be extremely sadistic. He appropriated large quantities of money, valuables, clothes, etc., taken from prisoners sent to the camp. During the operation of exterminating Jews he plundered on such a large scale that he was finally transferred to Brünn as head of an Auschwitz subcamp. Later he was arrested and brought to an SS court. Nothing is known of his subsequent fate.

Pohl, Oswald,
SS-Obergruppenführer
(born June 30, 1892)

Member of the NSDAP (no. 30842) and the SS (no. 137614). Head of the SS Economic and Administrative Head Office (WVHA-SS). He was condemned to death by the American Military Tribunal No. IV in Nuremberg on November 3, 1947, in the trial of WVHA-SS functionaries. The execution took place on June 8, 1951, at Landsberg.

Sauther, Erich
(born August 8, 1905)

Doctor of Medicine. Employed in the Dental Station of the SS hospital at *KL Auschwitz* until October 1942.

Schebeck, Franz,
SS-Unterscharführer
(born September 15, 1907)

Member of the SS (no. 301333). He was transferred, on June 25, 1940, from *KL Oranienburg* to *KL Auschwitz* where he was in charge of the food store which supplied the prisoners' kitchen. He was brought to court in Vienna after the war and sentenced to 10 years' imprisonment.

Scheffler, Hans,
SS-Oberscharführer
(born December 8, 1912)

Member of the SS (no. 218602). He was transferred, on May 16, 1940, from *KL Buchenwald* to *KL Auschwitz* where he was a cook in the SS kitchen. On July 1, 1944, he was appointed chef of the SS kitchen.

Scherpe, Herbert,
SS-Oberscharführer
(born May 30, 1907)

Member of the NSDAP and the SS. He served at *KL Auschwitz* from the summer of 1940, first as sanitary orderly in the SS hospital and between early 1942 and March 1943 in the prisoners' hospital in the base camp. He supervised the prisoners' hospital in the Auschwitz sub-camp *Golleschau* between April 1943 and March 1944, and the *Blechhammer* subcamp from April 1944. As an SS sanitary orderly he took part in selections among prisoners in the respective camp hospitals and he also used to kill them with phenol injections through the heart. The Court of Jury in Frankfurt am Main sentenced him to four years and six months in prison on August 19, 1965, and deprived him of civil rights for the period of four years.

Schillinger, Jozef,
SS-Oberscharführer

At *KL Auschwitz* he held the following post: *Rapportführer*, leader of a labour squad at the sub-camp Chełmek, and manager of the kitchen in the men's camp at Birkenau. He helped escort Jewish transports from the ramp to the gas chambers. On October 23, 1943, he was shot dead at the unloading ramp by a Jewess brought that day with a transport from *KL Bergen-Belsen*.

Schmauser, Ernst Heinrich,
SS-Obergruppenführer
(born January 18, 1890)

Member of the NSDAP (no. 215704) and the SS (no. 3359). In 1941—1945 he was commander of the south-eastern SS district in Wrocław and Higher SS and Police Leader for that district. He was responsible for the course of evacuation of prisoners from *KL Auschwitz* and its sub-camps.

Schumann, Horst,
Luftwaffen-Oberleutnant,
SS-Sturmbannführer
(born May 11, 1906)

Member of the NSDAP and the SA from 1930. Obtained his M.D. degree in 1933. In August 1939 he was appointed director of the Grafeneck Euthanasia Institution at Württemberg, in which mental patients were killed with carbon monoxide. After the liquidation of the Grafeneck centre he became director of a similar institution at Sonnenstein near Pirna in Saxony. When the programme of eliminating the so-called incurables was formally discontinued by Hitler and in fact extented to include prisoners in the concentration camps (under the cryptonym " 14 f 13 "), Schumann was a member of medical commissions the task of which was to select prisoners not fit for work or of little productivity in the concentration camps of Auschwitz, Buchenwald, Dachau, Flossenburg, Gross-Rosen, Mauthausen, Neuengamme and Niederhagen. He came to *KL Auschwitz* for the first time on July 28, 1941, when he selected 575 prisoners—invalids, cripples and chronic cases—and directed them to the Euthanasia Institution at Sonnenstein where they were killed with carbon monoxide. His next visit to *KL Auschwitz* in November 1942 was connected with research the aim of which was to test and develop a cheap and rapid method for the mass sterilization of men and women. Schumann sterilized men and women prisoners with X-rays in Block 20 of the women's camp at Birkenau, while castration operations were performed by him in Block 10 of the base camp at Auschwitz. The victims of such experiments mostly died of exhaustion, mental breakdown and burns sustained during the "treatment." Those who were found unfit for further work were killed with phenol injections or with gas. Only few victims had survived. In April 1944 Schumann forwarded his study on the effects of X-rays on human genitals to Hitler's chancellery, whence it was sent on to *Reichsführer SS* Himmler. Around mid-1944 Schumann left for *KL Ravensbrück* where he continued his experiments in sterilization and castration using Gypsy children as material.

After the war he lived in the Federal Republic of Germany until 1951. On the eve of his arrest he fled to Yokohama. He was a physician on a ship for four years. From 1955 he worked in the Sudan, in 1959 he escaped to Nigeria and then to Liberia. In 1960 he settled in Ghana where he practised medicine. On June 14, 1961, the University of Halle divested him of his M.D. degree. In March 1966 Schumann was arrested in Ghana and extradited to the judicial authorities of the Federal Republic of Germany. He was taken to prison to Butzbach on November 16, 1966. His trial before the Court of Jury in Frankfurt am Main began on September 23, 1970, and was adjourned in April 1971 due to the illness of the defendant.

Schumann is charged with having sentenced to death 13,720 mental patients in the euthanasia institutions at Grafeneck and Sonnenstein, and 765 Auschwitz and Buchenwald prisoners who, as unfit for work, were killed during the "14 f 13" operation. In additional indictment he is charged with conducting sterilization and castration experiment on men and women prisoners at *KL Auschwitz*. Of the 115 witnesses for the prosecution, 54 had died before the trial began.

Schwarz, Heinrich,
SS-Hauptsturmführer
(born June 14, 1906)

Member of the NSDAP (no. 786871) and the SS (no. 19691). After the outbreak of World War II he was detailed to the SS military formations (*Waffen-SS*) and assigned to serve at *KL Mauthausen*. In November 1941 he was transferred to *KL Auschwitz* to fill the post of head of the Employment Section (*Arbeitseinsatz*—IIIa). In November 1943 he became commandant of *KL Auschwitz III* (Monowitz), supervising also other Auschwitz sub-camps. After the evacuation of *KL Auschwitz* he succeeded Hartjenstein as commandant of *KL Natzweiler*. Charged with crimes committed at *KL Natzweiler*, he was sentenced to death by the French Military Court in 1947. The sentence was carried out.

Schwarzhuber, Johann,
SS-Obersturmführer

Member of the SS. Served at *KL Dachau*, *KL Sachsenhausen*, *KL Auschwitz* and *KL Ravensbrück*. On November 22, 1943, he became *Lagerführer* of the men's camp at Birkenau (*KL Auschwitz II—Männerlager*) and on January 12, 1945, *Lagerführer* at *KL Ravensbrück*. Arrested after the war he was brought to court in Hamburg, which for his crimes committed at *KL Ravensbrück* sentenced him to death on February 3, 1947. He was executed on May 3, 1947.

Seidler, Fritz,
SS-Hauptsturmführer
(born July 18, 1907)

Member of the NSDAP (no. 3693999) and the SS (no. 135387). In November 1940 he succeeded Franz Maier as second *Lagerführer*. Between October 1941 and March 1942 he was also deputy *Lagerführer* of the Soviet POW camp. He was subsequently transferred to *KL Mauthausen-Gusen*.

Speer, Albert
(born March 19, 1905)

In 1942—1945 he was minister for armaments and war production of the Third Reich. At the same time he headed the Main Office for Technology in the NSDAP, was president of the National-Socialist Union of German Technicians, General Inspector for German Road Building, and General Inspector for the Water and Power Supply. He was sentenced to 20 years of prison by the International Military Tribunal in Nuremberg on October 1, 1946, at the trial of the leading war criminals. He was released in 1966 after having served his sentence.

Streicher, Julius
(born February 12, 1885)

Member of the NSDAP, *Gauleiter* of Franconia until 1940 and editor of the anti-Semitic weekly *Der Stürmer*. Sentenced to death by the International Military Tribunal in Nuremberg on October 1, 1946. The sentence was carried out.

Thilo, Heinz,
SS-Obersturmführer

Doctor of Medicine. He was a camp physician at *KL Auschwitz* from October 9, 1942. He conducted

. (born October 8, 1911) — selections on the ramp at Birkenau and in the camp hospital, sending the sick and unfit for work to the gas chambers. Towards the end of 1944 he was transferred to *KL Gross-Rosen*. According to contradictory information, he died either on May 13, 1945, at Hohenelbe or on November 20, 1947, in Berlin.

Uhlenbrock, Kurt,
SS-Sturmbannführer
(born March 2, 1908)

Doctor of Medicine. In August 1942 he was garrison physician at *KL Auschwitz*. At that time he selected sick prisoners to be sent to the gas chambers. He was charged at the first Frankfurt trial, but released on bail. The inquiry was suspended.

Vetter, Helmuth,
SS-Obersturmführer
(born March 21, 1910)

Doctor of Medicine, camp physician at *KL Dachau*, *KL Auschwitz* and *KL Mauthausen*. As an associate of the firms IG-Farbenindustrie and Bayer, he tested medicines by using prisoners of concentration camps as guinea-pigs. He was sentenced to death by the American Military Court in 1947, at the trial of the garrison of *KL Mauthausen*. He was executed on February 2, 1949.

Weber, Bruno,
SS-Hauptsturmführer

Doctor of Medicine, bacteriologist, head of the SS Hygiene Institute at Rajsko near Auschwitz. He died in Homberg upon Saar on September 23, 1956.

Wiebeck, Gerhard,
SS-Untersturmführer

Doctor of Laws, judge of the SS court, member of the special SS commission investigating corrupt practices in the concentration camps.

Wigand, Arpad,
SS-Oberführer
(born January 13, 1906)

Member of the NSDAP (no. 30682) and the SS (no. 2999). He was an inspector of the Security Police and Security Service (*Sipo und SD*) in Wrocław. The government region in Kattowitz also came within his jurisdiction. Subsequently he took the post of SS and Police Commander in the Warsaw district. He was transferred to the Reich Main Security Office towards the end of the war.

Wilhelmy, Anton,
SS-Oberscharführer
(born October 26, 1912)

Between the summer of 1940 and September 1942, he was *Spies bei der Dienststelle SS Standortarzt* (company leader in the garrison physician's office) at *KL Auschwitz*. Later he served in the Auschwitz sub-camp at Budy.

Wilks, Martin,

He was *Rechnungsführer bei der Dienstelle SS Stan-*

SS-Unterscharführer (born 1916) — *dortarzt* (chief accountant in the office of the SS garrison physician) at *KL Auschwitz* from October 1941 until the evacuation of the camp.

Wirths, Eduard, *SS-Obersturmbannführer* (born September 4, 1909) — At the beginning of the war he was called up as army surgeon to the SS Military Formations, and was sent to the front. In 1942 he was assigned to work in the Inspectorate of Concentration Camps and on September 6, 1942, he took over the post of garrison physician at *KL Auschwitz*. He was in charge of all SS physicians, dentists and sanitary orderlies in the Auschwitz camps and sub-camps, also of the medical and nursing staff among the prisoners. When a medical experimental station was opened in 1943 in Block 10 of the base camp, to be used by Professor Carl Clauberg, M.D., Wirths conducted research work into cancer and operated on Jewish women suspected of having the disease. After the evacuation of *KL Auschwitz* he was camp physician at *KL Mittelbau-Dora*, *KL Bergen-Belsen* and *KL Neuengamme*. After his arrest by the British authorities he wrote a report on his activities. He committed suicide in prison in September 1945.

BIBLIOGRAPHY

Adelsberger, Lucie, *Auschwitz. Ein Tatsachenbericht*, Berlin 1956.

Adler, H. G., Langbein, Hermann, and Lingens-Reiner, Ella, *Auschwitz. Zeugnisse und Berichte*, Frankfurt a.M. 1962.

Amidst a Nightmare of Crime. Notes of Prisoners of Sonderkommando Found in Auschwitz, Oświęcim 1973.

Batawia, Stanisław, Rudolf Höss, komendant obozu koncentracyjnego w Oświęcimiu. *Biuletyn Głównej Komisji Badania Zbrodni Hitlerowskich w Polsce*, Warszawa, vol.7, 1951.

Biuletyn Głównej Komisji Badania Zbrodni Hitlerowskich w Polsce, Warszawa, vols. 1—20, 1946—1970.

Bullock, Alan, *Hitler: A Study in Tyranny*, London 1952.

Commandant of Auschwitz. The Autobiography of Rudolf Höss, London 1961.

Crankshaw, Edward, *Gestapo, Instrument of Tyranny*, London 1956.

Cyprian, T., and Sawicki, J., *Materiały norymberskie*, Warszawa 1948.

Czech, Danuta, Kalendarium der Ereignisse im Konzentrationslager Auschwitz-Birkenau. *Hefte von Auschwitz*, Oświęcim, nos. 2—4, 6—8, 1959—1964.

Eisenbach, Artur, *Hitlerowska polityka zagłady Żydów*, Warszawa 1961.

From the History of KL Auschwitz, Oświęcim, nos. 1—2, 1967, 1976.

Hefte von Auschwitz, Oświęcim, nos. 1, 9—15, 1959, 1966—1976.

Hefte von Auschwitz. Sonderheft (1). Handschriften von Mitgliedern des Sonderkommandos, Oświęcim 1972.

Henkys, Reinhard, *Die nationalsozialistischen Gevaltverbrechen*, Stuttgart—Berlin 1964.

Kąkol, Kazimierz, *Sąd nierychliwy. Frankfurcki proces oprawców z Oświęcimia*, Warszawa 1966.

Kalmar, Rudolf, *Zeit ohne Gnade*, Wien 1946.

Kamiński, Andrzej Józef, *Hitlerowskie obozy koncentracyjne i ośrodki masowej zagłady w polityce imperializmu niemieckiego*, Poznań 1964.

Kaul, F. K., *Ärzte in Auschwitz*, Berlin 1968.

Kempner, Robert, *SS im Kreuzverhör*, München 1964.

Kiedrzyńska, Wanda, *Ravensbrück, obóz koncentracyjny*, Warszawa 1961.

Kłodziński, Stanisław, Esesmani z oświęcimskiej "służby zdrowia." Wykaz wstępny, *Przegląd Lekarski*, series II, Kraków, no. 1, 1966.

Kogon, Eugen, *Der SS-Staat. Das System der deutschen Konzentrationslager*, Düsseldorf 1946.

Kolb, Eberhard, *Bergen-Belsen. Geschichte des "Aufenthaltslagers" 1943—1945*, Hannover 1962.

Kommandant in Auschwitz. Autobiographische Aufzeichningen von Rudolf Höss. Eingeleit und kommentiert v. Martin Broszat, Stuttgart 1958.

Landau, Leon, *Oskarżenie*, Warszawa 1963.

Langbein, Hermann, *Der Auschwitz-Prozess. Eine Dokumentation*, vols. 1, 2, Wien 1965.

Mitscherlich, Alexander, and Mielke, Fred, *Medizin ohne Menschlichkeit. Dokumente des Nürnberg Ärztprozess*, Frankfurt a.M., Hamburg 1962.

Musioł, Teodor, *Dachau 1933—1945*, Katowice 1968.

Nyiszli, Miklós, *A Doctor's Eye-witness Account*, New York 1960.

Piotrowski, Stanisław, *Misja Odilo Globocnika. Sprawozdanie o wynikach finansowych zagłady Żydów w Polsce*, Warszawa 1949.

Poliakov, L., and Wulf, J., *Das Dritte Reich und die Juden. Dokumente und Aufsätze*, Berlin 1961.

Poliakov, L., and Wulf, J., *Das Dritte Reich und seine Diener. Dokumente*. Berlin 1956.

Reitlinger, Gerald, *Die Endlösung. Hitlers Versuch der Ausrottung der Juden Europas 1939—1945*, Berlin 1956.

Reitlinger, Gerald, *The Final Solution*, London 1953.

Reitlinger, Gerald, *Die SS. Tragödie einer deutschen Epoche*, Wien 1956.

Russell (Edward Frederick Langley) Lord of Liverpool, *The Scourge of the Swastika. A Short History of Nazi War Crimes*, London 1955.

Russell (Edward Frederick Langley) Lord of Liverpool, *The Trial of Adolf Eichmann*, London 1962.

Ryszka, Franciszek, *Państwo stanu wyjątkowego. Rzecz o systemie państwa i prawa Trzeciej Rzeszy*, Wrocław—Warszawa—Kraków 1964.
Scenes of Fighting and Martyrdom Guide. War Years in Poland 1939—1945, Warsaw 1968.
Schnabel, Reimund, *Macht ohne Moral. Eine Dokumentation über die SS*, Frankfurt a.M. 1957.
Sehn, Jan, *Oświęcim-Brzezinka (Auschwitz-Birkenau). Concentration Camp*, Warszawa 1961.
SS im Einsatz. Eine Dokumentation über die Verbrechen der SS, Berlin 1960.
Weliczker, Leon, *Brygada śmierci (Sonderkommando 1005)*, Łódź 1946.
Wielka Encyklopedia Powszechna PWN, Warszawa, vols. 1—13, 1962—1970.
Zych, Gabriel, *Oranienburg. Rachunek pamięci*, Warszawa 1962.

Typeset prepared by INTERPRESS
Printed by Cieszyńska Drukarnia Wydawnicza, Poland
Zam. nr 1521/K-98